D1035820

BY ANTHONY EVERITT

Nero (with Roddy Ashworth)
Alexander the Great
The Rise of Athens
The Rise of Rome
SPQR: A Roman Miscellany
Cicero
Hadrian and the Triumph of Rome
Augustus

NERO

MATRICIDE, MUSIC, AND MURDER IN IMPERIAL ROME

NERO

ANTHONY EVERITT
AND
RODDY ASHWORTH

RANDOM HOUSE
NEW YORK

Published in the United States by Random House, an imprint and division of Penguin Random House LLC, New York.

Random House and the House colophon are registered trademarks of Penguin Random House LLC.

Photograph credits are located on pages 405–406.

LIBRARY OF CONGRESS CATALOGING-IN-PUBLICATION DATA
Names: Everitt, Anthony, author. | Ashworth, Roddy, author.
Title: Nero: matricide, music, and murder in imperial Rome / Anthony Everitt and Roddy Ashworth.
Other titles: Matricide, music, and murder in imperial Rome
Description: New York: Random House, [2022] | Includes bibliographical references and index.
Identifiers: LCCN 2022018557 (print) | LCCN 2022018558 (ebook) | ISBN 9780593133200 (hardback) | ISBN 9780593133224 (ebook)
Subjects: LCSH: Nero, Emperor of Rome, 37-68. | Emperors—Rome—Biography. | Rome—History—Nero, 54-68.
Classification: LCC DG285 .E84 2022 (print) | LCC DG285 (ebook) | DDC 937/.07092 [B]—dc23/eng/20220429
LC record available at https://lccn.loc.gov/2022018557
LC ebook record available at https://lccn.loc.gov/2022018558

Printed in Canada

randomhousebooks.com

2 4 6 8 9 7 5 3 1

FIRST EDITION

Book design by Simon M. Sullivan

For Luke Butler

CONTENTS

Maps · xii

Julio-Claudian Family Tree · xvi

Preface · xix

1
THE NEW ORDER
3

2
A FAMILY AT WAR
15

3
THE IMPROBABLE EMPEROR
34

4
YOUNG HOPEFUL GENTLEMAN
55

5
A DISH OF MUSHROOMS
79

6
BEST OF MOTHERS
95

7
"MY FOOLISH LOVE"
126

8
FREE AT LAST!
146

9
THE TURNING POINT
161

10
THE QUEEN IS DEAD
183

11
FIRE! FIRE!
237

12
ALL THE CONSPIRATORS
259

13
THE ARMENIAN QUESTION
294

14
"I DREAM'D THAT GREECE MIGHT STILL BE FREE"
313

15
DOWNFALL
328

16
LOOSE ENDS
347

Acknowledgments · 355

Timeline · 357

Glossary · 363

A Note on Sources · 367

Bibliography · 373

Notes · 379

Photograph Credits · 405

Index · 407

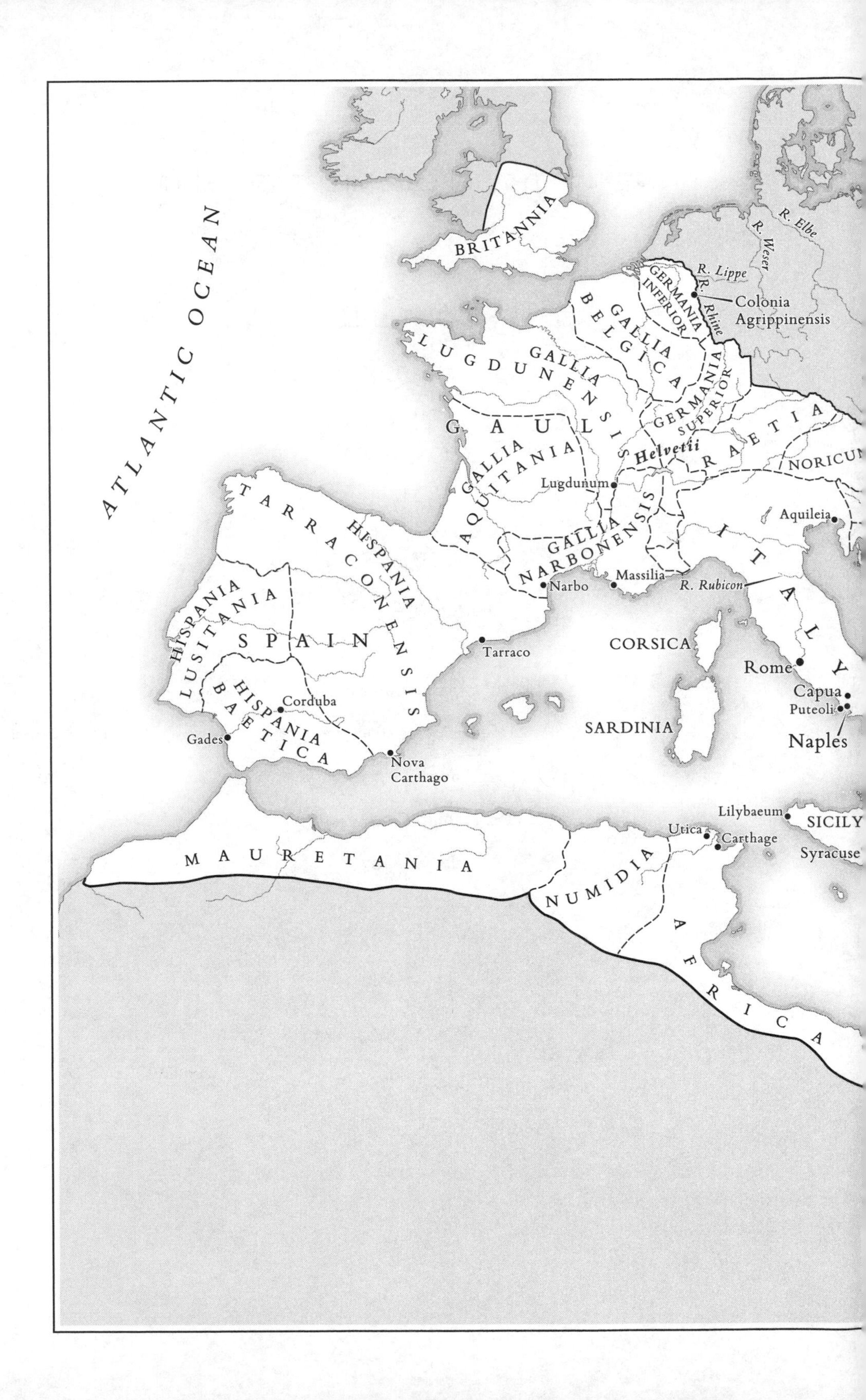
ATLANTIC OCEAN
BRITANNIA
R. Elbe
R. Weser
R. Lippe
R. Rhine
GERMANIA INFERIOR
Colonia Agrippinensis
GALLIA BELGICA
GALLIA LUGDUNENSIS
GERMANIA SUPERIOR
GAUL
GALLIA AQUITANIA
Helvetii
RAETIA
NORICUM
Lugdunum
Aquileia
HISPANIA TARRACONENSIS
GALLIA NARBONENSIS
ITALY
Massilia
Narbo
R. Rubicon
HISPANIA LUSITANIA
SPAIN
Tarraco
CORSICA
Rome
Capua
Puteoli
Naples
HISPANIA BAETICA
Corduba
Gades
SARDINIA
Nova Carthago
Lilybaeum
SICILY
Utica
Carthage
Syracuse
MAURETANIA
NUMIDIA
AFRICA

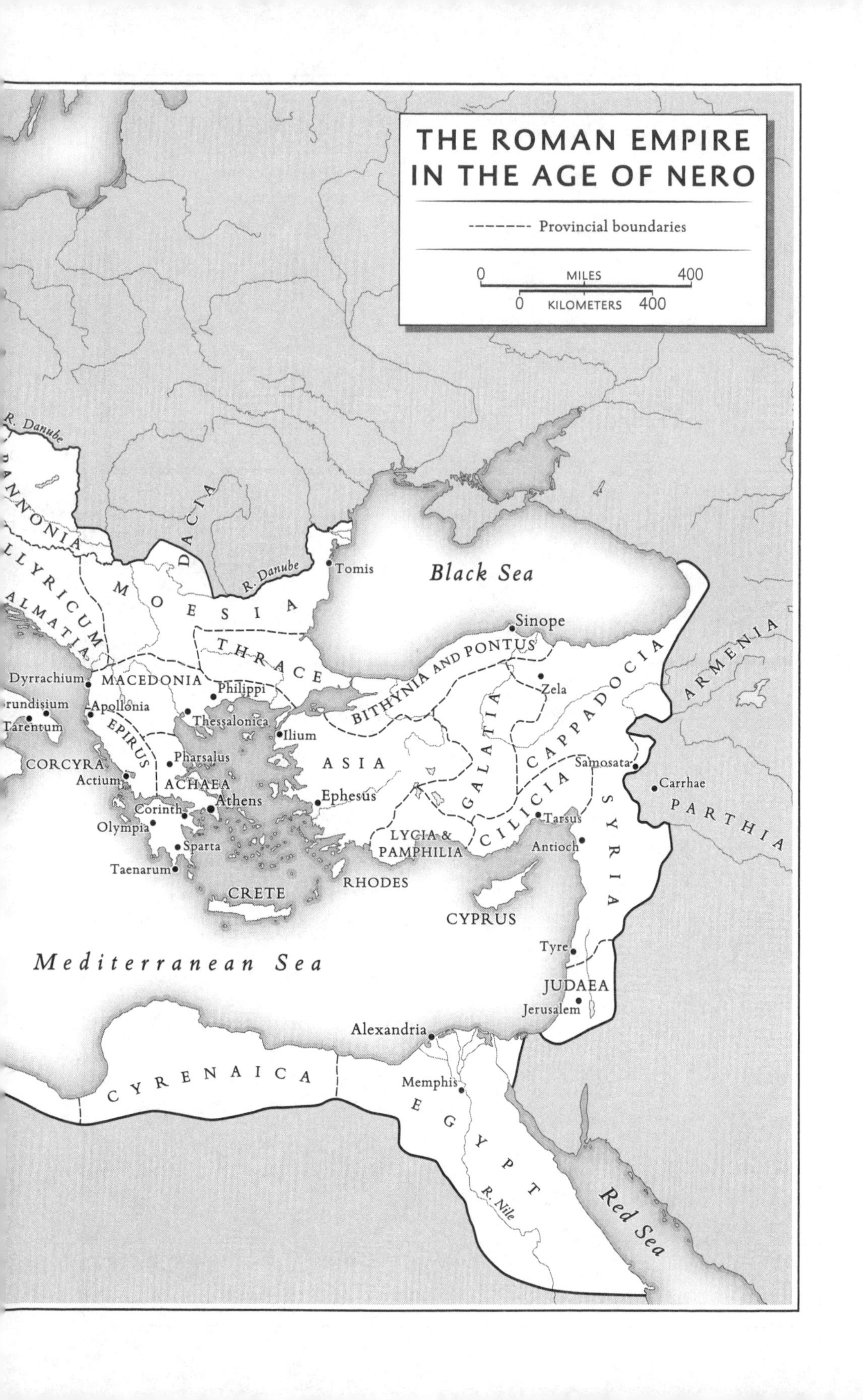

THE ROMAN EMPIRE IN THE AGE OF NERO
Provincial boundaries
0 MILES 400
0 KILOMETERS 400
R. Danube
PANNONIA
DACIA
ILLYRICUM
DALMATIA
MOESIA
R. Danube
Tomis
Black Sea
Sinope
THRACE
BITHYNIA AND PONTUS
ARMENIA
CAPPADOCIA
Zela
GALATIA
Dyrrachium
MACEDONIA
Philippi
Brundisium
Apollonia
Tarentum
Thessalonica
EPIRUS
Ilium
CORCYRA
Pharsalus
ASIA
Actium
ACHAEA
Athens
Ephesus
Samosata
Carrhae
PARTHIA
CILICIA
SYRIA
Corinth
Olympia
Tarsus
LYCIA & PAMPHILIA
Antioch
Sparta
Taenarum
RHODES
CRETE
CYPRUS
Tyre
Mediterranean Sea
JUDAEA
Jerusalem
Alexandria
CYRENAICA
Memphis
EGYPT
R. Nile
Red Sea

ROMAN BRITAIN
Coloniae or municipia
Tribal capitals
Other towns
Fortresses
Tribal boundaries
ICENI — Tribal name
Eboracum — Roman name
York — Modern name
Watling Street
0 MILES 100
0 KILOMETERS 100
CALEDONIA
SCOTLAND
Scetis
Skye
CALEDONIAN CONFEDERACY
North Channel
DAMNONII
SELGOVAE
VOTADINI
NOVANTAE
North Sea
Luguvalium
Carlisle
CARVETII
LOPOCARES
TEXTOVERDI
BRIGANTES
Cataractonium
Catterick
Isurium Brigantum
Aldborough
PARISI
GABRANTOVICES
Eboracum
York
Monapia
Isle of Man
Irish Sea
SETANTII
HIBERNIA
IRELAND
Mona
Anglesey
ORDOVICES
GANGANI
DEGEANGLI
Deva
Chester
CORNOVII
Lincoln
Lindum
CORITANI
Pennocrucium
Water Eaton
Derventio
Little Chester
Viroconium Cornoviorum
Wroxeter
Manduessedum
Mancetter
Ratae Corieltauvorum
Leicester
Venta Icenorum
Caistor St. Edmund
ICENI
St. George's Channel
Watling Street
Durovigtum
Godmanchester
DEMETAE
DOBUNNI
Glevum
Gloucester
CATUVELLAUNI
TRINOVANTES
Camulodunum
Colchester
Corinium Dobunnorum
Cirencester
SILURES
Isca
Venta Silurum
Verulamium
St Albans
Londinium
London
Durovernum
Rutupiae
Richborough
ATREBATES
CANTII
Aquae Sulis
Bath
Cunetio
BELGAE
Calleva Atrebatum
Silchester
Dubris
Dover
Lindinis
Ilchester
Venta Belgarum
Winchester
Portus Lemanus
Lympne
DUMNONII
DUROTRIGES
REGNENSES
Gesoriacum
Boulogne
Isca Dumnoniorum
Exeter
Durnovaria
Dorchester
Noviomagus Regnensium
Vectis
Isle of Wight
English Channel
FRANCE

GREAT BRITAIN TODAY
Chester—Modern name
Deva—Roman name
0 MILES 100
0 KILOMETERS 100
ATLANTIC OCEAN
North Sea
Skye
Scetis
SCOTLAND
CALEDONIA
Glasgow
Glasconium
Edinburgh
North Channel
NORTHERN IRELAND
Belfast
Carlisle
Luguvalium
Newcastle
Durham
Scarborough
Isle of Man
Monapia
York
Eboracum
Blackpool
Bradford
Leeds
Hull
Irish Sea
IRELAND
HIBERNIA
Liverpool
Manchester
Lincoln
Lindum
Anglesey
Mona
Chester
Deva
ENGLAND
Wroxeter
Viroconium
Cornoviorum
Leicester
Ratae Corieltauvorum
Norwich
Caistor St. Edmund
Venta Icenorum
WALES
Birmingham
Coventry
Aberystwyth
Cambridge
St. George's Channel
Gloucester
Glevum
Colchester
Camulodunum
Oxford
St Albans
Verulamium
Swansea
Cirencester
Corinium
Dobunnorum
Cardiff
Bristol
London
Londinium
Bath
Aquae Sulis
Winchester
Venta Belgarum
Dover
Dubris
Strait of Dover
Dorchester
Durnovaria
Portsmouth
Brighton
Exeter
Isca Dumnoniorum
Boulogne
Gesoriacum
Isle of Wight
Vectis
Plymouth
English Channel
FRANCE

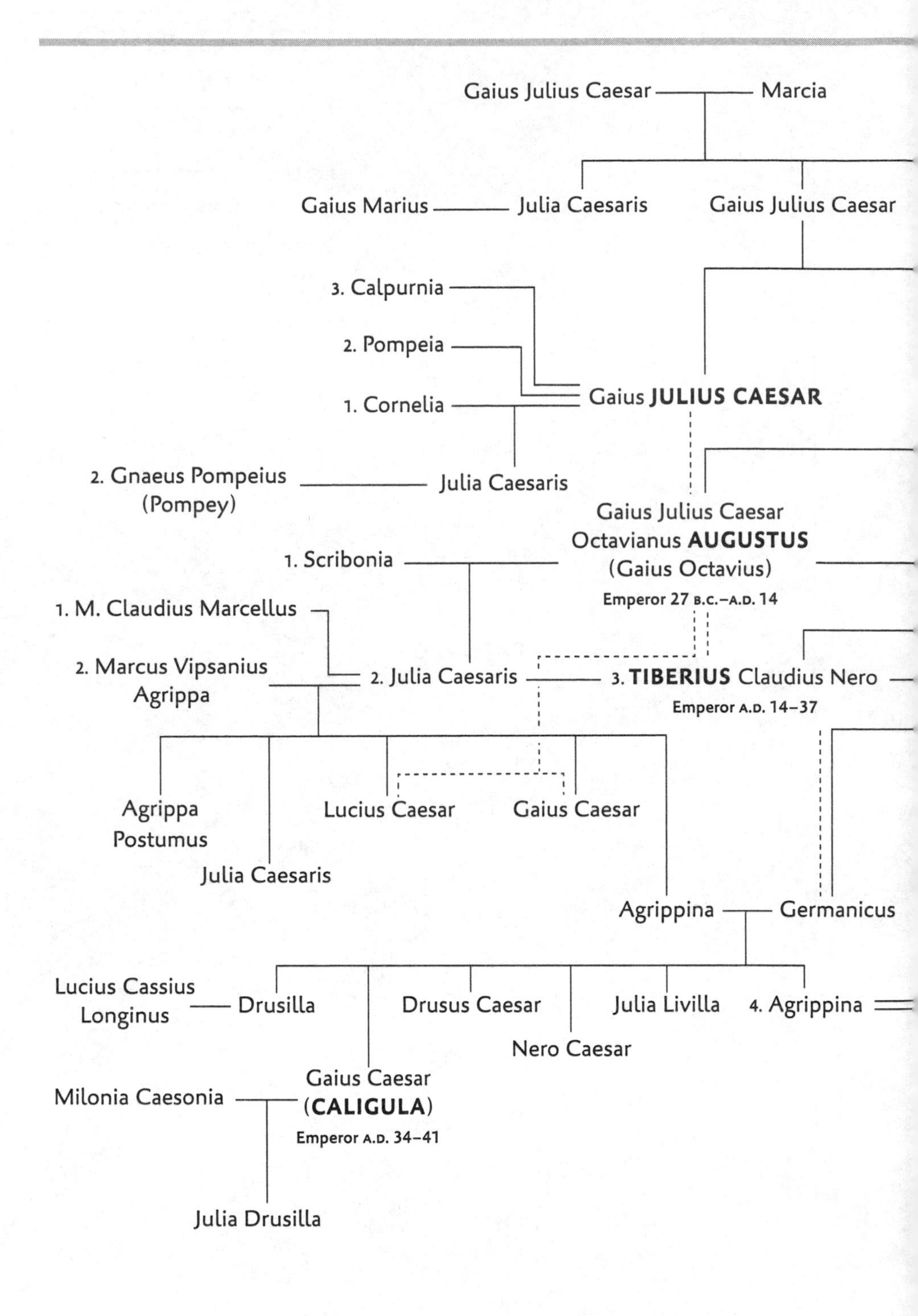
Gaius Julius Caesar
Marcia
Gaius Marius
Julia Caesaris
Gaius Julius Caesar
3. Calpurnia
2. Pompeia
1. Cornelia
Gaius JULIUS CAESAR
2. Gnaeus Pompeius (Pompey)
Julia Caesaris
Gaius Julius Caesar Octavianus AUGUSTUS (Gaius Octavius)
Emperor 27 B.C.–A.D. 14
1. Scribonia
1. M. Claudius Marcellus
2. Marcus Vipsanius Agrippa
2. Julia Caesaris
3. TIBERIUS Claudius Nero
Emperor A.D. 14–37
Agrippa Postumus
Julia Caesaris
Lucius Caesar
Gaius Caesar
Agrippina
Germanicus
Lucius Cassius Longinus
Drusilla
Drusus Caesar
Nero Caesar
Julia Livilla
4. Agrippina
Milonia Caesonia
Gaius Caesar (CALIGULA)
Emperor A.D. 34–41
Julia Drusilla

JULIO-CLAUDIAN FAMILY TREE

(ABBREVIATED)

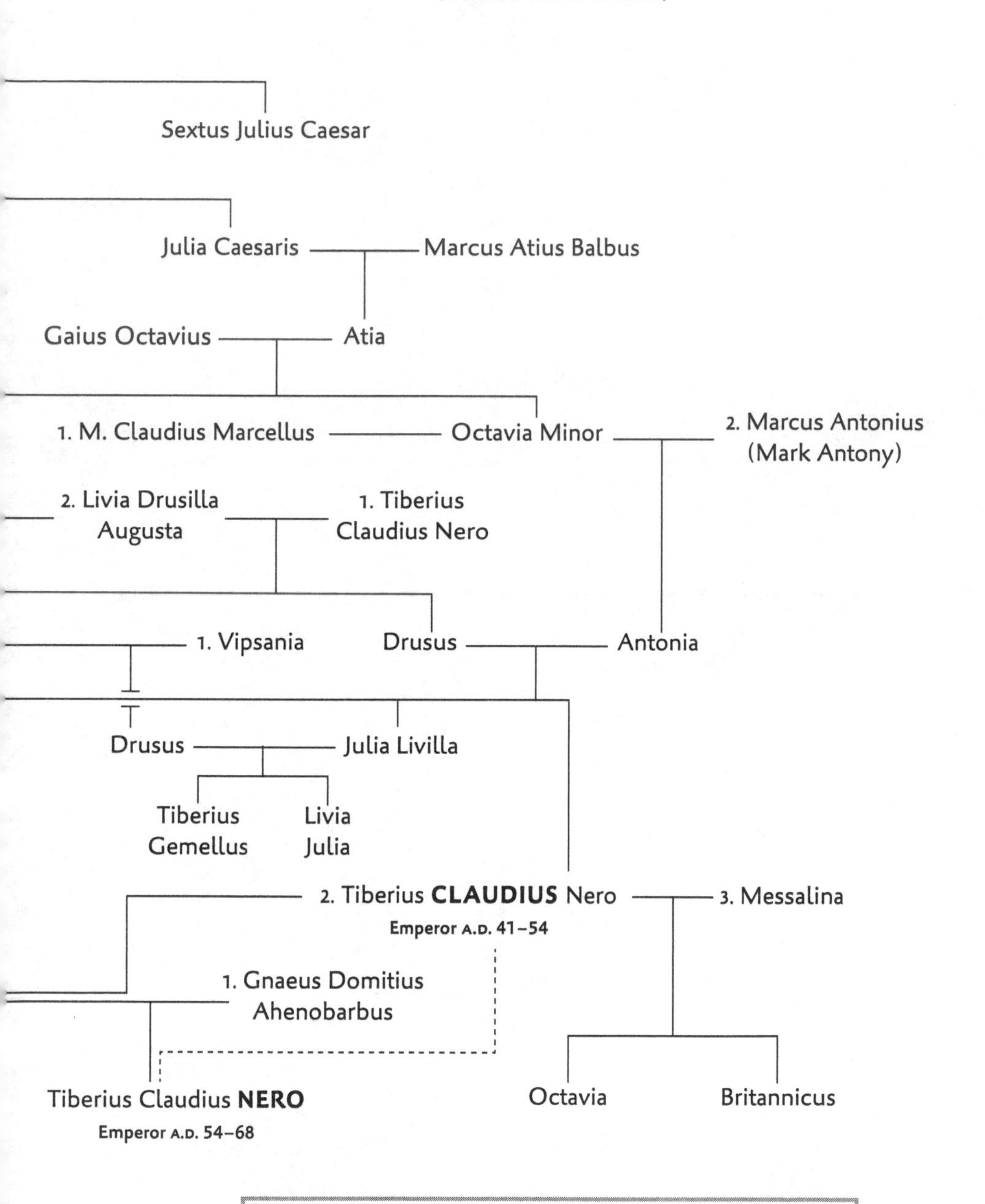

KEY

Marriage: —— Son/Daughter: | Adopted Son: ⋮

Number of Marriage: 1., 2., ...

(*Note: Only those unions discussed in the text are counted.*)

PREFACE

The people love Nero. He inspires in them both affection and respect. . . . One can discern the reason for this popular feeling: Nero oppressed the great and never burdened the ordinary people.

—Napoleon Bonaparte

When Nero perished by the justest doom
Which ever the destroyer yet destroyed
Amidst the roar of liberated Rome,
Of nations freed, and the world overjoyed,
Some hands unseen strewed flowers upon his tomb —
Perhaps the weakness of a heart not void
Of feeling for some kindness done when power
Had left the wretch an uncorrupted hour.

—Lord Byron

EVERYBODY HAS HEARD of the Roman emperor Nero.

He is the image of the bad ruler, cruel, vain, and incompetent. He was sexually voracious and the breaker of the most sacred taboos. He committed incest with his mother and murdered her.

He set fire to Rome, his own capital. Then from a convenient vantage point he fiddled while the city burned and sang an aria about the Sack of Troy. He cleared the charred ruins of the city center and in their place built a vast palace, the Golden House. He blamed the fire on a new religious sect, the Christians, some of whom he turned into human torches to illuminate an evening at the races.

He believed he was a great musician and singer but in fact had no talent, the Florence Foster Jenkins of his day.

These are some of the stories about Nero that have come down to us. But there is a mystery. For a long time after his deposition and suicide, anonymous hands laid flowers on his grave. In the eastern half of the Roman empire, a succession of men claiming to be Nero appeared and caused trouble for the authorities. There was a widespread belief that the dead emperor would return to his people and confer peace and harmony. *Rex quondam, rexque futurus,* the once and future monarch.

The monster was loved.

This biography will explore the contradiction. Nero did some terrible things, but the empire was well managed under his rule. He presided over a diplomatic triumph when he ended an on-and-off cold war and established a long-standing entente with Rome's rival superpower, the Parthian empire, which lay beyond the river Euphrates. He managed well a surprise insurrection in the new province of Britannia. While not a man for administrative detail, he kept the imperial show on the road. That was to his credit, but the bloodstained collapse of his relations with the ruling class gave him an indelible name for despotism.

As a matter of fact, he was quite a good singer and musician. The secret of Nero's personality lay in his commitment to art. He was no dilettante and took music and drama extremely seriously. Audiences loved him. He was the prototype of a pop star.

As emperor, he placed culture at the heart of his politics. Arts festivals, the enormously popular sport of chariot racing, and to a lesser extent gladiatorial shows and athletic games were aspects of a strategy of spectacle. They allowed the emperor to convey political messages to his subjects and to mark important events with celebrations. They were evidence of his affection for the ordinary citizen. Nero appears to have promoted a union of Greek and Roman culture.

Nero's story cannot be told without evoking the world from which he sprang. Without understanding his times, we cannot understand his life. So I touch on the imperial system that his great-great-grandfather Augustus created, the personality of his predecessor in the purple, his great-uncle Claudius, and above all the career of his hypercompetent mother, Agrippina, who tried to form him as a sculptor carves a block of stone. She deserves her own book, and I give her my opening chapters.

Nero became emperor at her behest. The fact is that he did not really want the job. Given the choice, he would much rather have been a poet and professional musician. But thanks to her he was doomed to power.

His life was wasted. We remember him as a failed despot and as an entertainer. Had he lived today he might have scraped a living as a mediocre rock musician—and been happy.

The ancient sources make much of the exotic sex lives of the emperors, and modern scholars tend to discount their stories as incredible or at least exaggerated. In fact, much is very probably true. With a few horrific exceptions (the castration of Nero's favorite slave boy, Sporus, is a case in point), the antics of ancient Romans are not greatly out of step with the variety of sexual attitudes and practices today. What the Victorians considered the overheated product of filthy minds and Edward Gibbon (perhaps with some reluctance) "left in the decent obscurity of a learned language" is now a matter of general report.

In this book all licentious passages are left *in*.

Wivenhoe, England

NERO

1

THE NEW ORDER

THE YOUTH WAS seventeen years old. His face had the temporary good looks of the teenager, but an observant eye could detect the unappealing lineaments of the man-to-be. He was of average height, with light blond hair and blue eyes. He was somewhat shortsighted. His neck was too thick, his body spotty and, apparently, malodorous. His legs were spindly and his stomach protruded.

This was Nero—or, to give him his full name and titles, Nero Claudius Caesar Augustus Germanicus. It was the autumn of A.D. 54 and he had just become emperor of Rome. Surrounded by senior politicians, all wearing the dark togas of mourning, he was leading the funeral rites of his predecessor and adoptive father, Tiberius Claudius Caesar Augustus Germanicus, whom we know more succinctly as Claudius.

The ceremony unfolded on the Campus Martius, the Field of Mars, a five-hundred-acre grassland that stretched away north of Rome's city walls. It was a lung for the world's first megalopolis, which was home to an estimated one million inhabitants. The Campus was a park, dotted with temples and other public buildings, and people of every class escaped there from the city's noise, crowds, and smells and engaged in leisure pursuits. The wealthy raced around in chariots or exercised their horses, while those of lesser means amused themselves with playing ball games, trundling hoops, or wrestling.

When necessary, there was plenty of space for military maneuvers, as the field's name in honor of Mars, the god of war, indicates.

Some of the ground was marshy and there were frequent inundations. A central swamp was organized into a small lake. In the west, the river Tiber rolled along on its way to the sea, and to the east and southeast, hills closed off the scene. A commentator of the day observed that these distant features "present to the eye the appearance of a painted backdrop." Indeed, the overall impression was of a very large stage set, with a fine panorama from the vantage point of Rome's citadel, the Capitol.

Today the mood was melancholy and given over to state solemnities. A long procession wound its way through the city to the music of a funeral march. The late emperor had lain in state for five days and now was conveyed on a flower-festooned bier, made from ivory and decorated with golden fittings and purple cloth. The body lay in a concealed coffin and a life-sized wax image of Claudius was visible above. Senators carried another gold statue of him, and a third represented him on a chariot.

Behind the bier walked his relatives, led by Nero, their heads veiled. Women of the family expressed, or pretended, their uncontrollable grief by wailing at full throttle, ripping their clothes and tearing at their cheeks. In shocking contrast, a group of specially hired comedians clowned around; in a long-standing tradition of extracting farce from tragedy, one of them mercilessly caricatured the late emperor.

Next in the cortege came, one might say, the resurrected dead. Down the generations leading aristocratic clans commissioned realistic death masks, or *imagines,* made from wax, of their most distinguished members. These were worn at funerals by men who resembled the originals in body shape and size. They rode in chariots and were preceded by functionaries carrying the insignia of the public offices they had held in life.

The long line of mourners paused in the Forum, the city's main square, and Nero, as his heir and next of kin, delivered a eulogy.

Claudius's "ancestors" sat in a row on ivory chairs and listened to the youthful emperor deliver a polished speech in praise of his adoptive father's achievements. An impressed Greek historian asked who would not be inspired by the sight of these personalities from the past "all together and as if alive and breathing?"

Eulogy over, the cavalcade left the city and entered the green plain. It came to a halt beside an open-air crematorium, or *ustrinum*, reserved for the imperial family. Between a circular iron fence and a white marble inner wall, black poplars shaded an enclosure where Claudius's pyre, an assemblage of wooden logs arranged in the shape of an altar and papered with dark leaves, was waiting. The corpse and the couch were placed on the top of the pyre, and Nero put a torch to the whole elaborate ensemble. Perfumes were thrown on the flames, also cups of oil, trinkets, well-used clothes, dishes of food that the deceased had especially liked, and other items of sentimental value.

When the pyre had burned down, the embers were soaked in wine. The bones were gathered up, placed in an urn, and carried to the place of burial. This was the vast Mausoleum of Augustus, founder of the ruling dynasty.

Erected about seventy-five years previously near the river Tiber, it was a short walk from the *ustrinum*. One of the largest tombs in the ancient world, the monument stood about 150 feet high and 300 feet in diameter. Above a high drum, built solidly of concentric rings of concrete faced with marble, rose an earthen mound covered with low-spreading evergreen junipers. On its apex stood a statue of Augustus that overlooked the city of which he was once the absolute ruler.

A tunnel led from the entrance to an internal corridor that encircled a hall with wall niches that housed the burned detritus of the imperial dead in golden urns. In the center of the Mausoleum a final chamber had been set aside for Augustus himself. Years had passed and his descendants were numerous. There were few spaces left, but room was found for a new occupant. Nero watched as leading businessmen, barefoot and wearing unbelted tunics as tokens of grief, deposited what was left of Claudius in its niche.

Nero's reign had well and truly begun.

The teenaged ruler would be forgiven if he felt nervous and ill-equipped for the task ahead. He had no experience of politics and governance. However, at the Mausoleum he had at his disposal an invaluable learning tool. Just outside the entrance he could see two pillars with bronze plaques on which Augustus had had his memoirs inscribed, proudly on public display. Copies had been widely distributed throughout the Roman empire, which stretched from Spain in the west to the river Euphrates in the east.

The memoirs (called *Res Gestae,* or Things Done) are concise and exemplify propaganda at its finest. They must have featured in Nero's educational syllabus. Augustus's rules still ran the empire, and his descendant needed to master them if he was to make a success of his reign.

Res Gestae was not simply a self-serving account of a life, for it set out an agenda for future emperors to consider and offered some attractive policy solutions. Nero would be wise to pay attention, and his career suggests that that was exactly what he did. He admired his great-great-grandfather and felt a special link to him.

Little in the document is obviously untrue, for knowledgeable contemporaries would have cried foul; but there are slippery omissions and elisions. The author conceals as much as he reveals, as when he writes:

> At the age of nineteen [in 44 B.C.] on my own responsibility and at my own expense I raised an army, with which I successfully championed the liberty of the Republic when it was oppressed by the tyranny of a faction. . . . I drove into exile the murderers of my father, avenging their crime. . . . I undertook many civil and foreign wars by land and sea throughout the world, and as victor I spared the lives of all citizens who asked for mercy. . . . The whole of Italy swore allegiance to me of its own free will and demanded me as the leader in the war in which I was victorious at Actium.

In these few deceptively simple sentences Augustus encapsulates the brutal civil war that followed the assassination of his adoptive father, Gaius Julius Caesar, on the Ides of March in 44 B.C. It is remarkable that he came to prominence while still in his teens; we may guess that this boosted his juvenile successor's self-confidence, for it showed that so far as Romans were concerned, youth was no bar to supreme power.

When discussing his victories over other Romans, Augustus tactfully names no names and makes a point of stressing his clemency. This is because when peace came, he knew he would need the active support of the political class, or what was left of it after long years of bloodletting, if he was to govern successfully his vast and sprawling inheritance. Also, he had learned from Caesar's violent death and meant to avoid the assassins' knives. Safety lay in forgiving his enemies.

The gods rewarded this commitment to reconciliation with a long life—a lesson that Nero took to heart and that was to be the keynote of the early years of his reign. There was much he would be wise to learn from his forebear's style of government—a mix of innovation with convention, openness with discreet despotism.

In 31 B.C., Augustus (or Gaius Julius Caesar Octavianus, as he was then known) defeated his rival, Marcus Antonius (our Mark Antony) and his lover and political partner, Cleopatra VII Philopator, Queen of Egypt, in a sea battle off the promontory of Actium in northwest Greece.

He was now the last man standing and had the power, if he so wished, to act as an outright tyrant. Instead he devised a new constitutional settlement that he hoped would win broad approval and enable him to rule by consent.

For nearly five centuries Rome had been a republic. Its operating rules were complicated. Male adult citizens voted candidates into public office for periods of one year. They were almost invariably drawn from a handful of highly competitive noble families. Executive authority rested with two Consuls who were heads of state and government. When their time in office was up, they usually went abroad to govern a province (as did a second tier of officials, the Praetors). The Consuls were authorized to veto each other's decisions, and ten Tribunes of the People could veto those of any public official and of the Senate, a large committee comprising all past and present officeholders.

This ramshackle constitution gave carte blanche to corrupt and quarrelsome politicians and was totally unsuitable for a complex imperial nation. In the first century B.C., a succession of powerful generals browbeat the Senate and brought the state to its knees. The last of these was Julius Caesar, who defeated the armies of the republic in a series of battles, Roman on Roman. Victory cost him his life, for he was struck down by embittered members of the Senate when in official session. His authority and his legions passed to his adoptive son and heir, Gaius Octavius (later, as we have seen, to become Augustus and Rome's first emperor), who eventually brought the strife to a close.

Despite the fact that their constitution was the ultimate cause of the civil wars, Romans were inexplicably proud of it. So Augustus obediently brought it back into being. In 27 he announced that he was returning all his powers and provinces to the Senate and People of Rome. He wrote in his memoir:

> After I had extinguished the civil wars, and at a time when with universal consent I was in complete control of affairs, I transferred the Republic from my power to the dominion of the Senate and People of Rome. For this service of mine I was named Augustus by decree of the senate. The door-posts of my house were publicly wreathed with bay leaves and a civic crown [a wreath of oak leaves awarded for saving citizens' lives in battle] was fixed over my door. A golden shield was set in the Curia Julia [the Senate house]. . . . After this time I excelled all in influence, although I possessed no more official power than others who were my colleagues in the several magistracies.

All was not quite as it seemed. At first sight, it looked as if the whole complicated system was indeed restored, but in fact Augustus remained in charge. This was because he allocated to himself a very large superprovince including Spain, Gaul (roughly speaking, today's France), and Syria, which he governed through proxies (he also held Egypt as his private fief). It was no accident that these areas were where most of Rome's standing army was stationed. Augustus controlled the legions and, it followed, he controlled Rome. The apparatus of the republic masked a military autocracy.

With the Ides of March in mind, Augustus arranged for legislation that his person should be inviolable. This offered no guarantees but would at least give the law-abiding assassin pause for thought. He was also granted the various and useful privileges of a Tribune of the People (in particular, the right to veto the activities of any other officeholder).

To make assurance double sure, Augustus founded the Praetorian Guard. These were five cohorts totaling about four and a half thousand men. Elite household troops, they maintained law and order in Italy (from which ordinary legions were barred) and protected the emperor in Rome, where their barracks were located.

The essential point was that while all these powers were unusual, even exceptional, they were perfectly legal and consistent with convention. Nobody could object, and nobody did. Roman politicians could appreciate a good conjuring trick when they saw one. Above all, they had had their dignity returned to them and their grand elective posts. After many years of conflict, most people were willing to make concessions for peace. They agreed to work with Augustus and help him govern the empire. He himself was scrupulously polite to the Consuls, the Praetors, and the rest and took care to consult the Senate on the issues of the day. He insisted on the modest everyday title of "first citizen," or *princeps*.

———

There was more to politics than government, Augustus believed, and the wise ruler paid attention to subjective factors. This was a truth that Nero, interested as he was in the arts and culture, in the life of the imagination, could very well understand.

Rome, the teeming capital of the known world, was unruly. Most of its inhabitants were poor and many were unemployed or could find only part-time work. They lived in squalid housing. These were the *plebs,* or common people, and Augustus realized that they could be pacified, even satisfied, by a program of spectacle. He boasted of the competitive and often cruel entertainments he or his supporters financed and presented:

> I gave three gladiatorial games in my own name and five in that of my sons or grandsons; at these games some 10,000 men took part in combat. Twice in my own name and a third time in that of my grandson I presented to the people displays by athletes summoned from all parts. I produced shows in my own name four times and in place of other magistrates twenty-three times. . . . I gave beast-hunts of African beasts in my own name or in that of my sons and grandsons in the circus or forum or amphitheater on twenty-six occasions, when about 3,500 beasts were destroyed.

Perhaps the most spectacular of these extravaganzas was a marine version of gladiatorial combat. Augustus wrote: "I produced a naval battle as a show for the people." His idea was to restage the famous battle of Salamis between the Athenian victor and the Persian aggressors. On the right bank of the river Tiber an artificial lake was dug, eighteen hundred feet long and twelve hundred feet wide, supplied with water by a purpose-built aqueduct. A high bridge led to an islet in the center. Thirty warships, beaked triremes or biremes and still more smaller vessels, were joined in battle. The "beaks" were metal prongs attached to the prow, which were used to ram enemy ships below the waterline and swamp or sink them.

About three thousand men, in addition to the oarsmen, fought in these fleets. The numbers of wounded and killed are not revealed. The financial cost is also unknown, but must have been colossal. The battle may have been fake, but men really did die to make a Roman holiday. History repeated itself, for the Athenians carried the day.

Spectacle materialized not only in flesh and blood but also in stone. Augustus is well known for ambitious building projects. On his deathbed, he boasted that he found Rome a city of brick but left it a city of marble, a claim with some truth in it. He was proud of what he had achieved and left out of his memoir no new development, large or small. He renewed aqueducts that were essential to Rome's water supply but had fallen into disrepair. He improved the drainage system and a major road running north out of the city and up the Italian peninsula. Eighty-two temples of the gods were refurbished.

Civic landmarks such as the Capitol and the theater of Pompey on the Campus Martius were renovated. A brand-new theater was dedicated to the memory of a beloved nephew. A business center, or *basilica*, was constructed after a fire as well as a new forum or public square, where lawsuits were heard and commercial and retail activity conducted. All of these works are itemized on the bronze plaques, an indication of the importance he placed on them. We shall see that Nero too was to become a great builder and, like Augustus, to maintain the transformation of Rome into the fitting capital of a great empire.

The years of carnage had had emotional and social consequences. A conviction that Roman values of virtue and courage had been undermined was widespread. The most famous historian of the age, Titus Livius, whom we call Livy, pointed to

> the personalities and principles of the men responsible at home and on the battlefield for the foundation and growth of empire and will appreciate the decline in discipline and in moral standards . . . down to the present day. For we have now reached a point where our degeneracy is intolerable.

To promote this gloomy (and somewhat overstated) analysis and to call for a cleansing, the princeps gathered poets around him, one of whom, the great Quintus Horatius Flaccus (our Horace), explicitly linked the chaos of recent times to moral collapse:

. . . riven by civil faction, Rome came near
To her annihilation and eclipse.

Bad sex coincided with, perhaps helped to cause, the crisis:

The age has proved fertile in evil. First
It stained the marriage vow, and then the home,
And thence impure blood; and from this fouled source burst
The river of ruin that flooded Rome.

Horace imagines a young woman's debasement. She "perfects the arts of provocation" and

Careless of whom
She chooses, hugger-mugger she confers
The illicit pleasure in a half-lit room.

One of Augustus's concerns, almost an obsession, was to purify morals and promote family values. He passed social legislation, among which measures a woman's adultery was for the first time made a public offense as distinct from being a private matter. Husbands were compelled to divorce their adulterous wives. Bachelors and childless couples were penalized.

The emperor's efforts seem to have borne little fruit, though, and the tone of Roman society remained as louche as ever.

The Forum Romanum was the city's meeting place. Lined by temples and shops and crowded with statues of the famous men of old, this was where businessmen met and bargained, where politicians surrounded by hangers-on schemed and gossiped. Here, too, litigants attended the open-air law courts.

The observer could be forgiven for failing to notice a tiny building, which may have originated in a bridge over the city's drain, the Cloaca Maxima, once an open culvert but now covered over. It was dedicated to Janus, god of beginnings and endings, of comings and goings, of passageways and doors. More particularly, he presided over transitions to and from war and peace.

At each end of the shrine were double doors that stood open in times of war and were closed only when Rome was at peace. Augustus writes:

> It was the will of our ancestors that the gateway of Janus should be shut when victories had secured peace by land and sea throughout the whole empire of the Roman people. From the foundation of the city down to my birth, tradition records that it was shut only twice, but while I was the princeps the senate resolved that it should be shut on three occasions.

The princeps was an aggressive ruler for whom peace was not worth having unless on his own terms. He believed in the superiority of Roman civilization and endorsed his court poet Vergil's claim: *"Tu regere imperio populos, Romane, memento"* (Roman, remember by your power and authority to rule the peoples of the earth).

By the time Augustus died, exactly forty years before Nero's accession, the empire had expanded to include northern Spain, parts of North Africa, the Alps, and territories along the Danube. He writes:

> I extended the territory of all those provinces of the Roman people on whose borders lay peoples not subject to our government.

Along the frontiers of empire the princeps relied for defense on client rulers. He lists two kings of the Britons, Dumnobellaunus and Tincommius, as "suppliants." However, a serious setback east of the Rhine thwarted his ambition to annex the Germanic tribes east of the Rhine. On this his memoir is deceitfully, if understandably, silent, but thoughtful Romans began to wonder whether endless expansion was sensible.

Augustus's greatest foreign policy coup was not military but diplomatic. This was the peace he negotiated with Rome's only serious competitor in the ancient world—the Parthian empire, which stretched from the river Euphrates to the river Indus. The two great powers quarreled about which of them should control the buffer kingdom of Armenia. Neither wanted all-out war, and a settlement was hammered out.

Somewhat overegging his cake, the princeps declared victory:

> I compelled the Parthians to restore to me the spoils and standards of three [previously defeated] Roman armies and to ask as suppliants for the friendship of the Roman people. Those standards I deposited in the innermost shrine of the temple of Mars the Avenger.

In fact, the entente was fair to both sides, but the problem of Armenia remained a thorn in the relationship between the empires. The strategic landscape across the empire had changed little since Augustus's day, and Nero would find himself having to deal not only with the difficult neighbor beyond the Euphrates but also with the savages on their foggy northern island beyond the uttermost ends of the earth.

The ceremonies were over. Nero and his party emerged out of the torchlit tunnel into the light of day. They passed between the twin columns and, the first emperor's legacy to his successors, his biography in bronze. The doors of the Mausoleum closed behind them and the great dead were left alone in the dark. The young emperor turned back toward the city, processing along the Via Flaminia, the Flaminian Way. The colossal temple of Jupiter Best and Greatest frowned from the heights of the Capitol as Nero walked through a gateway in the city wall into the Forum and entered his palace.

2

A FAMILY AT WAR

IT WAS A BRIGHT winter's dawn in the year 37. The sun's beams shone down on the exhausted woman and her newborn son. For want of antiseptics and anesthetics, giving birth was as dangerous as contracting a serious disease. It has been estimated that infant mortality stood at about three hundred for each one thousand live births.

On this occasion, the baby came into the world feet first, and the night had been terrible. Not only had the pain been hard to bear, but the mother's health, indeed her survival and that of her child, were at grave risk. Worse almost than that, a breech birth was widely held to be a bad omen. A contemporary observed: "It is in the due order of nature that man should enter the world with the head first, and be carried to the tomb in a contrary fashion."

For this pregnancy to have a successful outcome was of some importance, for the mother in question was Agrippina, sister of Rome's emperor, the erratic, some said mad, Gaius (most people know him as Caligula, or Little Boots, the nickname his father's soldiers gave him when he was a small boy).

She chose for her lying-in the splendid imperial villa at Antium, a popular seaside resort about thirty miles south of Rome, which offered relief from the noise, smells, airless heat, and crowded streets of the capital. Terraces gave onto the sea and included a roofed open-air loggia surrounded by a colonnade. Not far away was a small private theater; a civilized Roman was expected to write poetry, or at least verse, in the Greek manner, and here he could give recitations, sing arias, and act in semistaged tragedies.

To be bathed in sunlight at life's beginning was certainly auspicious, but other portents seem to have been adverse. A celebrated soothsayer, interpreting the date, time, and manner of his birth, cast a pessimistic horoscope for the little prince. He predicted that he would one day become emperor and murder his mother. Agrippina was not one to be easily daunted, and we are told that she replied: "He can kill me but just let him rule." (This famous remark is more terse and brutal in Latin: *Occidat dum imperet*.)

She was strong and fearless, but the experience was traumatic, both psychologically and physically. Her son, who was indeed to become the emperor whom we know as Nero, caused her so much suffering during his arrival that we can understand why, in spite of two further marriages in the future, she bore no more children.

The ruling dynasty was divided into two families, the Julians and the Claudians. The patriarch was Julius Caesar's great-nephew and adopted son, Augustus, who had a daughter, Julia, by his first wife. His second marriage, to Livia, produced no male offspring. He married Julia off to his best friend and comrade in empire, Marcus Vipsanius Agrippa, by whom she bore three boys and two girls.

As the years passed, the question of the succession inevitably loomed. Although his powers were in theory personal to him, the princeps decided that heredity was the only sure guarantee of political stability. Otherwise Rome's incurably competitive politicians would fight among themselves for the throne and very probably set off another civil war.

Julia had produced a plenitude of heirs, but the fates had other ideas. First of all, a nephew and then two of Julia's sons died in their late teens or early twenties, while a third suffered from some kind of personality disorder and was deemed unfit to rule.

Fortunately, Augustus's wife, Livia, had had a first marriage to a certain Tiberius Claudius Nero, both of whom were members of one of Rome's most ancient clans, the Claudii. They had two capable and loyal sons, Drusus, who also died young, and Tiberius, the sole survivor of all the hopeful inheritors. When Augustus died in A.D. 14 at the age of seventy-seven, Tiberius followed him as emperor. (Julia's unsuitable boy was not allowed to survive into the new reign.)

It was troublesome that the second princeps had not a drop of Julian blood in his veins, and before he left the stage, the old puppet master, Augustus, laid a plan to put this right. Tiberius was obliged to adopt his brother's son, a glamorous general called Germanicus, who in turn was obliged to marry one of Julia's daughters, Agrippina (called the Elder to distinguish her from her daughter, also called Agrippina, whom we have seen give birth to Nero). At last the two genetic streams were united in Germanicus's children.

Augustus had moved family members like pawns on a chessboard, whatever their personal feelings, but finally he had had his way. The Julians and the Claudians had blended into the Julio-Claudians.

The dynastic problem was solved, but once again, the fates thought otherwise.

The story of the empire's early decades is in large part one of masterful women, who faced difficulties if they were politically ambitious and wanted to make their way in the world outside the home. One of these was the younger Agrippina. Whatever the obstacles, she meant to succeed.

Public life was exclusively masculine. The Roman male was master of all he surveyed. When head of the family or paterfamilias, he held absolute power over his dependent relatives and the slaves that were an omnipresent feature of life in the ancient world. In theory, albeit only occasionally in practice, he was entitled to put his son to death and to kill his wife on the spot if he caught her in flagrante delicto.

Women were expected to be chaste and obedient, to behave modestly and tend their reputation. Their main functions were to wed a man, give birth to children, and manage the household. Protection of the bloodline was essential, so love affairs were out of the question. They were citizens but not allowed to vote or hold state office. That said, they enjoyed certain freedoms; they shared their husband's social life, met women friends, and attended public entertainments. Best of all, women were entitled to own and manage property (albeit sometimes with a male guardian).

Those women who openly ignored convention and intruded on male territory were punished by the destruction of their good name. They were represented as sexually voracious and subversive of the family.

Marriage was simply an agreement between families or, more precisely, between fathers. A wedding was no more than the ceremonial expression of a financial or political deal. Sexual passion was irrelevant to the choice of either bride or groom.

Girls married in their early teens, sometimes before puberty and as early as eleven years (a kind husband might delay sexual relations for a year or two). One consequence was that their schooling was rudimentary and would come to an abrupt end with the arrival of a spouse. Divorce was a fairly straightforward matter. A wife simply took back her dowry and left her husband's house, often returning to her father's care. The procedure was socially respectable, but a couple was wise to consider the consequences for the two families on the breakup of their alliance.

Although the minimum age for men to marry was fourteen, they were usually in their twenties before they did so. Because of the large age gap, they tended to die long before their wives, who could remarry if they chose or be guided by a guardian. However, many widows were at last able to live merrily, free of interference from their male relatives.

Faced with such constraints, what was an able and ambitious woman like the younger Agrippina to do with her life? A couple of role models presented themselves to her. The first and closest to hand was her mother.

Tiberius, tired and aging, did not seek the throne, but after Augustus's death, he implemented his wishes out of a gloomy sense of duty. Despite the fact that he had a son of his own, he appointed Germanicus to major foreign commands. Germanicus was young and attractive, in contrast to the melancholy princeps, but he was not a very talented general. However, he and his wife, the elder Agrippina, were a glamorous and (for an imposed union) devoted couple and very popular with the army. Agrippina accompanied her husband to the Rhine frontier and then to Asia, with a growing tribe of children. On one occasion her decisiveness rallied discouraged troops: she staved off panic and saved the day by acting as if she were their commander. She was evidently the dominant personality in the partnership. From a traditional Roman's point of view, she behaved like a man. This was the height of impropriety.

Germanicus was commissioned to reorganize the eastern provinces, which he accomplished successfully, but in 19, he died, suddenly and in doubtful circumstances, at Antioch. His grief-stricken widow was sure he had been poisoned and that the emperor was behind the deed. When she returned to Rome with the dead man's ashes, she was greeted by huge mourning crowds.

She was aware that as a woman she could never reign herself, but she distrusted the princeps and did everything possible to promote the cause of her three sons, the eldest of whom, Nero Caesar (not our Nero but his uncle), she regarded as Germanicus's heir and hence as the next emperor. She overplayed her hand, depending too heavily on her and her family's immense popularity and being furiously impolite in person to the emperor.

Her campaign claimed a scalp: The governor of Syria, who had feuded with Germanicus, was tried for his murder and committed suicide before a verdict was announced. He had had the emperor's ostensible backing, but maybe he knew too much. Agrippina did not stop there and aroused grave suspicions in Tiberius's mind. Once he took her by the hand and quoted a Greek saying: "If you are not empress, my girl, do you think you have been wronged?"

The final insult came when the princeps asked her to dinner, during which she refused an apple he proffered her. This was a grave insult, for the implication was that Agrippina feared, or pretended to do so, that the fruit was poisoned. Perhaps Tiberius was being too sensitive and there had been no such subtext, but the incident exposed the breakdown of a familial relationship.

The emperor's favorite and unofficial deputy, Lucius Aelius Sejanus, did all he could to discredit Agrippina, and her followers, further. His allegations eventually led Tiberius to lose patience, and he exiled her to the windy little island of Pandateria (today's Ventotene) off the Naples coast. Absence did not silence Agrippina, and to punish her contumacy, a centurion was ordered to give her a good flogging, during the course of which she lost an eye. Two of her three sons fared no better: They were both imprisoned and died. Nero, on another of the state's prison islands, was frightened into suicide. Drusus was locked up in a palace cellar in Rome and denied food. It was reported that hunger drove him to chew the flocking from his mattress.

In due course, Sejanus, who had been largely responsible for the fall of Germanicus's family, himself fell. He was executed by strangling, and an angry mob tore his body into pieces so small that the executioner could find no part left large enough to drag, as was the custom, to the Tiber.

Although he was now fully briefed on Sejanus's crimes, Tiberius did not rehabilitate Agrippina, and she remained on her little island. After a few years she had had enough of life and starved herself to death.

Tiberius was an experienced politician and not liable to indulge his emotions. It is hard to resist the suspicion that there was more than bluster to Agrippina's conduct and that she had been not only complaining in public but also secretly plotting against the princeps.

In that case, this unlikable woman got what was coming to her.

As we shall see, the younger Agrippina's career suggests that she had studied her mother's political methods and found much to admire in them. But she learned to avoid the irritability and rashness that had brought her down. Fortunately, there was another role model close by, one who deployed subtlety rather than bluntness and ended her life full of years and honors. This was her great-grandmother Livia, Augustus's widow, with whom she and her siblings had lived for a while after their mother's disgrace. Agrippina was fourteen and already married when the old lady died in 29.

In public, Livia was the model of a Roman matron, dressing plainly and (we are told) making her husband's clothes. She took care not to offend custom and practice.

Actually, she was very active behind the scenes. She was always at Augustus's side. He often consulted her and wrote notes for himself of her thoughts on topics he intended to raise.

Livia was officially released from male supervision and proved to be a good businesswoman—with copper mines in Gaul, estates in Asia, properties throughout Italy (including a brickworks, papyrus marshes, vineyards, and arable farms), and granaries in Egypt. She became very rich in her own right.

When her son assumed the purple, he was irritated to find that she had fingers in many political pies and often warned her to "remember that she was a woman and must not interfere in affairs of state." Caligula liked her but called her "Ulysses in a frock" (Ulysses, the Latin form of the name Odysseus, was the hero of Homer's epic *The Odyssey,* and a byword for cunning).

There can be no doubt that the younger Agrippina was her mother's daughter; she too was proud, ambitious, and sure of herself. But there was much to learn from the aged Livia—the importance of advice given (and strictly kept) in confidence, and above all the value of patience, a quality that often brings with it luck. Augustus's relict had played a long game and thrived. Although it took some unpleasant experiences to drive the lesson home, Germanicus's daughter learned when to lie low and when to pounce. She differed from Livia in only one respect—she was determined to have a public career whatever the men said. Were she ever to become empress—and as a member of the imperial family, why should she not?—she would re-create the partnership between Augustus and his beloved Livia.

And she would take her time.

Tiberius, who disliked the chaos and compromises of the capital city and now resided in reclusion on the island of Capri off the Campanian coast,was unforgiving to those members of his family who he believed were guilty of conspiring against him. However, he did not pursue those he felt were blameless.

The younger Agrippina was not old enough to be entangled in plots. Destined to be Nero's mother, she was born on November 6, 15, in a new town on the west bank of the Rhine.The baby girl's first months were spent surrounded by soldiers in an army camp, after which she accompanied her parents back to Rome and their grand house on the fashionable Palatine hill. When Germanicus left on his doomed expedition, he brought his wife and Caligula with him, leaving the other children behind, probably in the temporary care of their grandmother, Antonia Minor.

The girl was four years old when her father died and was among the procession of dignitaries who greeted her anguished mother on her return to the city. It must have been a momentous encounter and may have been among Agrippina's earliest memories. For some time she was brought up at home. As we have seen, in 27, after her mother's disgrace, exile, imprisonment, and death, the aged Livia took Caligula, now aged fifteen, and the other surviving Germanican children into her house close by. For her, family came first; if the dynasty was to survive, the only likely heirs were to be found among the offspring of Germanicus.

Agrippina's stay with her great-grandmother was an introduction to the practice of politics behind the scenes, but unluckily it was not to be for long. In 28, at the age of thirteen, she married Gnaeus Domitius Ahenobarbus and took up residence in her husband's home at a smart address on the Via Sacra (the Holy Way), which led into the Forum. The Domitii were among the oldest of Rome's clans, having flourished in those distant days when immortals still walked the earth.

The two young men on horseback were taller and more beautiful than ordinary human beings and had just grown their first beard.

They seemed to have come from nowhere. They plunged headlong into the ranks of the enemy and helped win the battle of Lake Regillus for the Romans, a mythical encounter between the small city-state and the neighboring tribe of the Latins. The fighting was over by the late afternoon.

Immediately afterward, two youths are said to have appeared in the Roman forum, very similar to those at Lake Regillus. In military dress, they looked as if they had come from a battle. They watered their horses, which were in a lather, and washed them down in a spring that rose from the ground near the temple of Vesta, goddess of the Roman hearth, and formed a small but deep pool.

A bystander asked them if they had come from the camp and what was the result of the battle. They replied that the Romans had won the day, and to confirm the truth of what they had said, they stroked the man's beard, which changed its color from black to a reddish bronze. As a result, he was dubbed Ahenobarbus, or Bronze-Beard. He was a member of the *gens Domitia* (the Domitius clan), and his descendants used the epithet as a hereditary cognomen (a Roman citizen's third name, which often originated from a nickname).

The mysterious riders vanished and were never seen again. They were believed to be the demigods Castor and Pollux, heavenly twins (and brothers of Helen of Troy). They were friends of humankind and helped people in times of crisis. A temple was built in their honor on the spot where they had materialized.

The family that claimed this legend, and into which Agrippina married—the Domitii—run like a russet thread through the weave of Roman history. They acquired a name for arrogance, violence, and corruption. Perhaps they passed down a genetic predisposition to their descendants, or perhaps they were the victims of prejudiced ancient historians. Alternatively and plausibly, having acquired a terrible reputation, they told themselves to live up to it generation by generation. They certainly behaved badly. (Not that they were alone in this, for the venality of Rome's ruling class was endemic and eventually helped bring down the Roman republic.)

It was said of one of the Domitii in the second century B.C.: "Should his bronze beard really surprise us? After all, he has an iron face and a heart of lead." A later Domitius took part in the civil war against Julius Caesar, but without success. He was typical of his clan. According to Suetonius, he found it hard to make up his mind, although he had a violent temper. He once attempted to kill himself in a fit of despair and panic, but so shrank from death that he had second thoughts and vomited up the poison. He conferred freedom on his doctor (probably a Greek slave), who knew his master and had purposely given him less than a fatal dose.

Other sources speak well of him, but in unconvincingly general terms. He lost his life at the battle of Pharsalus in central Greece, which decided the outcome of the civil war in Julius Caesar's favor.

The next Ahenobarbus in line had a more attractive personality, but he too was indecisive. Having initially supported Mark Antony in his great quarrel with Octavian, he switched sides to the victor just before the sea battle of Actium in 31 B.C., which brought the long succession of civil wars to a close. He diverted attention from his betrayal by instantly dying from natural causes.

His son reverted to type, being "haughty, extravagant, and cruel." Agrippina's Ahenobarbus had his full share of the family genes. According to Suetonius, he was "detestable in every aspect of life." Once, when driving along the Appian Way outside Rome, he purposely ran over a child playing in the road. When someone was rude to him in the Forum we are told he gouged the man's eyes out. We read of no court case, no conviction, and no punishment. Antonia, his mother, thought he was feckless for adding a bath annex to his family house when he should have been paying attention to his political career.

He was a passionate chariot driver in his youth and was better known for his successes at the racecourse than for his military campaigning in Germany. When elected as Praetor and later as Consul, he presented lavish public entertainments. These included a farce starring wealthy citizens and married women, to the scandal of respectable opinion. Wild animal hunts were staged at one of Rome's major venues, the Circus Maximus (or Great Racecourse), and in the city's neighborhoods. So great was the bloodletting at one gladiatorial display that Augustus had a quiet word with him about it; when he paid no attention, the princeps made his reservations public in an edict.

Social standing counted for more than bad behavior. Ahenobarbus was persona grata at court—so much so that his marriage was arranged to a daughter of Octavia, Augustus's much-loved sister. That brought him into the magic circle of the Julio-Claudians. He was now family. He will have been even more delighted when Tiberius agreed that his son should marry the little Agrippina. As a direct descendant of Augustus, she was a great catch. Their son is the protagonist of this book and the inheritor of the family genes. When he arrives in the world, he will have a reasonable claim to the throne were he to advance it.

Ahenobarbus did not remain in favor at court for long. He only just survived the reign of Tiberius. He was charged with impiety toward the emperor, adultery, murder, and incest with his sister Domitia Lepida. The sexual accusations were suspiciously generic and may have been confected to conceal a political intrigue. In any event, the sentence of execution was revoked when Tiberius died before it could be implemented.

What can Tiberius, the misanthrope of Capri, have been thinking of? He appeared to be running two mutually opposed policies—on the one hand, the destruction of Germanicus's family, and its rebirth on the other. The contradiction can, in fact, be resolved into a paradox. If the Julio-Claudian grip on power was to be maintained, it was essential to end the purges and cherish the few survivors—among them Agrippina. Tiberius had no choice but to be loving.

The other factor that will have weighed with him was the regime's relations with the Senate, the committee that represented the ruling class. Augustus and his descendants sought to bind the noble clans to them through marriages, that of Domitius and Agrippina being the latest. This practice worked well enough, although it did have the long-term disadvantage of producing numerous pretenders of the blood who could plot against the reigning incumbent. In later years they were to unbalance Nero's reign.

On top of it all, Tiberius was short of time. He had been in office for more than twenty years and was in his seventies. He was tired. Thanks to the purges over which he had presided, only two plausible candidates for the succession remained. One of them was the princeps's own grandson, a surviving twin and so nicknamed Gemellus; but he was only sixteen and a late developer. He had not yet reached puberty and was deemed too young for office. But he would soon be old enough to participate fully in public life and his future hung on the emperor staying alive.

His rival, Caligula, was Agrippina's brother and the only survivor of the sons of Germanicus. He brought with him the incomparable advantage of his late father's charisma. The princeps had both boys live with him on the island of Capri. We may presume that he wanted to keep them from nefarious influences. He cannot have supposed that either of them was qualified to rule, but took his duties seriously and must have spent time training them in the business of government.

Once he came across the two youths together. When he gave Gemellus a surprise hug with tears in his eyes, he noticed the grim expression on Caligula's face. He told him angrily: "*You* will kill him, and someone else will kill *you*." (The prediction was accurate: The lonely twin did not long survive the new reign.)

On March 16 in the year 37, time ran out for Tiberius. His health failed. His doctor took his pulse and opined that he had only two days to live. Letters were posted to provincial governors and commanders of the legionary armies. Plans were discreetly put in place to ensure a smooth transition of power. The princeps stopped breathing.

Then something terrible happened. His voice and vision returned. He shouted from his bedroom for some food. Caligula was surrounded by well-wishers and supposed he was now emperor. When the news arrived of Tiberius's recovery, panic ensued. Everyone fled except Caligula, who stood frozen with fear. His chief backer was the Prefect of the Praetorian Guard, the elite force tasked with protecting the emperor. He kept his calm and gave orders for the old man to be smothered under a pile of bedclothes. This was done, and the congratulations resumed. The young man relaxed. A new dawn had broken.

Caligula faced more than one conspiracy during his short, unpredictable reign. One of them was headed by those nearest and dearest to him.

He had grown up in a family under sustained attack from the state. Apart from himself, his three sisters were now the only members left. The eldest, Agrippina, was by this point in her early twenties.

Caligula awarded the siblings special honors. Perhaps the most remarkable of these was the appearance of the sisters on a coin minted at the beginning of the reign. They also enjoyed the same rights and privileges as the six priestesses of the goddess of the civic hearth, Vesta. These were the Vestal Virgins, the holiest women in ancient Rome, and the only ones with a senior public function. They had places of honor reserved for them at public games and performances. They could free condemned prisoners and slaves by touching them—if a person who was sentenced to death saw a Vestal on his way to the execution, he was automatically pardoned. Above all, a Vestal's person was sacrosanct. Nothing could be done that would harm her.

New wording was ordained for all official oaths:

> And I will not value my life or that of my children less highly than I do the safety of Gaius [that is, Caligula] and of his sisters.

In addition, he instituted a new formula for the Consuls to recite when introducing a proposition to the Senate:

> Good fortune and happiness attend Gaius and his sisters.

The goddess of luck had certainly been on Agrippina's side: She had suddenly placed her at the seat of power. She had also gained the inestimable advantage of an infant son. If childhood diseases spared him, he was likely to grow into an important addition to the imperial dynasty. A place in perpetuity at the top table of imperial politics was more or less guaranteed for his mother. All she would have to do was to encase him in her love.

So close was the emperor to his siblings that gossips, always looking out for the least favorable analysis, reported that

> it was his habit to commit incest with each of his three sisters. . . . They say that he violated his sister Drusilla's virginity before he came of age: their grandmother Antonia, at whose house they were both staying, caught them in bed together.

Strip away the veneer of sex and what may be left is deep familial affection and an end of loneliness.

Caligula marked his father's memory by renaming the month of September Germanicus; as for his mother and brothers, all the files of written evidence in their cases were taken to the Forum and burned. This was to lay to rest any fears former prosecution witnesses or informants might have for their safety, but the flames were also an act of rehabilitation.

What then is very odd is the discovery of a plot implicating the sisters. Much to Caligula's grief, Drusilla had died (of natural causes), but Agrippina and Livilla remained. They accompanied their brother on an expedition to the Rhineland. The course of events is unclear and fragmentary, but it appears that the general in charge of the province of Upper Germany was conspiring against Caligula. One of the emperor's closest friends, Marcus Aemilius Lepidus, with whom he was rumored to have had sex, was implicated in the conspiracy—and so, most remarkably, were the siblings.

This must have been a bitter blow. Suetonius tells us that the princeps accused them both of adultery with Lepidus and openly produced incriminating letters in their own handwriting. The guilty men were put to death and the sisters were banished to a small "prison" island. All their possessions were auctioned. As a culminating humiliation, Agrippina was commanded to place Lepidus's cremated bones into an urn which she then had to carry back to Rome in her arms—just as her mother had returned the ashes of Germanicus. He dedicated to Mars the Avenger three daggers with which, so an explanatory notice read, the would-be murderers had intended to kill him.

The sisters were lucky not to lose their lives, but their status as imperial women was lost before it had properly begun. Caligula issued a warning: "I have swords as well as islands."

Agrippina was intelligent, energetic, and interested in making her way in the great world, but her first foray had been a full-on catastrophe. Fortunately, she was given the time to reflect on the error of her ways. As it turned out, she was a good learner.

This is a mysterious story, and too much is missing in the ancient texts for it to be readily decipherable. It is clear that at the beginning of his reign, Caligula intended to break Roman convention and give Agrippina and Livilla public careers, an opportunity they will have welcomed.

There is only one credible explanation for their failed attempt to bring down their loving and all-powerful brother, and it has nothing to do with sex. The Julio-Claudians or their observers, or both, tended to account for political crises at court in sexual terms. It does not much matter whether Lepidus enjoyed the favors of all, of some, or of none.

Caligula was an intelligent young man with a wicked sense of humor, but inexperienced and overconfident. The son of Germanicus brought with him to the principate a fund of political capital, but after a couple of years on the throne much of it had been squandered. A wise emperor knew that he could try the patience either of the Senate or of the army chiefs who commanded legions and guarded the frontiers, but never both simultaneously. That was the mistake Caligula made, and in time it was to prove fatal.

Agrippina and the others saw the threat their brother brought to them. If he fell, they would fall with him. They too were intelligent, as well as being brutal realists. For them to continue enjoying power and privilege, the regime had to stay. In that case, Caligula had to go.

It was about this time that Agrippina made the acquaintance of a young man called Gaius Ofonius Tigellinus. The archetypal gigolo, he was poor but good-looking. He came from Agrigentum in Sicily (today's Agrigento). He got into some kind of trouble there and was exiled to a town in Calabria.

He slept with Agrippina and Livilla as well as with their husbands (whether serially or in groups we are not told). He was associated with the conspiracy against Caligula, but was only on its fringes, for he escaped execution and received a lesser penalty: banishment from Rome. He lived for a while as a fisherman in southern Greece. He then came into a fortune and was recalled on condition that he stay away from court. He bought land in Apulia and Calabria, where he trained horses for chariot races.

We will meet Tigellinus again, high in favor with Nero.

The island was volcanic, rocky and heavily wooded, and offered the exhausted mariners a small natural harbor. For two days they lay on the beach by their ship, recovering their strength after terrifying adventures. They were Greeks sailing home from the fallen city of Troy on the coast of Asia Minor.

The third day was heralded by a beautiful dawn. The group's leader was the crafty Odysseus. He slipped away from the ship and struck inland. In the *Odyssey*, Homer has his hero tell the tale:

> I made for a coign of vantage where I might look out for signs of human industry or hear male voices. I climbed a rocky height which promised a wide view, and on reaching the top I was able to see smoke rising from a distant spot.

Odysseus and his companions had inadvertently stumbled on the residence with its glowing hearth of the mythical goddess Circe, who amused herself by turning human visitors into animals—on this occasion into pigs. Odysseus managed to reverse her magic and went on his way.

Circe knew her sea-girt home by the name of Aeaea, but a millennium later Agrippina called it Pontia (apparently so named in honor of the family of Pontius Pilate, which owned a grotto there; today it is called Ponza). She did so with little pleasure, for this was to be her place of exile. But all was not so grim as it at first appeared.

Pontia is the main island, rocky and narrow, of an archipelago about seventy miles west of Naples (Neapolis, Greek for New City). It is some five and a half miles long. The ruins of two villas have been unearthed, one of them occupying more than nine acres. It stood on a headland overlooking a cove that was very probably the ancient harbor. A tunnel connected it to another cove on the far side of the island's narrow spine, where ships could also moor. At the foot of the headland, there were probably fishpools that provided fresh sea-food for the villa's occupants. Along the heights are the remains of terraces and a small theater or odeon, suitable for literary readings and chamber concerts.

Elsewhere an underground chamber contained niches for the cremated remains of the dead and for the inhumation of bodies. This must have been where little Domitius's uncle, Nero Julius Caesar, lay after his enforced suicide, until on his accession Caligula came in person to remove him and install him in the Mausoleum of Augustus.

Caligula may have selected Pontia for Agrippina's exile with a caustic smile, for, from his viewpoint, she was a modern Circe set on entrapping a man to his ruin. However, he had no intention of making her life uncomfortable. What we know of the island of Pontia and its extensive villa strongly suggests that the emperor's sister lived there in some style with numerous staff.

Her punishment was not so much painful as tiresome. There was nothing to do except brood on the failure of her schemes and wait for the future—if there was to be a future.

She must have nearly died of boredom.

———

The flamingo struggled but was held in place so that the princeps was able to kill it cleanly. Unluckily, blood spurted out from the wound and splashed onto a bystander's toga. Caligula, holding his bloody knife, laughed good-naturedly.

However, his underlying mood was savage. In the four years since he had succeeded Tiberius he had become unpredictable and, it would appear, unbalanced. Relations with the Senate, so friendly at the outset, had deteriorated badly. Plots and rumors of plots rose and ebbed around the city. The authorities caught as many would-be assassins as they could find and put an end to them. But there were always more.

The sacrifice of the flamingo was in honor of Augustus and was conducted at an altar on the Palatine hill. It was the ceremony which opened the third and last day of the annual Palatine games. A temporary theater had been built for the specially invited audience, including women and children. People sat where they wanted. The mood was easy and informal. A program of dramas, mimes, and musical recitals was presented.

Just after midday the princeps was in two minds. Should he or should he not adjourn for lunch? Eventually his retinue persuaded him to return to the palace along a covered passageway. Once inside, he decided to wash rather than eat and took a corridor, where there happened to be no guards, that led to his baths. He paused in a temporary greenroom to watch a troupe of boy dancers rehearse their moves while waiting to be called for their act.

An officer of the Praetorian Guard who was in attendance asked Caligula for the watchword. "Jupiter," he replied. "So take this!" shouted the officer, a military tribune called Cassius Chaerea, and struck the princeps from behind, inflicting a deep wound where the shoulder joins the neck. According to another version, he drove his sword through the jaw.

Caligula fell to the ground and writhed with pain. "I am still alive," he shouted, hopefully. The only people who came to his aid were his bearers, who tried in vain to defend him with their litter poles. A mêlée of blood and metal ensued. More than thirty wounds were counted on his corpse, some inflicted after he was dead. They included gashes through his genitals. Some spat on the man whom a few minutes previously they had greeted with the utmost respect.

The princeps had inadvertently become separated from a detachment of his close personal bodyguards. Distinct from the Praetorians, they were loyal German mounted infantrymen, between five hundred and a thousand strong. Carrying weapons but not wearing armor, they looked like paramilitaries. Most of them were Batavi, tribesmen from the lower Rhine. They were loyal to the emperor of the day. When those who were on duty learned of the attack they went berserk, killing at random anyone they came across, including three luckless Senators.

Members of the audience did not know how to react to the assassination. Most of them were probably pleased but suspected that the report of his death was the kind of half-crazed practical joke that the emperor might have staged for his amusement. Without more ado they scrambled from the theater as fast as their legs would take them.

A former Consul, Decimus Valerius Asiaticus, was a friend of the imperial house but privately loathed Caligula, not merely for sleeping with his wife but for boasting about it in his presence. He had been chatting with the princeps in the auditorium before the show and knew nothing of what was afoot. People asked him later who had done the deed, to which he replied: "I wish I had."

3

THE IMPROBABLE EMPEROR

AFTERWARD, people thought it a little odd that Claudius had left the show early for lunch. Everyone knew he liked his food, being a gourmand rather than a gourmet. But to vacate his seat before the emperor, who was notoriously touchy, was taking a risk. Intelligent observers, thinking later on the day's events, raised their eyebrows and held their peace.

According to the official account, Claudius made his way from the theater to a hall in the palace called the Hermaeum, and there he first learned of Caligula's assassination. He heard guards going from room to room on the lookout for valuables to purloin. Footsteps approached. Curtains hung across a door that gave onto a balcony and for want of time to escape Claudius hid trembling behind them.

A Praetorian private noticed a pair of feet beneath the curtains. He dragged their owner out for identification. Claudius dropped to the floor and begged for mercy. The man recognized him and immediately acclaimed him as emperor.

This was tantamount to a death warrant, for he was surrounded by enemies on all sides. He was uncomfortably aware of being the last surviving male member of the family of Germanicus. Senators hostile to the regime would want him out of the way. So would the assassins, fearful of revenge. So would candidates for the purple. Being a prisoner of the Praetorians was probably the safest place to be. Apart from the conspirators, most of them were loyal to Caligula and furious at his death, but they lacked an obvious target on which to relieve their fury. So they brought Claudius, frightened and in despair, back to the Guards barracks by the city wall in the north of Rome. The soldiers took turns carrying his litter because all his bearers had run off. Unable to resist the temptation of being kingmakers, the Praetorians offered Claudius the throne at a mass meeting. At first he declined but eventually accepted the proposal.

Meanwhile the Consuls took charge of the Forum and transferred the treasury reserves from the temple of Saturn to Rome's highly defensible citadel, the Capitol. It was here too that they convened an emergency meeting of the Senate at which they would decide what to do next.

Some members of the house believed that the moment had come to dismantle the autocracy and restore the tumbledown, semidemocratic republic—some, but not a majority. The Senators could not agree on a common course of action, except to adjourn.

When they learned that Claudius had survived the day and was spending the night with the Praetorians, they sent two junior politicians to instruct Claudius to attend the Senate. He declined the invitation on the grounds that he was "detained by force." The delegates threw down their cards, asking him at least to accept the principate from his peers, not from the soldiery.

Senators met again the following morning but bickered. Outside, a crowd called for them to appoint a new emperor and shouted Claudius's name. Eventually they lost their nerve and voted Claudius all the powers of the princeps. Wisely, he gave each Praetorian a generous bonus and administered an oath of loyalty.

The rise of Claudius was a surprise. His childhood was marred by persistent illness, and it is possible that he suffered from cerebral palsy. He had a dignified presence when standing still or seated, but his head and hands shook slightly and he dragged his right leg. He had a speech defect and an unpleasant laugh. When his emotions ran high, he slobbered and his nose ran.

His family was embarrassed by Claudius, Livia had as little to do with him as possible and his mother, Antonia, called him "a monster whom Nature had not finished but merely begun." So far as feasible, he was kept out of the public eye.

Augustus understood that Claudius's disabilities posed a problem for the regime, but he had time for him. In a letter he wrote to his wife he commented: "The poor fellow is unlucky, for in serious matters, where his mind does not wander, the nobility of his character is apparent enough."

In fact, Claudius was not the fool he appeared. If he was to be excluded from the family business, namely the exercise of power, then he would devote himself to the study of history, the exercise of power in the past. Among other books he wrote a history of the Etruscans, a civilization of ancient Italy that had played an important part in the foundation of Rome. He also began work on a history of the empire from the murder of Julius Caesar, but he realized that he would not be allowed to give a true and frank account and so left out the period of the civil wars. A substantial autobiography was criticized, Suetonius reports, "more for want of taste rather than style."

Caligula's erratic behavior had become a threat to good government. From late 39 onward, his assassination was in the cards and became a topic for nervous gossip among the political class. A well-informed observer such as Claudius, who had everything to win or lose, will have wanted to make his dispositions. It is possible that he stood in the shadows of the conspiracy or, more accurately, conspiracies. Unlike the groups of complicit Senators, the guardsmen who were the actual killers may well have agreed in advance to "discover" Claudius in the Hermaeum and whisk him away to their barracks. We shall never know, for an ungrateful emperor took care to have them quickly executed for treason.

The most dangerous time in the life of an infant such as Agrippina's son Domitius was not during his birth (in the year 37) but in the days following it. The child would be reared only if the father acknowledged it, but should it be deformed or unwanted for some reason, he could have it exposed in a public space. If it was not found and taken away by a childless couple or the organizers of a prostitution racket, it would die and be eaten by dogs or wild animals.

Ahenobarbus saw that his son was healthy and agreed that he should be accepted into the family. He was a less than enthusiastic father, though, for he is said to have remarked brutally: "Any child born to me and my wife is bound to be a public disaster." As was the custom, a ceremony called the *lustratio* was held to purify him on the ninth day after his birth (the corresponding ceremony for girls took place on the eighth). A procession walked around him to ward off evil spirits, and an animal, a pig perhaps, or a ram or a bull, was sacrificed. Finally, a small gold charm in a leather bag called a *bulla* was hung around the boy's neck (to be put aside when he became an adult).

Agrippina had not been allowed to bring her son with her when she went into exile. She had had to leave him in the care of his father and his dysfunctional family. Ahenobarbus appears not to have been implicated in his wife's adventures. Most probably he had been too ill for plotting, for we know that he suffered from dropsy, a swelling of soft tissues caused by an accumulation of excess fluid. This condition led to his death in 40 at the ancient Etruscan town of Pyrgi, a popular seaside resort.

Little Domitius inherited one third of his estate, but Caligula seized it. His upbringing was skewed by his parents' unhappy fates. In principle, a Roman child was looked after until the age of six or seven by his or her mother, but in Agrippina's unavoidable absence, her son was handed over to his aunt Domitia. Like her brother she was fabulously rich, but also tight-fisted and touchy.

She got along badly with her brother and ended up in court suing him for the recovery of a sum of money. She saved on legal costs by having her then husband represent her, but his plea was not on message. Addressing the two parties directly, he referred to their wealth: "There is nothing either of you needs less than the subject of this dispute."

Domitia seems to have applied her fabled stinginess to the infant placed in her care. He lived in her house, but apparently in real want.

Two not obviously suitable tutors—a dancer and a barber—were appointed to teach him the rudiments of Latin and Greek. Perhaps they charged low fees.

Ahenobarbus had a second sister, Domitia Lepida, who was just as much an irritant in Agrippina's eyes, but in a different way. She too was rich, but her sins were those of the flesh rather than of the counting house. She enjoyed sex and meant to have a lot of it. She believed that she was as wellborn as the great-granddaughter of Augustus. She presented more of a threat to Agrippina than Domitia, the elder sister, did. This was because she had become very fond of her nephew. When he entered his teens she offered a sharp contrast to the attitude of his mother, who was a strict disciplinarian. Tacitus called her "grim and threatening," whereas his aunt was kind to him and openhanded with her money. Her charm showed him that life could be fun.

Agrippina, irritated, bided her time.

To have been without his mother during some of the formative years of early childhood and to have exchanged her for an unloving aunt left a mark on Domitius. And then absence through illness and death removed his irascible father. We know almost nothing about the boy's emotional development, but we may well wonder if early insecurities influenced the adult man. Did he blame his domineering mother, subconsciously or even consciously, for the trauma of a miserable infancy, and if so did he ever forgive her?

If Agrippina turned her thoughts to the subject, she will not have cared greatly one way or the other. She had other matters to deal with, for on his accession, Claudius immediately recalled his nieces from their comfortable but tedious islands. Her possessions and estates were restored. She was now twenty-five and life opened up before her again.

Although the details are missing, Agrippina was ambitious for herself and was once more a player in the great game. She had confidence in her competence, and rightly so. However, she realized that, in light of women's exclusion from politics, she would be obliged to pursue open power through her son. Like most members of the Roman upper class, she placed a high value on education and we can be sure that she did all she could to ensure Domitius received the best possible schooling. Whether or not she acknowledged it to herself, she set her sights on the throne and she needed Domitius to win it for her. It was essential that her son acquire the skills and cultural attitudes of a noble Roman. To achieve this end, attention had to be paid to his beginnings.

A father had absolute authority over his children and as paterfamilias was entitled to manage their education himself. However, many boys were sent away to primary schools. They were placed in the charge of a *paedagogus* (a trusted house slave or former slave), who gave them simple instruction at home and accompanied them to and from their school. There was usually only one schoolmaster, or *ludi magister,* who taught reading and writing, in Greek as well as in Latin, and elementary arithmetic. Discipline was strict, beatings frequent, and holidays rare.

Some pupils, especially those from very wealthy and very grand families, were taught at home by private tutors. They studied a similar curriculum to that in the schools. But parents often preferred the competitiveness of the public classroom. As the educationist Quintilian, who flourished in the second half of the first century, astutely observed: "I prefer the broad daylight of a respectable school to the solitude and obscurity of a private education. . . . a boy should have companions whom he will desire first to imitate and then to surpass: thus he will be led to aspire to higher achievement." Which course of action did Agrippina choose for her son? There is no evidence either way, but it seems that he was gregarious and she was sensible, from which we can infer that he was sent to school.

At about eleven or twelve Domitius, alongside his contemporaries, progressed to secondary education. Here a *grammaticus* taught grammar and syntax by the detailed study of the masterpieces of Greek and Latin literature—among them the epics of Homer and Vergil and the brief evocations of everyday life by Horace. This meant reading texts aloud, learning passages by rote, and lashings of grammatical analysis. For the average student, it also meant hard work and the driving out of enthusiasm.

So Domitius will not have been too disappointed when a huge political scandal interrupted and transformed his life.

One of the curiosities of an elite Roman's life was a propensity to kill himself when he faced adverse circumstances.

Without doubt the most famous suicide of the civil wars that preceded Augustus and the imperial system was that of Marcus Porcius Cato (the Younger, to distinguish him from his famous ancestor of the same name). A leader of the republican cause, he was defeated by his enemy, Julius Caesar, whose victory (as we have seen) led to the creation of the Augustan autocracy.

In April 46, he was holed up in the capital of the province of Africa called Utica, with the enemy approaching. He made sure that his death was a public act that would resonate across the Roman world—and, as it turned out, down the ages. After a bath, Cato attended a last supper and over wine discussed philosophy with the other diners. As an adherent of Stoicism, a popular if gloomy creed of the day, he believed that nature or the universe was the supreme reason. Everything that happens is consistent with reason and should be accepted as the divine will. Nature was what Stoics called god. Virtue in a human being was to act in harmony with the laws of the universe. Cato mentioned a famous Stoic "paradox" according to which only the good man is free, because he acts in accordance with reason, and by definition bad men resist reason and are all slaves.

After discussing the topic, he went to bed and twice read the *Phaedo,* a dialogue by the great Athenian thinker Plato, in which he describes the calm and courageous death of his philosophical master Socrates and argues for the immortality of the soul. He slept for a short time, checked that his sword was sharp, discussed some business with a freedman, had his doctor dress a sore hand, and then fell into a deep sleep. He awoke to birdsong. Shortly afterward he stabbed himself below the breast, but missed the heart. He fell over with a crash.

His son and others ran into the room and found Cato unconscious and smeared with blood. Some of his intestines were protruding from a gash in his stomach. The doctor stuffed them back in and sewed up the wound. Cato came around, tore open the gash, and furiously pulled the intestines out. In this gruesome manner he ended his life.

In the world of Greece and Rome suicide was often seen as a respectable, even a virtuous act. Men and women killed themselves in many different ways and from very different motives. Among the upper classes and in the army there existed what might be called a culture of suicide.

Two main justifications could be claimed for a "noble" suicide. The first was *desperata salus*—namely, no hope of rescue, escape, or survival. Julius Caesar gave a spectacular example of this in the commentaries he wrote on his Gallic campaigns. Roman survivors of an ambush were faced with an impossible situation. He writes that they "had hard work to withstand the enemy's onslaught till nightfall. In the night, seeing that all hope was gone, every single man killed himself."

The second rationale was *pudor,* or shame. This did not mean that a Roman who was considering self-destruction was racked with guilt over some wicked thing he had done; rather, he recognized a catastrophic collapse in his social or political standing. Such reversals of fortune happened from time to time and were a hazard for the professional politician.

Emperors exploited the culture of suicide to their advantage. Instead of the death penalty, they let it be known that a political offender should kill himself rather than await trial, conviction, and sentencing. As we have seen, that was what happened to Piso, governor of Syria and the alleged poisoner of Germanicus. Nobody rejected the suggestion from the palace and those asked to do so obediently cut their veins or fell on their swords. They acted on the understanding that their possessions would be untouched and their families safe.

On one celebrated occasion, a noblewoman was obliged to stiffen her husband's failing resolve. In 42 a plot against Claudius was discovered. When ordered to do the decent thing, one of the conspirators, Aulus Caecina Paetus, wavered. His wife, Arria, grabbed the dagger from his hand and stabbed herself. Before expiring she said: "It doesn't hurt, Paetus"—*Paete, non dolet*. She became a byword for loving loyalty.

There was something in the arrangement for both sides, almost collusion. On the one hand, it saved the emperor a deal of trouble, while, on the other, the melancholy glamour of martyrs such as Cato or Julius Caesar's assassins, Brutus and Cassius, inspired generations of *résistants* to follow their example.

Many critics of the imperial system had Cato in mind as a model of virtue. The young poet Lucan famously wrote of the opponents in the civil war: *"Victrix causa diis placuit, sed victa Catoni"* (The gods backed the winners, but Cato the losers). His specter walks these pages.

Agrippina was delighted to be back in Rome, but she realized that even a princess would benefit from a rich and protective husband. She knew she was a catch, and this time she was able to choose for herself.

Her eye first of all fell on the able Sulpicius Galba, now in his forties and serving with distinction as commander of the legions in Upper Germany. Already married, he rejected her "shameless" advances; his mother-in-law was so incensed that she slapped Agrippina's face in front of a gathering of married women.

Retiring hurt, she turned her attention to her brother-in-law, Domitia's husband, the witty and well-heeled Gaius Sallustius Passienus Crispus. He willingly divorced his wife, presumably because of her disagreeable nature, and married Agrippina perhaps as early as 41. As a recent widow with a small son, she may well have been attracted more by the money than by the jokes.

Passienus was the type of man who was on the best of terms with those he loathed—until they were safely dead. Caligula thought he was a friend and asked him in confidence whether he had ever slept with his sister as he himself had with his. Passienus was in a spot. If he said no, he would have criticized the princeps by implication; if yes, he would have shamed himself and admitted a crime. He cleverly replied *"Nondum"* (Not yet). Referring to Caligula's silence about the persecution of his family when he was living with Tiberius on Capri and his cruelty when princeps, he coined a famous epigram: "There never was a better slave nor a worse master."

He understood the flaws in human character, including (one suspects) his own. He was fond of saying, "We leave the door against flattery ajar, just as we do with a mistress. If she gives it a push, we're delighted, and even more so if she forces it open."

Passienus lived to regret his union with Agrippina, for we are told that she poisoned him for his estate. He died sometime before 47, and his wealth, or a large part of it, passed to his widow and her son. No opportunities at the time presented themselves for advancement, but mother and son now had a bulging treasure chest in case of future need.

A Roman boy had to have a male parent in his life, and with the death of his natural father and now of his stepfather, it may have been about this time that the nine-year-old Domitius was assigned Asconius Labeo as a guardian. His family came from Padua, and Agrippina may have spent time in that area of northern Italy, attracting no attention and waiting quietly on events. Two Greek freelance teachers for her son were also hired, Anicetus and Beryllus. The child liked them all and later in life rewarded Labeo with a signal distinction, an honorary Consulship. He made Anicetus an admiral. It was an attractive feature of Domitius's character that he remembered with fondness most of the adults who helped raise him—except (as we shall see) his mother.

It is impossible to understand Rome, and in particular how the empire was run, without recognizing that, like other communities in the ancient world, it was a slave society—or, more precisely, a slave-dependent society.

Centuries of warfare during the republic produced many thousands of captives who were sold, and their children brought up, as slaves. They worked in the fields of Italy, often in chain gangs, in manufacturing trades, and services of one kind or another. In cities, they were barbers, builders, shoemakers, potters, bakers, fast food chefs, male and female prostitutes—in fact, any urban occupation. If they were unlucky, they worked in mines and quarries, where conditions were so backbreaking and brutal that life was short. They might also fight as gladiators or charioteers, the sports stars of their day. If they were lucky they were household slaves, working as accountants, secretaries, maids, valets, seamstresses, and, as noted, children's tutors. They often enjoyed a higher quality of life than many working-class freeborn citizens. Good looks might facilitate a position in a wealthy household but also entailed unwelcome sex.

A slave had almost no rights or status. As the respected Roman scholar Marcus Terentius Varro observed, he or she was no more than "a speaking tool." There were others who took a kindlier view, but they were in a minority. The Stoic philosopher and statesman Lucius Annaeus Seneca observed: "Though the laws allow a slave to be ill-treated without limit, there are nevertheless some things which the common laws of life forbid us to do to a human being." He wrote to a friend:

> I am glad to learn, through those who come from you, that you live on friendly terms with your slaves. This befits a sensible and well-educated man like yourself. "They are slaves," people declare. No, rather they are men. "Slaves!" No, comrades. "Slaves!" No, they are our everyday friends. "Slaves!" No, they are our fellow-slaves, if one reflects that Fortune has equal rights over slaves and free men alike.

Seneca noted with disgust the sexual abuse of slaves. He mentions a wine waiter at a dinner party who had been his master's plaything as a teenaged boy. Despite the fact that he had now grown up, he was not allowed to

> get away from his boyhood; he is dragged back to it; and though he has already acquired a soldier's figure, he is kept beardless by having his hair smoothed away or plucked out by the roots, and he

must remain awake throughout the night, dividing his time between his master's drunkenness and his lust.

Over the years more and more slaves were brought to Italy and to Rome. It has been estimated that by the end of the republic between 30 and 40 percent of the Italian population were slaves, in Rome itself perhaps four hundred thousand out of a million. Their living and working conditions, and above all their loss of liberty, were making them restless, so thought respectable—and nervous—opinion. A proposal was debated in the Senate to compel slaves to wear a uniform that would identify them. This was rejected when it was pointed out that slaves in the city streets would realize how numerous they were and might join forces to rebel. Indeed, from time to time there were slave uprisings that were suppressed only with difficulty.

In the previous century, a Thracian slave and gladiator called Spartacus defeated the legions and came within an ace of overthrowing the republic. In 64 B.C. there was an attempted outbreak by gladiators at Praeneste (today's Palestrina), which a company of soldiers on guard over them was able to put down. A shiver must have run down many Roman spines.

A slave's evidence in court could only be heard if obtained by torture. A particularly cruel law ordained that if a slave were to murder his owner not only the culprit but also all the fellow slaves in the household were to be executed.

A terrible case occurred in 61. A slave with a grievance murdered his owner, the city Prefect. His entire household of four hundred slaves was sentenced to death. Public opinion was shocked and crowds gathered with stones and torches to prevent the mass slaughter from going ahead. The Senate debated the issue. A conservative member argued that slaves could not be trusted. "Nowadays our huge households . . . are multinational. The only way to keep down this medley of humanity is by terror." The Senate regretfully agreed. Nero issued an edict reprimanding the protesters, and on his orders, troops lined the route along which the condemned men were taken for execution.

The Roman system not only punished but also rewarded. Although this was not compulsory, slaves were often given their freedom. Relations could be close; a tomb inscription of a boy of sixteen called him "slave and yet son." Some slaves saved pocket money and bought their liberty; others set up businesses in which their former owners invested, a few even inherited their estates. In a simple ceremony in front of an elected official, a rod was laid on the slave's head. The owner took hold of him and explained his motive for manumission. He pronounced the words "I wish this man to be free" and let him go.

The freedman, or *libertus,* was now a Roman citizen, although he was not allowed to hold public office. Any son of his, however, enjoyed full legal rights and could stand as a candidate in elections. A freedman would adopt the family name of his onetime owner. He might be employed by him and become one of his patron's "clients," or supporters.

The system of patron and client was one of the essential components of Roman life. In return for assistance when he needed it, the client, whether freed or free, would back his patron's political campaigns and render other services as required. The relationship resembled that between a parent and child. Leading politicians would have hundreds or thousands of clients, who created a network of mutual loyalties, stabilized Roman society, and bound the provinces to the center.

Situations varied, but some *liberti* were good businessmen and made fortunes. A handful worked for emperors and amassed wealth beyond the dreams of avarice. Freedmen were very unpopular with ordinary citizens and some were alleged to behave disrespectfully to their former owners. The Senate debated a draft motion allowing former owners to revoke their enfranchisement, but it was dropped. A general law was felt to be unnecessary and any cases of misbehavior were best judged on their individual merits. The fact of the matter was that freedmen were too useful to be antagonized.

Rome did not have a permanent civil service open to Romans, and that was how emperors (including Nero in due time) liked it.

As the empire expanded to include all the lands around the Mediterranean, so did its administrative workload. Under the republic, elected officials such as Consuls and Praetors used the manpower in their households to fulfill their obligations. When Augustus took over he did the same; he switched slaves and freedmen from domestic duties in the *familia Caesaris,* or Caesar's household, to state business, and over time formed a basic bureaucracy. These men usually came from the Greek-speaking or eastern end of the empire and were stereotyped as decadent scoundrels and cheats. However, they were not bought for their morals but for their sharpness of mind. They were literate in Latin and Greek and highly numerate.

To govern through freedmen brought the princeps three solid advantages—they had no political base and were entirely reliant on his favor; they became so rich that their loyalty could not easily be bought; and there was no need to trouble senatorial nobility with the detailed creation and implementation of high policy. Unsurprisingly, it loathed the intruders. To be ordered about by former slaves was an offense to its collective dignity.

The most famous freedman of the age was Gaius Julius Callistus. He rose from the humblest of origins, as Seneca, a contemporary of his, recalled: "I have seen standing in a queue outside Callistus's front door, his former owner. I have seen the owner himself turned away while others were welcomed in—the owner who once fastened the 'For Sale' ticket on Callistus and put him on the market." The freedman took his revenge late and cold.

He caught the eye of Caligula, who gave him his liberty (hence the "Julius" from the emperor's family name). He became his closest adviser, making a huge fortune in the process. The encyclopedist Pliny the Elder records having seen for himself a scandalous example of conspicuous expenditure—thirty large onyx columns in Callistus's dining room, or perhaps more accurately, banquet hall. Callistus was a fixer rather than an innovator, in Tacitus's judgment: "Experience had taught him that power is maintained by cautious rather than energetic measures."

He attracted envy and calumny. He was once denounced for conspiring against the princeps. He talked himself out of trouble, but the writing was on the wall. If he was to be accused of treason, it would be safer to be guilty. He was one of the men in the shadows during the planning of Caligula's death, of which some said he was the prime mover. It is conceivable that he discussed the succession with Claudius in advance of the assassination. Tellingly, once he was princeps, Claudius appointed the freedman to hold one of the great offices of state as the secretary *a libellis,* who was in charge of all petitions and grievances addressed to the emperor.

Claudius, inexperienced in government as he was, made full use of foreign freedmen and paid for it with unpopularity in the Senate, which he increasingly excluded from decision making. He cordially returned the sentiment, knowing that many Senators had opposed his emergence as princeps. As well as Callistus, there were two other leading imperial *liberti,* Marcus Antonius Pallas and Tiberius Claudius Narcissus.

Claudius paid heavily for their labors. Suetonius writes that

> when one day Claudius complained how little cash was in the treasury, the witty answer was made that he would have enough and to spare, if only he were taken into partnership by Narcissus and Pallas.

Pallas was secretary *a rationibus*—in other words, finance minister—a role he played so effectively that he was "in virtual control of the state." He became extremely rich while cultivating a reputation for economy. He drafted a law regulating the status of women who had sex with slaves and was rewarded by the Senate with an honorary Praetorship together with the very large sum of 15 million sesterces. Pallas astutely refused the money, saying that he was "content with the honor." The phrase was carved on the freedman's tomb. Tacitus reports with dry sarcasm:

> The Senate's decree was engraved in letters of bronze. It loaded praises for old-fashioned frugality on a former slave who possessed three hundred million sesterces.

Pallas came to be on good terms with Agrippina as she reestablished herself in Rome after her exile. They were rumored at a later stage in their careers to have been lovers. This may or may not be true, but he probably befriended her soon after her return and looked out for her at court. Once again we may guess that a peccadillo in the bedroom stands in for recognition of a political alliance.

The third freedman was Tiberius Claudius Narcissus. Another Greek, he was a slave in the household of Antonia, Claudius's mother, and devoted his loyalty to the family. He delivered a crucial message from Antonia to the emperor Tiberius that led to the fall of Sejanus. He was the secretary *ab epistulis* and was responsible for the correspondence of the princeps. By virtue of his job, Narcissus had to know everything—and this made him the most powerful of Claudius's ministers.

One particular thing he knew was that Agrippina and her little boy Domitius were better placed on the imperial family tree than Claudius himself (who had not a drop of Augustus's blood running through his veins) and so posed a potential threat to the regime. However, there is no record of her playing a part in public life, and (as we have seen) she may have spent much of her time in the country. Her invisibility persuaded the princeps and his wife, Messalina, that there was no cause for alarm.

Politics in a palace can be poisonous, and Claudius's court was no exception. The three *liberti* were usually at daggers drawn, but they saw a grave threat both to the emperor and themselves. In 48, Callistus, Pallas, and Narcissus agreed to meet, urgently and in private. The only item on the agenda was the overthrow of the empress.

Valeria Messalina was Claudius's third wife, whom he married before he became princeps. There was a seventeen-year age difference between them. A member of Rome's upper crust, she was the daughter of Domitius's favorite aunt, Domitia Lepida. Messalina was beautiful and, we are told, a nymphomaniac.

The savage satirist Juvenal, who flourished in the early second century, has left an indelible portrait of her slipping out of the palace when her husband was asleep to prostitute herself in a brothel "reeking of ancient blankets." She stood in her cubicle naked and up for sale. Her work name was She Wolf. At the end of an evening's session she left reluctantly, "with her clitoris inflamed and stiff." She brought back to the palace, Juvenal sniffs, the stench of sex.

The ancient writers present Claudius as a bumbling figure under the control of his wives. He was certainly uxorious, and there is no reason to doubt the word of the ancient sources that Messalina was highly sexed, even if we reject the historicity of an imperial Belle de Jour. However, from the moment of his bizarre accession, his position was insecure, and the reign saw a running battle with dissident Senators. Messalina organized a number of senatorial executions and political suicides, but she was acting as a partner with her embattled husband rather than as an independent agent pricked on only by desire.

If Messalina was a she-wolf sexually, she was also a fierce defender of her cub. She had given Claudius a son, Britannicus, whom she expected to follow his father on the throne once he grew up. For a time she had underestimated the threat that Domitius posed to the interests of Britannicus, but now she began to scheme against Agrippina.

Messalina's change of heart followed an incident of no significance in itself. The two little boys, nine and six years old respectively, took part in the Troy Game, an equestrian dressage display by aristocratic youngsters. The watching crowd applauded the grandson of Germanicus far more loudly than they did Britannicus. The boys descended from different sisters of Augustus and so were equal princes of the blood. Domitius, being a few years older, would reach adulthood first, and the more she thought about it, the more the empress worried about the long-term threat he could pose to her son.

Consequently, few people in political circles will have been taken aback when a report circulated of an attempt on Domitius's life. Hit men were sent to strangle him while he was having his afternoon nap. We must assume that they were either intercepted or betrayed, for nothing came of the affair. On another occasion, a snake was placed in his bedroom with malign intent. The snake was shy and slipped away unseen, but its sloughed skin was found by the boy's pillow. His relieved mother had it set in a bracelet, which he wore for many years.

But now Messalina went too far. On this the three freedmen were in complete agreement.

Messalina had fallen in love with Gaius Silius, a handsome nobleman and the following year's Consul designate. She began an affair with him, although at the outset he was less than enthusiastic. As Tacitus put it, he "understood the scandal and the peril." However, to extricate himself was more certainly dangerous than to proceed. Preferring to be a ram rather than a lamb, Silius took the lead, and the couple decided to get married.

First, the empress had to divorce her husband. This was easily done, for according to Roman law, a simple declaration would do, without necessarily informing the other party. Then, on a specified date when the princeps was out of town inspecting new building developments at Rome's harbor of Ostia, their union was solemnized in front of invited witnesses. A great party was held in the gardens of a royal residence. Appropriately enough, the fancy-dress theme for the celebration was that of a Bacchic revel. The emperor had decided to prolong his visit to Ostia and was one of the few people in the city to know nothing of what was going on.

The three freedmen debated the crisis but failed to agree. Callistus took the view that most problems solve themselves if left to themselves. Pallas feared for his skin. Despite the fact that he had worked with Messalina in the past, Narcissus decided to act on his own. How should the news of the wedding be broken to Claudius? The problem was the emperor's timidity and pliability—and the fact that he loved his wife.

Narcissus dispatched the emperor's two favorite mistresses to Ostia to break the news. They urged him to summon Narcissus. He did so. The freedman is almost to be imagined standing behind the door awaiting the call. "Act promptly," he counseled, "or Silius controls Rome."

Meanwhile, at the party, a guest climbed a tree. Someone asked him what he could see. "A terrible storm over Ostia," came the prophetic reply.

Claudius set off for the city at once. "Am I still emperor?" he kept on asking. He did not trust the Praetorian commander, and for one day only, Narcissus, a former slave, was put in charge of the Guard. This astonishing innovation reveals the seriousness of the situation. The freedman insisted on traveling in the emperor's carriage to prevent another passenger who had been given a lift from weakening Claudius's resolve.

Messengers carried news that the government was set on restoring order. The partygoers scattered. Silius went to the Forum like any ordinary Senator, as if nothing had happened. Messalina made her way across town to the Gardens of Lucullus, a splendid park on the Pincian hill which sloped down to the Campus Martius. As well as greenery it featured terraces, banqueting rooms, and a library open to the public. In her heyday the empress coveted the Gardens and had extorted them from their owner, whom she drove to suicide.

The chief Vestal Virgin, a figure surrounded by a force field of taboos, insisted that Messalina be allowed to talk to Claudius, and even Narcissus dared not disobey her. The encounter did not go well for Messalina. She cried and cried, hoping to soften her husband's heart by showing him their children, Octavia and Britannicus. Narcissus, who had taken control, shouted her down with the story of Silius and the wedding. He had the children removed.

Then he took the emperor to Silius's house and showed him imperial heirlooms stolen from the palace. The emperor had been silent till then, but now he lost his temper. After this detour, he made his way to the Praetorian barracks, where he briefly addressed the men and won their support.

Silius was arrested; he did not try to defend himself, but only asked for a quick death. The request was granted. As for Messalina, Narcissus knew his Claudius and feared his forgiving heart, especially after an early dinner. Ostensibly by order of the princeps he ordered a Guards officer to put the empress to death. The officer found her in the Gardens in a state of collapse and filled with indignation at her downfall. Her mother, Domitia Lepida, was estranged from her daughter but let bygones be bygones and joined her in her extremity. She advised suicide in the high Roman fashion: "Your life is over. It only remains for you to die honorably." *Desperata salus* indeed. Messalina was not up to the task. She took a dagger but could not bring herself to use it. The officer, who had stood silently waiting, ran her through.

When the news of her death reached Claudius, he showed no emotion. The following day he inquired where she was—as if she were still alive and well. He had momentarily forgotten the events of the previous day.

This is a very odd episode. It seems certain that what is said to have happened did indeed happen. Tacitus, a writer at the top of his game, insists that his narrative, however incredible it may appear, is accurate: "I have added no touch of the marvellous. I truly relate the oral and written evidence of my seniors."

What was going on? It begins as a romance but evidently grows into something darker. Once again sex intertwines with politics. Perhaps we have a plot led by an ambitious Consul designate to dethrone the emperor. That was what Claudius believed. Silius is reported as saying: "We don't have to wait until the princeps dies of old age!"

But, equally, perhaps Messalina was the guiding force. She wanted her little son, Britannicus, to succeed to the throne in due course, but she saw an obstacle in the approaching adulthood of Agrippina's son Domitius, now in his tenth year. It would not be very long before he became a new and powerful player of the political game, backed by his ferocious mother. With his clear ancestry back to Augustus, he would have every chance of overshadowing her son—and even

Claudius himself. Once Messalina realized that her husband was unwilling to destroy this threat, Messalina decided to replace him with Silius and eliminate her rival from a position of strength.

A traditional coup was out of the question. However, a tentative explanation does suggest itself, which fits the facts albeit unsupported by direct evidence. It derives from Claudius's personality, or rather his personality as perceived. He was eccentric, absent-minded, and fearful. It was easy to change his mind. He understood his reputation and acted up to it. In a murderous age he knew that survival lay in not being a threat to anybody.

Silius and Messalina made the mistake of judging the princeps to be biddable. Their plan was to negotiate an imperial ménage à trois. The deal had him stay on as emperor while adopting Silius as his son, deputy, and heir. Silius would at the same time adopt Britannicus, who would inherit the purple on Silius's death. This device of a princeps adopting an adult heir who simultaneously adopts a child or youth as his heir is not so fanciful as it might at first appear. We recall that Augustus adopted Tiberius while insisting that *he* in turn adopt Germanicus.

The lovers believed that Claudius would go along with their proposal, and the nervousness of Narcissus on the fatal day strongly suggests that they could well have been right. They failed because they underestimated the presence of mind of a former slave.

The true winners of the scandal were those whom Messalina had most feared—Agrippina and Domitius. The removal of the empress transformed their chances. It cleared the stage. From the lowest of profiles and after years of disappointment, Agrippina now had the opportunity to seize a starring role. She was ready.

4

YOUNG HOPEFUL GENTLEMAN

THE HANDSOME SHEPHERD watched over his flock on the slopes of Mount Ida not far from the city of Troy. In fact, he was an incognito son of the king. In one of the classical world's most famous legends, he was asked to judge which of three goddesses was the most beautiful. They were Juno, queen of heaven; Minerva, patron of wisdom; and Venus, embodiment of the art of love. The prize was a golden apple inscribed with the legend to the fairest.

The contest was too close to call, so the deities stripped to the buff to allow Paris a more complete idea of their charms. They also shamelessly offered bribes—rule over Europe and Asia; skill in wisdom and war; and the person of the world's most beautiful woman, Helen of Sparta. Paris chose beauty.

In a rare case of life imitating art, or (more exactly) history imitating myth, Claudius found himself having to choose his next wife from among three women. Beauty was in the mix, for he did not like to sleep alone at night.

The three leading imperial freedmen understood this very well. They disagreed on many things, but on one point they were firm: To ensure domestic contentment and calm at court, the princeps needed a wife. Each had his own candidate. Tacitus summed up the situation:

> The execution of Messalina convulsed the imperial household: for the freedmen quarrelled among themselves about who should select a consort for Claudius, with his impatience of celibacy and his

docility under wifely government. Competition was no less fierce among the women. Each paraded for comparison her high birth, her beauty, and her wealth, and advertised them as worthy of that exalted alliance.

The first great lady to be up for consideration was Lollia Paulina. She was phenomenally rich and happy for everyone to know it. The encyclopedist Pliny the Elder recalls seeing her "at a perfectly ordinary dinner party" wearing a cascade of jewels, rubies alternating with pearls, glittering all over her head, hair, ears, neck, and fingers to the value of 40 million sesterces. She used to carry around with her written proof of her ownership of the gems. They were family heirlooms, Pliny adds acidly, "obtained from loot gained in the provinces."

In a sense, she was used goods, for she had been briefly empress once before. Caligula had compelled her husband to divorce her and married her in his place. The experiment was a failure. Within six months Caligula had discarded Lollia.

The second rival for Claudius's bed had actually slept in it before. She was Aelia Paetina, who had been his second wife. She was the adoptive sister of Sejanus, the sinister helper of the emperor Tiberius. In his heyday she was a catch; and Claudius married her in 28. They had a daughter. Sejanus fell from grace in 31, sometime after which Claudius wisely divorced Aelia.

The third and final contestant in this updated Judgment of Paris was Agrippina. She had the distinct advantage of being a member both of the Julian branch of the imperial family through her mother and of the Claudian through her father Germanicus, but she suffered the crippling drawback of being her putative husband's niece. Romans did not approve of incest, which they regarded as a decadent oriental vice, to which the Ptolemies of Egypt had been prone.

Each of the women had their supporter at court. Callistus argued for Lollia, mainly on the grounds of her wealth. Also she had no children of her own and was sterile. This would solve the stepmother problem. Stepmothers were universally held to favor their own children by an earlier marriage and to act cruelly toward their new husband's progeny.

In a word, Lollia would be no trouble, which suited Callistus's do-nothing theory of government.

Narcissus made the case, as best he could, for Paetina. She shared with Claudius the parenthood of a child, their daughter Antonia. There would be no upheaval in the domestic arrangements, for they had lived together once before, and (pure assertion) Paetina would cherish Octavia and Britannicus as if they were her own children.

Pallas spoke for Agrippina. He made the most of her ancestry. If Claudius married her, she would bring along her son Domitius, grandson of Germanicus and a descendant in a direct line from Augustus; being both a Julian and a Claudian, he would be an eminently suitable successor and unite a divided dynasty.

Pallas was making a dangerous pitch, for he was implicitly excluding from the throne the princeps's own offspring, the little Britannicus. He calculated that Claudius was aware of his unpopularity and would see how an alliance with Agrippina and her son would stabilize his regime and, indeed, the dynastic project Augustus had devised and launched many years ago. Would Claudius be willing to pay the price?

The princeps could not make up his mind which woman to choose. He agreed with whoever had spoken to him last. Agrippina did not let the grass grow. Using the excuse of already being a family member she made a point of regularly visiting the princeps and having heart-to-heart chats with him. She used to kiss him and give him other little endearments, even, according to gossip, sexual favors.

She is often presented as a beautiful seductress, but the evidence of coins that feature her profile and a marble bust suggest that Agrippina was no more than presentable. Her face was rather jowly and she had a prominent nose. She was tall, and the overall effect of her appearance was slightly masculine. Her true attractions were her bloodline and her brains.

Lucius Vitellius was an intelligent man, and an outstanding administrator and general. He was also a toady and a court favorite. When Tiberius moved to Capri, he bought a villa for himself on the island, where he could be on hand to please. He had been the first to address Caligula as a god and was now close to Claudius. He sedulously greased the wheels of the autocracy. In a word, he was a typical senior politician of the day. (On the credit side, as a very effective governor of Syria, he dismissed the Prefect of Judaea, one Pontius Pilate, for using excessive force when putting down a religious riot.)

The Senate had no real power, but it often provided cover when a controversial decision was in view. One day in 49 Vitellius had a carefully scripted (we assume) audience with the princeps, during which he asked Claudius whether he would obey the will of the Senate. He replied, "I am a citizen among citizens and I will bow to unanimity."

Vitellius proceeded to the Senate House and sought permission to speak on a matter of the highest national importance. He said:

> In his exceptionally arduous duties, the emperor needs support. Could there be a more respectable comfort to our Caesar, a stranger to dissipation and self-indulgence, than a wife?

Loud applause. Vitellius then gingerly approached the nub of the matter. His audience will have guessed what was coming. Sometime previously Claudius had decided to choose Agrippina from the three spouses on offer and an informal partnership had been struck and immediately went into operation. However, they held back from solemnizing a marriage, for the obstacle of incest stood obstinately in place.

Vitellius itemized Agrippina's virtues:

> Her exceptionally illustrious birth is undeniable. Her morals are equally outstanding. She has proved her fecundity. She is well known for her purity of character.

The speaker emphasized the respectability of what he was proposing—a union between a virtuous widow and a man who had had no experience of women otherwise than of his wives.

More applause. Vitellius at last touched on the fact that bride and groom were niece and uncle.

> I admit that marriage with a brother's child is a novelty for Rome. But it is normal in other countries and not prohibited by any law. Here too union between cousins, long unknown, has become more common over time. Customs change as circumstances change. This innovation will take root.

Some excited Senators ran out into the Forum and shouted that if the princeps hesitated they would force him to marry. A crowd gathered and Claudius waited no longer. He left the palace, crossed the Forum and joined the Senate session.

He had no trouble persuading the Senate to legalize the marriage of uncles with their brothers' daughters.

The coup was a kind of improvised theatrical performance with Senators acting the role of enthusiasts, but there is no doubt that the marriage was popular. The impact of Agrippina's elevation was immediate and profound. Tacitus tells the truth, despite the garish misogynist coloring:

> From this moment, the state was transformed, and everything obeyed a woman—but not a woman who, like Messalina, treated the Roman empire as a toy in order to satisfy her sexual appetite. It was a severe, almost masculine tyranny: in public there was austerity and not infrequently arrogance; at home no trace of unchastity, unless it might contribute to power. A limitless passion for gold created a bulwark, as it were, of supremacy.

In effect, she and Claudius became partners, even co-rulers. When they appeared at public ceremonies she sat on her own dais alongside that of her husband. Within a year she was the first woman after Livia to be awarded the prized title of Augusta (Revered One). She was given permission to ride in a *carpentum,* a traditional two-wheeled carriage with an arched roof that was drawn by a brace of mules. This was a valuable privilege, for wheeled vehicles were banned in the city during the daytime. But even Agrippina could not lift the bar on women attending the Senate; so arrangements were made for her to listen to debates behind a curtain thick enough to conceal her from view but not to prevent her from hearing.

In the first half of the reign, relations between palace and governing elite had almost broken down. Claudius and his brilliant Greek bureaucrats saw no need to involve the Senate in important decisions and often bullied it. Discontent erupted on occasion into botched plots. Over the period, thirty-five Senators were executed or forced into suicide. The equestrians (the class below the Senate, consisting mainly of businessmen and nonpolitical aristocrats) are reported to have lost, variously, more than three hundred members.

Relations with the Senate swiftly improved after the entrance of Agrippina on the political stage in 49. She brought a new professionalism to government and a genuine willingness to consult. Before announcing a new measure, she would operate behind the scenes to win consent. It was possible to disagree with Agrippina without risking one's life. Dio writes:

> She realized her policies partly by getting the freedmen [who managed the regime] to win over Claudius and partly by arranging in advance that the Senate, the people at large, and the military should join together in shouting their approval of her demands on every occasion.

However, when vital interests were at stake, she did not hesitate to take action with extreme prejudice. For reasons not perfectly understood she and Claudius destroyed her rival in the marriage competition, Lollia Paulina. She was accused of sorcery and of consulting astrologers and magicians, presumably to learn the future fate of the princeps or other members of the imperial family.

Astrology linked events on earth with the motion of planets in the sky and rested on the idea that the universe was an interconnected whole. It flourished during the republic and the early empire. Its predictions were a popular feature of daily life, be it in the palace or on the street. Horoscopes gave precise details about an individual's past, present, and future. In an age when astrology was regarded as a science, great ones objected to this kind of scrutiny, for obvious reasons.

Claudius prosecuted Lollia in the Senate, saying that she was a threat to the state. Her property was confiscated and she was banished from Italy. When the dust had settled, a Praetorian officer was sent to enforce her suicide. Dio adds gruesomely that the empress requested sight of her head; she did not recognize Lollia until she inspected the teeth, which apparently had certain known peculiarities. Lollia was not alone in toying with criminal clairvoyance, for three years later Claudius expelled all astrologers from Italy. It was neither the first nor would it be the last time that the authorities sought to suppress the craft.

Now that Agrippina had assured her own position, she needed to establish that of her son. Even before their wedding, she persuaded the princeps to drop the fiancé of his daughter, Claudia Octavia, and betroth her instead to Domitius. At ten years old she was too young to marry, but the formal ceremony could wait.

More importantly, in marrying Agrippina, Claudius had accepted Pallas's argument that Britannicus's claims to the succession must be set aside in favor of Domitius. As the son of the disgraced and dead Messalina, his place in his father's heart was compromised. Worse, not a drop of Augustus's blood flowed through his veins. For the greater good, Britannicus was to be silently set aside.

Pallas goaded Claudius to adopt Domitius. Tacitus put suitable words into his mouth:

> "[The princeps] must consult the national interest and supply the boy Britannicus with a stable protector. . . . [The emperor] Tiberius had children of his own, but he adopted Germanicus: Let Claudius also provide himself with a young partner.

Eventually the princeps yielded to the pressure. On February 25, 50, he brought Domitius legally into his family by adopting him. At the age of thirteen, Lucius Domitius Ahenobarbus was hardly a grown man, but now he became, cumbersomely, Tiberius Claudius Nero Drusus Germanicus Caesar. (From this point in these pages he will be called by the more familiar name of Nero.)

It was essential that any latent support in the Praetorian Guard for Claudius's son of his own loins was stamped out before it became a threat. Agrippina scoured the army lists to identify and remove, through tactful promotions, Guards officers (military tribunes and centurions) who might favor Britannicus. She distrusted the two Praetorian Prefects and persuaded Claudius to remove them. In 51, they were replaced by a single Prefect—one Sextus Afranius Burrus, a man (in Tacitus's phrase) "of the highest character as a soldier, but well aware [to] whose pleasure he owed the appointment." Here we have another Vitellius.

Agrippina made an effort to seem kind to Britannicus, but when she took charge of Britannicus's upbringing, it had baleful consequences. A minor incident exposed the tensions running beneath the surface. The children of the imperial family ate regularly in the company of the princeps, among them Titus, son of an up-and-coming general, Titus Flavius Vespasianus (or Vespasian), who had caught Agrippina's eye.

At one such meal, Britannicus mistakenly greeted Nero by his old name, Ahenobarbus. It is unclear whether he did so accidentally or on purpose. He seems to have been an intelligent child who understood his situation and saw through his stepmother's maneuvers. He may have disapproved of the adoption. In any case, Nero was upset by the misspeaking and tried, eccentrically and unsuccessfully, to persuade Claudius that Britannicus was a changeling.

The empress complained loudly to her complaisant husband. He feared factional fighting at court and agreed to a purge of Britannicus's advisers. Agrippina kept him strictly out of the public eye, replaced his tutors with her own followers, and ensured that his father had as little to do with him as possible. She held the boy, writes Dio, in "a kind of imprisonment, though one without bars."

When planning her son's education, Agrippina accorded him more sympathetic attention than she did Britannicus. She was aware how close Nero was to the throne, and she meant to get him onto it. It was essential that she find a tutor who would train him in the art of government. In Lucius Annaeus Seneca, thinker, bestselling author, and rising politician, she believed she had found just the man.

Wealthy Romans used slaves with physical disabilities or attractive naked children as entertainers. They were given the run of the house and, like medieval court jesters, were expected to make amusingly candid remarks or satirical insults. Seneca's family employed a female clown called Harpaste, whom Helvia, the philosopher's mother, had inherited from an aunt. Her son disapproved, writing primly to a friend: "If I wanted to hear a clown's jokes, I don't have to look far. I can laugh at myself."

However, he was astonished by a medical disaster which befell her. She suddenly became blind, but with a twist. She suffered from a rare condition known today as Anton's syndrome. The main symptom is that patients deny their loss of vision. Harpaste insisted that she could still see. "The story sounds incredible, but I assure you that it is true," remarked Seneca. "She keeps asking her attendant to change her quarters; she says that the rooms are too dark."

Harpaste's illness reminded Seneca of a contradiction in his own life that he was never able to resolve—namely, between being rich and being good:

> You can see clearly that what makes us smile in Harpasté's case happens to all the rest of us; nobody understands that he himself is greedy, or that he is covetous. Those who accept that they are blind ask for a guide, while we wander about without one, saying: "I am not self-seeking; but it's simply not possible to live in Rome in any other way. I am not extravagant, but just living in the city is extremely expensive."

Seneca knows that he is guilty as charged, and his defense is half-hearted. His reputation for inconsistency and hypocrisy dogged him throughout his career. He summed up his position in his essay *On the Happy Life,* bringing forward as witnesses the great philosophers of the ancient world:

> "You talk one way," you say, "and live another." . . . This was the criticism flung at Plato, at Epicurus, at Zeno: for all these described how they ought to live, not how they did live. I speak of virtue, not of myself, and when I blame vices, I blame my own first of all.

Seneca's forebears were emigrants from Italy who settled and made their fortunes in Corduba (now Córdoba), capital of Baetica, a province of southern Spain centered on the river Baetis (today's Guadalquivir in Andalusia). After two and a half centuries of Roman rule, it was thoroughly Romanized, and Latin had become the dominant language. Baetica's prosperity depended on the export of wine and olive oil and is represented to this day by the Monte Testaccio in Rome; this substantial artificial hill is made from broken and discarded *amphorae,* or ceramic storage jars, indestructible survivors of this long-ago trade.

Seneca's father and namesake lived the civilized life of a gentleman who did not need to work. He belonged to the equestrian or business class. A provincial as well, he would have found it difficult to develop a career in politics and, in fact, had no desire to do so. Instead, he spent many years in Rome enjoying the city's cultural life and being trained in rhetoric, the art of public speaking. He wrote a history of the civil wars but wisely left it unpublished in his lifetime. He left his wife, Helvia, probably a native Spanish woman, to look after the family business.

Seneca himself was born at some point between 4 and 1 B.C., the second of three brothers. Their father devoted his energies to his boys' education, which they completed in Rome under his supervision. He was both loving and strict, and they turned out well.

Upper-class Romans often adopted young adult males if they had not produced sons themselves. In this way they could preserve the family name and prevent the breakup of their fortunes. Seneca's elder brother was adopted into the Gallio family and, as Lucius Junius Gallio Annaeanus, became a successful politician in Rome. He makes a cameo appearance in the Acts of the Apostles, when as a provincial governor he dismisses a lawsuit against the apostle Paul. This impartial judgment suggests that the Roman authorities were not prejudiced at this stage against Christianity, a new and little-understood sect.

By contrast, the younger brother, Annaeus Mela, his father's favorite, avoided the existential dangers of a political career. He chose to be the eternal student and lived a life of philosophical retirement. Seneca was impressed by his siblings. He wrote:

> In each of them [there is] cause for delight: the one by his energy has won the distinction of public office, the other with his wisdom has treated it with contempt.

Others were less charitable about Mela's motive for not seeking office. What he really wanted was to make quick money as an imperial *procurator,* or finance officer, handling private business of the emperor. According to Tacitus, he nursed "a perverse ambition to achieve a Consul's influence while remaining a non-senator."

Seneca was the most brilliant of the trio. He studied at a philosophical school in Rome, which was less interested in theory than in the practical application of Stoic principles, especially where they overlapped with old-fashioned republican values. These were expressed, for example, in two Latin words packed with meanings for the patriot: *pietas* (loyalty, duty, filial and religious piety, respect) and *virtus* (manliness, bravery, excellence, character). He wrote many essays, dialogues à la Plato, and letters. He was what we would call today a "public intellectual," and he became as well known throughout the ancient world for his Stoic principles and his writings on morals as for his stellar political career.

Educated Romans were proud of their literature and gloried in their epic poets, above all Vergil, and the love poetry of Catullus and Ovid, and Horace hymning private pleasures; but ever since they had encountered Greek culture hundreds of years in the past, they had felt chastened and inferior. Of course Vergil was great, but Homer was incomparable. Most of them spoke Greek fluently and learned to compose imitations of Greek writers. These they performed at fashionable, if frequently tedious, literary readings.

Like many of his contemporaries, Seneca stood in awe of the Greeks, and he wrote a number of tragedies in Latin on mythological themes inspired by the works of Aeschylus and the other Athenian tragic poets. One of his dramas, *Octavia,* had a contemporary theme and told of the fate of Claudius's daughter.

He was also a persuasive orator and, like other ambitious young men, made a name for himself speaking on behalf of clients in the open-air law courts in the Forum. Although Rome was governed by laws, there was no state prosecution service and it was up to individuals to bring criminal and civil cases. A citizen with a grievance would commission a Senator or someone with a good legal background to present his case. It was illegal to charge a fee, but a successful barrister could expect handsome presents or favors later. He might receive a portion of a losing defendant's property (mandatory in the event of a conviction for treason). The emperor made use of such men, called *delatores,* to gather information and to assemble and present charges with a view to punishing or, not infrequently, liquidating his opponents. They would be generously rewarded but were despised by many of their peers. Prosecutors pursued a dangerous trade. If their case failed, they would be subject to the same penalties as the accused, and friends and relatives of those convicted would look for revenge when the political climate changed or a reign closed.

Seneca's success as an orator won him fame, but it also got him into trouble with the emperor Caligula, who regarded himself as expert in the subject and is said to have been jealous of his success. He called the upstart a mere "school textbook orator" who used "sand without lime." Apparently, he ordered Seneca's execution but canceled it when told that Seneca had contracted tuberculosis and would die soon in any case.

The prognosis was a helpful error, although, as a matter of fact, Seneca had been in poor health since childhood. We cannot diagnose with certainty the disease he suffered from, but it may have been tuberculosis or more probably asthma or some other kind of respiratory disorder. He was brought to a standstill by attacks of breathlessness that he described as "a sort of continuous last gasp." At times he was so ill when a young man that he seriously considered suicide: "Only the thought of my kind old father kept me back." He spent some time in Egypt, where an aunt was the governor's wife. His condition improved with the years, but he was always delicate. He was something of a hypochondriac and was not shy about discussing his illness in his writings nor of using it as a political excuse.

Agrippina's decision to hire the brilliant Seneca as her son's tutor met an immediate obstacle, for he had been banished by Claudius and had spent the last eight years languishing in Corsica.

He was highly sexed and is reported to have had an affair with her (the customary accusation) at some unknown date and, separately and more plausibly, with her sister Julia Livilla, if the hostile sources are to be believed. Nothing came of the first allegation (signifying probably that nothing had happened—or, if it did, that the lovers were very discreet).

But Livilla was trouble. To sleep with women of the imperial family outside marriage was lèse majesté. Female promiscuity could damage the pedigree, a matter of moment where dynastic integrity was concerned. Convicted of adultery with Livilla after a trial in the Senate, Seneca was sentenced to death. This was an unusually severe punishment for the offense, and, perhaps after lobbying by his friend Agrippina, the sentence was commuted to exile in Corsica, where he devoted most of his time to writing and reading. Seneca insisted on his innocence and, as already noted, nursed a grudge against Claudius ever afterward. We will never know whether he was guilty as charged or whether, as usual, a personal scandal veiled a political crisis of some kind, now irretrievable.

Agrippina succeeded in persuading her husband to agree to Seneca's recall. It is unclear why he changed his mind, but he may have decided that it would be wise to win a celebrated author and thinker to his side and help promote the entente with the Senate that he and his new wife had in mind.

Agrippina knew that Nero needed to be educated to avoid the mistakes made by her brother, Caligula, that had led to the breakdown of relations with the Senate and the military.

A princeps who had not mastered the techniques of persuasion, of addressing large groups effectively, would not last long. But while Agrippina insisted that the art of rhetoric should be instilled into her son, she vetoed a related subject, philosophy. She may well have had personal sympathy for Stoicism, but it was clearly associated with opponents of the imperial system who argued for the restoration of the republic and who admired Julius Caesar's formidable enemy, Cato.

From the age of thirteen or fourteen, upper-class boys studied the theory and practice of public speaking, either at schools or with tutors at home; this was a little early for Nero, who was only twelve, but Claudius was getting on in years, his mother must have felt, and there was no time to waste. He had already been introduced to the basics of grammar and of Greek and Roman literature.

Seneca had charm, a quality that helped him form a warm bond with Nero. In fact, their relationship had an erotic or at least flirtatious content. Dio has it that Seneca was bisexual and "took delight in adolescent boys beyond their prime, a practice he also taught Nero to follow." Complaints were lodged against him, but he rejected them, saying that he had excused himself from kissing his pupil. Perhaps, the historian speculates faux-naively, "they were the wrong sort of lips."

Seneca's method as a teacher was imaginative and enlightened, even by today's standards. He had recently published an essay *On Anger,* in which he discussed how best to manage privileged children:

> By freedom a boy's spirit grows, by oppression it is crushed. If he is praised and led to expect well of himself, he improves. However, this technique can breed insolence and hot temper; so we must

guide him between the two extremes, using now the bit, now the spur.

We may assume that Agrippina had read the pamphlet and approved.

What curriculum Seneca used for Nero's secondary schooling is uncertain, but it is likely that he employed the kinds of course his father outlined in a memoir he wrote of famous rhetoricians he had known in his younger days and of the educational systems they deployed.

Suitable boys of Nero's age probably joined him in the classroom. They were taught to declaim fluently and persuasively texts or *suasoriae* they prepared themselves. These addressed historical themes. For example: After his victory at Cannae, Hannibal, the Carthaginian general, debates the pros and cons of marching on Rome.

Instruction was also offered in *controversiae,* or disputations. In these exercises, a fictional law was stated and a dilemma posed. Here is an example.

> Law: A son who strikes his father shall have his hands amputated.
>
> Dilemma: A tyrant summons a man and his two sons to his citadel. He orders the young men to beat their father. One of them throws himself off a high place and dies. The other beats his father, as he has been told. Later he becomes a friend of the tyrant and takes the opportunity to assassinate him. He receives a reward for the deed, but his hands are to be cut off. His father defends him in court.

Boys were called on to speak for one side of the case or the other. Ingenuity in argument was expected. This is a pity, for whereas the *suasoriae* dealt with real-life situations from the past, the *controversiae* tended to be artificial and irrelevant to the concerns an orator was likely to encounter on his daily round. It was arid work and Nero may have agreed with the protagonist of Gaius Petronius's great novel, *The Satyricon,* who condemns teachers of rhetoric "for making complete fools of our young men, because they see and hear nothing of everyday life in the schools."

So what did Seneca do that helped his charge understand the principles and conduct of power? We are not told, but there must have been informal conversations or seminars on constitutional and political matters. The underlying theme was good government. He wrote: "I shall state the best paradigm on which a prince may mould his life, that he deal with his countrymen as he would that the gods may deal with himself."

Years later, when discussing Seneca's retirement from public life, Tacitus has Nero tell him: "You did what the situation at the time demanded. First of all you fostered my boyhood, then my youth, with reason, advice and rules. Your gifts to me will be imperishable, so long as life may last."

There was another side to the story. Boys will be boys. Nero was the victim of great expectations, with unremitting pressure from his ferocious mother as well as his army of tutors. Dio reports that he developed a technique for getting his own way.

> In case those looking after him ever said anything to him by way of advice or his mother by way of instructions, he would appear abashed in their presence and promised to improve. But as soon as they had gone, he would become the slave of his desires and would do as his friends told him who were leading him in the opposite direction downhill.

On March 17, 51, Nero came of age. He was in his fourteenth year. As a rule, a boy entered adulthood at fifteen or sixteen. As with his secondary education, the date had been advanced to prepare him for the purple.

He removed the hollow gold amulet or *bulla* that he had been given eight days after his birth and worn around his neck ever since to ward off evil spirits and to mark his Roman citizenship. He also discarded his *toga praetexta,* which sported a purple stripe and was reserved for children and Senators. He replaced it with an all-white adult *toga virilis*. A toga was a large semicircular cloth of woven wool whitened with chalk that a Roman draped about his body over a loincloth and tunic rather than worn as one would a garment. It was inconvenient and liable to slip off; it was too hot in the summer and uncomfortably draughty in the winter, but it was the citizen's distinctive costume and was de rigueur on formal occasions.

Nero now dedicated both *bulla* and toga at the little shrine that honored his household gods, or *lares*. His genitals were inspected (presumably to check for visible obstacles to fertility before he was declared an adult, and we hear of nothing untoward).

Annually on this day an ancient fertility festival, the Liberalia, was celebrated. Nero and other newly confirmed adults joined a procession through the city's winding streets. Priests and aged priestesses brought with them wine, honey, cakes, and confectionery in honor of Father Liber (another name for the wine god Bacchus) and his consort, Libera. An outsize phallus was carried to protect crops in the fields from failure. From time to time sacrifices were burned in a small frying pan on a mobile altar. At some stage Nero himself conducted a sacrifice, probably at the temple of Jupiter Best and Greatest on the Capitol.

A respectable middle-aged woman was chosen to bring the proceedings to a close when she crowned the phallus with a wreath. Small prizes or gifts called *sportulae* were distributed among the young men's friends and relatives who were present as witnesses.

Sometime during the day an earthquake rumbled and shook. Looking back, people saw it as a signal of disasters to come.

Agrippina and, we suppose, the princeps were determined that the political importance of this event was understood. Under Nero's name, bonuses were paid to the troops. The Senate pressed a willing Claudius to appoint Nero Consul Designate; he would hold the office only when he attained the age of twenty. In the meantime, he was awarded the powers, or imperium, of a Proconsul (usually a provincial governor who had executive authority in his territory) throughout the empire outside the bounds of Rome itself. This was a rare and clever distinction, for it gave Nero interim power that would not lapse in the event of Claudius's death. He was also to be styled *princeps iuventutis,* or first citizen of youth.

After the Liberalia festivities, games were held at the Circus Maximus, again in his honor and designed to enhance his popularity with the crowd. Britannicus wore his child's striped *toga praetexta,* while Nero was splendidly costumed in the *toga picta* (painted toga). This was a purple toga picked out with gold wire embroidery. It was believed originally to have been the official dress of the Roman kings and was later worn by victorious generals at their triumph. The contrast between the two boys was striking. It was visual theater at its most dramatic—and most instructive.

Nothing was said, no announcement was made, but the crowd received the message: Nero was being silently announced as Claudius's heir. Onlookers felt sorry for Britannicus, who seemed a nice boy, but they were relieved that an awkward situation had been resolved: Two pretenders to the imperial throne promised instability—even civil war. One heir was sufficient.

The handling of this affair had been carefully planned. It bears the empress's imprint. She had persuaded Claudius to approve an expensive and potentially controversial project. It looks very much as if there was consultation in advance with the Senate. The "hijacking" of the Liberalia festival to promote Nero was neatly managed.

Of course, everyone could see what was going on—even Britannicus, who had been compelled to witness the decay of his prospects. But Agrippina's main objective had been attained. Her boy Nero, great-great-grandson of Augustus and grandson of Germanicus, had been introduced to the citizens of Rome, and they had decidedly warmed to him.

All was not exactly as it appeared. Seneca was not Nero's only tutor. A team of Greek specialists was recruited. They did not seem to be the kind of expert or role model that the empress had in mind. One of them was a scholar and cultural administrator who was summoned to Rome from Alexandria in Egypt.

The great city founded by Alexander the Great four centuries earlier had taken over Athens's title as cultural capital of the Mediterranean world. Performing artists, musicians, and writers flourished there. The city's Mouseion (whence our "museum") was a unique residential center for scientific and literary research (an ancient version of Princeton's Institute for Advanced Study or All Souls College, Oxford). One of the city's glories was its library, where manuscript copies of tragedies by the great dramatists such as Aeschylus, Sophocles, and Euripides could be found (borrowed from the Athenian authorities and never returned).

One of the Mouseion's senior officials was Chaeremon; he was superintendent of an offshoot collection of the library stored in the immense temple of Serapis, a popular Greco-Egyptian deity. Something of a polymath, he was the author of a history of Egypt and published research on comets, Egyptian astrology, and hieroglyphs. Most abstruse of all was his treatise on expletive conjunctions (conjunctions that connect two thoughts that are not expressed in the same sentence).

He was a well-known Stoic, whom a wit ribbed gently for his austere principles: "You won't be so keen on dying if you live a life of luxury. It is much easier to give things up when you don't have many things."

It is hard to explain Chaeremon's presence on Agrippina's list of appropriate instructors in the art of being a noble Roman. It may be relevant that Claudius was a great admirer of the Mouseion and had donated a new building to the campus. He had a particular interest in arcane scholarly disciplines. He could have insisted on interfering in Agrippina's dispositions.

Nero was fascinated by everything he heard about the city, and he presumably besieged Chaeremon with questions. Later in his life, he never succeeded in visiting Alexandria despite his best intentions, but it seems to have become his great good place, the metropolis of his imagination.

To his mother's annoyance, Nero's extracurricular enthusiasms were distractions from his education. From his earliest years he had a passion for horses. As time passed he followed in his grandfather's footsteps and discovered chariot racing.

Ludi, or games, were Rome's mass entertainment. They were essential opiates for the population of a megalopolis, much of which was unemployed or underemployed and demanded amusement. They were festivals in honor of the gods and were sponsored by the state or leading political personalities. More than fifty days a year were devoted to *ludi*. Events included public banquets, athletic competitions, plays and dance or mime performances, wild animal hunts, and gladiatorial combats. Sometimes public executions were scheduled—not crowd-pleasing, though, so often staged during the lunch breaks. To enliven dull material, myths could be relived for real. For instance, a criminal under sentence of death starred in a retelling of the story of Prometheus, who stole fire from the gods and gave it to man. For this offense he was chained to a mountain crag, where a bird ate his perpetually self-renewing entrails. The condemned man was bound to a cross and a wild boar stood in for the bird. It was a popular show and could be repeated—with a different cast of course, though sometimes reenactments were staged with artificial blood and nobody died.

Horse and chariot races were the most popular attractions and usually took place in the vast Circus Maximus, which could seat 150,000 spectators in three tiers. Entry was free.

The Circus was contained in a rectangular structure more than two thousand feet long and four hundred wide. Down the middle ran a barrier, or *spina,* around which the chariots raced. In its center stood an obelisk that Augustus had brought from Egypt at colossal expense after defeating the forces of Antony and Cleopatra and annexing the kingdom.

On race days excited crowds assembled. In an arcade that ran around the outside of the circus building, they were laying bets, buying fast food from booths, patronizing shops or brothels. Prostitutes cruised, jugglers busked, fortune-tellers guessed. Twelve chariots waited in brightly painted spring-loaded starting gates for the princeps if he was present, or the officiating patron of the games, to drop a white cloth, for the gates to open and the race to begin.

Charioteers belonged to one of four teams or factions, the Whites, the Reds, the Greens, and the Blues. They were usually slaves or former slaves, but they attracted ferocious loyalty among the public. They became celebrities like today's football players.

In the eyes of wealthy aristocratic parents, chariot racing was a thoroughly disreputable sport. It was not only beneath a Roman citizen's dignity but also expensive and dangerous. It brought their male offspring into close contact with untrustworthy slaves and what they saw as the dregs of society. Blue-blooded young tearaways (Nero's grandfather had been one such) who relished driving a chariot rather than simply being investors or spectators put their lives on the line. Accidents were frequent, especially at the ends of the *spina,* where chariots had to make an abrupt U-turn and risked collisions. The drivers carried knives with them in case they got entangled in the horses' reins and the wreckage and needed to cut themselves free.

In the event of serious injuries or death, little practical assistance would be forthcoming from doctors, if a remedy prescribed by Pliny the Elder is at all typical. Wounds from being dragged on the ground by chariots or lacerations by the wheels would be cured, he claimed, by the application of wild boar's dung, either pure or in vinegar

---

The young prince was an avid follower of the races and of the careers of charioteers. He chattered endlessly to his school friends about the latest charioteering gossip—despite the fact that he had been warned that this was strictly forbidden. One day he was bemoaning the fate of a charioteer for the Greens, who had fallen from his chariot and been pulled along by his team of horses. Nero's tutor overheard the remark and reprimanded him. A quick-witted boy, he replied that he had in fact been talking about an incident in Homer's *Iliad* when the dead body of Hector, prince of Troy, had received the same treatment at the hands of the Greek warrior Achilles.

This is an instructive incident. Nero's taste for dissolute diversions will have been discussed not only among his teachers. We can speculate that Seneca raised the subject with Agrippina, who will not have been amused. Now that he was an adult, her son was proving to be a typical Ahenobarbus. She will have been especially worried by his potential for making shady friends at the Circus.

The first sliver can be detected of a sign that mother and son were not always in accord.

Despite the prevalence of charlatans, many Romans believed in the power of magic, chiefly as a means of controlling their personal situation by charms and spells. Knowledge of the future threatened the authorities, who reacted sharply. Unfazed by Lollia Paulina's fate and Claudius's disapproval, Nero was fascinated. So claims Pliny the Elder, who adds that magic came in many forms, mixing conjuring tricks with rituals for accessing the supernatural world. It was

> practiced with water, for instance, with balls, by the aid of the air, of the stars, of lamps, basins, hatchets, and numerous other appliances; means by which it promises to grant a foreknowledge of things to come.

Mediums offered an opportunity to converse with ghosts and receive messages from the dead. (Later in life, though, Nero lost faith in the dark arts, which he came to believe were "fraudulent" illusions.)

Once again, he allowed himself an inappropriate enthusiasm. Whether either emperor or empress were aware of it is unknown. If they were, the heir apparent would have found himself in serious trouble, but we do not have even a distant echo of it.

Nero was a clever boy. From his childhood he turned his "lively mind" to artistic interests. Tacitus reports that he carved, painted, sang, and wrote verses showing that he had in him "the rudiments of culture."

There was nothing out of the ordinary about this. Upper-class Romans were expected to participate in cultural activities. In addition to their native Latin, they spoke and read Greek fluently and wrote verses in the manner of the great poets of old. Some, like Claudius himself, produced prose histories. Others, like Seneca, might compose essays on philosophical or ethical topics or carefully studied letters to friends which (of course) they took care to publish. Authors would meet at public readings of their work.

Nero's fellow pupil Titus was typical of his class. Suetonius notes that as an adult, he "gave speeches and wrote poems in Latin and Greek with equal ease and fluency. He was something of a musician too, sang pleasantly and had mastered the harp."

However, all these artists and authors were strictly amateurs. It did not do to take the life of the imagination too seriously. Nero disagreed with the dilettante approach of cultured Romans like Titus. As he grew up he became increasingly convinced of the superiority of Greek civilization. Fascinated, even obsessed, by its performing arts and literature, he dreamed of being a professional musician in Alexandria, where all the best Hellenic music was to be heard, as perhaps Chaeremon had told him.

Nero appears to have found Seneca's teaching of oratory dull; too much time was spent on his tutor's own work and too little on the masterpieces of the craft from earlier eras. Perhaps in search of expressive force, he turned to the writing of poetry. He discovered a gift for expressing himself rapidly and without effort.

Rumor had it that his verses were not his but were written by another hand. This was evidently not the case, as Suetonius conclusively established:

> Notebooks and papers have come into my possession which contain some of [Nero's] best-known poems in his own handwriting. It is perfectly clear that they were not copied or taken down from dictation, but worked out exactly as one writes when thinking and creating, for there are many examples of words rubbed out or struck through or added.

The ancient sources are unkind about Nero's poetry, but the unstated implication here is that it was well liked, at least by some, and that he was serious about his art. That he had talent.

Such evidence as we have indicates that Nero was not allowed to pursue his passion for the races nor for dramatic or musical performances, although he was not prevented from versifying. We have too little material to offer a psychological portrait, but it does appear that a conflict existed between the boy who was training for the role of princeps and the one whose dearest wish was to be a creative artist.

As his life unfolded, it would become clearer which course it was to follow—duty, or desire, or (daringly) both at once.

5

A DISH OF MUSHROOMS

CLAUDIUS MEANT to take full—and well-deserved—credit for the greatest engineering project of the age, the draining of the Fucine lake. He had placed his trusted freedman, Narcissus, in charge of the works and now that they were complete he looked forward to a grand opening in 52.

Most emperors commissioned grand edifices, temples, as often as not, and forums. Claudius was a builder too, but he invested in the useful rather than the splendid. He financed schemes that impacted on the lives of Rome's touchy and demanding inhabitants. Feeding them was beyond the capacity of Italy's farmers and the megalopolis depended on reliable imports of grain, mainly from Egypt, and the provinces of Africa and Sicily. As already noted, much of it was distributed in free subsidies. Shortages were rapidly followed by riots and the regime would totter.

Claudius oversaw massive enlargements of the port of Ostia where the Tiber flowed into the sea and also the harbor at Puteoli (today's Pozzuoli), which served the Alexandrian fleet. Fresh water was as essential as grain, and he repaired existing aqueducts and funded new ones (one of which, the Anio Novus, ran 55 miles from its source in the hills beyond Praeneste [modern Tivoli] to Rome). He took a personal interest in these developments, sometimes to his peril, for it was during a visit to Ostia that Messalina launched her bid for power.

The Fucine lake lay among the Apennines some fifty miles east of Rome in central Italy. It was a wide stretch of water, covering an area of about 87 square miles. Surrounded by hills, it had no natural outlet and after heavy rain flooded the towns around the lake's edge. In past years politicians had considered the problem, found it too difficult, and moved on.

Almost as soon as he assumed the purple, Claudius bravely gave the go-ahead for the construction of a tunnel three miles long, running from the lake beneath the Monte Salviano to the river Liris, through which the water would drain away. This would not only solve once and for all the problem of frequent flooding, but also create many jobs and reclaim much fertile land for food production.

According to Suetonius, thirty thousand laborers worked on the project, but the figure seems far too high; three thousand is a more realistic number. In any case, they labored, for much of the time in darkness, without mechanical assistance, for eleven years, and the final product, a brick-lined tunnel ten feet high, seemed worth the time and expense.

An inaugural gala was held that was to culminate in the unlocking of sluice gates and the gradual emptying of the lake. Claudius was splendidly dressed in military uniform and a gorgeous cloak, as was Nero, who looked every inch an emperor in waiting. None of the sources mentions Britannicus, who may not have been present, and even if he was, attracted no attention. Agrippina wore over her tunic a stunning cloth-of-gold Greek-style mantle fastened at her right shoulder by a brooch.

Tacitus describes the scene:

> The shores, the hills, the mountain-tops, formed a kind of theater, soon filled by a vast crowd, attracted from the neighboring towns, and in part from the capital itself, by curiosity or by respect for the sovereign.

A wooden barrier and stands were built around the lake and the audience took their seats to watch a spectacular and (in the Roman manner) blood-soaked entertainment.

This was a gladiatorial sea battle between two fleets of warships, the Rhodians and the Sicilians. There were nineteen thousand combatants, all of them convicted criminals. They were in effect a small army and security was tight. Rafts were stationed in the water carrying detachments of the Praetorian Guard who were able to operate catapults and stone throwers

Before the start of hostilities the combatants assembled in front of Claudius and said: "Hail Caesar! We salute you, we who are about to die." "Or not, as the case may be," replied the princeps amusedly.

The joke backfired. The men refused to fight, insisting that his words amounted to a pardon. Claudius was so angry that he seriously considered sending in troops to massacre them all or burning them in their ships. He had second thoughts, jumped from his throne, and hobbled to the lakeside. He threatened and coaxed the men to fight.

A mechanical silver Triton rose from the middle of the lake and blew a horn for the battle to start. Tentative at the outset, the struggle soon intensified. Tacitus reports:

> Despite being criminals the men fought with the spirit and courage of freemen. After much blood-letting, they were exempted from extermination.

The moment had arrived for the release of the water. An impressive outpouring had been expected but failed to materialize. The exit from the tunnel had mistakenly been set too high, and only a trickle flowed.

There was nothing more to be done that day, but after some redigging, dignitaries assembled at the Fucine lake once again. To attract a second audience, a gladiatorial display, mimicking an infantry battle, was staged on pontoons. A banquet was held at the outflow of the lake into the tunnel.

This time a roaring torrent swept away parts of the engineering works and flooded the area. A general panic ensued. The royal party was safe but had been alarmed.

This was more than a disaster, it was an embarrassment. If there is one thing a dictatorial regime fears it is laughter. Claudius had made himself look ridiculous, limping about and negotiating with criminals, and tales about the behavior of the water, now too little, now too much, must have been told and retold throughout the empire to gales of laughter.

Claudius was disconcerted and Agrippina was furious. She accused Narcissus, the manager of the scheme, of cupidity and embezzlement (in fact the contractors were probably the culprits). The freedman refused to be silenced and attacked "her feminine imperiousness and excess of ambition." That he was able to launch such an onslaught without penalty says much for Claudius's confidence in him. There was a danger signal here for Agrippina; however close the partnership was with her husband, she had not supplanted the freedmen who ran the government for him. If teased they could bite.

—

It would have been good to have Nero's account of these two unfortunate days. He had viewed the show from the front row. He was fascinated by civic spectacle and its value as a tool of policy, but he could see the ridicule created by managerial incompetence. When he came to power, he would show Rome what spectacle could really be like.

—

Nero was in his sixteenth year and it was judged time for him to put into practice all he had learned from Seneca and his other tutors. He needed to show that he was ready to rule. He made a number of carefully judged interventions.

At his formal introduction to public life, he gave a speech in the Forum, during which he announced a largess for the People and a bonus for the military. He headed a troop of cavalry that rode in a circle around armed foot soldiers (a ceremonial display called the *decursio*).

In the Senate, Nero took up the case of Ilium (or Troy, in present-day Turkey). This was where the Trojan War had been fought. He reminded Senators that it was the birthplace of the legendary Aeneas, the revered ancestor of Romulus and Remus, Rome's founders, and the (supposed) progenitor of the Julian clan, of which Nero was of course a leading member.

Ilium was no longer the capital of a once powerful kingdom, but a large tumulus where a down-at-heels village eked out a living as a tourist destination for cultured Romans with a taste for nostalgia. Nero addressed the Senate as its advocate and expatiated on its historic past, speaking "with grace" about its associations with Rome. He won approval for Ilium's application that it be freed from tribute and all community obligations.

The town of Bononia in northern Italy (today's Bologna) had been destroyed by fire and, thanks to Nero's advocacy, was awarded a handsome reconstruction grant of 10 million sesterces. His oratory also recovered the liberties of the troublesome island of Rhodes and a five-year remission of tribute for a Phrygian city devastated by an earthquake, successes that found him friends in the Greek-speaking parts of the empire.

Once a year the princeps and Consuls left the city and headed a long procession of dignitaries to the Alban Mount, a dead volcano in the Alban Hills, about twelve miles away. Near its summit stood a sanctuary to Jupiter, where the ancient rites of the three-day Latin Festival (or Feriae Latinae) were conducted. They reaffirmed an alliance between Rome when it was a small local power and other Latin-speaking city-states in central Italy. Each sent a representative who brought with him offerings of sheep, cheese, and other agricultural produce.

In 53 the officiant was, as usual, Claudius. He poured a libation of milk and presided over the sacrifice of a pure white heifer that had never been broken in and yoked. Its flesh was cooked and eaten by those present as a communal sacrament. Figurines of masks or faces were hung from tree branches to propitiate rustic deities.

Meanwhile, to ensure that the city of Rome was still governed in the brief absence of the political class, a temporary Prefect, or *praefectus urbi,* was appointed to maintain order. The post was largely ceremonial although it possessed legal powers. This year Nero was appointed as Prefect, but Claudius forbade any lawsuits to be heard. The veto was ignored, and the most celebrated pleaders of the day competed with one another to have Nero hear their cases.

As a rule, disobeying a princeps was not recommended; maybe Claudius issued his ban with a twinkle in his eye, merely wanting to distance himself in case Nero made any mistakes. No problems were recorded.

There can be little doubt that Seneca was Nero's speech writer and adviser, but, all told, the *princeps iuventutis* had acquitted himself well, no mean feat for a sixteen-year-old. For this he was rewarded when, after an engagement that had lasted five years, Nero finally married Octavia, one of Claudius's two daughters.

The problem of incest recurred, for after his adoption, Nero was Octavia's brother, albeit by law and not by blood. There could be no question of permitting marriage between siblings, so Octavia found herself adopted into another family before the wedding. The couple did not get along and the union was an unhappy one. When friends criticized Nero later for his treatment of her, he was dismissive: "Just being the princeps's wife surely ought to be enough to make her happy."

At some point in 53, Claudius fell ill. Nero's response, masterminded by his mother, enhanced an impression he was giving of competence and loyalty. It was uncertain that the princeps would survive. At Agrippina's prompting, Nero vowed to stage a horse racing festival, the people's favorite entertainment, if he recovered, and Claudius was persuaded to inform the Senate that, should he die, his adopted son was capable of conducting state business in his place. This was tantamount to announcing Nero as his heir.

Emperors tended, very sensibly, not to be explicit about the succession, so Claudius was taking an unusual and potentially dangerous step. As it turned out, he got better and the crisis passed. Fulfilling his promise, Nero presented a memorable series of horse and chariot races. Everyone was talking about him.

Meanwhile, nobody was talking about Britannicus. Agrippina was adept at the management of news, and more particularly of false news. The boy was seldom seen in public and many people did not know whether he was alive or dead. Some thought he was insane or an epileptic.

The atmosphere at court became poisonous. The impression grew that Agrippina was arrogating too much power to herself and that Claudius was coming to regret his partnership with her and her ruthless promotion of Nero.

What can have been in his mind? He was ailing again, and it would be extraordinary if at this late stage he were to reopen the matter of the succession and distance himself from the empress. And yet that was what may well have been happening. Only one factor in domestic politics would explain the new mood—Britannicus was maturing. In fact, in physical development he was in advance of his real age. If the princeps could stay alive for a couple of years, his natural son would be ready for public life. The two princes could rule together. There were precedents. Augustus had shared power with his school friend Agrippa, and in the following years there had been other hopeful pairings. But would Agrippina, fixated monomaniacally on her son, allow any move in this direction?

Coming across Britannicus one day, Claudius gave him a hug and advised him to grow up quickly. He quoted reassuringly a line from a Greek drama about the mythical heroes Telephus and Heracles: "The hand that wounded you shall also heal." Thinking on the matter, he decided to bring forward the boy's coming-of-age ceremony. We detect a campaign by Narcissus, who had opposed the marriage to Agrippina from the outset and whose suspicions of her were deepening. The shadowy outline of a faction in favor of Britannicus emerges.

Once again, the senior freedmen of the administration were at odds. Narcissus was close enough to his employer to be able to be brutally frank and go unpunished. He told one of his close friends: "Whoever comes to the throne, Britannicus or Nero, my fate is sealed. But Claudius has been so kind to me that I would give my life to help him."

He evidently believed that he had enough evidence of the alleged affair between Agrippina and Pallas to brief Claudius on the subject. According to Suetonius, when his freedmen congratulated the princeps, in his judicial capacity, on convicting a woman of adultery, he dropped a heavy, jocular hint: "I myself seem fated to marry wives who were unchaste, but remained unchastened." One evening in his cups, reports Tacitus, Claudius repeated the point: "It is my destiny to endure my wives' misdeeds, and then to punish them."

For her part, Agrippina was ready to move her queen and checkmate the king. She had long ago learned the art of patience, but now that all her pieces were in place and she had arrived at uncontested authority, she tightened her grip. Just as her mother had acted as if she were a man when she helped save an army, so the empress stepped out from behind her curtain and insisted that Rome's misogynistic elite recognize her openly as a ruler alongside her husband. Dio writes:

> Nothing seemed to satisfy her, though all the privileges that Livia had enjoyed had been bestowed upon her also, and a number of additional honors had been voted. But, although she exercised the same power as Claudius, she desired to have his title outright.

If that is true, it can only have been a daydream. She insisted on the trappings—hence the two equal daises for her and her husband at public ceremonies or use of the *carpentum* at festivals, a rare honor. However, she understood that she could rule only through her husband or her son. For all that, we sense her self-confidence, perhaps overconfidence, expanding to fill the available political space.

Agrippina picked up the signal of her husband's discontent and decided to take urgent action. It was time for Claudius to bid the world good night.

First, though, she had some unfinished business to settle. She arranged the destruction of Domitia Lepida, once upon a time her sister-in-law. She was charged with an attempt on the empress's life by magic and with failing to keep the slave gangs on her estates in Calabria in order.

Narcissus was outraged and vigorously opposed the accusations, but to no avail. Lepida was found guilty and executed. A nephew of hers was implicated. He was sent into exile, but was then ordered by a centurion heading a small military detachment to kill himself. Most unusually, the young man refused and fought for his life; the centurion ran him through. The entry wound was on his front—he had not turned to flee.

This is a perplexing business. Tacitus attributed Agrippina's motive for moving against Lepida to a "womanly quarrel." He may be right; both had domineering personalities and were used to getting their own way. They had probably been on bad terms since Agrippina wedded Ahenobarbus. In addition, the fact that Lepida was Messalina's mother and Britannicus's grandmother should not be overlooked. Did she support her grandson's claim to the throne rather than her nephew's?

Other factors should be taken into account. As we saw, Lepida had always been kind to Nero and generous with presents when he was a child. On the other hand, the empress was naturally short-tempered. Tacitus observed: "She could give her son an empire, but could not endure him as emperor."

She wanted no rival for Nero's affections once he had assumed the purple. To underline the point, she persuaded—or bullied—him to give evidence against Lepida. We are not told of the emotional cost he paid by betraying a women he was fond of, perhaps even loved. At the least, the incident can hardly have warmed him to his mother.

Finally, the slave gangs merit consideration. Slave rebellions were a Roman's recurrent nightmare, and it is plausible that Lepida as proprietor was criminally negligent. Her slaves were her property, and it was her duty to maintain discipline. The slave rebel Spartacus in the previous century was still a bogeyman. So Lepida may have gotten her just deserts.

To deal with Claudius once and for all, Agrippina needed some specialized support. If a Roman had serious marital problems or was suffering from financial difficulties or faced an awkward political challenge or had an eye on a promised legacy, he could apply for assistance to a woman from Gaul called Locusta. She possessed a rare skill that she was willing to place at his or her disposal, for an appropriate consideration. She was a professional poisoner and, according to Tacitus, "an artist in her field."

Many deaths were mistakenly attributed to poison when they were in fact a consequence of the regular appearance of diseases and epidemics poorly understood by doctors of the day. So when Claudius's father, Germanicus, fell sick and died from an unexplained cause in Syria, he and his wife were certain he had been poisoned, although it is just as likely that he succumbed to an infection.

However, in the last years of the republic and the early years of the empire, death by poison was not uncommon. The wealthy and powerful were so anxious for their safety that it became standard practice to employ food tasters. The great lawyer and orator Cicero in the previous century appeared as counsel in a number of poisoning cases. Poison was an effective way of killing oneself or being killed in the event of imperial disapproval. Tacitus reports that an official inquiry found Tiberius's favorite, Sejanus, guilty of murdering Drusus, his son and heir to the throne. He had

> chosen a poison so gradual in its effects as to mimic the progress of a natural illness. It was administered to Drusus with the help of a eunuch of his, Lygdus, [much loved by his master for his years and his looks]. All this was brought to light eight years later.

Animal poisons were seldom used (Cleopatra and her alleged asp may be an exception), and mineral poisons were little understood. A famous witch in Augustus's day called Canidia used to recommend hemlock in honey. Locusta will have specialized in vegetable poisons, such as the belladonna alkaloids including henbane and deadly nightshade, and aconite from hemlock. Mothers were supposed to loathe the women their sons married and aconite was nicknamed the "mother-in-law's poison." Strychnine was unknown to the Romans and they seem not to have realized that cyanide could be extracted from certain fruits.

Most poisonings appear to have been carried out by women, who, if we can trust the satirist Juvenal, "would happily see their husbands die to save their puppy's life." Clearly they are being stereotyped, but their subordinate position and lack of agency make it equally clear that some deployed poison to redress the unequal balance of power.

There may have been a positive side to this murderous craft. The Locustas of the ancient world were chemists expert in plants, and in their "day job" they may well have used their botanical knowledge beneficently to keep people in this world rather than dispatch them to the next.

Locusta was not hard to find, for she was in custody after a poisoning conviction. Agrippina sent for her. She had long meditated her husband's murder but did not know the kind of poison she needed. She explained her problem to Locusta. Something rapid and drastic would give her away, whereas a long and lingering agony might provide the princeps, faced with death, with time to renew his affection for Britannicus.

Locusta did not disappoint. Tacitus writes:

> What recommended itself was something recondite, which would derange Claudius's faculties while postponing his dissolution.

The recipe's effects were designed to mirror a typical Claudian evening—the ingestion of excessive quantities of food and wine followed by servants carrying the comatose emperor to his bed. This time, though, there would be no sleeping it off.

Agrippina assessed with care the correct time to dispense Locusta's potion. In October she had a stroke of luck. Narcissus's suspicion of her intentions was hardening into certainty, but the anxiety made him ill. He also suffered from gout, and Agrippina sent him—for his own good, of course—to Sinuessa Spa, a seaside town on the Appian Way well known for its mild climate and its thermal springs. While he took the waters and convalesced, the empress struck.

On October 12, 54, the annual celebrations of Augustus's birthday were held. There were horse races at the Circus Maximus; priests of the cult of Augustus, now an immortal god, and the Vestal Virgins conducted sacrifices; and, always a pleasure, the princeps presided at a banquet on the Capitol. His food taster, a eunuch called Halotus, was in attendance and suffered no ill effects.

The next day, dinner was served at the palace. This time there were consequences. Writers alive at the time recorded what happened. Cooked mushrooms were among Claudius's favorite foods and were on the menu. According to Suetonius, it was Halotus who sprinkled the poison on a particularly fine specimen and Agrippina who passed her husband the dish while he was watching a performance by some comic actors. As anticipated, the princeps picked up and ate the attractive but fatal fungus. To distract suspicion, his wife reached across and selected a harmless mushroom that she ate herself. She had strong nerves.

As on previous evenings, the emperor fell into a stupor. He vomited up the contents of his stomach and evacuated his bowels. In other words, for a palace banquet, nothing seemed out of the ordinary. To Agrippina's horror, the attempt appeared to have failed. The empress is said to have taken speedy remedial action.

The royal doctor, another pliable Greek freedman in her pay, gave Claudius a second dose, perhaps in a bowl of gruel, ostensibly to settle his digestion.

Other, less plausible versions have the poison introduced as an enema or as an envenomed feather plunged down the emperor's throat.

These follow-up measures are supposed to have been applied to an unconscious man and under the sharp-eyed gaze of courtiers. They are probably apocryphal. It looks as if Locusta had indeed devised a slow-acting poison that rhymed with Claudius's routine drunken binges. Despite the empress's alarm, it did its work during the night, and by dawn the princeps was dead. He was sixty-three years old.

What are we to make of Claudius as he leaves the stage? After his sickly and unhappy childhood, Augustus and Livia vetoed a political career for him and he had neither training for nor practical experience of government. Not being a direct descendant of Augustus, he was insecure on his throne and feared plots. However, he proved to be quite a successful ruler. He invested heavily in physical infrastructure, and the annexation and pacification of Britain were well managed. He supported, admittedly somewhat quirkily, the rule of law.

Claudius was an antiquarian and historian, a scholarly eccentric who had never expected to assume the purple, and he brought a fresh mind to the task. His civil service was run by highly intelligent Greek ex-slaves on the make; they amassed huge fortunes in his service, but they were efficient and, it follows, unpopular. He fell out badly with the Senate and much blood was spilled. However, he and his last wife made an excellent partnership and rebuilt relations with the aristocratic elite.

His final achievement was to arrange a trouble-free succession by placing his great-nephew on the throne. We shall see in due course whether this appears in the credit or the debit column.

Once again Agrippina learned from the example set by Livia, who concealed Augustus's death for a few days to facilitate an orderly handover to Tiberius. In the same way, she kept up the pretense that Claudius was still alive and doing well. This gave her time to make the necessary arrangements for the endorsement of Nero as the next princeps.

All entrances to the palace were guarded and no one was allowed in or out. The provincial governors and legionary generals on the frontiers had to be warned. A plan to ensure that the Praetorians in their camp at the edge of the city would be willing to transfer their loyalty to her son had to be agreed with Burrus, the Praetorian Prefect and the empress's inoffensive political appointee.

It was essential that senior members of the imperial family be separated from any supporters. Agrippina put on a shameless show with Britannicus. Tacitus writes:

> Apparently heartbroken and looking for consolation, she pressed Britannicus to her chest. She called him the very image of his fa-

ther. By this and other tricks she prevented him from leaving his room.

In the late morning of October 13, when everything was ready, the doors of the palace were suddenly thrown open and Nero, with Burrus beside him, walked out onto the front steps and met a battalion of Praetorians who happened to be on regular guard duty. His mother was tactfully absent.

On a hint from the Prefect, he was greeted with cheers and placed in a litter. One or two soldiers looked around hesitantly and were heard to ask: "Where is Britannicus?" Nobody followed their lead, so the men had no alternative but to acquiesce in the choice given them.

Nero was then carried in a litter to the Praetorians' camp where he said a few appropriate words, composed by Seneca, and promised a handsome bonus or donative of 15,000 sesterces for each guardsman, the same amount as that handed out at the start of Claudius's reign. This produced the obligatory cheer of "Imperator" (commander in chief, a title originally awarded after a battle to victorious generals by their soldiers).

In theory, the powers of a princeps were awarded by the Senate, but in truth that was a formality once the Praetorians had given their approval, on this occasion the sword being mightier than the pen. Nevertheless, Nero returned to the city center and addressed the assembled Senators.

The speech, again ghostwritten by Seneca, went down very well. It gave the clear impression that the new princeps would cooperate fully with the Senators, who issued the necessary decrees confirming his authority. A vote was unanimously passed that the address be inscribed on silver and read out aloud every time new Consuls entered on their year of office. This was not entirely sycophancy, for it would remind a straying emperor (not to mention citizens in general) of promises made during the honeymoon of his reign. Accolades were showered on Nero, all of which he accepted—except that of Father of His Country, which he declined because of his youth.

Claudius was voted divine honors, but his will was not read out as expected. We have no idea what it contained. It may be that the testator's partiality for his adopted as against his natural son would be embarrassingly obvious. Alternatively he may have made it clear, just as embarrassingly, that he regarded the two youths as being on an equal footing. Nero destroyed the document.

The princeps stayed in the Senate House until nightfall, after which he returned, exhausted but exhilarated, to the palace. It had been a long day and he had acquitted himself well. We know nothing of his emotions, but he could be pardoned for being pleased with himself. The transition of power had been smooth and uneventful. There had been hardly a whisper of dissent.

However, he knew whose day it had really been. Before going to bed, he gave the Guard its watchword for the night: *optima mater,* "the best of mothers."

Meanwhile the news percolated to all corners of the empire. Thus the mayor of the obscure Egyptian town of Oxyrhynchus announced to his people:

> The good spirit of the world . . . Nero has been proclaimed Caesar. For this reason, all of us ought to wear wreaths and sacrifice oxen, to show to all the gods our gratitude.

Some days later, after what Tacitus called the "mockeries of sorrow"—in other words, Claudius's funeral—were over, the new emperor returned to the Senate House in the Forum to set out his program of government. He made a polite reference to the authority of the Fathers, as Senators were called, and the backing of the army, before saying:

> I have advice at my disposal and examples pointing me to a good system of government. My early years have not been poisoned by civil war or family quarrels. I am bringing to my task no feuds, no resentment nor vindictiveness.

He then outlined the character of the coming reign and raised those issues which had recently provoked intense dissatisfaction. One of an emperor's duties was to preside at important law cases, but Claudius had done so eccentrically and too frequently. Nero vowed not to judge every kind of case, not to sit in camera whenever he wanted, and not to allow a few individuals too much influence.

> Under my roof will be no bribery and no legal loopholes: personal and state business will be kept separate. Let the Senate retain its ancient prerogatives! Let Italy and the Senatorial provinces have legal access to the Consuls, and let the Consuls grant them access to the Senate. As for the armies in my care: I myself will be responsible.

A cynic would raise his eyebrows, but the regime kept its promises. The entente between princeps and Senate was solid, and motions were laid before the house and approved without difficulty. Advocates in the courts were strictly forbidden to charge for their services, as had been the practice in the days of the republic (in fact, the situation had been murky even then, for—as already noted—counsel could expect generous gifts or services at some later date). Quaestors were the most junior elected public officials, and when a Claudian law required them to present a gladiatorial show at their own expense, it was felt to place an unfair financial burden on men at the outset of their political career. The Senate repealed the law.

Only Agrippina objected, on the grounds that her husband's legislation had been undermined. It was a small defeat, but a red flag waved warning of troubles to come.

6

BEST OF MOTHERS

THE STORY of Claudius's last supper was too entertaining to conceal. It soon became an open secret and was absorbed, with guffaws, into the popular culture.

It was the mushrooms that attracted the wits, among whom Seneca counted himself. In a letter to a friend, he observed: "You are afraid of death; but how magnificently heedless of it you are when tackling a dish of choice mushrooms!"

When the satirist Juvenal criticizes the stinginess of a dinner party host, he cannot resist a dig at the greedy princeps:

For the lower-income guests, some dubious toadstools:
for my lord, a rare mushroom, the kind that Claudius guzzled
(until his wife fed him one that wrote finis *to his eating).*

To give the reader a frisson of fear, the poet warns wealthy young wards to be on their guard: "Accept no dish at dinner; / those pies are steaming black with Mummy's poison."

Nero enjoyed a joke, especially if it was tasteless, and joined in the fun himself. After Claudius had been deified, he liked to quote an old Greek proverb about mushrooms being the food of the gods. "It's true," he used to say; "my father became a god from eating a mushroom." Another favorite quip of his was that Claudius could no longer "play the fool on earth," lengthening the initial syllable of *morari,* "to linger," so that it meant "play the fool."

Claudius hobbled down the Sacred Way and approached the Forum.

He saw a huge gathering of people. A gorgeous procession was passing by. Trumpets blared, horns boomed, an immense brass band was clashing and blowing every kind of instrument. The din was tremendous. The public mood was ecstatic. Everyone, except for a few corrupt lawyers and businessmen, was smiling and laughing. It was clear to Claudius that what was passing was his own funeral train. Only now did he understand that he was dead.

This posthumous Claudius was the satirical product of Seneca's teeming brain. He had never forgiven the emperor for sending him into tedious exile in Corsica. His skit, *Apocolocyntosis Divi Claudii,* or *The Pumpkinification of the Deified Claudius,* was published shortly after his funeral and was an act of revenge. It would have appealed to an adolescent with a scatological sense of humor, especially the adolescent who now ruled the empire. He will have fallen about laughing at Seneca's account of the emperor's final moments:

> His last words heard on earth came after he'd let off a louder noise from his easiest channel of communication: "Oh damn! I think I've shat myself." For all I know, he did. He certainly shat on everything else.

Mercury, the divine messenger and psychopomp, was Claudius's guide on this imaginary tour. A choir chanted a dirge in Claudius's honor; he would have liked to stay and listen to them singing his praises, but Mercury led him out of the city and across the Campus Martius until they reached a spot between the Tiber and a street called the Covered Walkway. There they descended into the underworld.

In real life Agrippina had arranged Narcissus's "suicide" soon after Nero's accession; by an odd chance he died near the tomb of Messalina, whom he had destroyed. (Professional to the last, he burned all his papers to avoid incriminating anyone he had done business with.)

Seneca has the freedman somehow travel to the land of the dead by a shorter route than his late master, for on Claudius's arrival, there Narcissus was, waiting to welcome him. They walked past Cerberus, the three-headed dog, and were greeted by a large crowd of people whom Claudius had either executed or forced into self-murder.

> "Friends everywhere! How wonderful!" he exclaimed, absent-mindedly. "How did you all get here?"
>
> "You killed us!" came the reply.

He was hauled off to hell's criminal court and prosecuted for multiple murders. The defense was not given a chance to speak (an echo of his own occasional practice as a judge). After conviction a long discussion ensued about an appropriate punishment. Perhaps Claudius could replace Tantalus forever stretching out for food and drink or Sisyphus endlessly pushing a rock up a hill. Instead, a completely new penalty was devised. An inveterate gambler, he was to rattle dice in boxes without bottoms for all eternity.

Just at this moment Caligula turned up and claimed Claudius as his slave. He donated him to the court judge who passed him on to his Greek freedman. This petty bureaucrat employed him as a lowly law clerk—a humiliating fate for a man used to being the empire's chief judge.

So who was now in charge? Certainly not the young emperor.

Agrippina was enjoying her heyday. She saw herself as a kind of regent. Her son had apparently left to her the management of both public and personal business. Everyone realized that the pair were on loving terms when they saw him sharing her litter or walking alongside it.

If a Roman paid a bill at this time, he could find himself extracting from his purse a brand-new silver coin, the denarius. If he looked at it, he would have been surprised, even shocked. It showed on the obverse two emperors facing each other in profile. One of them was Agrippina, and her titles circled the two heads, all in the nominative case. Nero's titles appeared only on the reverse and in the dative—

Neroni, or "for Nero." She was clearly the senior colleague in a joint enterprise. This conclusion was backed by anecdotal evidence of their closeness.

Other signs demonstrated that the empress was riding high. The Senate awarded her a pair of lictors and appointed her a priestess of the newly founded cult of the Deified Claudius. Lictors were attendants for elected officials with imperium—that is, executive authority—such as Consuls and Praetors. They carried bundles of rods tied around ax blades to symbolize that authority. For an unelected woman to be honored in this way was an offense against tradition.

Building on her practice when Claudius was alive, Agrippina arranged for meetings of the Senate to be held in the palace on the Palatine hill. Here she could station herself at a newly added doorway in the rear, across which she hung her discreet curtain.

Being a woman, Agrippina did not possess imperium, the constitutional authority to tell people what to do. It was a grave weakness. She was obliged to govern indirectly, and she did so in the main through three men. The freedman Pallas was in her pocket (and possibly her bed), and as *libertus a rationibus* he controlled the imperial finances, both the state treasury and the private *fiscus*. She had persuaded her husband to appoint Burrus as sole commander of the Praetorians, who guaranteed the security of the dynasty.

Finally, another of her placemen, Seneca, was promoted from tutor to political adviser. According to the ancient sources, he did not sponsor legislation in the Senate and held no official post. He was one of a select group of semiofficial *amici principis,* or friends of the emperor. It seems that he and Burrus exercised power according to the confidence the emperor had in them. Nero liked and respected Seneca and for a long time did as he was told.

We have seen that the Augusta worked hard to be on good terms with Senators, but there was one exception to prove the rule.

Marcus Junius Silanus was appointed Consul in 46 and went on to govern the province of Asia as Proconsul. According to Tacitus, he was both bad-tempered and lethargic, a combination of qualities unsuited to a manager of people. However, he suffered from a more serious disability. Like Nero, he was the son of a great-grandchild of Augustus, and so a member of the imperial family. This meant that he was qualified either for the purple or for death. Because he did not have the relevant political or personal skills, previous emperors counted him as harmless; because of his great wealth, Caligula nicknamed him "the golden sheep." But Agrippina's guiding political principle was that one can never be too careful.

Silanus was also unlucky enough to be the elder brother of the Silanus who had been the onetime fiancé of Claudius's daughter, Octavia, until forcibly and permanently removed. Agrippina feared that he might be looking to avenge his sibling's death.

She happened to have left over some of the poison with which she had terminated her husband. Two officials, an *eques* and Helius, a freedman who was the province of Asia's treasurer, administered the poison at a meal. Although he fails to give details, Tacitus writes that no attempt was made to conceal the killing. Perhaps a report was circulated after the event, or, less likely, the Proconsul was forced to eat what he knew would kill him.

A curious aspect of the incident is that Nero was neither consulted nor informed of what was afoot. Perhaps the empress and her staff were unable to predict or control a headstrong boy's reaction. But it is more probable that Agrippina, at the apex of her power, had decided that the image of the princeps should be pacific, forgiving, and law-abiding. To have his name associated with a murder or execution at the outset of his reign would not sit well with this approach. She was willing to take the blame.

Meanwhile flattering publicists were transforming the young emperor into a figure of myth. In his *Pumpkinification,* Seneca, cleverly picking up one of Nero's enthusiasms—the races—envisions his pupil as the divine charioteer of the Sun:

The shades of night dispersed, [he] brings back the day,
Looks on the world and starts his chariot off:
So Caesar comes, so Nero appears to Rome,
His bright face fired with gentle radiance,
His neck all beauty under his flowing hair.

Nero informed the Senate that he would rule according to the principles of Augustus, and he let slip no opportunity for acts of generosity and mercy, or even for displaying his approachability. Once, when asked to sign the usual death warrant for two convicted brigands, Nero replied: "Oh, if only I had never learned to write!" On another occasion the Senate offered him their thanks, but he demurred, saying: "Wait until I have deserved them!" He exercised in public on the Campus Martius and took to reading aloud his poems to selected audiences (the Senate toadily voted that they should be inscribed in gold letters and dedicated to Jupiter, king of the gods, in his great temple on the Capitol).

His attempts to show a compassionate side to his personality seem artificial and forced, as if he had learned a script in advance. He almost certainly had, for he was following a strategy agreed by Agrippina and articulated by Seneca, the ideologist of the new regime.

The statesman-sage wrote a substantial essay for his pupil to study and his princeps to implement. Called *On Clemency,* it set out principles of government that favored cooperation rather than compulsion, mercy rather than punishment. It offered sound practical justifications for a lenient government, for leniency "makes princes safer as well as more respected."

As often when Romans debated such matters, the conversation soon turned to Augustus, founder of the imperial system. Seneca evokes a vicious young terrorist who, after years of violence and crime, "dyed the sea with Roman blood" at the decisive battle of Actium—but later matured, sick of sin, into a kindly and popular ruler, ashamed to recall his pitiless youth.

In his essay he tells the story of a young Roman aristocrat, Gnaeus (or Lucius) Cornelius Cinna Magnus, grandson of Pompey the Great, who in 16 B.C. plotted to assassinate Augustus. He was betrayed and arrested. The princeps passed a sleepless night worrying whether to put Cinna to death.

The next day he had Cinna brought in for an interrogation. The room was cleared and the two men faced each other alone.

> "The first request which I have to make of you is that you will not interrupt me while I am talking," said Augustus, opening the conversation. "You will have a chance to speak later."

He reminded Cinna that he had already spared his life once, when he had been found in the enemy camp after Actium, and the family estates had been restored. In peacetime, he had awarded Cinna a coveted priesthood notwithstanding stiff competition from men who had fought on his, Augustus's, side in the civil wars.

"Despite receiving such kindnesses from me you decided to take my life," said the princeps.

Cinna protested. "I would not have been such an idiot."

"You promised not to interrupt. I repeat, you are preparing to kill me."

He then proceeded to tell Cinna of the location for the attempt, the names of his accomplices, the day of the attack, the detailed plan, and which of the conspirators was to deliver the fatal wound. Cinna's eyes were fixed on the ground in silent acknowledgment of his guilt. Apparently the princeps spoke for two hours before informing his relieved listener: "Cinna, I grant you your life for the second time." He added: "From now on let us be friends."

Augustus won from Cinna his lifelong loyalty and even nominated him for the Consulship in A.D. 5.

Seneca claimed to tell truth to power, but he was highly skilled at wrapping up candor inside flattery. He drove home the value of clemency by comparing Nero to Augustus—to the latter's disadvantage.

> I certainly do not give the name of mercy to weariness of cruelty; this mercy that you exhibit, Sir, is true mercy . . . that has never shed the blood of one's own countrymen. When one exercises su-

> preme power this is self-control in the truest sense and a love that embraces all one's fellowmen as oneself.

For five years Nero followed the advice of the "grown-ups in the room" and won golden opinions.

An aged, penniless, and licentious poet called Eumolpus recalled the days of his youth when he joined the staff of a public treasurer (procurator) in the province of Asia (today's western Turkey). He lodged by invitation at a home in the city of Pergamum. The owner's son was a good-looking adolescent, and Eumolpus determined to seduce him.

His first step was to win the family's trust, so whenever the topic of conversation touched on affairs of the heart, Eumolpus objected strongly to loose talk. Soon he was acting as the young man's tutor, taking him to the gymnasium and arranging his studies.

One evening the two of them were resting on the dining room couches, everyone else having gone to bed:

> "In a cautious whisper," said Eumolpus, "I made a vow. 'Venus, goddess of love, if I could kiss this boy without his being aware of it, I will give him tomorrow a pair of doves.' The boy proceeded to snore and I placed several kisses on his lips. I stopped there."

The next day Eumolpus bought and delivered the doves. In the evening he said in a soft voice that if he could fondle the boy, he would give him a pair of fighting cocks. Events proceeded as before. Eumolpus took his pleasure and paid his debt.

On the third night he whispered close to the ear of the restless sleeper that in return for full union he would buy him a thoroughbred horse. Never did a boy sleep more soundly. But this time Eumolpus did not fulfill his promise. "Please, sir, where's my horse?" Receiving no answer, the boy was angry and resisted further advances. He said: "Leave me alone or I will tell my father."

However, gradually the boy began to yield, and his protests—"I'll wake Father"—began to weaken. He was of an age to enjoy sex, and now he thoroughly did so. It was what he had always in fact desired. Eumolpus eventually tired of unremitting pleasure and dropped off.

> Less than an hour later he was poking me with his hand and complaining: "Why aren't we doing it?" I was infuriated to be disturbed so often, and turned his own words against him. "Go to sleep or I'll tell your father."

Eumolpus tells this cheeky story to three footloose bisexual young men on the make: Encolpius, who narrates their adventures; his teenaged lover, Giton; and his friend Ascyltus, rival for Giton's affections. They are the protagonists of a most remarkable work of fiction, *The Satyricon,* written by a close friend of Nero called Gaius Petronius. He was a valued courtier and his role is well expressed by his nickname, Elegantiae Arbiter, arbiter of elegance—or, in today's terms, fashion guru. Smartness and taste were restricted to what Petronius approved. Tacitus has left a memorable sketch of his character:

> He spent his days sleeping and his nights in the social duties and amenities of life. Energy raises some men to greatness, but he idled his way into fame. Yet unlike some who waste their wealth, he was not profligate or debauched but the finished artist of extravagance. People liked the apparent freshness of his unconventional and unself-conscious sayings and doings. Nevertheless, as governor of Bithynia and later as Consul he displayed a flair for hard work.

Through the pages of Petronius's book we hear the day-to-day language of ordinary Latin-speakers. Much of it is lost, but much luckily remains in numerous fragments. It was a combination of Menippean satire—a picaresque potpourri of attitudes, parodies, mythological burlesque—and sentimental Greek romances. *The Satyricon* contains plenty of sex and much of it is transgressive. The result reads very much like a modern comic novel.

Insofar as we can detect an overall theme it centers on Encolpius, the narrator. He has in some way offended Priapus, a rustic fertility god who specialized in protecting male genitalia, and is punished with impotence. He and his two fellow travelers are the ancient equivalent of French *flâneurs:* they saunter around Italian towns observing humanity—mostly the social underclass. They are probably educated freedmen and appear to have just about enough money to get by without earning a living. They find themselves in trouble and they create trouble. They have sex with men and women, and one of them deflowers a little girl. A punitive priestess of Priapus has them tied up, drugged with an aphrodisiac, and sexually assaulted.

We walk down the mean streets of the ancient world, and we taste the low-life atmosphere. On one typical occasion, our three antiheroes are struggling to their inn after attending an absurdly opulent banquet given by a nouveau riche multimillionaire, a freedman called Trimalchio:

> We had no torch to light us on our way as we wandered, and the lateness of the hour—it was now the dead of night—blocked all hope of meeting someone with a light. Worse still we were drunk, and so unfamiliar with the area that even in broad daylight we would have lost our way. So for nearly an hour we stumbled about, dragging our bleeding feet over the shards and splinters of broken crockery scattered along the streets, and it was only Giton's remarkable act of foresight that saved us in the end. Terrified of getting lost even in the daylight, the boy had shrewdly blazed every column and pilaster along the route with chalk. . . . At last we reached our inn, only to find that our ordeal was not yet over. For the old landlady had spent the night getting drunk with her lodgers and I doubt she would have stirred if her bed had been on fire.

We do not know whether Nero ever read *The Satyricon,* but as he was on good terms with its author, it would be surprising if he did not. Like Petronius, he had a pronounced taste for low culture and for nocturnal adventures that rivaled those of Encolpius.

At the outset of his reign, he was neither the innocent youth nor the ideal ruler that Seneca would have him be. Like the boy in Eumolpus's anecdote, and indeed like many throughout history, he was greatly looking forward to having sex and much else besides. He was waiting to be awakened. Now with supreme power he could do as he wished.

And so he did. Two years into his reign, Nero, still in his teens, used to dress up as a slave and go out at night. He wore a cap or a wig to disguise himself. His idea was to have fun in the anonymous dark. He and a group of friends would prowl the unlit streets. They called in at brothels and drank in wine bars; they pilfered goods from shops and attacked wayfarers as they came home from dinner, stabbing any who resisted him and throwing them into the sewers. The emperor's identity was unsuspected, and sometimes his victims gave as good as they got. On such nights, the emperor returned to the palace looking the worse for wear.

Eventually it became known that it was he who was behind the outrages, with the result that attacks on distinguished men and women increased. Once it was clear that this kind of disorder was tolerated, Neronian copycats recruited their own gangs and behaved in much the same way.

Matters came to a head one night when a Senator, Julius Montanus, was walking home with his wife and came across Nero and his friends in the dark. They pounced on him, but he reacted so fiercely that the princeps was badly bruised and had to stay indoors for several days nursing two black eyes.

Nero took the incident with good humor and let the matter drop, until he received a letter of apology from Montanus. The gesture backfired. "So he *knew* that he was hitting Nero," the emperor noted grimly. This was lèse majesté at best, treason at worst. The Senator saw that his case was hopeless and killed himself.

Nero also enjoyed the raffish company of theatricals. He encouraged brawls between claques favoring rival ballet dancers. He waived penalties and gave prizes, and riots ensued.

After a few years the princeps seems to have grown out of these violent, delinquent escapades. However, he never lost his broad Petronian tastes. Simply, from now onward, he expressed them mostly on the stage and at the racecourse.

Two of Nero's highborn but disreputable friends give a flavor of the company he kept in his leisure hours. One was Marcus Salvius Otho: Early wildness earned him many beatings by his father. According to Plutarch, he was "corrupted by luxury and the pursuit of pleasure as few Romans were."

He was flat-footed and bandy-legged, but almost feminine in the care of his person. He had his entire body depilated, and because he was balding wore a wig so carefully made and fitted to his head that no one suspected it.

Not unlike Nero, but less lethally, he enjoyed roaming around the city at night. He would seize and toss in a blanket any drunk or disabled person he came across. According to Suetonius, he pretended to fall in love with an influential but decrepit freedwoman as a means of worming his way into the emperor's presence. The two men became great friends and were rumored to masturbate each other. Otho knew all Nero's secrets.

Another court habitué was Aulus Vitellius, son of the able but servile courtier Lucius Vitellius. Suetonius claims that as a child and a teenager he was a member of a group of youngsters whom the emperor Tiberius sexually abused. Apparently Vitellius deployed his charms to help advance his father's career. He became a regular at the palace: Caligula admired his charioteering and Claudius his luck at gambling. He governed the province of Africa honestly, but as curator of public works at Rome and the holder of important priesthoods he pilfered temple offerings, replacing gold and silver items with brass and tin.

Vitellius acted in a sentimental and thoroughly un-Roman manner by falling passionately in love with one of his slaves, a good-looking young man with a mind of his own named Asiaticus. He had used him for sex since a boy, "to their mutual pleasure," comments Suetonius. Eventually, Asiaticus tired of his situation and ran away. He was found selling cheap drinks (*vin ordinaire* and water) at the port of Puteoli and retrieved. His owner put him in irons, but his heart softened and he set him free, and Asiaticus became one of his favorites again. But he behaved in such an overbearing manner that Vitellius lost patience and sold him to the manager of a troupe of itinerant gladiators. But when he heard that Asiaticus was reserved for the final match of a gladiatorial show (the spot in the program where the fighting was for real), he bought him back on an impulse.

What did a Roman princeps do day to day? How hard did he have to work? The ancient sources do not show much interest in the diurnal minutiae of public administration. Their attention favors accounts of offbeat sex, senatorial persecution, and military campaigns.

That said, we can identify factors that constrained the power of the central government in Rome. Communications were very slow. The empire was extensive and nothing could travel faster than a horse. Sailing was uncomfortable and only (relatively) safe in the spring and summer. Emergencies on some remote frontier or in a distant city had to be dealt with in the first instance by the local governor or military commander. A network of well-constructed roads and regular post-houses was invaluable, but it could still be weeks before Rome received news and even more weeks before any imperial response to crisis or query could reach the relevant provincial authority, by which time it had probably been overtaken by events. The emperor was best advised to wait patiently and pick up the pieces afterward.

During the republic there had been no permanent civil service, apart from a few finance officers. Senior elected officials, such as Consuls, used servants and slaves from their households to provide administrative support. Augustus followed this practice during the long decades of his reign. Eventually a small permanent civil service came into being, largely dominated, as already noted, by Greek freedmen. Most of their time was spent reading and replying to letters and petitions that flooded in from all corners of the empire. Everyone was asking for help, for money, for adjudications.

A major task was to run the treasury methodically and profitably. It was not feasible to centralize financial management. It would have been fruitless to transport tons of specie to Rome only to return it to the provinces and in particular pay for the legions. Taxes were collected locally (either by state officials or commercial companies that bid for tax collecting powers) and spent locally. Presumably any surpluses were delivered to Rome from time to time.

Emperors tried to draw a line between the exchequer, the home of tax receipts (wherever the actual cash was to be located), and the *fiscus*, the emperor's vast private wealth, drawn from the revenues of the provinces under his direct control, confiscated property and income from his estates. But it was a distinction without a difference. At times of crisis, the *fiscus* topped up the usually hard-pressed treasury.

There is very little talk in the sources of emperors developing active policies. It would appear that they reacted rather than initiated. They did what circumstances demanded and hoped for the best. That is a half-truth. By examining what they did, we can deduce priorities, even strategies. The fact that no strategy papers have survived does not mean that they were never written or that long-term plans were not discussed. Conversations took place behind palace doors where they were not overheard.

So, for example, Augustus and his generals pursued a long-term policy of pushing the imperial frontier from the Rhine to the Elbe. This was to create a *cordon sanitaire* between the provinces of Gaul and hostile Germanic tribes. The project was abandoned only after the loss of three legions ambushed in the Black Forest in A.D. 9. Claudius was also an expansionist and, as already mentioned, had conquered Britannia. A policy to improve the flow of food imports to the city of Rome underpinned his massive enlargement of the port of Ostia.

A dutiful princeps was extremely busy. He must surely have delegated responses to incoming mail to his senior staff, drafted according to preset policy guidelines. Even so, he will have had to deal with some of the important ones himself.

Romans liked important decisions to be made collectively. Augustus and his successors made use of his emperor's council, or *consilium principis*. Its tasks were to advise him and chair its meetings. It was not a standing committee; the members were men of relevant knowledge or skills (or, it seems, women, such as Agrippina), and they were summoned as and when their particular expertise was required.

The system that Augustus had designed was tough, flexible, and long-lasting. However, he could see its flaws. In the prime of his life he spent many years touring the empire and making decisions based on close inspection rather than remotely from the center. He recognized that his job was too big for one man; throughout his reign he made sure to have an experienced and trusty deputy. Later emperors were not so wise.

So how efficient was the imperial system under the Julio-Claudians? In a sense the empire could run itself. Although there were rebellions, it was seldom seriously tested. The *pax romana,* the peace imposed by Rome, was surprisingly popular—despite the arrogant or at best condescending behavior of many governors, procurators, and businessmen. It created certainty, encouraged trade, and fostered economic development. Provided they paid their taxes, local communities were largely left to run their own affairs. The Romans shared their citizen status with upper-class provincials, a growing number of whom were appointed to official posts and even joined the Senate. Most people of substance and influence throughout the empire were satisfied imperialists.

From the point of view of the princeps, the situation was less satisfactory. The machine its creator had devised was insensitive to command. Senators kicked against the pricks, frontier armies were too far away to trust, and he himself was exhausted and frustrated.

And where was the time for fun? This was a question Nero must have asked himself. We know nothing of his working life, but it is safe to assume that he had little time for the detail of government except in emergencies. According to Suetonius, he took care when making senior appointments, for which there was hot competition. He served in the annual, largely ceremonial, post of Consul four times during his reign, but only for part of a year before handing it over to a Suffect Consul.

> For a long time Nero excluded sons of freedmen from the Senate and forbade those who had been admitted under his predecessors from high office. Candidates who were in excess of the number of vacancies received the command of a legion as compensation for the postponement and delay. He commonly appointed Consuls for a period of six months. . . . He conferred triumphal regalia even on men of the rank of Quaestor [the most junior job in the *cursus honorum,* or "ladder," of public administrative posts], as well as on *equites,* and sometimes not for military services.

He sat as a judge in court, though he seems to have kept his legal work to a minimum, and presided over numerous civic and religious ceremonies. He could not easily escape from these functions—for instance, in his role as *pontifex maximus* (high priest), although in that case he employed a representative who stood in for him when necessary. He was expected to attend and be seen to enjoy the numerous *ludi,* or public entertainments, in Rome's annual calendar.

Nero devoted much if not most of his working day to writing and performing poetry and to composing music as well as to training as a charioteer.

> He acquired some knowledge of music in addition to the rest of his early education. As soon as he became emperor he sent for Terpnus, the greatest exponent of the *cithara* or lyre at that time. He listened to him sing after dinner for many days on end until late at night. Little by little he began to practice himself, and undertook all the usual exercises artists of this kind used to follow. He used to lie with a slab of lead on his chest and purge himself with an enema syringe, make himself vomit and avoid any kind of food that could damage his voice.

As we have seen with his charioteering, a result of this punishing regime was that he must have been physically fit and not at all the effete aesthete of more recent imaginings.

As an outgoing young man, he expected to enjoy generous amounts of leisure. It follows that the detailed business of political administration must have devolved on his advisers, such as Seneca and Burrus. However, as he gained in experience and years, he developed clear ideas of what should be done.

Fun was what a young man of seventeen, who ruled most of the known world, was determined to have. To Agrippina's disapproval, Nero felt that money existed to be spent. He ordered the treasury to pay Doryphorus, a favorite freedman in charge of petitions (*a libellis*), 10 million sesterces. His mother heard about this, and to dramatize the vast size of the gift, arranged for the money to be piled in a heap. She hoped the sight would make him change his mind. Out of perversity and to annoy her, he remarked, "I didn't realize I had given him so little," and doubled the sum.

A more serious quarrel disturbed the palace. During his first year in office, Nero fell in love with a beautiful freedwoman called Acte. Apparently she originated in Asia Minor and may once have been a slave in Claudius's household. The affair was conducted in secret, for the princeps knew that his mother would violently disapprove. He was tired of having to put up with her tirades and then trying to do his own thing away from her omnipresent gaze.

He confided in two of his intimates, Otho and a freedman, Claudius Senecio, who were, Tacitus observes sourly, "partners of his dissipation and of his questionable secrets." They helped the couple arrange their trysts.

Nero also poured out his troubles to Seneca, who took the matter in hand. He arranged for a young friend of his, Annaeus Serenus, who, as *praefectus vigilum* about this time, was in charge of the city's firefighters and police, to pretend that he was Acte's lover. The emperor's presents were routed discreetly through him so that, in the eyes of the world, they had been lavished on the freedwoman by Serenus.

It was hard to see what the fuss was about. The Roman male, as already observed, was entitled to have sex out of wedlock with any woman provided she was not a citizen. Acte was well-to-do and ran a substantial household. She was not a gold digger and was genuinely fond of Nero. If he was uninterested in routine state business, it was helpful for those who were running the government that he had an enthusiasm which distracted his attention and dampened any temptation to meddle. It was a bonus that the princeps had another woman in his life apart from his interfering mother.

Of course, Agrippina soon found out what was going on. Tacitus has her react "as women do." She was furious and, like a possessive mother, raged at Nero as if he were still a small boy. She called Acte "my rival the ex-slave" or "my daughter-in-law the housemaid." She probably calculated that the relationship was a passing fling and that a firm hand would put a stop to it. This was a serious error of judgment by a stateswoman of her experience who had practiced the virtues of persuasion and long-term thinking for most of her career.

It is true that many parents find it hard to adjust when their newly adult children break away and set out on their own. Agrippina was certainly an overbearing parent. But there was a deeper, political explanation of her behavior. She was proud of the work she had done in partnership with Claudius and did not want to see it undone, as that would diminish her present high standing. She was on close terms with Claudius's daughter, Octavia, and was especially anxious that Nero's marriage, that symbol of unity between the Julians and the Claudians, should thrive. Unluckily the couple did not get along, as we know, and the arrival on the scene of Acte cast a cloud over their future. What if Nero divorced Octavia, Agrippina worried, and established Acte as his *maîtresse en titre* (it was illegal for a Roman citizen to marry a freedwoman)?

Roman sons were expected to pay their mothers the deepest respect, but Nero was furious with Agrippina and began openly to disobey her. He could do nothing right and he tried to retaliate by frequent threats to abdicate. As Tiberius had done in reaction to Augustus's excessive demands, he would go and live by himself on the island of Rhodes.

Agrippina quickly realized her mistake. It is perhaps a sign of panic that now she went to the opposite extreme. She apologized to Nero for her excessive strictness and offered him the privacy of her bedroom, where he could pursue his liaison away from prying eyes. As a further peace offering, she placed all her resources (hardly smaller than his own) at his disposal. The princeps's circle was highly suspicious of this remarkable démarche. According to Tacitus,

> This change from excessive severity to extravagant compliance did not deceive Nero—and it alarmed his friends, who warned him to watch out for the tricks of this ever-terrifying and now insincere woman.

If there is one general truth about young men, it is that they resent a mother's interference in their love affairs.

It did not take long for Agrippina's position to weaken.

A misunderstanding proved to be a turning point. One day Nero was looking through the wardrobe of dresses that had once glittered on the women of the imperial house. Picking out a gorgeous jeweled garment, he sent it as a present to his mother. It was a spontaneous and affectionate gesture. Agrippina regarded the gift as an insult. She protested loudly that her son had not meant the dress to be an addition to her wardrobe, but rather, he was depriving her of all the garments that he had *not* handed over. He was a thief, for they were really hers.

Two developments were running together simultaneously. Being fresh to power and without any experience, Nero was hesitant but exasperated. He knew that something had to be done to restrain his mother and her supporters. At the same time, Seneca and Burrus were recalibrating their risks. They owed everything to Agrippina, but common sense told them that whereas before Claudius's death, mother and son were a single item, now they were two, and increasingly at odds. The adviser and the Guards commander switched their loyalty to the person most likely to come out on top—the princeps.

The daughter of Germanicus was far too popular and authoritative a figure and the regime too new and precarious for them to attack her directly. In fact, neither Seneca nor Burrus wanted her removed altogether from the game. She was too useful as a bugbear to keep her son in order and, indeed, to support their role as his friends and guardians. Without her he would kick over the traces and no longer listen to them.

A blow had to be identified that would damage her without her seeming to be the target. The puzzle was readily solved. Nero, surely on advice from Seneca, dismissed from his service the inordinately rich Pallas, who, writes Tacitus, "exercised virtual control over the monarchy" and was the empress's closest ally at court.

Pallas was not in the least abashed by his fall. It is said that he made a grand exit from the palace surrounded by an army of followers and with his vast fortune intact. Nero remarked wryly that he looked as if he were a Consul leaving office and was about to take the regular oath high officials swore at the end of their term—*se nihil contra leges fecisse,* that he had done nothing contrary to the laws. In fact, rather than any such solemn declaration, Pallas had agreed to go quietly on condition that there would be no investigation of his past conduct and that the treasury books would be regarded as balanced. Pallas knew the location of the corpses, and it was in nobody's interest to see them rise again.

Of Claudius's three trusted freedmen, none were now left. Callistus disappeared from view before Nero's accession and, we guess, died in his bed; we have seen how Narcissus was destroyed by Agrippina; and now Pallas was gone. The unofficial triumvirate that had ensured the empire's smooth running was broken up.

For Agrippina to have the cup dashed from her lips seems to have been more than she could bear. She recognized that she was under attack, but once again her anger overrode her judgment. She issued insults and threats that she knew would be reported to her son.

The fourteenth birthday of Britannicus fell on February 12, 55. He would very soon exchange the *toga praetexta* for the *toga virilis*. In the empress's latest opinion, if we take her at her word, he was a true and worthy heir of his father. He would make a fine princeps. She let it be known that she would have no objection to revealing the imperial family's "whole dark history"—including her poisoning of Claudius and all the steps she had taken to "fix" Nero's succession to the purple. (She was in fact writing her memoirs.) If necessary she would pull the house down around her ears.

Tacitus has her say:

> Heaven and myself are to be thanked that my stepson is alive. I will take him to the Praetorians' camp. Let them listen to Germanicus's daughter pitted against the men who claim to rule the whole world—the cripple Burrus [he had a maimed hand] and Seneca the deportee with his professionally smooth oratory.

History was repeating itself. Having learned from her mother's failure that anger, threats, and emotions running high were not reliable methods of achieving a political objective, Agrippina junior was unexpectedly morphing into Agrippina senior.

A splendid welcome was laid on for the embassy from Armenia.

For many years, this kingdom of lofty mountain ranges, deep river valleys, and lava plateaus dotted with extinct volcanoes had been a bone of contention between the empires of Rome and Parthia. Apart from its position as a buffer between the two great powers, it was of only modest strategic importance. The historic deal negotiated by Augustus in 20 B.C. was fraying. The quarrel between the princeps and the monarch over who should be ruler was as arid as the Armenian landscape. Pro-Roman and pro-Parthian candidates alternated on an unsafe throne.

In 52 the Parthian king, Vologeses—"a Greek concubine's son," notes Tacitus scornfully—invaded Armenia and installed his brother Tiridates as king. A terrible winter ensued together with an epidemic caused by the Parthians' inefficient supply system. Vologeses withdrew from Armenia and left it without a stable government.

Two years later, just after Nero's accession, the king returned and his army plundered the country. The mood in Rome was anxious and irritated. Clearly the government had to react. Tacitus writes that in the city,

> where gossip thrives, people asked how a princeps who was only just seventeen could endure or repel the shock. A youth under feminine control was not reassuring. Wars, with their battles and sieges, could not be managed by tutors.

Many Romans were unclear at this point in the reign how big decisions were made. The empress mother was still a force to be reckoned with. She had played a part alongside Claudius in foreign affairs; to the annoyance of anti-female traditionalists, they had received foreign envoys together, each seated on their own tribunal or dais. The Augusta was determined to maintain her grip on the state.

However, it is certain that the authority of Seneca and Burrus was rising, and it may well be that all three worked together on a response to the crisis. Nero—that is to say, his advisers—ordered that the frontier legions in the eastern provinces be brought to full strength and sent to Armenia. Two local client kings were to recruit an army for an invasion of Parthia, and the river Euphrates was to be bridged. The able commander Gnaeus Domitius Corbulo, whom Agrippina had promoted in Claudius's day, was appointed to secure Armenia. He was universally recognized as the best man for the job—"a sign," observes a surprised Tacitus, "that promotions were to be by merit."

There was evidence, though, of strained relations. An embarrassing event occurred when a pro-Roman delegation from Armenia visited Rome. According to Tacitus,

> when its members were pleading before Nero, Agrippina was just going to mount the princeps's dais and sit beside him. Everyone was stupefied. But Seneca instructed Nero to advance and meet his mother. This show of filial dutifulness averted the scandal.

We should spend a little time unpacking this puzzling incident. This, or something like it, is what must have happened: A state ceremonial of this kind had to be carefully planned. We may assume that Agrippina was informed and invited to attend. She expected to occupy her own tribunal alongside that of her son, as in the days of Claudius. In fact, only one had been erected, for the emperor's use.

She will have realized that she had been tricked. Doubtless affecting not to notice anything amiss, she stepped toward Nero's tribunal. This breach of protocol took everyone aback, but it could have been predicted of a woman of Agrippina's self-will. Seneca, with great presence of mind, told Nero to come down from his tribunal at once and greet her, so preventing her from asserting parity with him. The ceremonial resumed with emperor and empress mother at ground level.

The plot must have been masterminded by Nero and Seneca. Its object was to teach Agrippina a lesson—namely that, although she remained an authoritative figure, her wings had been clipped.

It was late afternoon on February 11, the eve of Britannicus's birthday. As was usual, the children of the imperial family were joined by aristocratic contemporaries for dinner at the palace. Whereas adult males reclined on couches at meals, it was customary for women and minors to sit separately on chairs. Among those present on this occasion were Britannicus and Vespasian's son, Titus. Since all the gossip surrounding Claudius's death, poison must have been on people's minds, and senior personalities were attended by food tasters.

Britannicus's food and drink were tasted before he was allowed to start the meal. He was served a very hot drink, which had been tasted like everything else. He asked for it to be cooled, and some water was added. The boy drank and his body immediately convulsed. He could neither speak nor breathe. There was a shocked movement among those sitting near him. Titus had taken a sip from his friend's drink and felt distinctly unwell (he suffered aftereffects for a long time, but recovered). Some, uncomprehending, panicked and ran off. Others, who had a better idea of what had occurred, stayed rooted to their places, their eyes riveted on Nero. He remained where he was, lying on his couch with an innocent expression on his face. "This is nothing out of the ordinary," he explained. "He has been an epileptic since he was a baby. Sight and consciousness will soon return."

Agrippina could not control her features, and her obvious mental anguish was evidence that she had not been forewarned. Britannicus's sister Octavia had grown up in a palace and knew better than to show her feelings at a moment of crisis. The boy did not recover, and the body was removed. After a brief silence, dinner resumed. The funeral of Britannicus took place, with a minimum of ceremony, later that night during a heavy rainstorm. After cremation, his remains were lodged in the Mausoleum of Augustus.

So what actually happened? Tacitus is certain that this was a cleverly conceived assassination. What follows is a rational unwrapping of how the deed was done.

The fatal sequence of events began with Nero anxiously pondering Agrippina's latest hostile moves. He was also alarmed by the maturing of Britannicus's character as he reached adulthood. Tacitus charges Nero with having had sex with his stepbrother during the days leading up to his death; if this is so, the intention must surely have been to humiliate rather than to receive or give pleasure. Alternatively, but less plausibly, it might have been an attempt at seduction by Britannicus to disarm the person most likely to threaten his life.

Although Nero was content to let Seneca and Burrus administer the empire while he amused himself and developed his artistic practice, he was well aware of the ferocity of dynastic politics. There were other ambitious men with Julio-Claudian blood in their veins who were waiting in the wings. Fear of conspiracies prompted action.

Nero recalled a disturbing incident during the previous year's Saturnalia. This midwinter carnival saw the upending of regular norms. For instance, owners served food to their slaves. Named after the god Saturn, it gave a glimpse of the legendary golden age over which he had presided long ago before the triumph of crueler gods—Jupiter and the other Olympians.

It was customary to choose a "king" of the revels, and Nero's group of youthful merrymakers threw dice and (surprise!) the princeps won. As king he gave different individuals amusing tasks to complete. He commanded Britannicus to come into the middle of the room and sing a song extempore. He expected the boy to make a fool of himself, for he was unused to sober parties, let alone tipsy blowouts.

But, in fact, Britannicus acquitted himself well. He composedly sang a poem that hinted at his displacement from his father's house and throne. Night, alcohol, and misrule uncovered true feelings. To his profound irritation, Nero noticed that those listening looked as if they felt sorry for the lad.

It was obvious that his half brother understood the splendor of his lineage and was embittered by ill treatment. Under Agrippina's tutelage he had the potential to be a serious rival to the throne.

Nero determined that somehow the threat had to be eliminated. But he faced difficulties. He had no grounds for bringing a criminal charge against Britannicus and dared not simply order his execution. So Locusta, the celebrated poisoner, came to mind. She was still in custody, and through her guard, Nero commissioned poison from her. One of Britannicus's new, hostile staff (ironically, Agrippina's choices) administered a dose, but it only gave the victim an attack of diarrhea. Locusta's potion was too weak. She had diluted it on purpose in order to disguise or delay the effect. She may have calculated that neither she nor the princeps would welcome another poisoning scandal in the palace.

Nero was past caring about discretion. He had Locusta brought to him, threatened her with execution, and flogged her with his own hands. He complained that she had produced a medicine, not a poison. She replied that the crime should not be too obvious.

"So you think I am afraid of the Julian law against assassination and poisoning?" said Nero.

He then forced Locusta to mix on the spot as strong a potion as possible. According to Suetonius, Nero

> tried it on a young goat, but when it took five hours for it to die, he made her reduce the brew again and again. Finally he tested it on a pig, which died on the spot.

An ingenious scheme was devised to get the poison to its destination. The hot drink that we saw being served to Britannicus had been sampled by his taster and was found to be "clean." But it was guessed, correctly, that the boy would ask for it to be cooled. Cold water mixed with the poison was added to the drink without its being tasted again. Nobody noticed the omission.

Dio reports that an effect of the poison was that the corpse's skin darkened (this suggests arsenic). In an attempt at concealment, gypsum was smeared on the body, but it was washed off by rain as the body was carried through the Forum.

The hurried funeral looks suspicious and was probably designed to preempt adverse demonstrations, but that it took place at night is of little significance, for those who died prematurely in childhood were traditionally laid to rest during the hours of darkness.

The murder was planned to the last betraying detail. Britannicus's pyre had been built in advance. The princeps rewarded Locusta for her services with a full pardon and large estates in the country. He even sent her pupils to learn her craft.

The ancient sources are sure that Nero had his stepbrother killed, but modern scholars note that the boy was epileptic and may have died from a fit. This is certainly a possibility, but it must be set against the certainty of Tacitus and the others. The fate of Gemellus, Caligula's cousinly competitor, set a grim precedent. Crucially, the timing of Britannicus's death points to foul play. The public was saddened but did not object.

Two royal brothers would have boded ill for the state. As Tacitus put it, "autocracy knows no partnership."

Nero had not finished with his mother, although he knew he had to tread carefully. The blood of Germanicus ran in her veins, and his star still shone brightly despite his having been dead for more than thirty years. As we have seen, she had spent time, energy, and money cossetting the soldiers of the Praetorian Guard. Over the years she had made her own handpicked appointments, not only of the Prefects but of junior officers, military tribunes, and centurions. This was her impregnable power base, and Nero feared it.

Undaunted by Britannicus's death, she began to cultivate Nero's wife and Britannicus's sister Octavia (bad news for *her,* one would have thought) and took to holding confidential meetings with her own friends. She raised funds from all sources, ostensibly to deal with emergencies. She cultivated members of the nobility as though she were canvassing for a political leader.

Nero took small steps to a distant goal, his mother's downgrading. To counter disapproval of his stepbrother's murder and to disarm Agrippina's schemes, he distributed lavish gifts to senior personalities. Tacitus observes sharply that he was

> conscience-struck by his crime but hopeful of forgiveness, if he could place the powerful under an obligation to him by a show of liberality.

The Augusta still lived in the palace and Nero now transferred her to his late grandmother Antonia's house nearby. He wanted her under a different roof and a suitable pretext was found. Dependents and supporters of leading politicians used to gather every morning at their homes, offer their greetings, and then accompany them as they went about their business. Large crowds came to see Agrippina at her residence and created something of a nuisance. A separate establishment would solve the problem. After she had moved to her new home, the princeps visited Agrippina to see if she was settling in well, although he spoiled the gesture by arriving with a bevy of centurions. He gave her a cursory kiss and stayed for only a few minutes.

The next phase in decoupling the empress mother from her central position in the regime could now be implemented. Detachments of the Praetorian Guards used to watch over her residence. Ostensibly as part of a wider reorganization, the Praetorians were now restricted to purely military duties and withdrawn from service to Agrippina. Also, ever since she married Claudius she had been used to personal protection by the princeps's special German bodyguard. This too was withdrawn.

There were defensible reasons for these changes, but the underlying message was clear. Most people got the point and reacted accordingly, as Tacitus notes:

> Veneration of power, when that power depends on someone else, is the most precarious and transient thing in the world. Agrippina's house was immediately deserted. Her only visitors and comforters were a few women, there because they either loved her—or hated her.

Matters came to a head. We are told that Agrippina fell out with a close woman friend of hers, a certain Junia Silana, about her plan to marry a young nobleman. She made her objection only too clear, calling Silana "a woman of no morals and uncertain age." This put a stop to the courtship.

Silana, furious and aware of Agrippina's weak political position, devised a plot to bring her down. She joined forces with another enemy of the empress, the avaricious and penny-pinching Domitia, one of Nero's paternal aunts. Two of Silana's dependents, or *clientes,* laid serious charges against Agrippina; they avoided familiar chatter about Britannicus and Octavia and accused her of encouraging a young nobleman, Gaius Rubellius Plautus, to launch a coup d'état, depose Nero, and take his place. She would marry him and resume her rightful place at the head of affairs.

If the story had been true this would have been a serious matter. Rubellius Plautus had a pedigree as portentous as that of the princeps, for he descended from Octavia, Augustus's elder sister. The emperor Tiberius and Mark Antony were among his forebears.

How should the news be broken to Nero? One of his favorite drinking partners was Paris, a famous pantomime actor and a freedman of Domitia. He was persuaded to tell Nero of the alleged plot. He walked into the room where Nero had spent a long evening drinking. He usually arrived at about this time to enliven the somewhat befuddled mood. This time his face was gloomy, and as he went through the details of the conspiracy, Nero grew so terrified that he decided not just to put to death his mother and Plautus, but even to dismiss Burrus as commander of the Praetorians, on the grounds that he owed his promotion to Agrippina and was in her debt. Letters patent appointing a successor were prepared.

At this point Seneca stepped in. He insisted in the strongest terms on Burrus's loyalty. Nero was reassured, but was unnerved by what he had heard and called for the immediate execution of his mother. However, Burrus had now joined the gathering and calmed him down. Whatever the facts of the case, he knew very well that the Praetorians' loyalty to the Augusta would make this a suicidal move, unless it could be shown that she had definitely engaged in sedition. A trial, however informal, was essential. He promised Nero that he would cross-examine Agrippina and if he was convinced of her guilt she should die. He added, according to Tacitus:

> But everyone must be given an opportunity for defense; above all a parent. No prosecutors are present, just one solitary voice from the household of an enemy. Let the princeps take into account the darkness, the night spent in conviviality. The whole story has an air of recklessness about it, and ignorance of the facts.

The arraignment of the empress mother began without delay. At daybreak, Burrus and Seneca called on Agrippina to inform her of the accusation and tell her that she must refute it or pay the price. The proceedings were watched by some freedmen from the palace to check that they were being conducted properly and to brief the princeps. Adopting a threatening air, Burrus itemized the charges and named the accusers.

In response Agrippina rose to the occasion. Attack was the best defense. She opened her remarks by firing broadsides at her accusers, Silana and Domitia. The former was childless and could not understand a mother's love of her offspring; the latter cared more for her pedigreed fishpond (highly fashionable among the upper class) than for her nephew. She then moved to a daunting climax. She said: "I defy anyone to accuse me of tampering with the Praetorians, of shaking the allegiance of the frontier legions."

This was a clever remark, barbed with implicit menace. Her listeners knew well that she had no need to tamper with soldiers who were overwhelmingly loyal to her. As for conspiring with Rubellius Plautus, she pointed out that her interest obviously lay with her son rather than with someone unconnected with her. Blood runs thickest. She wound up her speech by demanding to see her son.

The day ended with a predictable acquittal. Nero agreed to a meeting with Agrippina at which she did not protest her innocence nor remind him of all she had done for him. What she asked for—and obtained—was the punishment of her accusers. Silana was exiled (we do not know where to), as were her two clients who undertook the prosecution. His aunt was overlooked, but a freedman of hers who had suborned Paris was put to death. The princeps was too fond of the actor to touch him and he survived scot-free. At a later (uncertain) date Nero had him officially declared to be freeborn and so never a slave. Domitia, his onetime owner, was obliged to reimburse Paris for the price of his enfranchisement—no doubt much to her annoyance. Perhaps this was the penalty she had to pay for tangling with Agrippina. Rubellius Plautus, who had no idea what was being done in his name, was ignored.

As inquisitor and judge, Burrus looks to have been above the fray. But political stability depended on complete trust between emperor and Praetorian commander. Nero's confidence in him took a hit.

In fact, the empress mother was the surprise winner of a crisis that was intended to bring her down. Her position had been contested and found to be stronger than previously thought. For the next four years she remained a figure of immense prestige. Her birthday was officially celebrated and her powers of patronage, of giving jobs to her supporters, was undiminished. An inveterate networker, she avoided public disputes and operated more than ever behind the scenes. The princeps was reconciled with his mother, but whether he welcomed this state of affairs or was in some sense captured by it, the sources do not reveal. For the time being, though, the empire was well, or at least peaceably, governed, and the entente between the palace and the Senate flowered.

What can we tell at this stage of Nero's emotional development? Insufficient information and bias against him in the sources limit what can be said, but a tentative analysis can be ventured.

Timidity and anger, both born of fear, scarred his personality. He seems to have been a needy child who was fond of his caregivers and teachers and liked to have them around him in the world of grown-ups. We can assume he both loved and was oppressed by his monomaniacal mother, a combination that bedeviled their relationship.

In this early time, Nero may have flinched at the princeps's heavy workload, and his violent delinquencies on the streets of Rome make it clear that he greatly enjoyed the antisocial "perks" of uncontrolled authority.

He was a receptive pupil and "trained" for the purple with assiduity. He was good at ceremony, when he was the center of attention. At the same time he was stubborn where his deepest feelings were engaged. He rebelled against expectations and refused to give up the woman he loved.

His prime image of himself was of a would-be professional artist; he was addicted to popular entertainments as well as the products of high culture. He played the ruffian in his nocturnal excursions, but was brave only in the safety of a group.

Power came to him with little effort: How keenly did he want it? In his depths we have the impression of a personality at odds with itself. He made little effort to hide his criminal behavior. Rather, he advertised it in the hope of pardon. Remarkably, although his subjects were horrified by the murder of Britannicus, that is what they gave him. They allowed themselves the guilty pleasure of empathizing with him. For Nero, forgiveness was a kind of love, which made crime worthwhile.

7

"MY FOOLISH LOVE"

THE VILLA OCCUPIED an enchanting spot on the Bay of Naples, with a marvelous sea view, but it was rather crowded. Everybody who was anybody had a vacation home along the coast. Strabo, the geographer, wrote: "The whole gulf is quilted with cities, buildings, plantations, so united to each other, that they seem to be a single metropolis." Like the house at Antium, where Agrippina gave birth to Nero, the building was on such a grandiose scale that it probably belonged to the imperial estate. It dominated the small town of Oplontis, not far from the busy city and cultural center of Pompeii.

It was there in Pompeii that Nero's latest lover was born in 30, six years before Nero. Unlike her predecessor Acte, Poppaea Sabina belonged to a rich, well-known, and "new" family. Her father was a certain Titus Ollius, who unwisely tied his fortunes to those of Sejanus. She changed her name to that of her much more distinguished maternal grandfather, Gaius Poppaeus Sabinus, who served as Consul and won a hard-fought campaign against some Thracian mountain tribes.

Her mother was one of the beauties of the age, admired more for her looks than her character. Her daughter Poppaea inherited from her a property portfolio that included a brick and tile factory at Pompeii.

She was clever and a pleasant conversationalist, but Tacitus marks her down as immoral and venal.

> She paraded respectability, but was sexually unprincipled. She rarely appeared in public, but when she did she half-veiled her face—to leave the curious unsatisfied or because the look became her. For bedfellows married men and bachelors were alike. She was indifferent to her reputation—yet insensible to men's love and herself unloving.

This is Tacitus at his most unsparing, yet if we strip away his scorn we are left with an attractive and intelligent person who led an active sex life, much like many people today. Not an especially damning portrait.

Poppaea knew how to make a party go. Courtesy of her imperial lover, she treated the villa at Oplontis as her country residence and the perfect venue where she could play the generous hostess. There was a variety of gardens, a park (no doubt for hunting), echoing reception halls decorated with frescoes on mythological themes, a richly painted *triclinium,* or dining room, a massive outdoor swimming pool, and steam baths. Statues and fountains abounded. On the upper floor workrooms and dormitories accommodated slaves.

We are told that Poppaea tended her complexion by bathing regularly in asses' milk. This sounds uncomfortably viscous, but whatever the truth of the tale, it made her a byword in luxury.

Nero probably fell for Poppaea in 58, and the affair led to a quarrel with his best friend, Otho. There are two versions of what took place, although the outcome was the same.

Poppaea was married to an *eques* and former Praetorian Prefect when Otho seduced her. She was attracted not only by his youthful charms but, perhaps more, by his intimacy with and easy access to the princeps. A divorce was followed by a wedding, and the groom kept on praising his new wife's beauty and graces within Nero's earshot. As he rose from the table at the palace he could be heard to say: "I must get back to my wife." Perhaps Otho intended all along to share his prize with the emperor, but whether intentionally or not, this boasting had a predictable consequence.

Nero warmed toward Poppaea, and she quickly established her ascendancy. Her opening gambit was to be flirtatious. She pretended to be overwhelmed by Nero's beauty and to be unable to resist her infatuation. Once she had netted him, she grew haughty. After spending a couple of nights with Nero, she reminded him that she was a wife and wanted to maintain her marriage. Tacitus gives her an appropriate speech:

> I am devoted to Otho. . . . *There* is a man for whom nothing is too good. Whereas you, Nero, are kept down because the mistress you live with is of slave stock, Acte. What a sordid, dreary, menial association!

It was not long before the noblewoman Poppaea was installed as official mistress. Presumably Nero stopped seeing Acte regularly, although the relationship did not die and years later she reappeared loyally and lovingly at a moment of crisis.

There is a different account: Poppaea became Nero's lover. Just as with Acte, Agrippina feared that he would marry her. To allay her anxiety, Nero turned her over for the time being to his bosom friend Otho, and just as with Acte, a pretend marriage was declared. Dio claims that the two men then "enjoyed her together."

A large part of Otho's attraction was his impertinence. Nero loved being teased, often about his supposed stinginess (in fact, his prodigality was legendary), and Otho was happy to oblige. We are told that for some social event he was hosting, the princeps drenched himself with an expensive perfume and sprinkled only a little of it on his friend. The next day in his turn Otho entertained Nero at a party and suddenly turned on gold and silver pipes that had been installed on all sides of the room, from which perfume gushed as freely as water. Hoots of laughter. On another occasion, Otho emphasized some claim he was making with the phrase "as truly as you may expect to see me as princeps." This was lèse majesté and risked a severe punishment, but all Otho received was the good-humored response "I shan't even see you as Consul!"

But then he overstepped the mark. He fell in love with Poppaea and became increasingly jealous of Nero. In fact, he could not bear the thought of him as a sexual rival. Suetonius reports:

> We have every reason to believe that he would not let in messengers Nero sent to fetch Poppaea. On one occasion Otho even shut him out. The princeps was left standing outside Otho's bedroom door, ineffectually threatening and pleading.

One way or another, the friends never forgave each other. Poppaea was retrieved and her faux spouse was dispatched to the edge of the world. In 59, Otho was appointed governor of Lusitania (roughly, our Portugal). Nero could simply have banished him to Massilia (Marseille) in Gaul or some distant city in Asia Minor, as he did other dangerous noblemen. Their punishment was boredom, unemployment, and homesickness.

But by offering his former favorite a real job, the princeps was exercising clemency, as Seneca had taught him. Otho did not repine; instead he worked hard and built a reputation as a competent and disinterested imperial administrator. He returned to Rome only after the end of the reign years later.

The hooligan had grown up.

At some point in 59, Nero decided to kill his mother. We do not know why. The silence of the sources since her trial in 55 suggests amicable or at least cooperative relations. There is no talk of quarrels or complaints or scandals.

The immediate cause was Poppaea, who was eager to marry Nero at the earliest opportunity. Two obstacles prevented this ambition from being realized; the first was the empress mother, who opposed this union as vehemently as she did the affair with Acte. She regarded women as the gravest of threats to her power. Second, Nero already had a wife, Octavia, Claudius's daughter by Messalina. She too would have to be removed. Because she was a respected and unassuming member of the imperial family, who was not politically active, this would require cautious planning.

Poppaea's method of getting her way was to make her lover's life a misery. She

> nagged and mocked him incessantly. He was an emperor under orders, master neither of the empire nor of himself. "Otherwise," she said, "why do you postpone marrying me?"

Agrippina was not without resourcefulness. It was put about that an erotic, or at least an intimate, bond between mother and son persisted despite their political differences. A Consul during Nero's day and a respected historian, Marcus Cluvius Rufus, who will have known all the political players of the day, claimed that she committed incest with her son as a means of controlling him. According to Tacitus,

> Cluvius states that Agrippina's passion to keep her power carried her to the point where at midday, an hour at which Nero was beginning to experience the warmth of wine and good food, she presented herself on several occasions to her half-drunk son, coquettishly dressed and ready for incest. Already sexual kissing, and endearments that were the precursors of guilt, had been observed by their close circle.

It was whispered that the pair had sex whenever Nero shared her litter. Stains on his clothes when he emerged were cited as evidence. The only point of doubt was which one was the seducer.

Seneca was worried by the damage to the reputation of the princeps that this kind of talk was causing and called in the freedwoman, Acte. Nero was still on good terms with her. Their long friendship allowed her to raise sensitive matters without causing offense or endangering herself. And that was what she did. She told the princeps that Agrippina was boasting about their relationship and that this was upsetting the military.

It was of little consequence that the rumors of incest were very probably unfounded. The character of the two parties, as understood in the popular mind, was such that they could have been true, and that was enough to fuel the tale-telling. Agrippina and her emperor were putting on a show of affection to demonstrate that their partnership was in good working order. Flirtatiousness was misinterpreted as lust in action. It was perfectly possible, of course, that on one side or the other there was lust in thought.

Nero was alarmed by Acte's warning and began to avoid private meetings with Agrippina. He congratulated her when she announced her decision to take a break from politics and spend time at her garden villa or *hortus* on the outskirts of Rome or her estates at Tusculum and Antium. Finally, he became convinced that, wherever she might live, she was still too much trouble. She needed to be permanently removed.

In addition to his passion for Poppaea, Nero was having an affair on the side with a woman who looked very like Agrippina. He used to introduce her to friends and joke that he had been sleeping with his mother. If he was to lose the real person, he could always quip that at least he possessed the simulacrum.

When did the idea of matricide first occur to Nero?

Poppaea was right to regard the empress mother as a dangerous enemy, and wanted to see an end of her. However, this does not seem enough to have caused Nero to make the most momentous decision of his life. While she was eager to marry the emperor, in his view there was no great rush. The wedding did not in fact take place for a further three years.

A clue can be found in a throwaway sentence of Tacitus. He records the moment when the princeps finally makes up his mind to kill his mother and remarks: "Nero postponed no further the long-contemplated crime." Poppaea was recent news, and so must be excluded from consideration. But how long is long?

If the motive for murder was political, then five years, the time Nero had been on the throne, was the maximum. Despite their reconciliation and Agrippina's good behavior (after a difficult start), her presence as a dominant piece on the chessboard was infuriating for a young man of twenty-two who had found his feet and no longer wished to share power.

In fact, the motive may have been personal. In that case, its origin could lie deep in Nero's childhood and adolescence. The evidence is thin, but his mother's disciplinary insistence on training her son for the purple, when his passion was for the arts, is clear enough. What if she had always frightened him, and still did? It could well be that rage against his fear incubated slowly inside his breast before eventually forcing its way out.

The two scenarios are not mutually exclusive. Here is a possible one that brings them both together: Nero's mother had confiscated his life. The only practical way of taking control was to override her choices by choosing them for himself. To do this successfully he would have to assume the reins of power with real commitment and exclude her from having any role. She refused to be excluded. He was still afraid of her. Fear led to fury.

To quote a famous Latin tag, *hinc illae lacrimae,* hence all those tears.

The planning was tricky. It was important that Agrippina's death not be laid at his door and that, ideally, it should be regarded as an accident. Nero reviewed the options. Poison was possible. It had worked well enough in the case of Britannicus, but how many truly believed the official explanation of epilepsy as the cause of death? Another unexpected expiry at dinner would insult the public's intelligence. What was more, Agrippina recognized the risks and was vigilant. She protected herself with preventive antidotes. Her staff were loyal.

Nero could not think of a way to strike his mother down with a dagger or a sword without the assassin himself being killed or captured. Who would volunteer for such a suicidal task?

The problem was solved by one of his old tutors, Anicetus (appropriately enough, Greek for "undefeated"). As already noted, Nero had appointed him admiral of the fleet based at the naval port of Misenum, which lay south of Rome and was not far from the cities of Puteoli and Naples. The freedman was among the trusted protectors of his childhood whom Nero promoted to important positions. By contrast, between Anicetus and Agrippina there was mutual loathing.

One day the two men attended a theatrical show. The action involved a ship that automatically broke in two and released a number of wild animals. It then closed up and became seaworthy again. The idea came to them to prepare such a vessel in real life and persuade Agrippina to sail in it. There would be no trouble selling accidental death by shipwreck to the Praetorians.

Nero approved the project and Anicetus set to work designing and building a lethal ship. What this exactly consisted of is unclear, but the account given in *Octavia*, a play apparently written by Seneca in his lifetime (see A Note on Sources page 371) and presumably not published till after Nero's death, was the closest in time to the event itself, as well as being the simplest and most practical. The vessel appears to have been a splendidly decorated trireme; that is, a galley with three tiers of oars and a single square-rigged sail. It sat low in the water and was prone to being swamped in bad weather. The hull was a thin shell of planks joined edge-to-edge and then stiffened by a keel and light transverse ribs. Anicetus arranged for some of the trireme's timbers to be loosened so that once they encountered the currents of the open sea they would separate, and the vessel would take in water and sink.

Like most upper-class Romans, Nero enjoyed vacationing in the gulf of Naples. He was especially fond of the fashionable resort of Baiae, where he stayed at the imperial mansion on loan to Poppaea. Every March he used to attend a five-day festival of Minerva, the goddess of wisdom, which took place in the town. This year, 59, he enticed his mother to join him. He repeatedly remarked: "One has to put up with it when parents lose their temper. They should be humored." As intended, this generated a rumor of reconciliation, and in due course she agreed to come.

She sailed down from Antium (today's Anzio), where she had a family country house. Nero met her on the beach; he greeted her warmly and kissed her. He politely accompanied her, either by ship or by litter, to her own holiday villa at a place called Bauli, which stood on a headland not far away, before returning to his own mansion.

They stayed for the whole festival, meeting at meals. Other guests of the princeps included Seneca and Burrus. Also present was Otho, Nero's partner in excess (for the time being, still in favor). He was accompanied, unrecorded but presumably, by Poppaea. On the last day of the holiday, he threw everyone off the scent by inviting his guests to a farewell banquet.

The whisper of a plot to kill her had reached Agrippina, but she could not decide whether to believe it. A trireme awaited her, but for safety's sake she made the short journey to Baiae by land, carried on a litter. Once she had arrived, her fears were allayed by the warmth of her welcome. In the dining room she was given the place of honor above the emperor himself. Nero conversed freely, one moment boyish and intimate, the next with furrowed brow when making a serious point.

The party went on till late. At last Agrippina, who had drunk deep and was feeling tipsy, said: "I really must get back." Nero led her down to the quay. Tacitus reports that as he

> saw her on her way, he clung more closely than usual to her breast and kissed her eyes. This may have been a final touch of hypocrisy, or possibly the last sight of his doomed mother affected even that brutal heart.

Until the moon rose at about half past two, it was a black and starry night and the sea was flat. Nero offered the doctored trireme and said: "All best wishes, mother, look after yourself. I live for you and it's thanks to you I'm emperor." Agrippina, a much-loved servant, Acerronia, and another member of her household went on board without demur.

Anicetus had done his job well. Seneca's tragedy, *Octavia,* evokes the scene:

> The waves soon resounded with the plash of oars, and the craft shoving off, is quickly borne upon the sea. From the force of the waves it soon springs a tremendous leak, letting in the sea, the hull giving way on account of the looseness of its timbers, and it ships a heavy sea!

As the trireme became waterlogged, the crew (sailors under orders, from the fleet at Misenum) attacked the empress mother's party. Agrippina fell into the sea. She was wounded in the shoulder, but she was a strong swimmer and moved away in the darkness from the sinking vessel. She wisely kept quiet. Acerronia, also in the water, distracted attention from her mistress by bravely shouting: "Help, help! I am Agrippina." She was killed by blows from poles and oars.

The empress mother herself was swimming toward the shore when she came across some fishing smacks. They took her in and dropped her off at the Lucrine lake, a stretch of water farther along the coast. After waking the occupants of a nearby dwelling, she commandeered a litter and was carried home.

She thought hard about the events of the past few hours. The invitation and the extraordinary courtesy she had received had been treacherous. Why and how did the boat sink? There was no wind, no reefs; it must have been tampered with. This had been a serious attempt on her life, she was sure of it. Nero, her son, was evidently its author. This was too serious for anger.

She decided that her best course was not to notice there had been a plot at all. She sent a freedman to inform the princeps that thanks to divine intervention and his lucky star she had survived a serious accident. She knew how upset he would be and that he would want to visit her. She begged him to forbear. What she needed now was complete rest.

Meanwhile in Baiae the princeps was beside himself with anxiety as he waited for news of his mother. Information dribbled in that everything had gone wrong and that she had escaped with a wound from a light blow. She must have realized what was afoot and who was to blame.

This was the worst possible outcome. Half dead with terror, Nero insisted that she might arrive at any moment hot for vengeance. According to Tacitus, he protested:

> She may arm her slaves or inflame the troops! She may make her way to the Senate and the People's Assembly, and charge me with the shipwreck, her wound, and the death of her friends! What counter-resource is at my disposal? Could Burrus and Seneca help?

Asleep in their bedrooms, they were immediately summoned. They were probably unaware of the plot, which was the emperor's secret, and would have disapproved of it if they were. After being briefed on the situation, neither of them spoke for a long time. If they were to offer sensible advice they knew it would be rejected. They wondered whether matters had gone so far that Agrippina would have to be destroyed if the princeps was to survive. Most of all, they did not wish to be involved in Anicetus's mess.

Everyone in the villa was aware that they were protected by Praetorian Guards, who were enthusiastic supporters of Agrippina. Seneca glanced at Burrus and asked him what his Praetorians would do if they were ordered to put Agrippina to death. He replied that the troops were devoted not only to the princeps, but also to the imperial house as a whole and to the memory of Germanicus. They would take no measures against his descendants.

"Anicetus," Burrus concluded, "must live up to his promises."

The Praetorian commander had shown himself to be a weak reed, neither objecting to the murder nor applauding it. So Nero could not depend on the Guards nor on him, and was right to panic.

Nothing daunted, the freedman enthusiastically accepted Burrus's challenge. Put *him* in charge and he would deal with the matter once and for all. Nero's relief was palpable. "This is the first day of my reign, and a magnificent gift from a former slave," he said. "Go quickly and take men with you who scrupulously obey orders." Anicetus set off at once in search of his quarry.

Meanwhile, Agrippina's freedman arrived with the joyful news that she was safe and sound. Nero had one of his men drop a dagger surreptitiously on the floor beside him and then pick it up. This was to make it seem as if he had been sent to assassinate him. The princeps ordered his arrest as a killer caught in the act.

Word of Agrippina's momentous night filtered out, and as dawn gleamed, groups of people began to congregate on the seashore near her villa. They cheered upon learning that she was well and streamed up with torches to offer their congratulations. Then Anicetus's armed column suddenly appeared and dispersed the crowd. The freedman surrounded the house and broke in. He arrested anybody he came across and soon arrived outside Agrippina's bedroom door.

She had become increasingly troubled by the silence from Baiae. Nobody had come to see her, and, ominously, her freedman had not returned. And then, uproar. Her maid abandoned her. "Are you leaving me too?" she asked. Then suddenly, peering through the dim light, she saw Anicetus behind the maid, accompanied by a warship captain and a marine centurion. "If you have come to visit the sick, report back that I am feeling much better," she exclaimed. "If it is to commit murder, matricide can have been no part of your instructions." The captain hit her on the head with a club and the centurion drew his sword to finish her off. She jumped up, tore open her clothing, and cried out "Strike here!" pointing at her womb.

In his play *Octavia,* Seneca allows the Augusta's ghost to imagine what would have happened if wild beasts had torn at her womb and killed the unborn Nero. He knew her well and persuasively evokes a mother love that smothered its object. She says:

You would have died
Unknowing, innocent, exempt from sin;
You would have died all mine, flesh of my flesh.

Agrippina was speedily cremated on a dining couch, perhaps to remove evidence of her wounds. As the flames took hold, one of her freedmen, called Mnester, ran a sword through his body; whether from love of his mistress or fear of his own fate is unknown. The late Augusta was buried by her servants in an unmarked plot. Sometime afterward she was given a proper but modest tomb on the Misenum road near a villa that had once belonged to Julius Caesar, founder of the dynasty she had briefly led.

That long-ago prophecy that when he grew up her baby son would murder his mother was fulfilled.

What are we to make of Agrippina? She had something of her mother's capacity for unmanageable rage, although she saw how that had led to catastrophe. She was a fast learner. The embarrassing failure of the plot against her brother Caligula taught her the virtue of patience.

She was a gifted and professional politician. If a major policy initiative was contemplated, she would lay the groundwork, consult, and muster support. She was not seduced by power and understood that even in an absolute monarchy, it had its limits. Her life was spent in the heart of empire and she was familiar with the issues and the methods. She was surrounded by stupid people or, worse, clever incompetents, and knew that she deserved to rule.

The empress mother labored under two weighty disadvantages. First of all, as we have discussed, she was a woman in a misogynist society. She pushed back as far as she dared against the constraints and mollified the political elite in the Senate by taking its members seriously and by seeking consensus. She accepted that she could not take part in meetings of the all-male Senate but insisted on listening to its debates. She did not flaunt her authority, nor did she hide it.

But the tragic flaw that felled her was her attitude toward her own son. She seems to have assumed that he had no agency, that he was inert in the hands of a domineering puppet master. We do not know enough about Nero's childhood, but something appears to have happened to him, we cannot say what, that left him with a permanent wound. He found a way of easing the pain through the arts. They allowed him to create an empire of the mind that was all his own and where Agrippina held no sway.

Although generally observant and astute, she did not trouble to listen to him and take the measure of his unhappiness. Right until the end she believed that Nero would always give way to her. She failed to see, astonishingly, that once he became princeps, he was out of her hands. Had she understood her son better, her story might have ended differently.

A final question suggests itself: what would have happened if, after saying goodbye to the fishermen on that fearful night, she had returned to Nero's mansion at Baiae rather than her villa and placed herself under the protection of the Praetorians? Counterfactuals are risky, but with one throw of the dice the daughter of Germanicus might have regained mastery.

Instead, she could not quite allow herself to recognize the mortal danger she was in from her unforgiving son.

The long night was not yet over and the princeps was close to a complete breakdown. Although he had achieved his objective, he was sure he had precipitated his own deposition and death. According to Tacitus,

> Sometimes dumb and motionless, but often starting in terror to his feet in a kind of delirium, he waited for the daylight which he believed would bring his end.

He could not believe that such a huge event had taken place. He rushed off to inspect the dead woman's corpse before the cremation. According to Suetonius, who claims to be indebted to "reliable authorities," he had the body undressed and handled her limbs. Between drinks to slake his thirst, he debated her good and bad points. Apparently he said: "I had no idea I had such a beautiful mother!"

The news of Agrippina's death soon reached Rome, where it caused shock and awe. There were public demonstrations of disgust. A leather sack was hung on one of Nero's statues. This was an allusion to the traditional punishment of a convicted killer—namely, to be sewn up in a leather sack, together with an assortment of live animals including a dog, a snake, a monkey, and a chicken, and then thrown into the river Tiber to drown. A newborn baby was abandoned in the Forum with a tag that read: "I won't bring you up in case you murder your mother."

Matricide was a well-known topic of classical legend. Alcmaeon, a Greek leader, obeyed his father's order and put his mother to death. He was pursued by the Furies, ancient goddesses of vengeance. These were ghastly hags who carried studded scourges and whose victims died in torment. An even more celebrated assassin was Orestes, a young man whose mother had ensnared her husband, King Agamemnon of Mycenae, in a net and stabbed him to death. Orestes was ordered by the sun god Apollo to avenge him. This he did, activating the Furies, who chased him around Greece until at a trial in Athens his blood guilt was set aside.

Romans knew their Greek mythology. They were entertained by a blunt graffito, which appeared on walls everywhere in the city:

Alcmaeon, Orestes, and Nero are brothers.
Why? Because all of them murdered their mothers!

People said quite openly that Nero had put his mother out of the way.

In the ordinary course of things, satirical comments of this sort would be severely punished. But Nero treated jokes about him and insults with surprising leniency. He never tried to trace their authors and when an informer provided the Senate with a list of names he gave instructions that the offenders should be punished lightly.

In a song beginning with the line "Goodbye father, goodbye mother," the performer accompanied the words with gestures of drinking and swimming—references to the death of Claudius by poisoning and to Agrippina's near-death by drowning. Pointing to seats reserved for Senators, he sang the line, "The underworld awaits!" The singer was punished with no more than banishment.

This tolerance was the product of an abrupt transformation of Nero's mood after the first dizzy euphoria. Nero was overwhelmed by grief at the loss of his mother and did not care who knew it. His method of coping with his feelings was to luxuriate in his culpability. He did not forget that he was an artist and in the coming years gave many public performances. These allowed him to translate his remorse into the stuff of Greek legend. In other words, guilt for his crime became a dimension of his identity as an artist. Suetonius writes in terms of a theatrical performance:

> He often admitted that he was hounded by his mother's ghost and that the Furies were pursuing him with whips and hunting torches: and employed Persian magicians to conjure up the ghost and entreat its forgiveness.

The parts he most enjoyed playing were figures from myth who committed incest or murdered close relatives. In addition to the aforesaid matricides, Orestes and Alcmaeon, these included Canace, who slept with her brother (Nero acted her giving birth); Hercules, who in a fit of madness slaughtered his wife and children; Oedipus, who slept with his mother and killed his father; and Thyestes, who contrived the death of his brother. Through the make-believe of myth, Nero was able to confess his wrongdoing without suffering the usual consequences.

—

The occupants of the Baiae mansion realized that they had to get a grip on the situation. Seneca and Burrus had declined to be directly involved in the killing, but once it was over and done with, they would of course do everything possible to help. They agreed that Nero must be calmed down and the Senate informed. Support for Agrippina had to be suppressed.

Burrus persuaded some Praetorian centurions and military tribunes to present themselves to the princeps. At his suggestion, they shook him by the hand and congratulated him for escaping his mother's criminal plan. The Praetorians were willing to die for the daughter of Germanicus, but only so long as she lived. In the last resort they were practical men and always willing to do business with power.

Their compliments cheered Nero up, and he gave them money. Friends of the regime were deputed to visit temples in the neighborhood to spread word of the "conspiracy" and to welcome the emperor's survival. Towns in Campania quickly realized what was expected of them; they held grateful sacrifices to the gods and sent joyful delegations to the court at Baiae.

This was the first sign that an expected pro-Agrippina backlash might not be forthcoming. Her authority had been personal and vanished with her. Furthermore, without Britannicus, there was no one left in the immediate imperial family to whom it could be transferred.

Seneca drafted one of his perfectly judged letters to be sent to the Senate above the princeps's signature. "The fact that I am still alive, I can neither believe nor celebrate" was the lapidary opening sentence. The core argument reversed the roles of killer and victim. Nero's panicked invention on the night became the official explanation: namely, a confidential freedman of Agrippina had been arrested carrying a weapon in Nero's presence. He was under instruction from Agrippina to kill her son. The attempt failed and, conscious of her crime, she paid the price with her life.

This was a thin story (however poor their relations, Nero was her only source of authority, so why would she destroy him?), and Seneca added a long charge sheet to win doubtful minds. As Tacitus has it, it read:

> "She had hoped to be joint ruler of the empire. She wanted the Praetorian Guard to swear allegiance to a woman; and for the Senate and People to submit to the same humiliation. Then, her ambition foiled, she had turned against the soldiers, the Senate and the People and had opposed a military donative and civilian largesse. She contrived the ruin of eminent citizens. How hard I had to work to prevent her from forcing the door of the Senate and setting terms for foreign nations!"

The letter cleverly mixed facts with fiction. Agrippina *did* see herself as co-ruler, at least until Nero had gained the experience to do the job himself. She did try her hardest to secure for herself the loyalty of the Guards. In that light, though, it is incredible that she should refuse them donatives. She monitored senatorial proceedings and did business with foreign delegations, although these are surely venial complaints—even allowing for Roman misogyny. Every scandal of Claudius's reign was laid at her door, but there was nothing new in these half-forgotten imputations. In sum, Seneca's confection contained enough truth to be credible as a whole, and it was forwarded to the Senate in Rome.

Nero left Baiae and made the short journey to Neapolis. Founded by Greeks and originally called Parthenope, it had a population of something more than a hundred thousand inhabitants. With its two theaters, one open-air and the other enclosed, it boasted a thriving artistic scene. The great epic poet Vergil spent much of his adult life in the city and was buried there. However, if Nero had hoped for entertainment and distraction, he was disappointed. He slept badly, sometimes waking suddenly in the middle of the night and leaping in terror from his bed. He kept on changing his residence; he would settle in a house, panic, and move elsewhere. He put off returning to Rome for fear of a hostile reaction.

It soon became clear that he need not have worried. The political elite had cooperated with Agrippina and respected her, but they had never liked her. Now that she was gone they pretended to believe in her conspiracy to assassinate Nero. Decrees were drawn up and thanksgiving ceremonies held at all appropriate shrines. The festival in honor of Minerva, during which the conspiracy had been brought to light, was to be celebrated in future with annual games. A golden statue of the goddess, alongside the emperor, was to be erected in the Senate House. Agrippina's birthday was included among the unlucky dates on which political and judicial business was forbidden.

The letter from Nero was read out at a meeting of the Senate. It was welcomed with insincere warmth. Only one Senator showed his disapproval. This was Publius Clodius Thrasea Paetus, a member of a wealthy senatorial family who served as a Consul in 52. He belonged to a group of kindred noblemen who disliked one-man rule and hankered after the republic. They accepted the imperial system through gritted teeth and from time to time tried to overthrow it. Emperors endured them with poor grace. Many were believers in the Stoic philosophy, which taught them to accept whatever the moment brings as being part of nature's plan.

Thrasea was disgusted by the letter and the Senate's fawning reaction. Public life was a danger zone and he held that flattery was no protection against an angry princeps. He rose from his seat and left the meeting without a word. Open opposition could cost a man his life, but, being the good Stoic that he was, Thrasea used to say: "Nero may kill me, but he cannot harm me."

At last Nero overcame his timidity and set off for Rome. He had been worried that people might not cheer him, but his staff reassured him. He would see how popular he was. An advance party left early to prepare the ground and when the princeps approached the Appian gate he saw vast applauding crowds. Senators were present in force, wearing their finest togas. Groups of wives and children were marshaled according to sex and age. Tiers of seats rose along the route for citizens to have a good view, just as when victorious generals marched in their triumphal processions.

Tacitus at his scornful best evokes the spectacle: Nero,

> flushed with pride, victor over the nation's degradation, made his way to the Capitol, and paid his grateful vows. He then gave himself up to all the wildest improprieties. Until now they had been hindered, though scarcely repressed, by some sort of deference to his mother.

The princeps recognized the general mood of permission by rescinding the decrees of banishment imposed on those responsible for the failed attempt by Silana to bring down Agrippina. Silana herself did not benefit from the recall. Hearing that Agrippina's position was weakening she had decided to risk a return to Rome and died en route of natural causes at the port of Tarentum in southern Italy.

Apparently, her co-conspirator, Nero's avaricious aunt, the elderly Domitia, who had survived the failure of the plot scot-free, was mortally ill from a severe constipation and on her sickbed. The princeps dutifully paid her a visit. The first time a Roman shaved was an important milepost in his life, often marked by a religious ceremony. Nero had not yet lost his downy beard and she told him: "When you shave, I shall die happy and at peace." Ever one for an unkind joke, he turned to the people with him and said: "I'll shave it off at once then." The remark probably gave rise to an unlikely piece of gossip, retailed by Suetonius, that her nephew had his eye on her property and told her doctors to administer a lethal dose of laxative.

—

The late empress mother's statues were pulled down, and soon she and her grisly end faded into history—or would have done so had her son not performed a remarkable volte-face. Contradicting her official transformation into an unperson, he staged an extravagant festival expressly in her honor. An ambitious program of events was presented over several days in five or six venues in the city.

The pièce de résistance was an elephant carrying a mahout and walking down a tightrope. The princeps threw tokens in the shape of tiny balls among the crowds. These could be redeemed for generous surprise prizes—among them horses, slaves, teams of oxen, gold, silver, and garments of many colors. The festival required a huge outlay, and respectable opinion (at work again) condemned it as a waste of money. Ordinary Romans, though, were impressed and asked for more.

Nero was very pleased that the festival was a popular success, and it turned out to be a sign of things to come. It was in essence a peace offering. Fearing the Furies, he sought to appease Agrippina's angry shade.

The best of mothers was to linger as a presence throughout her son's restless, guilt-ridden reign.

8

FREE AT LAST!

THE GREAT WARRIOR Achilles was doing battle on the windy plain of Troy. He drove his chariot invincibly through the ranks of his Trojan enemies. He ran amok with his spear, sings the Greek poet Homer in *The Iliad*, his epic on the siege of Troy, "like a driving wind that whirls the flames this way and that." His horses trampled dead men and their shields.

> The axle-tree under his chariot, and the rails that ran around it, were sprayed with the blood thrown up by the horses' hooves and by the tires and Achilles pressed on in search of glory, bespattering his unconquerable hands with gore.

Like other young Romans, Nero knew his Homer. He had studied him at school, and these lines from *The Iliad* evoked the thrill of driving a chariot. At last he was released from the potency of his mother's disapproval and was able to indulge his passion for the sport. This was not just for the excitement of speed, but also, as he was a philhellene, because it was Greek. One of the most thrilling contests of the Olympic games was the chariot race, and chariots were an integral component of warfare in the legendary age of heroes such as Achilles.

Centuries had passed and chariots were no longer to be found on the battlefield, but blood and thrills were necessary ingredients of chariot racing at the Circus Maximus, Rome's chief racecourse. The perilous pursuit of glory was not so different in its essentials for Greek hero and Roman emperor.

If only he could drive a chariot, he would share the experience of an Achilles or a Hector.

> The dust that rose from underneath the horses' chests hung in the air like a storm-cloud or a fog, and their manes flew back in the wind. At one moment the chariots were in contact with the fruitful earth and at the next were bounding high in the air. The heart of each driver as he stood in his car and struggled to be first was beating hard. They yelled at their horses, who flew along on a cloud of dust.

It was a dangerous sport. Pileups were frequent and accidents could be fatal. For a ruler without an heir, this was to take a chance with fate.

However, there was no stopping him. He intended not only to realize his long-standing ambition to drive in four-horse chariot races, but also to develop his career as a performing artist, as a singer of epic verse. For his critics, he prepared a carefully thought-out justification, which, writes Tacitus, ran as follows:

> Charioteering was an accomplishment of ancient kings and leaders, honored by poets, associated with divine worship. Singing, too, is sacred to Apollo: that glorious and provident god is represented in Greek cities, and also in Roman temples.

Seneca and Burrus, who felt they had lost control of Nero after the poisoning of Britannicus, decided that where there were two contested decisions they would concede one in order to gain the other. Direct involvement in chariot racing was undesirable in itself and also inordinately expensive, but they gave way on it.

Nero built a racecourse. Laid out by Caligula but left unfinished, it stood in the valley between the Janiculum and Vatican hills. Surrounded by a walled enclosure, the princeps was able to practice charioteering away from prying eyes. He trained hard to a professional level and was capable of driving a ten-horse racing team, no mean feat. The sport required a high degree of physical fitness, excellent eye-brain coordination, and a fine sense of balance.

Presumably, he agreed to practice in private as a concession to his advisers, but access to the racecourse was improved by the construction of a new bridge across the Tiber, and it was not long before ordinary racegoers were admitted, sometimes by invitation. Officially, these events were unofficial. They were also extremely popular.

The princeps invested in other ambitious projects. On the right bank of the Tiber lay a large artificial lake that Augustus had had dug in A.D. 2 for an enactment of real-life naval warfare. A new aqueduct had been specially built to supply it with water. A bridge spanned the lake to a small island in its center. All around was a wooded park or pleasure ground for public recreation. Here the princeps erected at great speed in 58 a wooden amphitheater, or perhaps a Greek-style semicircular theater. Audiences were protected from the sun by blue awnings spangled with gold stars.

The year of Nero's release from maternal control, 59, was proving to be packed with public entertainments, for this was the venue for a new kind of festival, the Juvenalia or Youth Games, which he founded in honor of his beard that, at the age of twenty-two, he now shaved for the first time (his late aunt Domitia would have been gratified). Bullocks were sacrificed to mark the occasion. The hair was placed inside a small golden globe decorated with pearls, which was dedicated to Jupiter in his great temple on the Capitol.

A program of plays and mimes was staged, some of them traditional Latin farces and dramas, others comedies and tragedies in the Greek manner. In addition, a gladiatorial display and chariot races appealed to lowbrow tastes. As a novelty act, chariots drawn by camels competed with one another. A sea battle was fought in the lake, which had been filled with salt water for the occasion and, as well as warships, featured large "sea monsters" (most probably dolphins).

In self-serving theory, armed combat in the arena was an object lesson in bravery and taught the spectator how to die well. However, it is better seen as a cruel kind of mass entertainment. Gladiators were usually slaves, although some were volunteers. They would fight only a few times a year and might expect to win at least ten encounters in their career. The economics of the "industry" and the practicalities of recruitment and training meant that killings were relatively rare, and duels were sometimes conducted with wooden swords. Winners usually kept their prize money, and a few became as rich and famous as today's soccer stars. Those who survived might be allowed to buy their freedom—and die in their bed.

Emperors were expected to enjoy the thrills of the arena and Nero gave a favorite gladiator called Spiculus houses and estates. To his credit, though, he did not take much pleasure in the spilling of blood. For the Juvenalia he ruled that no fighter should be killed. Being slightly myopic, he used to watch proceedings with the aid of an emerald, which operated as a mirror to produce a focused image. His distaste may have reflected the views of Seneca, who was revolted by an entertainment that damaged "good character."

Once Seneca attended a gladiatorial show by chance. During the midday break, he was expecting a light and witty entertainment. Instead, condemned criminals were brought out and put to death. "It was murder pure and simple." He said with dry humor that "when the games stop for the interval, they announce: 'A little throat-cutting in the interim, so that there may still be something going on!' "

Death occurred not only in the arena but also in the theater, albeit on this occasion by accident. The Juvenalia featured a version of the Icarus story. The actor cum dancer who played the title role headed a ballet mime group that presented the Pyrrhic dance, a dramatic presentation based on a traditional Greek war dance. Performers were usually imported from Asia, well-bred Greek-speaking boys and girls who were awarded certificates of Roman citizenship at the end of the show. Sometimes professionals were recruited, or, for dangerous acts, specially trained convicted criminals. The dance took as its subject (not unlike the Roman pantomime) mythological topics, often drawn from the life of Dionysus, such as the march of the god against the Indians or, as now, the legend of Icarus.

Icarus was the son of a master craftsman called Daedalus, who invented many ingenious mechanical devices. King Minos of Crete commissioned him to design the famous labyrinth. After it was finished the king refused to let him go, so Daedalus prepared two sets of wings made from feathers and wax to enable him and his son to fly away. He warned Icarus not to get too close to the sun, but the boy disobeyed. The wax melted and he plunged into the sea and drowned. The story was retold for the festival as a mime, but unfortunately the mechanical device enabling Icarus to "fly" was not ingenious enough and failed. The performer fell onto the theater floor near the imperial box and died. His blood spattered the princeps.

An original feature of the festival was the large number of amateur performers and stage managers recruited from the nobility. They were trained in advance and paid handsomely, and many seem to have enjoyed taking part. They were cast according to their talents, and those without any were assigned to the choruses. According to Dio,

> Some of them played the flute and danced in pantomimes or acted in tragedies and comedies or sang to the lyre; they drove horses, killed wild beasts and fought as gladiators, some willingly and some bitterly against their will.

A distinguished and wealthy old lady in her eighties caused a stir when she danced in a pantomime. Ordinarily actors and dancers in stage plays and mimes wore masks, but for this performance Nero ordered them to be removed, perhaps to allow spectators to identify well-known personalities.

Tacitus holds his nose:

> There were many volunteers. Birth, age, official career did not prevent people from acting . . . or from accompanying their performance with effeminate gestures and songs. Eminent women, too, rehearsed indecent roles.

As we have seen, all the ancient sources deeply disapproved, and so did senior Romans. To have an emperor who was a common entertainer was shocking and offensive. But they protested too much. There was nothing novel or uncommon about scions of the great families taking to the stage, racing in chariots, or even appearing in the arena. To take just one example, we hear of

> a man of loose morality, not without intellectual gifts, who by indulging in frivolity posed as a wit. In Nero's time he had acted in a farce at the Juvenalia, at first pleading compulsion, but afterwards voluntarily; his performances were clever rather than respectable.

He enjoyed a successful career and became the commander of a legion.

Thrasea Paetus, that most conservative of conservatives, had offended the emperor and was not invited to perform in the Juvenalia. However, we know that he sang in tragic costume at a festival in his native town of Patavia (today's Padua), apparently without attracting adverse comment. In his case, Stoics stuck together and the usual complainants fell silent.

An unspoken motive for involving fellow nobles was that Nero was himself eager to perform in public as an artist, and was looking for cover. How would he be received? Controlling his stage fright, he made an informal appearance at the climax of the festival. To ensure order and encourage the crowds, Praetorian officers were in attendance as well as their commander, Burrus, "with his sigh and his word of praise." One of Seneca's brothers, Gallio, announced the emperor under his own name, as if he were an ordinary citizen, rather than by his catalog of titles. Nero walked onto the stage wearing the long gown of a cithara player. He was nervous. He scrupulously tested his instrument and struck a few preliminary notes to the trainers at his side. Addressing the Senate, present in force, the princeps said modestly: "Honorable members, be so good as to give me a hearing."

He proceeded to sing a song he had written. Dio is unsure which of two likely compositions it was. Either *Attis* or *The Bacchantes* would have been an eccentric, even a scandalous, choice. Attis was the beautiful son of Cybele, the Asian mother goddess. She fell in love with him. He made good his escape and castrated himself. Bacchantes were female followers of the powerful god Dionysus, among whom was the mother of King Pentheus of Thebes. He offended the god, and the Bacchantes tore him to pieces. His mother pulled off his head.

It can hardly have escaped the audience's notice that their emperor's subject matter was an incestuous or a murderous mother, as portrayed by a mother killer. This was an early example of Agrippina's posthumous reappearance in her son's life, this time as nightmarish perpetrator rather than as victim.

To guarantee a warm reception, the princeps created a claque of youthful fans. A few were drawn from the equestrian class and were appointed as officers, but five thousand of them were sturdy, ordinary youths. They called themselves the Augustiani and were noticeable for their bushy hairstyle and expensive clothes.

Their task was to clap and shout rhythmically and generally to act as pumped-up cheerleaders. They conveyed an impression of latent violence; Nero divided them into three groups: the Bees (perhaps they made a sound like the humming of bees), the Roof Tiles, and the Bricks (the tool of rioters throughout the ages).

The Augustiani chanted: "Caesar is great! Our Apollo! Our own Augustus! Another god of music! Caesar, in your name we swear, you are the best!"

Unsurprisingly, Nero's performance was received with thunderous applause. Seneca and Burrus stood beside him, waving their arms and togas at every opportunity. Despite their deep embarrassment at the ruler of the Roman empire behaving as if he were a common player, they were there to support him. Senators and other dignitaries joined in the ovations. Only the incautious failed to follow suit.

Nero had his critics. They usually belonged to the upper class. Some complained of his "weak and husky voice." Before the day of the microphone this was a fatal disadvantage; but as we have seen he was a serious and (at least) competent musician and declaimer, who during his adolescence trained specifically to be audible. So far as we can tell, ordinary theatergoers enjoyed listening to him, which they would scarcely have done if they could not hear him, and throughout his reign his performances were apparently well liked by the Roman public. Nero's compositions were published in *The Master's Book,* and after his death, Suetonius records that some of them were reprised in public to an enthusiastic reception.

As an after-show diversion, Nero hosted a public banquet on boats in the artificial lake. Other entertainments were available. Among the trees and bushes of the park, booths were selling food and drink. Prostitutes plied their trade. Brothels and taverns were set up around the lake. Places of assignation were hidden in the glades. As night fell, so did inhibitions. The atmosphere was one of men in lust and of carnival, where rules were turned on their head.

At midnight the princeps left the party. He boarded a boat that sailed along the canal leading into the Tiber, then turned upstream. He disembarked at a convenient spot for the palace.

Nero had grounds to be well pleased with his day's work. He had disproved the naysayers.

The princeps looked back enviously at the reign of Augustus, which set a benchmark for cultural achievement. As well as establishing himself as a great artist, he was determined to be a patron of literature and inaugurate a new Golden Age to rival that of the first emperor.

Tacitus reports:

> Nero affected a zeal for poetry and gathered a group of associates with some talent for versification but not such as to have attracted remark.

"Affected" is unfair, for he was undoubtably sincere; what is more, his plan to identify writers at the outset of their careers was well-judged. Apparently they sat around in the palace and engaged in what sounds not unlike a modern-day creative writing workshop. They would string together verses they had brought with them or improvise poems on the spot. Sometimes they filled out suggestions put forward by the princeps.

As well as working with promising authors, Nero invited philosophers to dinner on occasion, so Tacitus tells us. He amused himself by listening to "their disputatiousness when explaining their conflicting doctrines. There was no lack of gloomy-browed and sad-eyed sages eager to figure among the diversions of majesty." Perhaps the not-so-gloomy Seneca approved of and joined these discussions; he may even have recruited the participants.

Developing creative talent could not remain a private activity conducted behind closed doors, if there was to be a renaissance. In 60 the princeps launched the Neronia. This quinquennial festival was modeled on the Greek games, such as those held at Olympia in southern Greece, where the program of events featured not only athletics and horse races, but also cultural contests in which sculptors, poets, and painters took part. To coincide with the Neronia, a new gymnasium, an open-air wrestling school, and baths (similar to today's Turkish baths) were opened. Here athletes were able to practice their various sports. Olive oil for rubbing down athletes' bodies was donated to all Senators and *equites*. During the festival, Greek clothing fashions became all the rage.

A conundrum presented itself. Nero competed for the prize for Latin oratory and verse. On the one hand, he regarded himself as but one contender among others, so naturally he ran the risk of not placing first. On the other, he was the emperor, whom protocol required always to be first. The dilemma facing the judges was made all the trickier by the fact that many of Rome's leading public speakers had put forward their names. In the event, they all withdrew from the race and allowed the emperor to take the prize—a neat outcome, for while he could claim the victory, it was obvious that there had been no competition. Everyone's amour propre was intact. When he was also offered the prize for lyre playing, perhaps simply an olive or laurel wreath, he knelt in front of a statue of Augustus and had it laid at its base.

Taken all in all, Nero's new plan for the arts had gotten off to an excellent start. This was due in no small measure to the sudden appearance of the brilliant, astoundingly prolific, insufferable twenty-year-old Marcus Annaeus Lucanus, Englished as Lucan. Nephew of Seneca and son of Annaeus Mela, Lucan was born in 39 in Corduba in southern Spain. As we have seen, his family was very wealthy and well connected. He was a year or so younger than Nero and may well have been his schoolfellow.

Like many upper-class men in their late teens or early twenties, Lucan was taught philosophy in Rome and completed his education with a stay in Athens, where he studied philosophy and rhetoric, the art of persuasion through public speaking. His poems were already attracting attention, and in 59, Nero recalled him to Rome to join a circle of close friends who were serious artists.

He delivered a poetic *Eulogy of Nero* at the festival and then gave public readings from his epic poem, *De Bello Civili* ("On the Civil War"—also known as the *Pharsalia*), his riposte to *The Aeneid*. Published in parts during the early sixties, this told the story of the first of the civil wars, when Julius Caesar defeated Pompey the Great (in Latin, Gnaeus Pompeius Magnus), that put an end to the Roman republic.

The author's sympathies were clearly on Pompey's side, and he condemned Caesar for his ruthless ambition. At first sight it seems odd that the regime allowed root-and-branch criticism of its founder. However, nostalgia for the republic was widespread and permitted, for Romans were realists and few seriously envisaged its return. They recognized that only a centralized state was capable of running an empire. The good old days appeared so only when viewed from a distance.

An epic usually included in its cast list the Greco-Roman gods who lived on Mount Olympus and constantly squabbled over human beings, but Lucan swept them away in favor of an impersonal Stoical fate or Nature. The action was usually set in a legendary past, whereas in *Pharsalia* it took place no more than a century before. Although Lucan's literary style was highly artificial, the story he told was realistic, although not exactly historical. He strains for rhetorical effect and the results are often grotesque, as when Julius Caesar enjoys a post-battle breakfast among enemy corpses. He had a talent for bleak epigrams: thus, "No one ever befriends the unlucky" (*Nulla fides umquam miseros elegit amicos*). Quintilian, the teacher of oratory and educationist, had his reservations. "Lucan is fiery and passionate," he commented, "and remarkable for the grandeur of his general reflexions, but, to be frank, I consider that he is more suitable for imitation by the orator than by the poet." In other words, he was better at making speeches than creating a poetic masterpiece.

Nero enjoyed banter, as did the roaring boys he assembled around him. Petronius and Seneca knew this very well. Their respective satires, *The Satyricon* and *Pumpkinification,* suited their employer's sense of humor and must have been, at least in part, tailored to tickle it. He himself wrote some scurrilous verses at the expense of a Senator notorious for his effeminacy, who neither forgot nor forgave the insult. Another of his targets was a promiscuous politician and former Praetor whom he slandered in a poem entitled *The One-Eyed Man* (unfortunately, neither work has survived).

Writers such as Suetonius did not always distinguish between badinage and serious intent. He reports that the princeps wished to throw living men to crocodiles, which liked to crunch raw flesh; also that he would massacre the Senate and replace it with *equites* and freedmen. These sound like bad temper or tasteless late-night jokes, which are not so funny in the light of day. Seneca warned Nero not to go too far. "In a ruler," he advised, "loud speech and unrestrained language ill accord with majesty."

The princeps got as good as he gave, but he only pursued a few of his mockers. In principle, speech was free under the Augustan system, but caution was advised. An astute observer of the day "cannot feel any sympathy for those who are willing to risk their lives rather than pass up a witty remark." On one famous occasion a nobleman read out at a dinner party some poems he had written that libeled the emperor. He was prosecuted in the Senate and sentenced to death by the old-fashioned method of garrotting. Without prompting, Thrasea Paetus intervened. Heaping praise on the princeps (most unusually), he argued for mercy—namely confiscation of his property and exile—and won his colleagues over to that view. The Consul who was chairing the session wrote to the princeps stating the opinion of the meeting.

The imperial displeasure was evident. Nero responded that the accused "had grossly abused the emperor." The Senate had been asked to punish him. It ought to have fixed a punishment fitting the enormity of the crime. "But I will not amend your leniency. Indeed I should not have allowed anything else. Decide as you please. You could have acquitted him if you pleased."

Tacitus believed that the princeps had planned to commute the death sentence all along, to illustrate his clemency. Seneca's influence still held sway. Annoyingly for Nero, Thrasea Paetus had as usual gotten in the way.

In another case, a promising young poet, Aules Persius Flaccus, loathed the fashionable literary world of the day. He imagined a poetry recitation as a sex show in which the listeners are brought to orgasm: "the poem enters their backsides and . . . their innermost parts are tickled by verse vibrations." Persius attacked Nero with a seemingly innocuous line of verse, "Midas has ass's ears." According to legend, Midas was king of Phrygia. One day he attended a music competition between the country god Pan and Apollo, god of music, who won the prize. Midas announced that he disagreed with the verdict. Apollo was infuriated and as a punishment transformed the king's ears into those of a donkey.

By applying the myth to Nero, Persius was poking fun at his poor taste. His Stoic teacher and friend Annaeus Cornutus advised him, if he wanted to avoid trouble, to change the line to "Who has not an ass's ears?" In the event, no offense was taken, but Cornutus himself was not so lucky. Not to be outdone by Lucan, we are told that the princeps planned to write an epic on the achievements of the

Romans. He asked his circle how many "books" (that is, chapters or sections) it should have. Some courtiers advanced the absurd number of four hundred. Cornutus commented that that would be far too many and nobody would read them. It was objected that another author whom Cornutus greatly admired had written at even greater length, "Yes," he replied, "but his books helped people to live better lives!"

To be told he was both unreadable and unethical pained the princeps, who sent the offender into exile. He was temperamentally disinclined to punish friends and colleagues for saying rude things about him, but he may have felt that Cornutus had struck at the respect he was owed as a public figure, as emperor. Nero's encouragement of promising young artists was sincerely meant and he took pleasure in their company. Nevertheless (like patrons throughout the ages) he was wounded by their ability to bite the hand that fed them. Beneath the carapace of command he was sensitive to insult.

Lucan was a case in point. His relationship with Nero was not political but purely personal. It began well, but he was too successful for his own good. He opened his *Pharsalia* with a flood of flattery so over the top that even Nero at whom it was aimed may have had difficulty taking it seriously. Here is a sample, which depicts the princeps as taking pride of place among the immortals on Mount Olympus.

You, when your duty is fulfilled
And finally you seek the stars, will be received in your chosen palace
Of heaven, with the sky rejoicing. Whether you choose to wield
The scepter or to mount the flaming chariot of Phoebus
And to circle with moving fire the earth entirely unperturbed
By the transference of the sun, every deity will yield to you.

The poem was praised to the skies, but a friend's good fortune does not always please. It appears that Nero became irritated and in time jealous. It is telling that both men wrote poems on the Trojan War;

comparisons were inevitable and, if not odious, at the very least upsetting. Affection chilled.

Lucan lost patience. According to Suetonius, he was

> piqued because Nero had suddenly called a meeting of the Senate and gone out while he was giving a reading, with no other purpose than to throw cold water on the performance. [Lucan] did not hold back afterwards from disobliging comments about the princeps and hostile acts, which people still talk about.

Public lavatories in ancient Rome could be grand marble edifices and were fashionable places where men of the world dawdled and defecated. One day Lucan was using one of these facilities and emptied his bowels with an uncommonly loud fart. He derisively shouted out a line from one of Nero's poems—"You would think it thundered underground" (*sub terris tonuisse putes*).

Having wiped his bottom with a wet sponge on a stick (Rome's unhygienic alternative to toilet paper), Lucan left the latrine, we can safely assume, thoroughly pleased with himself.

Word of the incident spread, and as a result he found he was no longer welcome at court. Worse, he was forbidden to recite or publish his poetry.

How successful was Nero's cultural policy? We have seen that emperors from Augustus onward knew that their survival depended on the backing, or at least the acquiescence, of the million or so inhabitants of the metropolis. A cynical but truthful politician of the following century summed up what was required:

> The citizens of Rome are kept in line by two things above all else—the supply of free grain and public entertainments. The exercise of power meets with approval as much for amusements as for serious projects. Important business is neglected with greater loss, amusements forgone with greater public resentment. Handouts are anticipated less keenly than shows. The grain allowances

please only the named individuals who receive them, whereas spectacles win over the masses as a whole.

Nero understood this as well as any princeps. His approach to spectacle was not original and he knew he built on foundations laid by Augustus. The difference between him and the first emperor was that he had a passionate and personal commitment to the arts, both high and low, and with his disapproving mother out of the way he could at last act on it openly. Creativity was his world. Audiences understood this and liked him for it. The bond between them was sincere and never entirely broken.

Nero's poem about the fall of Troy was a major project that consumed his energies. It was a well-worn theme and would attract praise from the critics only if he were able to give it a new edge. So, instead of doing the obvious thing and making the warrior Achilles his protagonist, he focused on Paris, an antihero who was more interested in sex than war and was a coward on the battlefield.

The unmilitary Nero seems to have seen his art as a coded confessional. Did he recognize a little of himself in the willful young prince who stole the loveliest of women and brought shame on his city?

9

THE TURNING POINT

THE WATERS LAY like a tranquil pool and were a deep green. They were a confluence of springs in the Apennine mountains, famous for their purity and coldness, from which the Aqua Marcia, Rome's longest aqueduct, originated. Built at colossal expense between 144 and 140 B.C., it conveyed water by force of gravity for more than fifty miles, in places through subterranean channels and elsewhere on arches spanning valleys, until it reached Rome. Once inside the walls the Aqua Marcia and the city's other aqueducts, eventually eleven in all, returned underground or ran along existing walls and bridges. They supplied many public bathhouses and *nymphaea,* richly decorated stone fountains. These masterpieces of engineering ensured that, in principle, every citizen had plentiful access to running water. Indeed, without them Rome could hardly have grown into an imperial megalopolis.

One day in the year 62 the princeps visited the Aqua Marcia's source. The pool looked inviting. He stripped down and swam in the refreshing water. The public, when it heard of the incident, was outraged, for the source was held to be sacred and swimming in it impious. There may have been more to this than a high-spirited jape. Despite the copious springs, the aqueduct produced only a few trickles of water when it reached its destination. This was because private individuals, especially those rich enough to own private houses, installed their own illegal pipes and siphoned water into their homes, leaving little for the ordinary citizen. After Rome's Great Fire (see chapter 11), the princeps took measures to improve supply and eliminate the scandal. His efforts appear to have been successful, for we know that at the end of the century the Aqua Marcia was distributing fifty million gallons a day in the city.

Nero paid a high price for his dip. Soon afterward he fell gravely ill, and people linked the two events. He recovered, but this was the second time he had recently had a problem with his health.

Earlier in the year, a comet was seen in the sky for several nights running, and lightning struck and broke the table at which the princeps was dining. As was customary in the ancient world, unusual or alarming natural events were seen as portents of an important person's death. They tended to send Nero into a rage and make him look around for enemies. Seneca tried to calm him with a grim bon mot: "No matter how many people you kill, you cannot kill your successor."

Not long afterward, Nero took to his bed. We do not know the nature of his ailment, but it was evidently serious. What would happen if he were to die? Who would fill the empty throne? Nobody could say. Courtiers gathered around and put the question to him. He replied that the state did have one resource. "Tell us what or who was that" was the general cry. "Memmius Regulus" came the ironic response. Memmius was an eminently respectable Senator nearing the end of a long life. He had helped Tiberius through the Sejanus crisis and had been married for a time to the society beauty Lollia Paulina, whom we have met before when she was considered as a possible wife for Claudius. Memmius was a "new man" (that is, the first member of his family to hold the Consulship) and had no genetic connection to the ruling dynasty. He did not have much money and lived in quiet retirement. A less likely candidate for the purple could hardly be imagined. The princeps was joking, of course, for he knew better than to identify a plausible successor while he himself was still alive.

Despite these bouts of sickness and a third unspecified malady, Nero's health was generally good, but neither that nor his sarcastic naming of an heir made the issue of the succession go away. Until it was settled, he could not sit easy on his throne.

The obvious solution to the conundrum was for Nero to produce a son. There was an obstacle, his wife Octavia. She was only nine when she was engaged to the eleven-year-old Nero. Their wedding a few years later in 53 did not signify a love match but was, as we have seen, a case of raison d'état. Tacitus reports that the husband could not bear to touch his aristocratic and virtuous wife, "whether from destiny or the greater pleasures of forbidden fruit."

Nero decided to divorce Octavia and marry his long-established lover, Poppaea, who proved her fertility by announcing that she was pregnant. His senior advisers were unenthusiastic. Burrus was a mild-mannered man who liked to avoid trouble, but he seems to have treated the princeps as a lazy pupil. When Nero asked him to give his opinion on a matter of importance for a second time, he replied brusquely: "When I have spoken about something, don't ask me to repeat myself." He did his best to prevent the divorce and in one heated exchange told him: "All right then, but give back her dowry." By this he meant the Roman empire. Octavia was popular with the general public and brought with her the legitimacy of her father's imperium. Divorce could cast doubt on Nero's right to rule.

The matter was still open when Burrus died in 62. Inevitably, there were rumors of poison, but they are unlikely to be well founded. The timing was suspicious, but against that the Praetorian commander was aging and known to be sick. He suffered from a large goiter on his neck, which pressed against his windpipe. The princeps came to see him and brought some medication—an ointment or a cough mixture. It was said to be envenomed, but the risk of discovery would surely have ruled this out. More plausibly, the goiter was a fatal symptom of thyroid cancer.

The visit appears not to have been a success. When Nero inquired how he was, Burrus turned his face away and said: "*I* am doing well," as if to say that nothing else was and that the empire was in bad shape.

Nero had worried about the loyalty of a sole *praefectus* of the Praetorian Guard, who would be able to build a power base among his soldiers without being easily detected. Now that he had the opportunity, he replaced Burrus with two appointees, who did not get along and could be counted on to compete with each other rather than conspire against him. As one of them he chose Lucius Faenius Rufus. He was a competent and well-respected administrator who had managed the grain supply to Rome to the satisfaction of the populace and, unusually, without making a profit for himself. His co-commander was a man we have met before, Gaius Sofonius Tigellinus. He shared Nero's louche lifestyle and love of chariot racing, and they became good friends. Before joining the Praetorians, Tigellinus had headed the city's paramilitary Urban Cohorts (a position roughly equivalent to chief of police).

He was despised by the ancient historians. Tacitus has it that he was evil incarnate, licentious and rotten to the core, but this judgment should be treated with caution. It can be argued that Tigellinus was a clear-sighted and ruthless opportunist and a hardworking manager who served his master well (albeit after he had served himself).

The passing of Burrus left his political partner Seneca in an exposed position, and he decided to leave the government.

Nero seems to have tired of his sententious adviser, if we can judge from attacks that people close to the princeps launched against him. They probed his weak spot, namely his wealth, which was excessive in any subject of the emperor and was still growing. Tacitus has them claim that "the grandeur of his mansions and the beauty of his gardens . . . outdid even those of the emperor." The detractors had a point, for throughout a long career Seneca wrote and spoke at length on the austere teachings of Stoicism. As we have seen, he himself recognized the contradiction between the principles he preached and his practice—but could not bring himself to make the necessary changes to his way of life that would harmonize them.

This was not all. "He allowed no one to be called a good orator but himself," the charge sheet continued. "He was always writing poetry now that Nero had taken it up. Of the emperor's amusements in general he was an open critic, saying he was no good as a charioteer and laughing at him for singing out of tune!"

The most persuasive critique was that the princeps was no longer a boy. He was a man in his midtwenties and it was time to discharge his schoolmaster. Seneca took the point. He could no longer control Nero and did not wish to be implicated in acts with which he disagreed and for which he was not responsible.

He heard what was being said about him and noticed that Nero was increasingly avoiding his company. He asked for an appointment to see him and the request was granted. At the interview Tacitus has him say:

> It is nearly fourteen years, Sir, since I was first connected to your rising hopes, and eight since you inherited the empire. During that time, you showered me with such distinctions and wealth that if only I could retire to enjoy them modestly, my happiness would be complete.

He accepted that this would be impossible and offered to hand his fortune back to the princeps. He was old and incapable of the lightest work. He sought leave to withdraw into private life. He could have quoted the apt words he gave the Chorus in his tragedy, *Thyestes*,

> *Let others scale dominion's slippery peak,*
> *Peace and obscurity are all I seek.*
> *Enough for me to live alone, and please*
> *Myself with idleness and leisured ease.*

Nero responded graciously and warmly. He expressed no interest in acquiring his former tutor's wealth. He resisted, but did not in so many words refuse, his resignation offer. "You are enjoying a vigorous old age and appear to be adequate to office—and to its rewards. I myself am only starting out on my reign." His remarks concluded with a hug and kisses. Seneca expressed his gratitude.

An innocent observer would think that nothing had happened, nothing had changed. In fact, each man recognized that a chapter had closed. From then onward, Seneca abandoned his official administrative routine, canceled his grand receptions and dismissed his entourage. He spent most of his time in the country and rarely visited the capital. Poor health and his philosophical studies kept him at home, he used to say.

We know that Nero was fond of the adults who had supervised his youth. But Seneca was afraid that his enemies would stir up trouble for him. He needed to remove himself entirely from the political scene.

Tacitus tells us that in fact the princeps was annoyed by what he regarded as rejection. He was not taken in by the pretense of illness and suborned one of his old tutor's freedmen to poison him. Seneca was told (or figured out the plot himself). Thereafter he kept himself alive on a diet of wild fruits and water from a running stream.

Seneca and Burrus had spent the previous five years and more managing their youthful emperor very effectively. They had provided him with political guidance and at the same time trained him in statecraft. The purpose of both the guidance and the training was to produce an autocrat who worked within the law. They taught him to collaborate constructively with the Senate, whose members played an essential role in the imperial system, governing the provinces and commanding the legions.

The plan worked out well. Nero was no fool and broadly followed Seneca's policy of clemency. In particular, he was on good terms with the Senate (in this respect, maintaining Agrippina's consultative approach to government, which had reinvigorated the second half of Claudius's reign).

But a weakness in Nero's character finally brought the predominance of Seneca to a close. He appreciated his contribution and was grateful to him and Burrus for giving him the free time in which to write his poems and rehearse his music. But they did not share his tastes and frowned upon his escapades. He was drowning in good advice and probably felt anxious and insufficient to his duties as emperor.

Seneca saw that with the passing years the princeps was escaping from him. He had disapproved of Agrippina's murder and even more of Britannicus's poisoning. He viewed inaction on the succession with deep foreboding.

Perhaps he had left his withdrawal from the stage until it was too late. Despots dislike resignations, and Seneca worried for his future.

The crisis of the succession did not simply reflect the troubling absence of an heir, who would ensure continuity and stability. It also threw a treacherous light on those Roman noblemen whose parents or grandparents had married into the imperial family and who may have felt they were as entitled to power as the current wearer of the purple.

Chief among these was Gaius Rubellius Plautus. Born in 33, he boasted a dangerously rich dynastic inheritance. He had been mentioned, without his knowledge, in the supposititious plot to depose Nero, attributed falsely to Agrippina (see page 122). She had triumphed at her trial, and the devisers of the scheme had been duly punished.

As we saw, Plautus's name had been passed over in silence. However, he recognized the peril that threatened him and was not politically active. He led a contented private life and was reputed to be an affectionate husband and father. Like Seneca he was that uncomfortable thing, a rich Stoic. He was on friendly terms with a group of noblemen who were critical of one-man rule, but he accepted the imperial system. Plautus was a thoughtful and upright young man. He would happily have sunk into obscurity.

That was not to be. The appearance of the comet in 62 stimulated tactless prognostications of the fall of Nero, and Plautus's name came up in conversation as a possible new princeps. This undercurrent of discontent alarmed Nero, although not to the point of taking punitive action. For a second time, he must have judged Plautus to be innocent of any offense, but he wanted him safely out of the way. He wrote him an ostensibly friendly letter in which he suggested that Plautus

> consider the importance of calm in the capital and extricate yourself from the scandalmongers. You have family estates in Asia where you will be able to enjoy your youthful years in peace and quiet.

So off to Asia Plautus went, uncomplainingly, along with his wife and a few close friends.

There was another man, without talent but burdened with a glittering pedigree, who caught the eye of the princeps. He was Faustus Cornelius Sulla Felix. Descendant of a famous republican political leader and born in 22, he was the son of Nero's aunt, Domitia Lepida, and so the emperor's first cousin. His maternal grandmother was a daughter of Augustus's sister Octavia. The emperor Claudius married him to one of his daughters, Claudia Antonia. In 55 his name was cited in a conspiracy to replace Nero with himself. Burrus and the freedman Pallas were also implicated. It turned out that the whole affair was a malicious invention. Its author was banished and no further action was taken.

Nero could not stand Sulla, whose inveterate stupidity he mistook for well-concealed cunning. His suspicions seemed to be confirmed by the disclosure of a new conspiracy linked to an incident during one of the princeps's nocturnal rambles. He enjoyed visiting the Milvian bridge (today's Ponte Milvio), which crossed the Tiber north of the city. The area enjoyed a deserved reputation for prolific sex after dark. Here Nero could pick up a partner or (less riskily) enjoy "dogging" with fewer awkward consequences than in Rome itself.

On his way home one night, he and his party were thrown into a panic by a handful of noisy revelers and took a detour to avoid them. This should have been the end of the story, but a malevolent imperial freedman reported the incident in exaggerated terms, transforming a contretemps into a full-blown attempt on the emperor's life—masterminded by Sulla.

However, none of his slaves or dependents were identified at the scene, and the allegation was completely out of character. Sulla was too fainthearted for such a dangerous enterprise. Nevertheless, he was tried, found guilty, and exiled to the city of Massilia (today's Marseille) in Narbonese Gaul.

Far from Rome, at least he was safe. Or so he hoped.

Tigellinus, trainer of horses for chariot racing and now Praetorian Prefect, was becoming more influential with each passing day, but he needed to find a joint project that would bind him closely and permanently to the princeps. He realized that Nero's deepest fears were of Plautus and Sulla. However peaceable their intentions might be, they were standards behind which rebels would happily march.

With great care Tigellinus laid out the case against them. Plautus was not far away from the legions of the East under Corbulo and Sulla was within striking distance of the armies of the Rhine. They could easily tamper with the troops without Rome knowing anything about it. Exile had exacerbated rather than resolved the challenge they posed.

According to Tacitus, Tigellinus fed Nero with untruths and half-truths:

> Sulla doesn't have any money, which makes him impetuous. He pretends to be lazy, but is merely waiting for an opportunity to strike. Plautus, with his vast wealth, doesn't even affect to want peace. He parades his mimicries of the ancient Romans, takes on himself the arrogance of a Stoic and cultivates a sect which breeds sedition and political intrigue.

The princeps was persuaded. No time was lost. An execution squad, presumably some of Tigellinus's Praetorian Guards, set sail for Marseille. On arrival six days later, they disembarked and went quickly to Sulla's house. He had just sat down to dinner when they entered and was completely taken by surprise. He was dispatched on the spot.

His head was cut off and taken back to Rome for inspection by Nero, who was amused to see its premature gray hair. Postmortem decapitation was seldom motivated by gratuitous gloating; rather, in an age of unreliable communications, it gave the commissioner of a death the absolute assurance that his order had been carried out.

Young Plautus was better known and respected than Sulla, and more people were concerned for his safety. Eliminating him was to prove a much more difficult task.

Evidently security at the palace was weak, for word got out that Plautus was to be put to death. A false story spread that Plautus had escaped to Corbulo, then campaigning to save Armenia from the Parthians. With his mighty army and a high military reputation, it was said that the general feared falling from grace in a jealous emperor's eyes and welcomed a chance to replace him. In fact, Plautus had stayed put on his Syrian estate and Corbulo had had his hands full loyally repairing the damage done by a fellow general whom the Parthians had recently defeated (see page 298). In another case of fake news, unenthusiastic soldiers ordered to kill Plautus had failed to carry out their task and joined the rebellion.

What *was* true was that a detachment of a centurion and some sixty soldiers set out from Rome for Syria with orders to execute Plautus. Its commander was a court freedman, a eunuch called Pelago—an appointment which strongly suggests nervousness on Nero's part that an army officer could not be trusted to carry out the execution warrant.

Plautus's family in Rome had heard what was afoot and sent a freedman to forewarn him. He traveled faster than the soldiers and reached Plautus before they did. He delivered a letter from his father-in-law recommending resistance:

> Escape a passive end while there is a way out. Sympathy for your great name will make decent men back you and brave men help you. Meanwhile do not despise any possible support. Sixty soldiers have been sent. If you repel them, much can happen, even a war may develop.

Plautus was unmoved. He may well have judged that a military solution was impractical. He loved his family and will have calculated that Nero would not punish them (for instance, by confiscating his property) if he accepted his fate. His Stoic friends advised him to choose a courageous death in preference to an uncertain and harassed life.

The killers found Plautus early one afternoon. He was stripped for exercise. The centurion cut him down and decapitated him while the eunuch Pelago looked on. His widow clasped his spouting neck and kept his bloodstained clothes.

When the princeps was shown his head, he said: "I had no idea he had such a big nose!"—as much as to say that he would have spared him had he only known this mitigating fact. He did not admit the executions, but wrote a letter to the Senate naming Sulla and Plautus as "turbulent spirits." He went on to say that he was watching with great care over the safety of the state.

In response, a national thanksgiving was voted and Sulla and Plautus were expelled from the Senate, as if they were still alive.

To cancel an imperial woman's marriage vows was to take a serious and possibly fatal risk, as the Messalina affair had demonstrated. The introduction of a new princess into the family was almost equally dangerous, to which the competition for Claudius's hand bore witness. Nero had been waiting patiently for years, but he now felt that he could at last safely discard his wife, Octavia. With Burrus dead and Seneca neutralized, there was no longer any opposition at court, and he was willing to risk popular disapproval. He was still in love with Poppaea, who with her advantage of years may have played the role of a mother as well as of a sexual partner. She was eager for marriage.

Nero divorced Octavia for barrenness and twelve days later married Poppaea. He hesitated to take further measures against her, for she was known to lead a quiet and blameless life. However, the new empress would not feel secure unless Octavia was eliminated from the scene once for all. She incited a member of Octavia's household staff to accuse her of adultery with a slave, an Alexandrian flute player. According to the law, the slaves of an indicted Roman could only give evidence under torture. Although pain drove a few of Octavia's people to make false admissions, the majority steadfastly maintained her innocence. Under cruel interrogation by Tigellinus, one of her lady's maids retorted: "My mistress's cunt is cleaner than your mouth!"—the most memorable put-down in the records of Roman history.

The prosecution failed. Nero was generous in defeat and made over to his onetime wife Burrus's mansion and Plautus's estates. If the news reached the young Stoic in the Elysian Fields, he will have learned that his self-sacrifice had been in vain.

It was not long before Nero, prompted by Poppaea, returned to the charge. Octavia was dismissed to Campania. The masses were infuriated by this constant bullying of a well-liked princess and took to the streets on her behalf. This badly frightened the princeps, and a rumor spread (presumably planted) that the emperor repented of his decision to remove Octavia from Rome and intended to remarry her.

Immediately, cheering crowds ascended the Capitol. They overturned statues of Poppaea and carried those of Octavia on their shoulders, setting them up in the Forum and the temples and scattering them with flowers. Even Nero was loudly applauded with ear-shattering vows of loyalty. Demonstrators burst into the palace until military detachments drove them out with beatings and drawn swords.

Soon everyone went home and the city calmed down. Like a summer storm, the crisis had been fierce but brief and was suddenly over. Poppaea's statues were reinstated. It was decided to find a suitably distinguished man who would admit to having an affair with Octavia. For this service a handsome reward and a pleasant place of retirement would be provided. Refusal would be punishable by death. The choice fell on Anicetus, admiral of the Misenum fleet and mastermind of Agrippina's murder. The fates had been unkind and he was no longer in favor. Nero could not bear to look at him, for he brought agonizing thoughts to mind.

However, he made an exception now. He summoned Anicetus and laid out his terms. The freedman accepted the commission and in fact went beyond his instructions when he made a full (and entirely invented) confession before a specially convened council of the emperor's *amici*. Nero was as good as his word, and the freedman was sent to Sardinia, where he lived out a not uncomfortable existence and died a natural death.

Octavia was caught in a deadly trap. The princeps announced that she had seduced Anicetus in the hope of winning the loyalty of the fleet; then, worried about her infidelity, she had procured an abortion (the previous charge of sterility was forgotten). Octavia was banished to the tiny island of Pandateria off the Bay of Naples; Augustus had built a holiday palace there, which he and other emperors used as a luxurious *oubliette* for locking up inconvenient or badly behaved imperial women.

A few days followed, after which orders arrived for her to kill herself. She protested that she was no longer Nero's wife but his half sister and nothing more. In other words, she was no threat. Octavia's guards acted. She was tightly bound with cords, and veins in each of her limbs were opened. Her blood flowed out too slowly, so her killers suffocated her in the steam of a bath heated to its maximum temperature. Her head was cut off and sent to Rome, where it was viewed by Poppaea.

Suetonius reports that years later, Nero had a nightmare about Octavia. She dragged him down into thick darkness where hordes of winged ants swarmed over his body.

It is time to pause and pose a question. With the deaths of Plautus, Sulla, and Octavia, following closely on those of Agrippina and Britannicus, has Nero made himself into the monster of myth?

The point to note is that his victims were all relatives who in one way or another threatened his position as princeps—at least potentially so. Agrippina had wanted to share his throne and expected to do the ruling while her son had a good time. When he pushed back, she cultivated dynastic rivals, perhaps not seriously, but who was to know?

Plautus was unwise to have been in touch with the Stoic Opposition, but it is very probable that he and Sulla had no idea that conspirators were promoting them as the next princeps. But innocence made them no less dangerous from Nero's point of view, perhaps even more so.

Octavia is a special case. We can accept that she was imprisoned inside an unhappy marriage, but what brought her down was the imperial couple's inability to have children. Nero disliked her heartily, but he would not have had her killed had they been sexually compatible and she had produced a male heir. Poppaea would have had to go whistle.

Tigellinus's advice was brutal and, as realpolitik, probably correct. Despite these grisly events, Nero's popularity with ordinary Romans held up. The palace had its own rules of behavior; the street looked on—always with interest, sometimes with surprise and seldom with disapproval.

If challenged to justify their use of state violence, the princeps and his counselors could plead cruel necessity. This defense fitted what we can guess of Nero's psychological makeup. In him fearfulness was accompanied by feelings of guilt and inadequacy, which could only be assuaged by further bloodletting.

However, Augustus and the dynastic system he invented deserve as much blame as Nero himself for the horrors of his reign. The first emperor's descendants posed a genuine threat to those who followed him. Admittedly, a princeps more confident of himself might have been able to cope with a Plautus or a Sulla without taking extreme measures.

Poppaea's fertility brought her no good. On January 21, 63, she gave birth to a daughter, Claudia, in the imperial retreat at Antium, Nero's birthplace. Joy was unconfined, and the Senate traveled from Rome en bloc to offer congratulations. The baby was awarded the honorific title of Augusta. Gold statues were placed in temples and circus games were held in her name. However, she died in April. Her father's overwhelming grief was mitigated by her instant deification. A shrine and a priest were dedicated to her shortly afterward.

Once more, Senators streamed down to Antium to pay their respects (except for Thrasea Paetus, who was, ominously, barred from going). They will have spoken kind words while thinking to themselves that the absence of a male heir, indeed an offspring of any kind, was as embarrassingly obvious as ever. The succession remained wide open.

The empress was soon in an interesting condition again.

Despite this setback, Nero had grounds for satisfaction. The recent arranged deaths had strengthened his hold on power: as we shall see, he soon added to the lengthening list one more luckless inheritor of Augustus's genes.

A growing self-confidence allowed Nero to brook no further delay and advance his artistic career. His plan was to graduate from being an amateur to fully professional status and to appear regularly on the public stage. He had waited until his mother was out of the way and then made a cautious start, performing in his gardens and at his personal theater. In theory, he appeared in private, by invitation only. In practice, anyone who wished to attend was able to do so, but he longed for the regular applause of a mass audience.

Nero specialized in playing the *cithara,* a seven-stringed version of the four-stringed lyre. It had a sound box and is best understood as an early guitar (the names are etymologically related). Like many Romans, he regarded Hellenic culture as superior to his own and onstage presented himself in a long tunic like a Greek instrumentalist or *citharoedus*.

He was nervous about his reception, and it was not until 64, ten years after his accession, that Nero chose Naples as the venue for his professional debut. He enjoyed its Hellenic atmosphere and believed its citizens would be flattered if he invited them to witness this unique event. The concert attracted not only Neapolitans but also people flooding in from the countryside, and the emperor played to a full house.

Nero often went back to Naples to perform. According to Suetonius, even when he took a short break to rest his voice, he could not keep out of sight but went to the theater after bathing and dined on the stage with people all around him, promising them in Greek that when he had had a drink he would sing something good and loud.

The reception of his debut was gratifying but appears to have caused a disaster. The theater in which he performed had probably been overloaded and suddenly collapsed. Luckily the show was over and the audience had already left. There were no casualties. The princeps responded with an ode of thanks to the gods for a lucky escape. All in all, the visit had been a triumph.

Now that he had surmounted this first hurdle, Nero's confidence grew, and he conceived the idea of a tour of Greece, where he would compete in the Olympic games and other famous festivals of arts and athletics. He would also stop over at the culturally abundant city of Alexandria in Egypt. It was there, he felt, that his talents would be fully recognized.

Not many miles away from Naples lay the highway from Rome to the port of Brundisium (today's Brindisi), where travelers could embark for eastern destinations. It would seem that in the euphoria generated by the concert, Nero decided to put his idea into immediate practice, joined the road, and proceeded south. He soon arrived at the town of Beneventum (now Benevento), where he attended a gladiatorial display.

Nero chose this moment to eliminate a nobleman called Decimus Junius Silanus Torquatus on trumped-up charges. His true crime was to be another of Augustus's great-great-grandsons. Accusers were instructed to prosecute him for an extravagance so egregious that he must have had a coup d'état in mind to restore his ruined fortunes. To make matters worse, Torquatus ill-advisedly gave his senior freedmen the same job titles as those of the princeps—*ab epistulis, a libellis,* and *a rationibus* (secretaries for correspondence, petitions, and accounts). The prosecution alleged that this betrayed a treasonous ambition to replace Nero and his officials. Torquatus anticipated his conviction by opening his veins. This allowed the princeps to claim his regret that the guilty man had not awaited the indulgence of the court.

So yet another nobleman joined his ancestors. With each such death, however rational, the good work accomplished by Agrippina and Seneca was being dismantled. The years of clemency on the emperor's part and willing cooperation on the Senate's were over and done with. The welcome of the arts and entertainment world and Nero's popularity with the plebs hid from him the dread and hatred with which the ruling class increasingly regarded him.

Without warning, Nero decided to postpone his journey to the eastern provinces and went back to Rome. He made no firm announcement and gave no explanation, but an imperial expedition entailed complicated logistical arrangements that required notice, and he may have yielded to practicality. It is also possible that the Torquatus affair had unsettled senatorial opinion and that Nero felt it would be wise to wait until the political atmosphere calmed.

Once back home, he made it clear that if he did leave the city, he would not be away for long, and that the departments of state would ensure administrative stability and the empire's prosperity.

Seeking divine advice about his voyage, writes Tacitus, he proceeded to the Capitol, the city's symbolic heart, where he performed his devotions. He then went down into the Forum and made his way across the square to the small circular temple of Vesta, protectress of the city's hearth. Here her priestesses, the Vestal Virgins, tended a sacred fire that was never allowed to go out. Entry was forbidden to everyone else.

The princeps ignored the rule. He went inside the shrine and sat down. Something mysterious took place. The fringe of his garment caught on something when he tried to stand up. Seemingly terrified by an angry Vesta, he was temporarily blinded. He began to shake all over. If we are to believe Suetonius, at some unknown date he had raped a Vestal called Rubria, so he cannot have been altogether surprised if the goddess wanted to punish him.

Once recovered from this unnerving experience, the princeps officially canceled his expedition, giving patriotism as his excuse. In truth, the public disapproved. "I have heard the whispered complaints of my fellow-citizens about the extensive travels I have in mind," he announced. "They cannot bear even my shortest absence. . . . In the business of government, you, the Roman people, have first call on me and I must give way if you want me to stay."

It is difficult to know what to make of this curious episode. It may have been a fiction concocted to give the princeps cover for his volte-face. But the story of an unexpected panic attack rings true and should be accepted at face value. It may be linked to Nero's pangs of guilt for his past actions and his eagerness to do or say anything that would attract the sympathy of the ordinary Roman citizen.

This was not the end, though, of his yearnings for a foreign adventure, for a tour of Greece, and for recognition as a great artist. He would return to them on another day.

The emperor still balanced his vocation for high culture with a wholehearted enthusiasm for lowbrow entertainment, on which he spent large sums of money, enough indeed to strain the treasury's resources. He raced with chariots, an irresponsibly risky hobby for an emperor but one that caused widespread excitement among the people at large, if not among respectable opinion. On days when racing was not possible, he used to play with ivory horses and toy chariots on a table. On one never-to-be-forgotten occasion, he presented a wild animal hunt; when that was over, water was immediately piped into the arena and a sea fight was staged; the water then being let out, a gladiatorial combat concluded the program.

In the spring and early summer of 64, Nero held a series of open-air banquets in public places across Rome. They proved, remarks Tacitus sourly, that he was treating the city as if it were his own palace. As well as being his idea of fun, the banquets were surely designed as damage limitation; despite appearances to the contrary, they proved that Rome was, and always had been, his favorite place.

The most famous of them was promoted by Tigellinus. As at the Juvenalia feast, the venue was an artificial lake set in a wooded park. Created by Augustus's partner, Agrippa, it lay next to the Pantheon, temple of all the gods, on the Campus Martius. A great raft, made from planks on empty wine casks, was towed through the water by small rowing boats with silver and ivory fittings, which acted as tugs. The oarsmen were male prostitutes marshaled according to age and sexual speciality. The raft was moored in the center of the lake, and here the princeps and Tigellinus reclined on purple rugs and soft cushions and enjoyed the feast.

Sea creatures, again perhaps dolphins, had been captured and swam in the lake. Exotic birds and animals from faraway places had been hunted down and were also on display.

On the quayside stood "pop-up" brothels stocked with attractive noblewomen and girls (or so we are told), and opposite were booths where naked "working girls" plied their trade. To begin with, party-goers restricted themselves to obscene gestures and bodily movements miming coition. As darkness advanced, some had sex among the surrounding trees and in the houses around the edges of the park, which echoed with song and sparkled with lights.

Crowds of drunken men roamed about and fights broke out, on occasion with fatal results. Some women were taken away by force, and in the crush, others died of suffocation.

As for the princeps, he thoroughly enjoyed himself. So much so in fact that he allowed himself to go through a mock marriage ritual between himself and a favorite freedman. Tacitus fulminates:

> Nero himself was defiled by lawful and unlawful sex acts. He had left no outrage untested that could deepen his depravity—bar one. A few days after the banquet he married, in the manner of a proper wedding ceremony, a member of that gang of degenerates, whose name was Pythagoras [the emperor's sommelier]. A bridal veil was placed over the emperor's head, the augurs were called in, and dowry, marriage bed, and wedding torches were all there.

Suetonius adds the scabrous detail that "Nero moaned and groaned like a virgin being penetrated."

What are we to make of this remarkable claim that gay marriage was pioneered two millennia before its introduction in modern societies? Nero was not alone. There are reports of other male couples entering into long-term or lifelong unions. The poet Martial, who flourished later in the first century, wrote a poem on the topic:

> Bearded Callistratus married rugged [the Latin word, *rigidus,* is a double entendre, also meaning "stiff"] Afer in the usual manner in which a virgin marries a husband. The torches shone in front, the wedding veil covered his face. . . . Even the dowry was declared. Are you still not satisfied, Rome? Are you waiting for him to give birth?

Callistratus was presumably a Greek slave or freedman of a lower social status than Afer, an elite Roman. We may surmise that he enjoyed, or at least endured, penetrative sex, consent to which was taboo for a freeborn citizen. Elsewhere the poet refers to a man of masculine appearance with the remark, "Don't believe his looks. He took a husband yesterday."

The poet and public opinion at large disapproved of a practice that, while not routine, appears to have been a fairly familiar occurrence in Rome. So did the great satirist Juvenal, who was a contemporary of the emperor Hadrian. He wrote of a man, also from the aristocracy, who has set up house with a cornet player, "or perhaps I should say a straight horn"—yet another off-color joke.

> *Marriage documents were signed, felicitations offered, they sat down to a great banquet, and the new bride lay in her husband's lap.*

To understand these scenes, we should look carefully at the traditional Roman wedding in the first century. There were laws on aspects of marriage (for example, girls could not marry if younger than twelve years and boys than fourteen, although they could get engaged), but the state played no part in the administration of marriage, kept no register, and did not supervise the process. By the same token, the official religion and its representatives had no role. Marriage was simply an agreement between two people, usually a male and a female; it was also, and more significantly, a social and economic alliance between families. Its chief purpose was to produce offspring and so ensure the propagation of the family line.

The most striking feature of Roman marriage was its lack of required formalities. No particular ceremony was compulsory. So far as we can tell, a couple were married if they said they were, behaved as man and wife should, and intended a lifelong union. The woman would bring a dowry with her (repayable in the event of divorce) and a contract would be drawn up and signed. "Where you are Caius I am Caia," said the bride, citing a common forename, to which the groom replied: "Where you are Caia, I am Caius." Mutual consent having been given, the deal was done.

Roman weddings were lively affairs, involving a feast and a procession. The groom led his bride, her head covered by a flame-colored veil, from her home to his, where the couple were ushered into their bedroom and the door closed. Though these celebrations had religious significance, they were more like a boozy modern wedding party than a rite that approved and solemnized a union.

This lack of definition enabled two men to act as a married couple without obviously breaking any law, subverting any public institution, or attracting too much adverse comment. However, it is unlikely that they regarded themselves as properly married, for they were unable to fulfill the essential function of a traditional heterosexual marriage—namely, procreation. As Martial makes clear, this kind of ritual was not the real thing but was conducted "in the usual manner" of a traditional ceremony. What male lovers could do was to enjoy a colorful wedding procession and dedicate themselves informally one to the other.

Nero appears to be a different case. He was a serial monogamist who slept with Acte, married Poppaea, and later would marry Statilia Messalina (not to be confused with Valeria Messalina, Claudius's profligate empress). So far as we can tell, these were sincerely felt, loving relationships. It is unlikely that he took his marriage to Pythagoras altogether seriously. It was a pastiche, reminiscent of the escapades in Petronius's *Satyricon* or his nocturnal forays in search of trouble. In brief, Nero was having a laugh.

We may wonder what Poppaea, his great love, who was now pregnant again, made of all this. Perhaps she was not told. There seems to be little doubt that alongside straightforward heterosexuality, the princeps ran a second bisexual sex life, powered by the thrill of anonymous promiscuity, sometimes laced with violence. Suetonius recounts a famous anecdote:

> He so prostituted his own chastity that after defiling almost every part of his body, he at last devised a kind of game, in which, covered with the skin of some wild animal, he was let loose from a cage and attacked the private parts of men and women, who stood bound to stakes, and when he had satisfied his mad lust, was finished off by his freedman Pythagoras.

Gay marriage was a feature of the first century, and it is conceivable that the practice was invented by Nero and as a result became fashionable in advanced circles. At any rate, after two or three generations it died out—or was no longer mentioned in the sources.

10

THE QUEEN IS DEAD

AFTER THE MURDER of his mother, Nero was trouble-free. But just when he felt safest, he was confronted with the biggest crisis of his leadership.

Catastrophic news arrived in Rome. Britannia, one of the empire's most prized conquests, was now in flames, in the throes of widespread rebellion. Tens of thousands of Romans had been slaughtered. An entire legion had been wiped out. The island was suddenly in chaos and beyond his control.

The reason for the disaster stretched back centuries, but it was only now, when Britannia became a threat, that the Romans had to confront the reality of its existence. The idea of this mythical land had previously been incompatible with their concept of the world, yet now this remote outpost had become a direct threat to Nero's authority and that of the empire. Rome had not contemplated the cost of its contempt. It had misunderstood and miscalculated the power of savagery.

This predictable, arrogant error led to a decision that would define the very world we live in today.

The island of Great Britain, the largest in Europe and the ninth largest on the globe, rises in the North Atlantic just twenty miles northwest of its nearest neighbor, France.

But Britannia, as the Romans would come to call it, was a world away.

In some ways, for them, it was beyond even that—for centuries, they had believed that the western boundaries of the earth were confined by the raging, torrential Oceanus, effectively today's Atlantic, on the western shores of the continent. Oceanus was thought to be a vast, fierce, and unconquerable river, whose distant borders were the very rim of the world. To some living close to Europe's western coast, these turbulent waters were worshipped as a wrathful and tempestuous god.

The Romans had little understanding of geography beyond their bounds. Although it is not in doubt that Roman scholars from at least 200 B.C. were aware the world was a sphere—this had been established by Greek mathematicians and endorsed by both Aristotle and Plato—these truths did not percolate far from the private libraries of scholars. Even if the prospect were brought up in conversation, say, at a high-class banquet or symposium, the notion of the earth as a globe may have been a point of mild curiosity; but this was a matter for philosophy, and one of little consequence to them.

As for Britannia, it was a mythical, almost imaginary place, an idea, the stuff of legend or of fairy tales. But the centuries wore on, and it became more and more difficult to write it off as a complete fantasy. Merchants began to bring occasional goods into Rome from beyond the fury of Oceanus, and with them tales of a strange, savage, and distant land.

In fact, Britain had maintained a thriving relationship with non-Roman Europe, both mercantile and otherwise, for millennia. And Rome had received from the island both wool and wickerwork.

Toward the end of the third millennium B.C., populations began to move westward from lands north of the Black Sea, disturbing and dislodging native communities. In spite of its remoteness and terrible weather, many groups crossed over Oceanus to Britannia. Among them were peoples known today as the Bell Beaker Folk, because of the numerous drinking pots that have been unearthed in their sites. They were, we might surmise, hard drinkers.

Later waves of harried migrants sought refuge in Britannia, now named the Urn cultures. One of their inventions was the bronze short sword and they made innovations in agriculture and manufacturing. In the centuries during which Rome was establishing itself as a great power, the flood of new arrivals did not abate.

As Rome's boundaries grew, from about the third century B.C., the prevailing belief that the western Oceanus was an endless, treacherous monster of water at the meeting of the Mediterranean Sea and the Atlantic became awkwardly incompatible with the presence of Britannia, and of the goods flowing to and from it. No more were the Pillars of Hercules—today's Strait of Gibraltar, overlooked by their famous, daunting, mountainous rock—the gateway to the ends of the earth.

As a result, over generations, the idea that there was no land west of the continental shores morphed into a new belief—that of *terra inculta*—a lawless expanse of unforgiving waters punctuated by savage islands, without reason or civilization, filled with as much hazard, rage, and monstrosity as the surrounding seas.

This new belief system not only allowed acknowledgment of the existence of Britannia, but in the centuries leading up to its first direct confrontation with Rome gave a justification for its existence.

By around 100 B.C., most wealthy or reasonably educated Romans had an abstract idea of a land "beyond Oceanus." It was said, up to and including the time of Julius Caesar, to be the shape of a triangle with the flat end facing Europe. Even merchants had doubts of its size or shape, and Cicero (along with others) even mistakenly placed it opposite Spain.

An explanation of the myth of Britannia, however, was within easy reach, if only they had known it. The island had been mapped in some detail by a remarkable Greek merchant, navigator, and explorer, Pytheas of Massilia (today's Marseille), who, around 330 B.C., had circumnavigated the island. But again, none of this valuable wisdom seems to have traveled beyond Roman academics.

Pytheas's charts, maps, and observations in his book *On the Ocean,* save for a few fragments, have not survived. But the book is frequently referred to in many classical texts. In one of these the island is referred to as Pretannia—land of the painted people, or tattooed folk—which is the origin of the name Britannia.

Pytheas also established that there were trade links between southwest Britannia and Gallia (more or less today's France). The Britons, he wrote, exported tin and copper directly to Spain and beyond. In fact, Britannia's export of metals and stone to Europe dated back at least two thousand years before he wrote—there was even a tin mining boom in Cornwall between 1600 and 1400 B.C., due to overseas demand, during which British metal spread widely across the Continent. Flint axes and metals from Britannia suggest that trade with the Phoenicians, whose country lay on the east coast of the Mediterranean, was extensive even before this time. Throughout prehistory, Atlantic trade routes existed, and fashions, artifacts, and goods flowed between Britannia and the Continent.

Again, scholars would have known much more about this trade than any ordinary Roman citizen. The Greek historian Diodorus Siculus describes the Britannic tin miners based in the southwestern peninsula of the island as "very fond" of foreigners, and he details the route of their wares to Gallic markets in some detail:

> They prepare the tin, working very carefully the earth in which it is produced. The ground is rocky, but it contains earthy veins, the produce of which is ground down, smelted, and purified. . . . the merchants buy the tin from the natives and carry it over to Gaul; and after traveling overland for about thirty days, they finally bring their loads on horses to the mouth of the Rhone.

The Greco-Roman writer Strabo gives more detail of Britannia and its exports before invasion:

> It bears grain, cattle, gold, silver, and iron. These things, accordingly, are exported from the island, as also hides, and slaves, and dogs that are by nature suited to the purposes of the chase.

Some in Rome would, then, have known of Britain's existence, its armies having colonized the Rhône valley in about 160 B.C. Where were these merchants coming from with their wares? An island beyond Oceanus may not have been the answer expected. It is here we begin to see the trouble that challenged Roman belief in the riverine circle of Oceanus. *Terra inculta* it became.

That is not to say that awe of Oceanus vanished, however. It was still revered and still feared. The seas between mainland Europe and Britannia, Tacitus wrote, were filled with wild currents and tides that not only surrounded the island but penetrated inland via rivers up into its hills and mountains, almost as if Oceanus actually owned and ruled the country.

In the first century B.C., Rome began to accept that there was an uncivilized island, a realm of savages, constantly waging ugly and brutal wars to protect the territorial boundaries of their kingdoms, which constantly shifted depending on the might of either opposing force.

This land was foggy, laid out in mostly flat areas covered with dense forest, but with hilly and mountainous districts; outside of these wooded areas the land was supposedly made up of mired marshland.

The fierce inhabitants lived in mud huts, and, we are told, when cold and hungry they went into an entranced state, or perhaps even one of hibernation, standing in swamps up to their necks with only their heads above water, where they would wait until conditions improved.

The men either fought naked, smeared in colorful dyes, or wore nothing but animal hides, with their hair and their beards long. Bestial rites were performed after a battle—the victorious barbarians would hack off the heads of their slain opponents and present them to those who had fought on horses and chariots. Dark mystics with dangerous and diabolical powers would slice open these heads and pull out the brains to give power to their curses and commandments. Surrounding these magicians, the warriors and their women—for each man had several wives—would light huge fires and, entranced by ceremony, strong drink, and song, indulge in paganistic orgies which could last for days. They supposedly knew nothing of agriculture, or keeping domestic animals of any type, but lived on roots and berries—there were fruits, but no vines or olives.

Worse, though, were stories that deeply disturbed and repelled Romans of the time, as they flew in the face of their sensibilities. The first was human sacrifice: The Britons, they were informed, would ritually murder their kinsfolk to study human entrails for prophetic purposes. The second was even more alarming to Rome's ears: They would frequently eat the flesh of their enemies and drink their blood. Britannia was a land of cannibals.

But these stories of Britannia's inhabitants came mostly from merchants and traders who had deep commercial interests in keeping more and more lurid tales flowing into the ears of appalled but fascinated Romans. As today, narratives of violence, sex, and brutality capture the imaginations of their listeners with not only a sense of revulsion but also a morbid curiosity and delight in sensation. For those involved in commerce, the more appalled they were by the dangers and hazards of Britannia, the more unattractive the island would seem as a prize worth winning for Rome. An absence of Roman bureaucracy meant fewer duties and fewer taxes for them, while also encouraging greater advantage over less-exotic goods and, in turn, greater prices.

What became more evident as time passed was that the mercantile class, while dealing with Britannia's coastal traders, was itself afraid to venture more than a few miles from the ports and shores of Britannia. It is clear that, even as the purveyors of demonic romantic fiction, they were wary of exploring the island's forbidding interior.

By the middle of the first century B.C. the merchants were almost certainly not the only ones spreading these wild rumors. Other travelers probably also began reporting back to Rome yet more terrifying details of overseas barbarism, concreting the myths. It was almost as if, perhaps, a knowledgeable senior Roman was deliberately creating propaganda to increase the bloody reputation of a future foe in a forthcoming conflict.

Those Romans who heard news of Britannia would have learned one thing above all others: The island's natives were more animal than human. Their barbaric practices were so repellent they could never be civilized; as men they were lower than slaves.

Gaius Julius Caesar, an ancestor of Nero and the imperial dynasty, was a giant of the Roman republic, but at the age of forty-six he was in trouble. Born in 100 B.C., he was the dominant personality of his day. He was impatient with the inefficient republican constitution. Rome was governed by a rabble of rowdy aristocrats who tried to manage him but whom he constantly outmaneuvered. He was backed by ordinary citizens. After serving as Consul in 59 B.C., he obtained the combined governorship of southern France, northern Italy, and southeastern Europe, together with the command of four legions.

This is where we find him facing a crisis. Deeply in debt because of unpaid election expenses, Caesar needed a war to restore his finances. He judged that a tribal migration in Gaul could threaten Italy. A quick victory removed that danger, but other tribal groups rose up in arms. The Gauls were effective warriors but lived in communities that were fiercely independent. They were weakened in the field by political divisions.

Caesar viewed Gaul as three distinct regions and peoples, defined by location, culture, and language. There were the Belgae north of the river Seine and west of the Rhine. The area below was known as Gallia, whose people, he noted, referred to themselves as Celts and spoke the Celtic language. To the south were the Aquitani.

Caesar probably thought his Gallic wars would be finished quickly. Parts of Gaul were already on good terms with the republic, among whom were the influential Aedui. Southern France had already been colonized and was known as the Provincia (whence today's Provence).

Years of hard fighting ensued. Caesar engaged with the Gallic tribes piecemeal. He stamped out one fire only to find that another had ignited. By the end of the last campaign season perhaps a million Gauls had lost their lives. Over the coming years Gaul was not simply conquered but Romanized.

While Caesar was campaigning in the north against the Belgae, he encountered particularly fierce and determined resistance. Recognizing a common foe, the many Belgic chieftains of this area (including those of the Atrebates, Viromandui, and Nervii kingdoms) had formed a confederation not simply to challenge his invasion but also to resist Roman influence, which had been creeping into the area since about 150 B.C.

The Belgae were an unusually belligerent people and were not proving easy to win over. Pushing forward into Belgic territory, Caesar was prepared to resort to genocide. After one fierce and bloody confrontation with the Nervii, he declared in his memoir:

> This battle being ended, and the nation and name of the Nervii being almost reduced to annihilation, their old men, together with the boys and women . . . said that their senators were reduced from 600 to three; that from 60,000 men they [were left with] scarcely 500 who could bear arms.

During this time Caesar discovered that there was more than just the occasional trade link between the mythical land of Britannia and the Continent. Various groups from this supposedly backward isle were regularly, and on a large scale, sending significant aid to almost all of his Gaulish enemies: raw metals, weaponry, and other strategically valuable supplies. He also became aware that refugees from all over Gaul were arriving on British shores. But matters became more serious still. Caesar quickly discovered that a Britannic tribe called the Dumnonii, based in the southwest, was sending warriors snaking around the British coast and onto the continent to their aid. His soldiers were now engaging with Britons.

He learned that for at least three centuries there had been a continuous and far more systematic Belgic migration across the sea to Britannia. This dispersal of peoples under pressure from migrant populations in central Europe had probably begun on a small scale as early as about 400 B.C. and gradually crescendoed in the decades and centuries after. So this island beyond Oceanus was no more an object of curiosity. It was not simply a large but unimportant isle of swamps and mists, populated with fearsome but unsophisticated cave dwellers, hunting with spears and gathering roots and berries. It was, at the very least, a barbarian outpost that could present a tangible threat to whatever peace he could eventually bring to Gaul. At the very worst it could present a serious threat to the Continent. To Caesar's mind, Britannia was now officially an enemy of Rome.

Despite Rome's prejudices, Britannia had not been nearly as poorly developed as was thought. The assumption that its savage inhabitants inhabited only mud huts, caves, forests, and swamps was sorely mistaken. The clearing of woodland had begun in the Stone Age and continued through the Bronze Age, and through pollarding, shredding, and coppicing around 500 B.C., if not earlier, almost half of Britannia's wildwood had been cleared, some of it replaced by farmland and some by timber woodland.

This was used not just to fence in animals for clothes and food but to build roundhouses in small farmsteads, for heating, for cooking, for rudimentary vehicles, and, of course, for boats. In seats of power, more elaborate buildings could be found. Hill forts dotted the countryside, especially in the midlands and the west country. A common type of language had seeped in from the Continent and crept slowly across the country, and although there were variations of dialect, this allowed at least basic communication between kingdoms from the southeast, farther north, and farther west. It was no lingua franca, but it was a linguistic tool.

The Belgae exerted a profound effect on the island's development. They revolutionized the storage of corn and other staple cereals by using better-designed pottery, and their manufacture of metal goods created a huge demand for iron as well as tin and copper. The Belgae's import of agricultural tools and skills allowed cultivation of more and different crops as previously barren land became arable.

Even before the mass exodus from mainland Europe, Britannia's distinctive blacksmithery had advanced enormously in the last centuries of the Iron Age, soaked by but never drowning in styles from the Continent. The craft flourished so rapidly that some of the island's most beautiful pre-Roman jewelry—torcs, bands, necklaces, and brooches—were made from precious metals and highly prized enamels. Decorative plates, tankards, buckets, harnesses, and all manner of treasures displayed ever more grace and beauty as artisan skills improved. The representations of animals and humans on pots and cauldrons became more realistic. Even the neck chains for captives and shackles for slaves became objects of distinct style.

Neither Britannia nor its new Belgic enclaves (nor their spreading influence) ever, of course, reached anything like the peaks of sophistication found in Romanized societies. There were no villas, no baths, no underfloor heating, no aqueducts, nor anything close to the architectural splendors of Rome, with its Circus Maximus, Forum, and temple of Jupiter. Its transport system was rudimentary, its roads nothing more than unpaved trackways. But Britannia, with its long-established ability to absorb new customs, religions, and beliefs, had become a swirling mixture of new ideas, new cultures, and age-old tradition.

Before long, Caesar had extended his influence by establishing a rudimentary intelligence network among those Gauls who were loyal to him. He learned of the large kingdom of the Catuvellauni and their growing power in Britannia. The island had become a haven for Belgic and Gallic refugees and a gradual swelling of Catuvellaunian territory had begun, pushing back the boundaries of others through force. Further information gave him a broad, although not detailed, understanding of the two British kingdoms on the coast facing Gaul: the Cantii and the Trinovantes. Both of these were neighbors of the Catuvellauni, and to that tribe's west lay the smaller (but still considerable) Britanno-Belgic kingdom of the Atrebates. None of the three, he judged, would present much in the way of military resistance. They were almost certainly feeling the heat of the bulging Catuvellauni as they began to expand on to their territories and exert ever greater power.

The general began to eye Britannia carefully and to assess the prospect of an invasion. Landing a significant army on its shores would shock its inhabitants—new and old—into the realization that Rome was indeed capable of extending its might across the seas. But there were other prizes to be won.

The Gallic wars had so far done little to service his debts, and by now he would have known of the precious metals emanating from the island—gold, silver, copper, and tin—and there were even tales of rich pearls off the island's coast. Also, the Senate was no doubt becoming impatient of the seemingly stalled Gallic campaign.

To secure a foothold in Britannia, beyond Oceanus—even for a short time—would surely bring amazement and wonder to Rome's plebs and soldiery, while also silencing any criticism from his rivals for political and military power, who, he probably suspected, were already whispering in Rome about his problems in Gaul.

Technically, an invasion of Britannia would be illegal: Wars of aggression were forbidden by Roman law (although this was honored more in the breach than in the observance). But because the southern kingdoms of Britannia had meddled in the affairs of Gaul, he would probably be able to justify such a thing.

And so Caesar began to build a fleet, making no secret of his plans to cross the channel for an invasion. Before long, a line of ambassadors from small Britannic tribes arrived, submitting to Caesar and professing loyalty to Rome. The general simply sent them back across the sea along with a slippery character named Commius, a former Belgic chieftain who claimed good relations with his fellow countrymen. (In the event, the moment Commius landed, the local leader of one British tribe was more than happy to welcome this self-styled diplomat by having him locked in irons and thrown into a dungeon as a potential hostage.)

The arrival of these envoys gave Caesar great confidence. Before the war had started, he thought his enemy was suing for peace.

Shortly before sailing he sent out a reconnaissance ship captained by a certain Velosenus, who turned out to be either an incompetent or a coward; he returned after a week saying he had found no harbor, even though on the route taken he must have passed at least one.

In August 55 B.C., Caesar set out in the dead of night with eighteen warships and eighty transport ships, carrying an invasion force of some ten thousand men.

On his arrival a chaotic battle ensued. Eventually, after facing an avalanche of cavalry, swordsmen, archers, and spearmen, Caesar's army managed to push the Britons back and secure a beachhead.

Soon a gradual trickle of local tribal chieftains came to offer their supplication to Rome, offering their lands, their loyalty, and even hostages—probably young members of local aristocracy—to Caesar. The general even managed to secure the release of his hapless envoy, Commius.

A huge storm erupted, damaging the Roman fleet. Caesar realized that he was in a tactically precarious situation. Because of the terrible storm, he had no cavalry to flank and provide forward scouting for his infantry. He could neither proceed inland nor escape. His decision was to cut his losses, salvage and patch up those boats that could be repaired, and head back to Gaul.

That night, under cover of darkness, Caesar's remaining ships set sail from the beach and back to Gaul.

Given the danger of the mission, the obstacles overcome and the risks involved—and in particular Caesar's failure to scarcely move forward from a beach—his adventure abroad was hardly a success—in fact it had nearly ended in disaster. He had barely left the beach. But we go back to those Roman cultural values and beliefs. The simple fact that he had crossed Oceanus and returned alive with at least most of his men was greeted with marvel and amazement. He might as well have landed on the moon. Rather than punishing him for attacking a kingdom without provocation, the Senate was lavish in its praise, even if only to reflect the genuine awe of the republic's citizens and military. To praise this achievement, Senators voted a public thanksgiving of twenty days. With Caesar seen as the most formidable general Rome had ever produced, he was now more or less untouchable.

Typically, having reflected on the reaction to his supposed success, Julius Caesar decided to go one step further. In the next campaigning season he would not just revisit Britain—he would conquer it.

The following summer he sailed back with an army of twenty-five thousand battle-ready soldiers, along with two thousand cavalry and auxiliaries. They were transported by eight hundred ships, a spectacle so intimidating (it would appear) that this time the landing was not contested. Men and horses disembarked and the ships were left to lie at anchor on an open shore.

The ever energetic Caesar made sure that a base camp was speedily built and a substantial infantry force together with a few cavalry was appointed its guard. By midnight the rest of the army set off into the interior. By dawn they had marched twelve miles when they came under attack from a British force on a fortified hill. The Romans stormed the hill and drove off the enemy.

During the following night a tempest blew up and wrecked the Roman fleet. Undismayed, Caesar then resumed his march.

Meanwhile the southern kingdoms had united under the command of Cassivellaunus, king of the Catuvellauni, to resist the invader. Having lost a full-dress battle, the British leader attempted to outmaneuver Caesar and destroy his base camp and fleet. This also failed and Cassivellaunus sued for peace.

The Roman was happy to oblige, for summer was almost over and the season of autumn storms was approaching. It was time to return to Gaul.

While battling through Gaul, Caesar discovered a strange and mysterious class who seemingly transcended the rivalries and warfare so prevalent in the western zones he was trying to conquer. While most of the population, he noted, were little more than slaves to the nobles, this group paid no taxes, was exempt from military service, and was free to move unhindered from petty politics and internecine warfare. No matter which kingdom or tribe, they were not only able to travel unfettered but were treated always as revered guests. They were called Druids, and they hailed from Britain.

Caesar was almost respectful of these men, despite their deep animosity toward Rome. He wrote that the Druids were, if inclined, able to command mutual Gallic aggressors to lay down their weapons and then, with their apparent wisdom and divine powers, settle scores that may have lasted for decades. How often they used these powers for peace we do not know, but as they also had the right to plunder battlefields for anything of value (rings, torcs, sacred weapons, etc.), it may not have been in their interest to interfere too much.

Druids were not priests, nor seers, nor magistrates, nor intellectuals; instead they encompassed something of all those qualities, and more besides. They understood the movements of the stars and the planets. They were called into kingdoms and tribes to judge the most heinous of crimes; those they found guilty were excluded from society and effectively outlawed. They were shunned and not permitted to communicate with others. When encountered they were treated as pariahs.

They were scientists who could read and write Greek, had knowledge of medicine, and were versed in primitive surgery. However, their rituals and knowledge were a guarded secret and handed down only by oral tradition. This, of course, was how many sages and mystics retained their authority throughout the ancient world. Gauls or Britons may not have understood the concept of calendar. As astronomers, it is possible many Druidic predictions were often based on that knowledge: when to plant crops or when a season of cold would come.

The Druids kept their mystical order alive by adopting disciples and pilgrims, young men not from the aristocracy but the landowning class, to learn their practices. They were taught in sacred groves, then common around the country. These young men supposedly spent as long as twenty years as disciples and were taught that the soul was immortal.

The image of Druids we have today was created by Pliny the Elder, echoing a constant refrain about the Druidic belief in the sacred properties of a parasitic creeper called mistletoe, which wraps itself around trees to suck out nutrients and water from its host. The Druids valued oak trees above all others (it is suggested their very name is derived from "worshippers of oak"), and we are told of Druids dressed in white cutting from these trees their sacred mistletoe with golden sickles. Never mind that any Druid clambering up a tree or even a makeshift ladder would find his white robes covered in dirt, and never mind that a golden sickle would be useless to cut down almost anything:

> The Druids—for that is the name [the Gauls] give to their magicians—held nothing more sacred than the mistletoe and the tree that bears it. . . . clad in a white robe the priest ascends the [oak] tree, and cuts the mistletoe with a golden sickle, which is received by others in a white cloak. They then immolate the victims, offering up their prayers that [their] God will render this gift of his propitious to those to whom he has so granted it. It is the belief with them that the mistletoe, taken in drink, will impart fecundity to all animals that are barren, and that it is an antidote for all poisons.

But there was another, far darker side to the Druids. They were no tree-worshipping saints. Although the Romans sacrificed animals and examined their entrails, the Druids sacrificed humans. This was, to Rome, intolerable behavior. Their "sacred groves" were not circles of lush oaks but large huts made by bending in trees around an altar. These trees were then partially or wholly boarded with timber: Several sources speak of the interior of these groves as caked with human blood. The Druids were the exponents of the three-fold death, and Caesar talks of the wicker man—a huge statue made of dried rushes, grasses, and vines. Inside this structure, shaped like a massive human, the Druids would trap their sacrificial victim before the structure was set alight and burned to the ground.

The Graeco-Roman writer Strabo continues to say that human sacrifices could not take place without Druidic presence, and describes the nature of ritual killings:

> They used to strike a human being, whom they had devoted to death in the back with a sabre, and then divine from his death-struggle. But they would not sacrifice without the Druids. We are told of still other kinds of human sacrifices; for example, they would shoot victims to death with arrows, or impale them in the temples.

He goes on to elaborate on the Druidic idea of the wicker man:

> Having devised a colossus of straw and wood, [they would] throw into the colossus cattle and wild animals of all sorts and human beings, and then make a burnt-offering of the whole thing.

The Druidic forces also appear to have awe-inspired armed forces—Caesar remarks that within a Druidic hierarchy, they would sometimes fight to reach the top.

Who made up these warriors is difficult to discern. It may have been their Druidic students, but there were other young men (who were perhaps deemed unsuitable for teaching) who flocked to the Druids in awe of their powers. Perhaps some of these were trained as soldiers. Whichever is correct, with their belief in reincarnation these fighters were prepared to die for their spiritual masters; they were prepared to conduct suicide missions if necessary. The Druids may have ordered their followers to terrorize the advancing tide of Rome flowing toward their areas of authority. In some ways, they were the equivalent of today's jihadists.

However, they also encouraged headhunting among those who were not intimate members of their cult; to the warrior class of Gallic and British kingdoms and tribes their belief in reincarnation did not seem to apply. Instead they taught the non-initiated that the head was the center of the soul. They encouraged troops in battle to decapitate their enemies, whether wounded or dead. Heads were prized: A warrior was honored by the number he owned. Sealed in wax or oil, they were displayed as badges of honor either on the boundary of or in their homes. Heads could be conjoined; the greatest honor was to graft three heads together. British statues of the time reflect this, possibly as a nod to the three-fold death the Druids espoused.

Strabo was also clearly no fan of the Druids, or those supposedly governed by their laws:

> There is also that custom, barbarous and exotic, which attends most of the northern [Gallic] tribes—I mean the fact that when they depart from the battle they hang the heads of their enemies from the necks of their horses, and, when they have brought them home, nail the spectacle to the entrances of their homes. . . . the heads of enemies of high repute, however, they used to embalm in cedar-oil and exhibit to strangers, and they would not deign to give them back even for a ransom of an equal weight of gold.

The Romans were revolted by Druidic rituals and, as we have seen, human sacrifices in particular. History, of course, is almost always written by the victors, but the evidence of at least some of their practices pepper Roman history with similar tales of their abhorrent behavior. Perhaps the invaders enjoyed their disgust and exaggerated the squalor, but the repugnance was real. In his epic poem, *Pharsalia*, Lucan describes a sacred grove encountered by Julius Caesar, accompanied by some troops:

> *There was a grove, untouched through long centuries,*
> *whose interlacing boughs enclosed cold and shadowy*
> *depths, the sunlight banished far above,*
> *. . . gods were worshipped there with*
> *savage rites, the altars piled high with foul offerings,*
> *and every tree drenched in human blood. On those*
> *boughs, if ancient tales, respectful of deity, may be*

> *believed, the birds feared to perch; in those coverts no wild beast would lie; on that grove no wind ever blew, no lightning bolt from the storm clouds fell.*

Caesar's men were so frightened by the grove they were left petrified, unable to swing their axes to smash down the reeking grove, and it was left to the general to cut down the first tree before they could.

That the Druids held control of the religious sensibilities of the Gauls and the Britons may have seemed of little consequence to Caesar—perhaps he regarded them as an irritation, to be met with simple destruction of groves and shrines. As he pushed toward Oceanus they began to retreat westward from his lines. Perhaps their cover was blown by the advanced knowledge the Romans held of star-gazing and calendar. Perhaps the chiefs and kings were already becoming sick of these meddling magicians, who, despite their powers, were unable to halt the steady progress of the Roman war machine. Perhaps the Gallic population was relieved that the prospect of being burned to death in a giant flammable effigy of a man was becoming redundant. Whichever, the Romans came to lose patience with the Druids and their megalomanic sacrifices as well: Augustus made the practice of Druidism illegal, and Claudius went further. He introduced steep penalties for any association with the upstart priests, who were busy attempting to convince their communities to defy any interference from Roman troops or, in particular, the Roman culture that stripped them of their authority.

Whatever the weight given to those possibilities, they are ultimately mere speculation. By the time of Nero, the Druids had all but withdrawn from Gaul and retreated across the waves to their spiritual home, Britannia.

But more was to come of them as we shall see.

On the face of it, Julius Caesar had gained very little from his two expeditions to Britannia. He was lucky to leave the island with his army more or less intact. Bad weather and his own impulsiveness had contributed to military failure.

In fact, Caesar's fabled good luck held out. The general view in

Rome was astonishment that an army of theirs had reached the ends of the earth, even if the practical outcomes were meager.

Caesar had also impressed the British locals. Whatever mistakes he had made they could see clearly the long-term superiority of the legions. The Romans' departure for Gaul did not mean that they had gone away for good. Caesar and, in the long run, Rome was here to stay. Before leaving the island, Caesar agreed peace treaties with the various tribal kingdoms (including the Trinovantes) he had encountered. Tribute was imposed and (once more) hostages were taken to secure obedience. There is no reason to believe that on this occasion the Britons defaulted as soon as Caesar's back was turned.

The politics of the island was complicated and fluid. Small political units competed with one another for dominance with fire and sword. The most powerful were the landlocked Catuvellauni. Their territory stretched from the Thames northward to the midlands. They were ambitious and wanted to enlarge their realm. They trained their acquisitive eyes on their neighbors the Trinovantes, who inhabited a coastal region now comprising the counties of Essex, Hertfordshire and Suffolk, and adjoining the East Anglian kingdom of the Iceni. The Trinovantian capital was Camulodunon, modern Colchester.

The third leading kingdom was that of the Atrebates, an offshoot of a Gallic tribe of the same name, which settled in Berkshire and Hampshire. Their ruler was that devious fellow Commius who acted as Caesar's go-between when passing on messages for senior Britons. A few years later he was to turn coat and support Vercingetorix, leader of the last great but doomed revolt in Gaul against the Roman invader. For this Commius was not forgiven. One of Caesar's lieutenants tried to have him assassinated, but he escaped with a head wound. A second attempt failed too, and he appears to have fled to Britannia. Eventually he sued successfully for peace, promising to live where he was told and no longer to oppose Caesar—on condition that he would never again have to meet a Roman.

Caesar recognized that Cassivellaunus was a menace to the other local kingdoms and that he would assure his popularity with them if he punished him. He ordered him "in strong terms to do no harm to Mandubracius [king of the Trinovantes] or the Trinovantes."

This policy seems to have survived the civil wars and was adopted by Augustus. He sought to maintain Roman influence and keep warring rulers from one another's throats. He seems to have considered a new invasion from time to time, always to postpone it.

The court poet Quintus Horatius Flaccus (our Horace) writes that the great waterways of the known world revered Augustus's name and did not resort to war against him:

. . . the Nile, who still conceals her secret
springs, and the Danube and the hurrying Tigris
and the whale-burdened sea
that bursts on the exotic British coast
. . . pause at your name and lay their weapons down.

So in his relations with the British Augustus relied on diplomacy rather than force. So far as we can tell, he did his best to ensure a balance of power between the main British kingdoms. Some of the better-off Britons even sent their children to study in Rome. However, following a Roman defeat on the Rhine in 17 B.C., the Catevellaunian king of the day, a certain Tasciovanus, attacked the Trinovantes and captured Camulodunon. This broke the terms of a previous deal with Julius Caesar. The presence in Gaul at the time of the disapproving Augustus was sufficiently threatening to persuade Tasciovanus to withdraw.

The agile Commius was succeeded as king of the Atrebates by three sons, one after another. The eldest, Tincommius, was deposed for unknown reasons and made his way to Rome, where he presented himself to Augustus as a suppliant. The emperor thought this event to be important enough to mention in his memoir, *Res Gestae,* but he does not explain why.

We know little more about the politics of the time than that the Catuvellauni were still upsetting the neighbors. Their new ruler after Tasciovanus was his son, the able and long-lived Cunobelin (Shakespeare's Cymbeline), who held power for almost forty years. His name translates, not inappropriately, as Strong Dog.

Like his predecessors on the Catuvellaunian throne, he devoted his energies to expanding his kingdom. He conquered the Trinovantes and regained Camulodunon. This was strictly against Rome's British policy, but it may be that this had changed. Shaken by the loss in A.D. 9 of three entire legions at the hands of a German tribal army, Augustus and his successor, Tiberius, believed that the empire should be kept within its existing bounds. Foreign adventures were to be avoided. Cunobelin seems to have been appointed a Roman client king and officially allowed to style himself Rex on his coinage. He now had a free hand.

The last of Commius's sons to hold power among the Atrebates was Verica. Thanks to Catuvellaunian encroachments, he ruled only over the West Sussex coastline, and even that sliver of land was lost when Verica went to Rome to appeal for help.

He could not have arrived at a more convenient moment, for the new emperor Claudius was looking for a pretext to launch a war of aggression against the British.

Claudius would take a more aggressive approach. When he succeeded Caligula in 41, the disabled Claudius had had no military experience, but as the ruler of a military monarchy, it was essential that he be seen to lead his legions to a victory. He decided to annex southern Britannia to the empire. This was not a new scheme. Caligula had proposed an invasion. Suetonius claims that he drew up his army on the shore at Boulogne:

> No one had the least idea what he had in mind when, suddenly, he gave the order "Gather sea-shells!" He referred to the shells as "plunder from the ocean, due to the Capitol and the Palace," and made the troops fill their helmets and tunic fronts with them.

Perhaps this was meant as a joke, or perhaps it never happened at all. Either way, we can be sure that Caligula's military laid their well-thought-out plans and that Claudius took them over.

It was determined that an experienced general should fight and win the war, after which the princeps would arrive to receive the enemy's surrender in person. He would be hailed by his troops as a victorious general, or *imperator*.

In 43 a Roman expeditionary force gathered at Gesoriacum (today's Boulogne in France). Narcissus was sent out to be Claudius's eyes and ears, and he witnessed dissent among the legionaries. They did not know what to expect of a campaign in a strange land and were panicking. They went on strike and refused to listen to their officers, so Narcissus climbed the speaker's platform and started to address them.

For a former slave to act in this way was breathtakingly impertinent and went against every patriotic Roman's sense of propriety. It reminded the men of the winter festival of Saturnalia, when masters and servants reversed roles for a day. Instead of being angry, they shouted him down with the festival greeting of "Io Saturnalia," burst into laughter, and returned to work in good humor.

The army probably consisted of four legions with auxiliaries, or in total about forty thousand men. It crossed the Channel and after marching inland found the enemy lined up in large numbers on the far bank of the river Medway. The Romans met with fierce resistance, which they overcame only after two days' heavy fighting. They then established a solid bridgehead at the river Thames (from the British Tems).

It was time to summon Claudius. He had probably made his way from Rome before the campaign started. He was accompanied by many senior politicians (to prevent them from making mischief at home during his absence, we may surmise). He was within easy reach, and on being called, quickly sailed across the Channel and joined his army, which marched on Camulodunon. Once there, the emperor held an impressive victory parade featuring some war elephants he had brought with him. Elephants were unreliable on the battlefield, where they tended to panic and blunder onto their own side, but on ceremonial occasions such as this they made a profound impression. No Briton had ever seen such a huge beast. They must have been terrified.

The princeps was soon back in Rome, where he declared victory and held a triumph attended by defeated British leaders. In the old days, generals of the republic had celebrated military success with this colorful army procession through the streets of Rome, but under the empire, a triumph was awarded only to the emperor and members of his family. All military glory went to the commander in chief, the princeps of the day, whether or not he had fought in the battle. The best a general could hope for was triumphal insignia—that is, the dress and privileges traditionally granted to a *triumphator,* but without the procession at the head of his troops. Nero, too, would receive credit for his generals' successes as much as for his diplomatic wisdom.

Despite the official victory, hostilities dragged on. Cunobelin had died in about 40, and British opposition to Rome was led by two of his sons, Caratacus and Togodumnus. Togodumnus died at the Medway. After the invasion Caratacus went on fighting the legions, led by Britannia's second governor, Publius Ostorius Scapula.

As a commander Scapula was tactically astute but tactless as a politician. He announced that he intended to disarm all Britons south of the rivers Trent and Severn. This so infuriated the pro-Roman kingdom of the Iceni (today's north Norfolk) that they rose in revolt alongside their neighbors. Scapula defeated the rebels and went on to campaign successfully in Wales. The Iceni were allowed to maintain their independence, but it was doubtless now that, after checking with Scapula, they made the pro-Roman Prasutagus their king.

In 50, Caratacus, after years of guerrilla campaigning, sought refuge with Cartimandua, queen of the Brigantes, who headed a powerful confederation of tribes in northern England. This was an unwise decision, for the queen was loyal to the Romans, and she handed him over to them, along with his wife.

Cartimandua herself came to grief. She divorced her husband, Venutius, after falling in love with his armor bearer. He took this badly and led a number of rebellions against her. Her Roman protectors kept her in power until 69, when she was evacuated and disappeared from history. Her ex-husband took over the kingdom.

Brought to Rome under sentence of death, Caratacus had nothing better to expect than strangulation in the tiny prison overlooking the Forum, the Tullianum. His body would then be sluiced down a shaft into the river Tiber.

Before that could happen, he was presented to the Roman public. He stood in chains in front of two imposing daises, on one of which the emperor sat enthroned and on the other the empress. The Praetorian Guard stood at arms and a large crowd gathered to see the show. Caratacus was given leave to speak and plead for his life. His prospects were bleak.

He spoke politely but unrepentantly: "If my high birth and my luck had been matched with only a moderately good outcome, I would have come to your capital as a friend rather than as a prisoner."

What was to be done with him? He had cost the Romans time, treasure, and blood, but he was brave, loyal, and true. There was a word for these qualities in Latin—*pius,* which was often applied to Aeneas. The reputation of Caratacus had spread beyond Britannia and even reached Italy. He was the kind of enemy Romans liked to like.

Having listened to his speech, Claudius delivered a surprise: He announced that the prisoner was pardoned. Relieved of their chains, he and his family were free to go. The British chieftain thanked the emperor warmly and took care to offer Agrippina, seated in her separate state, the same homage and gratitude as he had given her husband. He had been well briefed.

Some time later Caratacus and his party were wandering about the city looking at the sights. He exclaimed to some Romans accompanying him: "And can you, then, who own such buildings, and so many of them, covet our miserable huts."

The ultimate fate of Caratacus is unknown. He will not have been allowed to return to his native land and probably ended his days in a comfortable villa in Italy.

Nero is likely to have attended this remarkable ceremony and will have watched with interest the clemency of the princeps. What could he have drawn from it? It looks very much as if the event, the parade, the speech, and the response were prearranged. Emperors do not enjoy surprises. Great enemies of the past—say, the Numidian monarch Jugurtha or Vercingetorix—had ended up dead in the Tullianum. But now the empire was stable and there was no need to be daunted by foreign barbarians. Forgiveness would help pacify conquered provinces and win over domestic public opinion.

There was a lesson here for the young prince, which he duly heard and digested. When he was in power he would seek an opportunity to present such a spectacle of mercy and of magnanimity, but even more splendid.

Camulodunum, the new capital of Britannia, was ten miles in area and occupied a strong defensive position on a ridge. It was protected by rivers on two sides and by earthen ramparts and ditches, perhaps the most extensive in Britain. Ships made their way a few miles up the river Colne bearing goods from the Continent. Soon new stone buildings would begin to rise. In time the settlement would contain all the features, the columns and the statues, that a Roman who lived in any part of the empire would expect to see.

Instead of liberating the settlement, the Romans took it, Latinized its name to Camulodunum, and began to build a camp, even with its own elephant enclosure. Within months this became a permanent barracks and perhaps in 44, a project to build a legionary fortress was begun at a vantage point that is today the town center. This, and the barracks, was to be home to about five thousand troops.

The Trinovantes were deeply unhappy with the Romans. After expelling the Catuvellauni from Camulodunon, they initially expected the Romans to hand them back their ancient lands. After all, Caesar had explicitly brokered a deal to shield them from further Catuvellaunian expansion and demanded yearly tribute to Rome in recompense. (Whether this was paid or not is unknown—there is no record. However, the kingdom, probably anticipating further Roman incursions within just a few years, would have been unwise to default.)

The Romans were unsentimental about money. They expected

the empire to bring in a profit. Ever a philosopher concerned with the virtuous life, Seneca willingly invested funds in the new province of Britannia, but he would be ruthless if he failed to make a good return. In an essay titled *The Happy Life,* he confides more candidly than he intended:

> To some I will offer assistance, *in certain cases actually forcing them to accept* [my italics]. . . . At no time do I register names more carefully than when making gifts. "What's that?" you say. "Do you give only to take back?" . . . one should store away a benefit like a deeply buried treasure, only to be dug up in time of necessity.

Seneca was only one of many unscrupulous investors who made money available to Britons that he could call in whenever he wanted after having given the impression that he was giving them a gift. Other money men also forced loans on powerless conquered peoples. Some were honest dealers who practiced mutually advantageous trade, but others paid for infrastructure or public works themselves in order to Romanize a province's way of life while still expecting a generous dividend.

Somewhere around or soon after the commencement of full-scale construction, Seneca forced massive loans upon both the Trinovantes and the Iceni, totaling 40 million sesterces, which they did not ask for or want. (To give an idea of the size of this loan, it would have paid fifty thousand troops for a year.) The lowest interest rate for loans such as these was 12 percent—but the more common rate would be 20 percent.

In 49, Claudius decided that Colchester was to become a full-blown urban community known as a *colonia* (the first in Britain). It would also become the capital of Britannia. There were two main functions of a *colonia:* One was to provide accommodation and housing for retired soldiers, and the other was to assimilate surrounding kingdoms and tribes into the new Roman way of life. It was also the highest status of a city outside Rome, as it was allowed to self-govern. Kings, aristocrats, and even local tribal leaders would be offered the prospect of Roman citizenship, provided they accepted their new rulers and imposed their values and legal doctrines on their subjects. The town was renamed Colonia Victricensis (City of Victory).

Using these *coloniae* on the edge of the empire as bastions of high Roman life and civilization was a common policy during the days of both the republic and the empire. It almost always succeeded. Villas, fine wines, olives, decorative tiles, and other luxuries generally attracted the wealthy and influential Britons. In a *colonia,* what else did the Romans offer conquered and obedient peoples? Sanitation, medicine, education, public order, irrigation, roads, and freshwater systems were just some of the inducements for locals.

Rarely did the Romans interfere with local religion and beliefs. Attempted conversion to the Roman gods was bound to lead to trouble. (A good example is Judaea, where the religious rights of the Jews had been more or less permitted even after their lands had been conquered.) But as far as Gaul and Britannia were concerned, the meddling Druids, who not only interfered with this assimilation but also vehemently discouraged it, were unacceptable.

The Gallic Druids, who had escaped across the sea to Britain during Caesar's war, had joined up with their British counterparts and fanned the flames of pocket tribal rebellions, which wasted time, money, and soldiers. More importantly, the Druids, as we have seen, had tremendous authority over every kingdom and every tribe. Because of this, the Romans hated the Druids: and, because of the threat to their powers, the Druids hated the Romans.

On his accession in 54, Nero inherited as governor of Britannia one Gaius Aulus Didius Gallus. He had served as Prefect of Cavalry in the province of Asia and as governor of Sicily. For ten years he held the unexciting but crucial post of superintendent of Rome's aqueducts. He thought his appointment to Britannia something of a comedown. He spent his time suppressing rebellions against Roman rule and was criticized for being reactive and defensive.

After five years in the post he was followed by Quintus Veranius, who abandoned the policy of simply maintaining the status quo. He had been chosen by Nero to conquer what is now Wales, in the hope of finding the elusive silver and gold he coveted. This campaign had been far more difficult than he had anticipated. The kingdom of the Silures had proven particularly resilient, using the art of forest ambush that so typified British tribal fighting of the time. After only a year in office, Veranius unexpectedly fell ill and died. Suetonius Paulinus was sent out to finish the job. In 59 he became the fifth governor of Britannia.

The new governor was highly regarded as a tough military leader and strategist. As a general he had suppressed a serious revolt in Mauretania (present-day Algeria and Morocco) and become the first man to lead an army over the Atlas Mountains.

Nero appointed Paulinus because of his record as an aggressive and energetic commander. The emperor needed somebody who could quickly subdue the west of the island. Paulinus was soon convinced his troops were battle-ready (this would not have taken long—they had been well trained by Veranius) and decided to fight his way across Wales. He had available for the purpose four legions: Legio II Augusta, Legio IX Hispania, Legio XIV Gemina, and Legio XX Valeria Victrix.

The legion was the most efficient war machine of its day. It was an infantry formation of about five thousand heavily armed Roman citizens, divided into ten tactically flexible cohorts, and was accompanied by a similar number of auxiliaries recruited locally, mostly cavalry and light-armed troops.

Before radical military changes made by Gaius Marius in about 107 B.C.—known as the Marian reforms—Rome's armies had been made up of militias of Italian civilians, called on as and when needed. They were followed by baggage trains hauled by mules, with a trail of merchants, suppliers, prostitutes, and various ne'er-do-wells. Although the soldiers were trained, at the end of any hostility they simply went back to their homes. But by the time Paulinus was fighting in Britannia, everything had changed. The legionaries were salaried, hardened, strong, committed, and highly professional soldiers.

It's worth taking a very brief look at the might, stamina, and strength of a single legionary by examining his training. After signing up to the army, he would spend the first four months on road marches until he was able to complete almost 19 miles in five hours. After that, he was kitted up in full gear and forced to complete a march of 22 miles—again in five hours. His kit included his helmet, armor, weapons, cooking utensils, rations, a wax bladder containing a mixture of water and vinegar, palisade stakes, a sickle, and entrenching tools (including a small pickax). Yet despite this staggering load, no military unit in the ancient world could match the speed of a legion.

Then came months of weapons training. The legionary would be taught to fight with a heavy wooden sword by running at and attacking a tall, wide wooden stake as his enemy while using an interlaced withe shield almost as tall as he was. He would be taught to thrust, not swing, his sword—a move senior soldiers thought too dangerous, as a slashing movement could easily be seen coming as well as exposing the soldier's body. At the same time as learning sword technique, he would be taught to throw heavy wooden javelins as far as 100 feet, ensuring they landed at the best possible angle to kill a man. Gradually he would be involved in one-on-one training, until he progressed to the lighter metal *gladius* (sword) and a *pilum*—a six-and-a-half-foot throwing spear. In the case of Claudian and Neronian campaigns in Britannia, it appears that the Romans carried two javelins (including, perhaps, the deadly *falcata,* although there is no firm archaeological evidence for this).

Finally the legionary would be tutored in Roman battlefield tactics, including formations on the command "Form a wedge" (*cuneum formate*), the *testudo* (tortoise), and the triple line. The wedge was one of the most important of these. If seen from above, it would look like an arrowhead made up of men, its tip facing the enemy.

In A.D. 60, Paulinus's legions were in key strategic areas. Legio II was stationed in Isca Dumnoniorum (today's Exeter), a town in the southwest peninsula of Britannia, at the lower end of the Fosse Way and south of the river Severn. Legio IX was in the newly established

Lindum (today's Lincoln, about 120 miles due north of London), while Legio XX was based in Usk, roughly twenty-five miles northeast of Cardiff.

Legio XIV was fighting with Paulinus, who had more or less subdued the Silures and was battling toward Mona (now Anglesey), the sacred island home and stronghold of the Druids, in the hope of destroying their power base by desecrating their most important shrines and sacred groves.

Meanwhile, back in Camulodunum, the retired Roman soldiers and their families were expanding their territory into Trinovantian lands. Every veteran was given not only a house but also a small parcel of land. As the population of Colchester began to grow, within the city itself there was no room for new land allowances so plots were allocated outside, which encroached on Trinovantian boundaries.

There was worse. Some of the Trinovantes were treated as underlings, others thrown into jail for the most minor of misdemeanors—or none at all. Part of the money the kingdom had been given in credit, both by Seneca and by loan sharks, was extorted from them to build a huge, ornate building in the town, the temple of Claudius. As if that were not injustice enough, the Trinovantes were forced to build it themselves—for no pay—under the instruction of Roman architects. They were effectively slaves, and this was something Britons bitterly resented. As Tacitus wrote:

> The Britons themselves submit to the levy, the tribute and the other charges of Empire with cheerful readiness, provided that there is no abuse. That they bitterly resent: for they are broken in to obedience, not to slavery.

The mistreatment of the Trinovantes no doubt played into the hands of the Druids, who were seeking to darken Rome's name across the country since the invasion. So as far as they were concerned, the exploitation of the Trinovantes was, at last, concrete evidence of the invaders' cruelty. Not only that, but the monstrous temple of the divine Claudius—"the very man who enslaved Britain"—became a symbol of hatred.

Druidism—regarded as something of an anti-Roman terrorist group—had become ever more elusive and clandestine.

In particular, the Druids did not want a repeat of their experience in Gaul of being gradually Romanized. Druidic plotting, interference, and violence in tribes had initially led to flare-ups, rebellions, and the ritual of human sacrifice. But as the years went by, the cult of the severed head all but disappeared, as tribal and internecine warfare became rarer and almost ceased altogether. As Rome's Gallic towns and cities flourished as mercantile centers with their new goods, buildings, and public services, Druidic influence not only weakened but became resented. The danger of annihilation led them to flee from Gaul back to their spiritual home, Britannia. The advance of Rome into the country threatened to push them into irrelevance.

The Druids, who had factions in every kingdom, probably further infiltrated the Trinovantian territory with their student followers—young men who could stir up and add fuel to the flames of resentment. This faction was known for its ability to twist the truth and for its ruthlessness in thwarting Roman progress at almost any cost. Having been promised immortality, these followers held such faith in the power of their dark arts, as we have seen, that they were not even afraid of death; if need be, they were prepared to undertake suicide missions for their cause.

At the same time that the Trinovantes' anger was growing, the governor was pushing forward to capture the island of Mona, the cult's nerve center and sanctuary, with the aim of destroying their shrines and in particular their bloodstained sacred groves. Mona appears to have been sent valuable and exotic tribute from every British kingdom throughout the land, holding a sacrarium of great treasures. Destroying the outpost, Paulinus believed, would show that Rome was invincible, and the myths of the fabled Druidic powers would quickly fade to nothing.

With Paulinus on maneuvers in Wales, responsibility for the day-to-day administration of Britannia fell to the procurator, or treasurer, of the new province, Catus Decianus. He was probably a former centurion, and, with the provincial governor away, would have been responsible for tasks such as the building of roads, the setting of boundaries, and the development of towns. He would oversee the building of the theater, the basilica, Roman baths, the forum, and of course the temple of Claudius in Camulodunum, while also enforcing taxation and tribute.

Because of his financial duties, the procurator's base had moved from the capital to Londinium (today's London), the location where most merchants were trading due to easy access along the Thames estuary and the network of roads that met there. After the Claudian invasion, the town started as a small and cramped place, covering an area of just half a square mile. Even though there had been no settlement there before the Romans arrived, the area had been contested territory and the site of many border wars. This was probably a consequence of its proximity to the river Thames, and it appears that the land was variously held by the Trinovantes, the Catuvellauni, and the Cantii.

The Romans originally classed Londinium as a *vicus,* meaning a village, and despite its rapidly growing population and convenience for mercantile activity it was not until 49 that it became a *municipium* (town). Tacitus writes that despite its commercial activity it did not have the same status in A.D. 60 as Camulodunum, which was still the capital of Britannia:

> Londinium, which did not have the distinction of being a *colonia,* was much frequented by a number of merchants and trading vessels.

The gradual worsening of the Trinovantes' relationship with Rome was summed up by Tacitus, especially the invaders' policy of forcing young men to take on more and more work for them or fight in their auxiliary army. Many were made to work as virtual slaves, quarrying for stone, stripping forests of their timber, or baking wet clay for tiles, all of which the Romans required for their Mediterranean-style buildings:

> "If," cried they, "we bend our necks to the yoke, the Romans do but lay on heavier burdens, as if we bore them lightly.
>
> "We used only to have one king at a time: now we have two; our lives are the prey of the military governor, while our goods are the prey of the civil commissioner. . . . as it is, a pack of effeminate cowards (for that is what the most of them are) plunder our homes, carry off our children, and then force us to serve in their ranks, as though we could face death well enough in any cause except our country's."

As if these feelings among them were not enough, the Romans further antagonized the Trinovantes by forcing them not only to build and pay for but also to worship at the loathed temple of Claudius, which had not yet been completed. The various tribes that made up the kingdom, especially those near Camulodunum, were expected to serve the imperial cult. But this was an expensive business, and it drained too much money from too few within the territory. "Men chosen as priests had to squander their whole fortunes under the pretence of a religious ceremonial," Tacitus tells us. Still more money was needed to help build the town, which the Romans were happy to lend; but a loan of money was not a practice Britannia's kingdoms were used to—their rudimentary society allowed only gifts, purchases, and none but the smallest items to be taken in trust. The idea of paying back such huge loans was something most tribes probably did not comprehend at all.

This presented Catus with a problem: There was too much lending going on in Britannia, and the population did not have enough hard cash to repay it. To make Catus's precarious situation even worse, Seneca, who had such huge investments in the country, was beginning to recognize the problem as well, and began to strong-arm the procurator to extract his remaining debts and send them back to Rome.

Becoming aware of this trouble, merchants and loan sharks also began to call in their loans. The amounts of money required weren't there—it was tied up in property, new country houses, villas, public buildings, the provision of education and the like. As the man responsible for servicing the province's finances he must have realized that Britannia's economy was heading for a credit crunch.

Fortuitously for Catus, at around this time a client king named Prasutagus died. He was the ruler of the Iceni, based in a large area to the north of the Trinovantes, covering today's Norfolk and parts of south Suffolk and east Cambridgeshire. This ruler had almost certainly been vetted by Scapula as a reliable leader of the wealthy Iceni kingdom and granted Roman citizenship, with the understanding that he was to act as a client king—that is, one who recognizes Roman rule but governs in a semiautonomous way, ultimately subservient to the governor of the province first and the procurator second. (Again, to take Judaea at the time of Jesus as an example, Herod Antipas was tolerated as the ruler of a client kingdom but lacked meaningful power, which ultimately lay with the governor, Pontius Pilate.)

The area then occupied by the Iceni is flat, or at most gently rolling, with huge skies. The rainfall is relatively low compared to much of Britannia, and the climate suits the growing of crops, as it has from the earliest times. The eastern coastline (which has been eroded over the centuries by up to one and a half miles) was then dominated by trading harbors, and spectacular Iron Age hoards have been unearthed, suggesting that the Iceni became wealthy through commercial exchange. However, some visitors from across the sea were unwelcome, and coastal forts were built to discourage raiders.

It appears the Iceni bred and broke horses not only for their local tribes but for export to other kingdoms and perhaps even to Gaul. Horses were a huge status symbol in Britannia and even more so when paired with elaborately decorative chariots, of which the Iceni produced many. With a large boundary of ocean to its north and east, huge quantities of salt could be extracted, ground, and sold—this was a valuable commodity across the empire, especially for preserving meat. The Iceni specialized in skilled pottery and metalworking; they also had ready access to iron.

The kingdom minted its own coins, mostly featuring horses (although some carried the impression of boars). The royal family and its tribes were extremely wealthy in comparison to those of most other kingdoms.

After Prasutagus's death, presumably as an attempt to please Rome and to secure the royal family's status, he left half of his fortune to Nero and the other half to his two daughters. His wife, Boudica, was cut out of his will altogether; why, we do not know. In Gaul and among the Belgae it was common for a king to leave his wife as sole heir.

For one reason or another it is clear that Boudica's accession to the throne had been seen as a problem by Prasutagus. It may well have been that she had made public some anti-Roman statements. Perhaps she had refused citizenship in the empire, or accepted it reluctantly. It may have been that the marriage to Prasutagus had been arranged for political reasons and she was originally from another kingdom. Tacitus says she herself was "a woman of royal race," which perhaps indicates that she was not brought up an Icenian. One theory is that Boudica was a Druidess, but there is scant evidence for this, although we do know she practiced Britannia's old traditions of divination.

In any event, the future of the kingdom was now in doubt. It was unusual for women to rule, and neither Boudica nor her daughters—who we are told were little more than children—were acceptable rulers as far as Catus was concerned. To cap it all, Rome had a growing habit of seizing the lands and property of client kingdoms after their rulers had died.

With the powerful Seneca on his back, now demanding that every last penny of his loans be repaid immediately, Catus proposed that the Iceni territory would lose its client kingdom status and be annexed to Rome. Nero (who may also have been under some gentle pressure from Seneca) simply rubber-stamped the deal. No doubt more eyes in Rome were watching the finances of the province, even if they had not yet realized the potential trajectory of Britannia's economy. So Catus, in his capacity as Roman treasurer, formally demanded the full contents of Prasutagus's will for the empire. No longer would the Iceni simply pay an annual tribute to the empire: Rome would impose laws and taxes across the population.

This was a delaying tactic in financial terms. Converting pigs and sheep into gold would take time. Catus needed to come up with something more substantial, and fast. He ended up with a clever and skulduggerous plan: He would start creating money from nothing.

His first move was one that would serve him well, with the added benefit of pushing the Iceni to virtual bankruptcy. When Prasutagus had been installed on the throne after the kingdom's battle with Scapula in 47, one of his first moves was to buy off his nobles, who obviously needed to be persuaded that an enemy one minute was a friend the next. Many of the Iceni tribes would have lost relatives in their rebellion against Rome, only to have their weapons confiscated and suddenly ordered to be allies of the empire.

Prasutagus had therefore given gifts (mostly land) to his barons to buy their cooperation. Details of these had at the time been meticulously detailed and submitted to Claudius, who approved and provided compensation to the new king. But, Catus thought, what if they hadn't been gifts from Prasutagus—but loans? The land "given" to the aristocracy would have to be paid back to him as part of the late king's legacy. This meant he could put up parcels of land for auction immediately.

This idea seems to have worked well for the procurator—so well, in fact, that he declared that all of the land and money Claudius had given to loyal kings across Britannia ("the foremost Britons") after the invasion of 43 had not been gifts, but *loans,* and Catus wanted them paid back.

But as Boudica would not surrender the Iceni's treasures nor its Royal Estate, Catus was on the horns of a dilemma. He did not want the valuables to be distributed elsewhere, and Boudica's refusal even to meet him may have suggested she was creating some kind of defense system—dykes, ramparts, and other fortifications—and calling in the finest of the kingdom's warriors to defend her.

Naturally, when they heard Catus's demand, any remaining pro-

Roman feeling among the Iceni people must have immediately turned to dust. Merchants to whom the Iceni owed money, along with their guards, moved in, seizing whatever of the kingdom's loot or lands they could. The proud tribes and their chieftains were being systematically impoverished.

Boudica, meanwhile, had been crowned as the queen of the Iceni in the kingdom's capital at Venta Icenorum (Market of the Iceni—today's Caistor St. Edmund). A proud and intelligent woman, she may have thought this kind of demand was not Catus's to make—it would be action that only the governor could oversee, and (perhaps rightly) she guessed Paulinus would never dream of instigating a large tribal standoff so close to Britannia's capital. Some suggest she may even have sent an appeal to Paulinus, but if she did, it either never arrived, was ignored by one of his staff, or was disregarded by him.

She was wrong about Catus's position as deputy. Catus's relationship to Paulinus was more complex. It was the procurator's duty to report back to Rome if he thought the governor was in error, especially over financial matters. He probably thought of himself as more of an official backstop, should the governor misbehave. Besides which, with the governor absent fighting a campaign, there was no doubt he was indeed in charge of the province.

Boudica defied his order and refused to hand over any of her treasures, lands, or citizens to Rome. She saw the throne as hers and the Iceni people as her subjects. Importantly, so did they.

But Catus was determined: She would pay up, and pay up fast. There was a chance that merchants and their vigilante militias would call in yet more of the Iceni's riches.

Boudica refused again, probably not fully understanding the power, determination, and greed of the procurator. Catus had a significant number of Paulinus's guards at his disposal—perhaps even as many as four or five centuries (that is, between four hundred and five hundred men, plus an equal number of auxiliaries, making eight hundred to one thousand men) barracked at a fort near Londinium.

What happened next was extraordinary, cruel, and brutal. It was the beginning of the domino effect that would cause a catastrophe for both Rome and Britannia.

It may be that Catus ordered his centurions to do it, that he spoke obliquely to them about the problems the Iceni were causing or told them to wrest whatever they could from the Iceni grip at any cost. Whichever it was, it was enough to spark one of the biggest uprisings and ethnic cleansing the Roman empire had ever faced in its entire history.

Frustrated by the lack of cooperation from Boudica, he sent the soldiers he controlled, along with moneymen, servants, and slaves, to confront her and demand payment. But as soon as they crossed the border into Iceni territory it became obvious these men were intent on more than just a march to Venta Icenorum. Instead they fought from tribe to tribe, forcing chieftains out of their lands, torching buildings, and leaving chaos, fear, and panic in their wake. They plundered, looted, and even made Iceni freemen slaves.

Because many of the Iceni's men had been dragged far away to fight as auxiliaries with the legions, each small farmstead or tribal group had less than its natural quota of young and fit defenders, and the kingdom's professional warriors, anticipating nothing of this sort of unruly behavior, were scattered over the kingdom. As the Romans careered across the territory almost unchallenged, the nobles were stripped of their rank, gold, and ancestral treasures—some of which would have been of deep religious significance to them. Using tactics more associated with barbarian ruthlessness than Roman discipline, they eventually pillaged their way to Boudica's palace.

However many guards Boudica had to protect her, they were not capable of or accustomed to dealing with the wanton violence meted out by these fit, maniacal, professional soldiers. Slaves and accountants ransacked the palace for its treasures. And it is here, according to Tacitus, that the most significant assaults took place. Prasutagus's entire family was enslaved. Boudica's two young daughters, almost certainly virgins, were gang-raped by the Roman soldiers. As for

Boudica herself, she was dragged out of the palace and publicly flogged. For a proud warrior queen, there was almost no greater humiliation than to be whipped half senseless in front of her own people.

Just before this extraordinary episode, every Druid would have been in a state of great trepidation.

Romanization had pushed the Druids west from Gaul back to Britannia, and now they were being pushed to the west coast there too. Their squalid, gory sacred groves in Gaul, the east of England, and then the midlands had been systematically destroyed.

As we have seen, the Druids had already feared they were on borrowed time as Paulinus pushed his way further west through Wales; but then came hard news confirming that both they and their island were Roman targets. Intelligence, probably from their own network, told them that Roman technicians had started building a fleet of flat-bottomed boats just over the border of what is now Wales. This made it obvious that they intended to assault Mona, as there was no other place they would need boats to reach. Those remaining Druids on the mainland would probably have flocked to the island, along with whatever resistance groups still existed after the conquest. If Tacitus's information is to be taken at face value, these groups would have taken with them as many Roman prisoners as were available to be the victims of human sacrifice. It would seem that only their agents, the young Druid acolytes, remained within Roman territory.

It is possible that over in the east of the province, taking advantage of the anger shared by the Iceni and the Trinovantes, those Druid agitators brought them together. There is no reason to believe that the kingdoms had much in the way of mutual respect—they shared a boundary, for a start, which in pre-Claudian Britannia was bound to cause great tensions. Also, the pro-Roman Iceni would have been very aware of the suffering of the Trinovantes, yet for years had done nothing to help them.

Why should they suddenly team up? We know too little of the background of these distant events; what follows is a reconstruction based on what we do know. After the Roman desecration of Boudica and her kingdom, any Druidic involvement would have been not only acceptable but welcome. Before long, as Tacitus puts it, the Iceni were relishing the prospect of spilling Roman blood alongside the Trinovantes, "who, not yet broken by servitude, had entered into a secret and treasonable compact to resume their independence."

When they had agreed on terms, and that they would collectively serve under the still wounded Boudica, it seems likely that throughout the winter of 60–61 the Iceni and Trinovantes, hidden from Roman eyes, began to build weaponry and equipment on an almost industrial scale. As this was outside the campaigning season, such manufacturing would hardly need to be clandestine. There may have been an occasional Roman patrol, but if so it would have been a rare occurrence—Legio XX had moved from Camulodunum to Usk, and the only available units would have been a very small town guard.

The Iceni had direct access to almost everything they needed to equip themselves for battle—iron, horses, and plenty of timber. Chariots were built, cavalry saddles and reins leathered, metal horse equipment forged, and swords hammered. (It is also likely that after Scapula's confiscation of weapons, secret arms dumps would have been filled.)

It was probably in early spring that, according to Tacitus, the veteran soldiers and their families in uptown Camulodunum (in the town center and to its east) began to see and experience strange and disturbing omens and portents:

> For no apparent reason, the statue of Victory at Camulodunum fell, with its back turned as if in retreat. . . .
>
> Women, converted into maniacs by excitement, cried that destruction was at hand and alien cries had been heard in the invaders' senate-house: the theater had rung with shrieks. . . .
>
> The ocean had appeared blood-red and the ebbing tide had left behind it what looked to be human corpses.

A fifth column—possibly made up of Druidic apprentices—had established itself in the town, perhaps even in the cult of the Divine Emperor itself. These infiltrators, along with senior Trinovantians, assured the city's Roman inhabitants there was nothing to fear, apparently demonstrating a great talent for and esoteric knowledge of divinity. Whoever these people were, they must have had almost hypnotic powers of persuasion.

At a date unknown in the spring of 60, the men, women, and children of the Iceni, in their wagons and with their loaded-down mules, moved down into the territory of Trinovantes. The two tribes mingled; the excitement of imminent vengeance against all things Roman must have set the air abuzz. Boudica and the military chiefs of both tribes would have been discussing a plan of action.

For the Trinovantes, in particular, the prime target was Camulodunum, their original town, which had been invaded first by the Catuvellauni and then by the Romans. Were it destroyed, there was a chance Nero would recognize that control of the island was not a done deal, and that native resistance was too strong for him to waste time and money on the province.

Many of the ditches, dykes, and ramparts that surrounded the town had been either filled in or pulled down. There were no cohesive defenses around the town. Perhaps after Claudius had showered the pro-Roman kingdoms and tribes with gold, the empire had taken it for granted that the tribes would accept Rome as their leader.

The final attraction, destroying Camulodunum, would be comic were it not so tragic. There was no military presence by the Romans of any note. With Paulinus and Legio XIV fighting in Wales, and Legio XX having moved on from the legionary fortress, the only soldiers there were those who had been pensioned off.

The decision then was easy. The men, women, infants, and children of two entire kingdoms would, as one force, take Camulodunum and, instead of holding the city, would wipe it off the map.

For a few days, people might have noticed unusual activity around the town—riders passing by on the outskirts of the city, the occasional face peering through the glades—but one thing must have struck some of those living in the town: The seemingly helpful, reassuring, and enlightened interpreters of omens and the like had disappeared.

Then, one day soon after, would have come something that will have struck fear into their hearts—the sound of distant horns and drums and shouting, the rumbling of hooves, and the screeching of faraway wheels.

The fifth column of Druidic apprentices had done its work well. Instead of being spotted as scouts and lookouts, these had been brushed off as nothing to worry about.

How the first attack began is unknown, but unfortunately for those living in Camulodunum, we do know it lasted for at least two days rather than a matter of hours.

> They [the city's population] were as carelessly guarded as if the world was at peace, when they were enveloped by a great barbarian host. All else was pillaged or fired in the first onrush.

Although some of the veterans would no doubt have put up a good fight, it is likely that the fittest men would have been on the front line encircling the weakest and so been the first to perish when the tribal warriors swarmed around them, hacking with their longswords and throwing incendiary torches over their heads. As retired soldiers (many of them from the Legio XX, which had originally been stationed there), these were the men who were most hated by the Trinovantes. But there was no distinction between man, woman, or child. This was a massacre.

Every human being living in the city was a target. Every building was spattered with blood, every pavement littered with corpses and body parts.

Before long, as the defense began to weaken, it became obvious there was only one place the town dwellers could seek sanctuary—the temple of Claudius.

The temple was a huge stone building, fronted in the classical style with eight tall marbled pillars and approached by a wide staircase. It stood more than 65 feet high and was as big as any in Rome. Behind its huge bronze doors was a space of around three thousand square feet. As many as a thousand (or possibly more) of Camulodunum's population scrambled inside until somebody—presumably on the outside of the building—must have realized there would soon be a fatal crush.

Whoever that person was would have had to gather enough men to push the crowds back and allow the temple's huge bronze doors to close—leaving themselves and everyone else remaining to be killed or, perhaps for the unlucky, to be captured. The British returned to their camp with their prisoners. The slaughter had ended. The human sacrifices began:

> Those who were taken captive by the Britons were subjected to every known form of outrage.
>
> The worst and most bestial atrocity committed by their captors was this: They hung up naked the noblest and most distinguished women, then cut off their breasts and sewed them to their mouths in order to make the victims appear to be eating them; afterward they impaled the women on sharp skewers run lengthwise through the entire body. All this they did to the accompaniment of sacrifices, banquets, and wanton behavior.

Meanwhile, some of the very few who escaped the attack on Camulodunum managed to send word to Catus in London, who knew nothing of the catastrophe he had caused. He was still fiddling the finances while Camulodunum burned.

Suddenly, he must have realized his days of wheeler-dealing and mismanaging Britannia's economy were over. The game was up. He ordered just two hundred men to help the stricken city—possibly not even soldiers, but again just clerks and slaves—to somehow deal with the problem. It is understood he quickly took to the Thames and chartered a boat to carry him to Gaul. He is never heard of again.

For those who remained in the temple, Tacitus says they managed to remain for two days until it was stormed by the impatient Britons outside. But it appears more likely that the Trinovantes, having constructed the building, knew that the best way to gain access to the interior was, in fact, through the roof. From there it is possible they poured in tar, boiling oil, and fuel to set the building alight from the inside.

Within five days the prosperous Roman *colonia* was in ashes. This sacred city, built as a beacon of Roman civilization, instead of drawing support from the surrounding kingdoms and converting Britons to its culture, with its theater, statues, grand houses, and temple, had instead been destroyed, looted, and burned to the ground. Not a single building was left standing.

Britannia's huge rebel army had displayed the barbarism and savagery that had always been simmering beneath Roman rule. But Boudica and her war chiefs were one step ahead of the occupying forces. With the mob carousing and indulging in the ways of the old religion, they anticipated the most likely Roman response to the attack on Camulodunum.

With Legio LIV attacking Mona under Paulinus's command, and both Legio II and Legio XX weeks away at full march, the only immediate threat would be an attack from the north, by IX Hispana, based in and around Lincoln. Tacitus tells us that the legate, Petillius Cerialis, mobilized his whole legion to march to Camulodunum. (It is more likely he had a vexillation of only about three thousand men, which can be divined from the number needed to replenish the legion after the rebellion.) Boudica's alliance had predicted this, and probably, on a rough track in forests northwest of the *colonia,* where the infantry may well have been having to walk in single file, a large force of hundreds of tribesmen launched a surprise attack. British warriors' greatest battle tactic was ambush in difficult terrain, and for the legionaries it was a weakness that had dogged them in almost every campaign across Britannia.

However, never had they met an assault as large as this. With the Roman soldiers carrying all their gear, their shields over their backs, the enemy was able to dart in and out of cover. They would have probably rushed the legionaries and tipped some of them off balance and to the ground, while others were scrabbling to grab their weapons and free themselves from their equipment. Tacitus writes:

> The victorious Britons routed the legion and slaughtered the infantry to a man: Cerialis with the cavalry escaped to his camp, and found shelter behind its fortifications.

Meanwhile, at the Menai Strait between Mona and the mainland, Paulinus launched his attack on the Druidic stronghold, in what appears to have been a night attack. But neither he nor his men were prepared for what they saw once they landed on the shore of the island. Rising in front of them stood a long line of armed men (some of them almost certainly Druidic acolytes, partway through their twenty-year training). Weaving in between their lines were a number of vicious and febrile women, dressed in black and brandishing torches. And behind them stood the holy men themselves, their arms outstretched above them, chanting and shouting curses and incantations and summoning up magical powers.

For a moment it looked as if some of these incantations were having an effect—the Romans froze in shock, as if paralyzed by some sort of supernatural power, and even as their enemy attacked, they could not move. When hit with weapons, the legionaries stood still, like statues, terrified. But Paulinus was having none of it. He promptly ordered his men forward, telling them not to be afraid of such mystical nonsense. The men snapped out of it:

> Reassured by their general, and inciting each other never [again] to flinch before a band of females and fanatics, they charged behind the standards, cut down all who met them, and enveloped the enemy in his own flames.
>
> What they found appalled them. The Roman prisoners, their former comrades, had been sacrificed by the Druids, their blood dripping from the walls.

The next step was to install a garrison among the conquered population, and to demolish the groves consecrated to their savage cults, for Tacitus claims that "they considered it a duty to consult their deities by means of human entrails."

Only when the Druids had been cut down, and every sacred grove had been destroyed, and the garrison camp built, did Paulinus receive news from a messenger: Britannia's *colonia* had been destroyed.

The news must have been devastating. But Paulinus didn't have time to hang around. He was told the mob—somewhere between 80,000 to 230,000 strong, the entire population of two kingdoms—had started moving and was heading on its way to the developing mercantile town of Londinium.

Quickly he spoke to his senior commanders. He had with him the entirety of Legio XIV and a large detachment of Legio XX at his immediate disposal. Some cohorts of Legio XX should be left to guard the garrison (along with those too wounded to leave), but the entirety of XIV and the remainder of XX must immediately gather forces and, with their auxiliaries, begin the long, grueling march back through the kingdom of the Ordovices (half of which was still enemy territory) to Londinium.

Paulinus would also need messengers, scouts, and possibly a very small cavalry attachment to ride down to Legio II (in Isca Dumnoniorum, today's Exeter). His initial orders would probably have been to meet at the junction between the Fosse Way and Watling Street (today's High Cross).

Other messengers would be sent along the various routes to Roman forts that were strung evenly along both roads, to buy or extort supplies for the legions en route. The general Paulinus himself would undertake what is now famously known as the Cavalry Dash with a small number of fast horses to London. In order to make up time, and to avoid the possibility of ambush, it is unlikely he himself would have traveled from Mona through the Ordovices' territory—instead it is probable he took one of the swift galleys that had accompanied the fleet of boats from Chester. From there he could gallop down through friendly territory. This would cut down his journey to about 180 miles—70 miles shorter than the marching route. It must have been a determined, hard ride, but it is conceivable that Paulinus reached Londinium after a three or four days' gallop, changing horses as he went.

When he arrived, the town was quiet. Many of the richer merchants would have chartered, stolen, or even had their mercenaries commandeer any available boats to flee. The townsfolk probably hoped he had come to save them. But as he looked at the confused street layout, the lack of defenses, and the shortage of men, he realized that any attempt to save it would be futile. His decision was simple, but steely cold: The needs of the many outweigh the needs of the few. Ignoring the pleas of those Londoners left in the town, he advised those who were capable to follow in the wake of his dash back to his troops. Tacitus says:

> The laments and tears of the inhabitants, as they implored his protection, found him inflexible: he gave the signal for departure. . . . all who had been detained by the disabilities of sex, by the lassitude of age, or by local attachment, fell into the hands of the enemy.

Luckily for Paulinus, Boudica's hordes had begun to run out of control. Rather than wreaking revenge on the Romans, their main aim was to avoid Roman forts altogether and instead to drink, pillage, and loot. Other than those who had directly suffered from the cruelty of the Romans, the Britons march—probably about seventy thousand strong—was turning into something of a roving, carnivalesque free-for-all. As well as this, it moved slowly—with women and children trooping along, on or accompanying their carts, it was no match for a legion. Still, it descended on London and torched it—and doubtless partied again after killing and sacrificing the remaining population, doubtless staying for a day or so as groups of men pillaged nearby villages and wassailed into the night.

Next on the list was the Roman settlement of Verulamium (today's St. Albans)—a Roman *municipium* (that is, a free town) and former Catuvellaunian power base, a doubly delicious target for those of the Trinovantes who could recall the ruthlessness of the kingdom—and then a decision needed to be made. Boudica and her advisers could either carry on up Watling Street to meet Paulinus, or return to their lands. They outnumbered the Roman force—and if they doubled back there was every likelihood each and every one of them would be hunted down and crucified. And so they chose to confront Paulinus. The jamboree-like movable feast of drinking, plundering, singing warriors, together with their women, their children, and their pets, headed northwest along this now paved, wide, but ancient road.

During the cavalry dash to and from London, Paulinus must have been keeping a close eye on his surroundings. He had every reason to expect that a battle would take place sooner rather than later, and every reason to recognize that he would lose it should the two sides simply meet in a head-on clash on an open plain.

The general must have made a number of observations and calculations as he rode. Where was an area for the Romans to take on the approaching mob of tribes somewhere along Watling Street? It was a prospect that would never before have been considered, so unlikely were the circumstances. He would have to make do with what he could improvise. As well as finding a location in which the Romans could, as far as possible, dictate military terms, it would have been essential that it be close to clean water for the men at his camp and his cavalry horses. Naturally, he would want to fight downslope (although not so much downhill, as that would stymie the fluidity of movement for his troops). Considering the size of the army moving to confront him, it was essential to protect the flanks of his army; perhaps an area with deep forest on one side and a river on the other could be found.

Tacitus tells us:

> He [Paulinus] chose a position approached by a narrow defile and secured in the rear by a wood, first satisfying himself that there was

> no trace of an enemy except in his front, and that the plain there was devoid of cover and allowed no suspicion of an ambuscade.

It's reasonable to extrapolate from what Tacitus was describing that Paulinus had found a David-versus-Goliath location. His troops would fight from the end of a narrowing gorge behind which was a large area of thick woodland, preventing any sort of attack from the rear. On each side the slopes were high enough to force the opposing army to funnel toward his men, with no possibility of its front line fanning out. Perhaps more important, because of the lay of the land, there was no way the Romans could be outflanked or ambushed from either side. The sudden widening of the plain at the end of the gorge meant that watch could be effectively taken by the Roman centurions and commanders.

Essentially, Paulinus was in a very strong defensive position. It at least gave him a safer spot for a small army like his to operate when facing a much larger one than a straightforward battlefield. He chose his place and waited.

Although he had sent orders to the southwest of the country for Legio II to march up from its base, its *legatus legionis* (the highest commander of a legion, second in command only to Paulinus) was absent. Why is not clear, although it is conceivable that hostile trouble in Winchester may have drawn him and some of his cohorts there. Even more inexplicable is that on receiving Paulinus's orders, Poenius Postumus, a deputy to the legatus, chose to disobey them and remained in place. His decision may have been one of cowardice, which would seem unlikely, given his rank; or, more plausibly, it may have been based on a knowledge of local tribes in the region and their capacity to ambush, making it, he thought, dangerous and impractical to march through it with such little notice. Postumus would later fall on his sword with shame after realizing the perils in which he had left his governor and fellow legionaries.

This almost spelled disaster for Paulinus as it left him about eight thousand men short. He would fight this feral mob with just ten thousand men.

Together the legionaries and their auxillaries met up at the location and made camp, and, on hearing the horns and shouts of the rabble coming toward them, he buckled down with his men. He stood his legionaries three deep and his cavalry ready to flank.

Their enemies appeared and gradually formed at the end of the field. The warriors pushed to the front, with other men—blacksmiths, farmers, builders, bakers—behind them. The two kingdoms were so assured of victory that as their army stood in front of them, the women and children formed a crescent-shaped line of wagons from which to watch the proceedings, stretching from behind them and on their flanks. Meanwhile Boudica was on her chariot, her daughters beside her.

Boudica, probably wearing an early tartan and a gold torc, made a speech to her army, moving from division to division to division.

Dio records this speech, which he almost certainly embellished with its unflattering reference to Nero.

> Recall this I say, not with the purpose of inspiring you with a hatred of present conditions,—that hatred you already have,—nor with fear for the future,—that fear you already have,—but of commending you because you now of your own accord choose the requisite course of action, and of thanking you for so readily cooperating with me and with each other.
>
> As the queen, then, of such men and of such women, I supplicate and pray thee [Boudica's goddess Andraste] for victory, preservation of life, and liberty against men insolent, unjust, insatiable, impious,—if, indeed, we ought to term those people men who bathe in warm water, eat artificial dainties, drink unmixed wine, anoint themselves with myrrh, sleep on soft couches with boys for bedfellows,—boys past their prime at that,—and are slaves to a lyre-player and a poor one too. Wherefore may this Mistress Domitia-Nero reign no longer over me or over you men; let the wench sing and lord it over Romans, for they surely deserve to be

> the slaves of such a woman after having submitted to her so long. But for us, Mistress, be thou alone ever our leader.

Tacitus records Paulinus as addressing his men thus:

> Now is the time, fellow-soldiers, for zeal, now is the time for daring. For if you show yourselves brave men to-day, you will recover all that you have lost; if you overcome these foes, no one else will any longer withstand us. By one such battle you will both make your present possessions secure and subdue whatever remains; for everywhere our soldiers, even though they are in other lands, will emulate you and foes will be terror-stricken.

And then the rush came from the rebel warriors, screaming, weapons drawn, and hurtling themselves unevenly. This was no longer a party. But the Romans, with their triple line at the front, stayed absolutely still, until the enemy came within reach of their javelins.

Then the first volley was thrown. The *pilum* is a deadly, well-designed weapon. About four feet of it was made of wood, and the tip, about three feet long, was metal. Its primary use was, of course, simply to kill. But were that not successful, it could cut through armor, and although it could not pierce a good shield, it could become lodged in it. This meant an opponent would have to throw down his main defense and fight without it. Whether by luck or design, the metal part of the pilum would bend on impact, rendering it useless to throw back.

Six thousand of these pila would have rained down into the tribesmen causing death, serious injury, and chaos. The Britons would have found themselves having to run over corpses and the dying. As it is likely that Romans often carried two pila, a second volley was thrown. Yet more chaos. Then the Romans rushed toward them for a first assault—the *gladii* thrusting and twisting into the bodies of the opponents. The rebels, running into the defile, found that while trying to wield their longswords broadside, they could not swing them—they were too tightly crushed together by the narrowing walls of the defile.

As the Romans began to beat down the dazed Britons, Paulinus' cavalry launched itself into the British flanks and attacked the weakest of the men waiting behind the warriors. Arrows and missiles were slung at the Romans, but with their helmets and breastplates they counted for little. Meanwhile archers would have begun to launch over the Roman front line while slingers fired blunt projectiles (mostly metal). The legionaries moved forward slowly in three divisions before forming into wedges, driving the warriors into deadly narrowing gaps, making it easy for the Romans to cut them down.

Then the Romans advanced across the pile of dead warriors and their weapons. By this time the rebels were finding it difficult to maintain a core army. The British had no real comprehension of field warfare, nor attack formations—their battle technique was concentrated on an individual enemy. They had no concept of fighting as units, no battle tactics, no commanders watching the movement of the mob. The only weaponry advantage was the chariot. This not only had screeching wheels, but two men could advance, one of whom could jump off to attack and then, when overwhelmed, jump back on to retreat.

"The barbarians would assail the Romans with a rush of their chariots, knocking them helter-skelter," writes Dio; but the mass of rebels pushing from behind made it impossible to pull back, forcing them to become shunted broadside against their own men. "All this was going on not at one spot only, but in all three divisions at once. . . . Light-armed troops exchanged missiles with light-armed, heavy-armed were opposed to heavy-armed, cavalry clashed with cavalry," Dio continues.

The Britons, who started with an army so much larger than the Romans, began to realize there was no hope. As they had dealt out massacre to those in London, Camulodunum, and Verulamium, it was now they who were being slaughtered. After much fighting the tribesmen, soldier and civilian alike, had either died, were lying in agony, or had become exhausted. They simply did not have the weaponry, the armor, the strength, or the discipline of the legionaries.

And so they tried to withdraw. But their luck had well and truly run out. As they ran back from the battlefield, the Romans gave chase, and here they took their bloody revenge. Savagery was to meet savagery. Those fleeing, whether running or on horseback, clattered into the wagon train. There was no escape through the carts, the ropes, the screaming women, their children, and their animals. The Romans had at them. For once, breaking the entire spirit of the civilization they had hoped to bring to the British, they become frenzied. Legio XX would not be stopped after the murder of their kith and kin at Camolodunum, and Legio XIV still had the memory of their comrades' blood dripping down the walls of the Druidic shrines.

Women, children, animals: The Romans slaughtered everyone they could find.

Boudica escaped into the forest with a small group of soldiers. But she knew these Romans would spare nobody in the east of England in hunting her down. She knew she was doomed. Facing torture and crucifixion in front of her own people was too much. She had faced such crushing humiliation being flogged in public. She would never be demeaned like that again.

Dio and Tacitus give different accounts of her death: She either became ill (probably from a wound) or she took poison. Either way, the Queen was dead.

> The triumphant Romans presided over a wasteland. Boudica was no more and forts were built in the land of the Iceni and elsewhere in the province. Those members of the Iceni and Trinovantes who had managed to escape the battle returned to their lands: but only to be executed or face famine. In the build-up to the rebellion the farmers had planted no crops.

Now that the fighting was done with, there were scores to settle and reputations to maintain among the victors.

Dio confirms that the rapacity of the procurator, Catus, with his trick to turn grants into loans, lit the flame of revolt. Recognizing his guilt, he fled and disappeared into Gaul. History hears no more of him.

His replacement, one Julius Classicianus, was a very different kind of public administrator. He argued that peace would return to Britannia if the survivors of the rebellion were treated sympathetically.

Paulinus strongly disagreed. He sought revenge and punishment rather than understanding and tolerance. According to Tacitus, any tribes that were vacillating or resisting were devastated by fire and the sword.

The new procurator put about the idea that the province should wait for the arrival of a new governor who would deal humanely with rebels who surrendered. At the same time he sent reports to Rome that Nero should expect no end to the violence, no genuine reconciliation and pacification, until a successor to Paulinus was found.

The princeps accepted Classicianus's advice but proceeded with caution. He sent out to Britannia one of his freedmen, Polyclitus, to review the situation and report back. His official instructions were that "harmony be established between governor and finance officer," but his real task was to remove the former without a fuss.

The freedman's findings were toned down and Suetonius Paulinus remained in charge of operations, but the loss of some boats and their oarsmen was used as a pretext to have him replaced by a kindlier successor. A few years later Nero brought the well-connected Paulinus (or perhaps his son) back into favor with a second Consulship.

There was to be fighting for control of the island in the future, but the battle of Watling Street settled the governance of southern Britannia once and for all. For this Nero and his advisers deserve much credit. In addition to the strategic military victory, they had handled a tricky personnel problem with competence and care. Above all, the princeps showed that he still believed clemency to be an essential ingredient of good government.

He spoke no more of abandoning angry provinces to their own devices.

11

FIRE! FIRE!

On the night of July 19 in the year 64, a hot wind was blowing across the city. The moon shone brightly. The population sweltered. The princeps had fled the summer heat for the fresher sea airs that cooled his coastal villa at Antium.

Rome was a maze of narrow, winding lanes and passages and tiny squares. The rich lived in inward-looking, windowless houses ringed with shops that distanced them from the noises and bustle of street life, while the poor rented rooms in gimcrack apartment blocks as many as eight stories high, which had a tendency to collapse unexpectedly.

In Seneca's opinion, there were simply too many people in Rome. "Turn your thoughts to this city," he remarked in a letter to a friend. "The crowd which flows endlessly through the widest streets is crushed utterly whenever anything gets in the way to impede its course as it sweeps along like a rushing torrent."

At the Circus Maximus, the evening was busy. Fast food establishments and any number of booths and workshops that lined the many entrances into the building were open and trading. A small fire broke out among some business units at the far end of the Circus by the foot of the Palatine hill, in which combustible goods were stored.

This was not an unusual occurrence in a city stuffed full of flammable materials, and we may guess that few passersby paid it much attention. Perhaps someone had heated their supper on a brazier and knocked it over or some embers had fallen from it to the ground.

Even the proprietor will have predicted no great trouble putting out the flames.

If so, this time he was wrong. Whipped by the sirocco, the flames quickly gathered strength and turned into a conflagration. It generated its own wind and scattered red-hot cinders over the sleeping city. At the top level the Circus's stands for spectators were constructed from wood, and there were no tall stone structures—mansions or temples—that could act as obstacles. In no time the entire structure was engulfed. Having spread horizontally, the flames now leaped vertically up the brickwork cliff of the Palatine hill, where they reached the residences of the imperial family and their officials.

The Romans were used to fires. They looked back with fear and loathing (and a degree of invention) to the incineration of the city in 390 B.C. at the hands of invaders from Gaul. In those distant times many of the buildings were made of wattle and daub and easily burned down.

During the republic we have reliable records of fifteen fires, of which seven were widespread and the remainder saw the destruction of at least one important public building. They tended to occur in the industrial and commercial quarter along the Tiber and the busy area around the Forum, where many people used to congregate. The empire saw an increase in the number and seriousness of fires, which we can attribute to Rome's population growth and the resulting overcrowding.

In 31 B.C., the year of Actium and the very beginning of Augustus's sole rule, a fire was set at the Circus Maximus by some freedmen who objected to a taxation assessment, or so it was claimed. It roared up the neighboring Aventine hill, where it destroyed the famous temple of Ceres and its priceless collection of paintings and sculptures. At least three other major fires took place during the reign, one of which devastated the Forum, the basilicas Aemilia and Julia, business and commercial centers which stood on the long sides of the square, and most serious of all the temple of Vesta, symbol of Rome's identity with its eternal flame.

Augustus lost patience and after a catastrophic conflagration in the year A.D. 6, which saw several fires occurring during a single day, he established a fire brigade whose members doubled as nightwatchmen and were called the *vigiles*. They were a substantial force of seven thousand freedmen, who would qualify for full Roman citizenship after twelve years of service. They were divided into seven cohorts. Augustus had already organized the city into fourteen administrative departments, or *regiones,* and beneath them local wards, or *vici*. Each cohort was made responsible for two of these *regiones*. The *vigiles* were lodged in purpose-built barracks and, clear evidence of their importance, their commander reported directly to the princeps.

Although they were an improvement, there was a limit to their effectiveness as firefighters. Their equipment was inadequate; they fought fires with axes, pikes, ladders, bucket brigades, and mats soaked in vinegar. Rome's aqueducts and the river Tiber ensured a plenitude of water, but not the means of delivering it in quantity and force. At some stage, perhaps in Nero's day, pumps were introduced.

Seneca observed:

> Should a fire appear in one particular dwelling, the household and neighbors throw water on it; but an extensive conflagration that has already consumed many houses is extinguished only by [sacrificing] part of the city.

In other words, the *vigiles* created firebreaks by intentionally demolishing buildings in the fire's path. They are reported to have employed *ballistae,* military siege engines in the shape of giant crossbows.

Emperors were expected to help generously with reconstruction costs. A fire consumed the Aventine hill and part of the Circus Maximus in the year 36. The then princeps Tiberius appointed Nero's father, Domitius, to a commission which processed applications for assistance. In total the privy purse found itself the poorer by 100 million sesterces, a considerable sum.

In 54, the last year of Claudius's reign, a stubborn fire leveled the southern part of the Campus Martius. The emperor and his wife, Agrippina, went in person to organize the efforts to put out the flames. We may assume that Nero as heir apparent helped out in some unrecorded way. As a philhellene he would have mourned the loss of statues of the Muses, the goddesses of literature, music, and dance, created by the great Athenian sculptor Praxiteles. For centuries, Romans had looted Greece of its artistic masterpieces, and many of them must have shared the Muses' fate.

In 62, well into Nero's own reign, the new gymnasium and baths complex he had commissioned was struck by lightning and burned down. A statue of him melted.

Two years later, from its modest beginnings at the Circus, the latest of Rome's fires caught hold and raged for six days. Tacitus writes:

> It outstripped all defensive measures because of the speed of its deadly advance and the vulnerability of the city, with its constricted alleyways twisting this way and that, and with its irregular blocks of buildings, which was the nature of old Rome.

Ancient temples and houses from Rome's early days, including the palace of Rome's second (legendary) king, Numa Pompilius, were consumed, together with the spoils of its victorious wars, original copies of literary masterpieces, and official archives deposited in the *tabularium* overlooking the Forum. The claim of these buildings to genuine antiquity is questionable, as many were reconstructions after earlier incinerations. Old documents, of course, vanished forever, vaporizing the historical record.

The terrified population flooded onto the streets, carrying what was portable from their blazing homes and impeding relief efforts. As they milled around, they were held up by human obstacles—the very old and the very young. Some were suffocated or trampled underfoot. The shouting and wailing were deafening and the smoke blinding. Many fled to other parts of the city, chased by the flames. Some left town for the safety of the moonlit countryside.

Dealing with city fires had been a regular feature of an emperor's life, and when Nero received news of the disaster, he must have thought: "Not again!" But past experience told him what he had to do. Abandoning his holiday at Antium, he hurried back to Rome, where he led the fight to extinguish the flames. Like his predecessors Augustus, Tiberius, and Claudius, he took the crisis seriously, and even his worst enemies allowed that he acquitted himself well.

He arranged temporary shelter for the destitute and homeless in his gardens across the Tiber and on the Campus Martius, which seem to have mostly survived unscathed. He opened up a group of monumental buildings completed by Augustus's partner Agrippa—including the Pantheon; some public baths; the Porticus Vipsania, a long portico or colonnade that displayed a map of the known world on its wall; and the Saepta Julia, a vast voting enclosure. Essential supplies were shipped up the Tiber from Ostia, Rome's port, and neighboring municipalities. The price of grain was reduced to 3 sesterces per *modius* (that is, between ten and fourteen pounds in weight). Also, some makeshift buildings were rapidly erected on open ground.

The *vigiles* were busy, to good effect. Tacitus reports that

> at last, on the sixth day, the blaze was brought to a halt at the foot of the Esquiline [one of the city's traditional seven hills]. Buildings had been demolished over a vast area so that the fire's unremitting violence would be faced only with open ground and bare sky.

However, the work of the firefighters was undone when the flames resumed their onslaught. Embers must have reignited. Apparently casualties were fewer than before, but the destruction of public buildings was greater. This suggests that the fire reached the Campus Martius, where there was little residential housing but a large number of temples, colonnades, and the like. Three days later, the ashes at last cooled and the immediate crisis was over.

Tacitus estimates that of Rome's fourteen districts, four were still intact, three had been entirely leveled, and in the other seven a few charred ruins were all that remained. Numberless houses and tenement blocks were blackened rubble. Modern archaeologists are more conservative than the historian. It is estimated today that between 15 and 20 percent of the city was totally destroyed. It is possible that at least two hundred thousand inhabitants, perhaps many more, were made homeless; at least ten to twelve thousand *insulae* and several hundred *domus* were rendered uninhabitable.

The princeps worked hard on the city's reconstruction. He was determined to turn a short-term catastrophe into a long-term gain. Rules for the construction of new buildings were introduced, including a ban on wooden beams. Poor quality limestone that was friable under great heat was to be replaced so far as possible by locally sourced fireproof stone.

Nero replaced the old haphazard street plan with a more orderly layout (something perhaps like his ideal city, the Alexandria he yearned for but had never seen). Rows of streets were to be properly surveyed, spacious avenues driven through where dense housing had been, height limits set for buildings, and open zones created.

Porticoes were added, too, to protect the façades of multistory buildings. Nero undertook to pay for them from his own pocket, and he also promised to return to their owners their property lots, cleared of debris. If the redesign is taken into account, lots equivalent to previous holdings were presumably negotiated, or else purchased by the state and resold. The princeps made grants available, prorated according to a person's rank and the market value of his house, and set time limits within which work had to be completed for applicants to qualify for the money.

According to a clever incentive scheme, a man with partial civic rights (he would be called a Latin) who was worth at least 200,000 sesterces could obtain full Roman citizenship if he spent half that sum from his own pocket on building a new house in the city.

The *vigiles* were instructed to watch out for householders who illegally siphoned off water from water pipes. Every house owner had to have firefighting appliances. Party walls between houses were banned; each property had to have its own exterior wall distinct from its neighbor's.

The marshes near Ostia were selected as the dumping ground for the city's debris, thus filling in marshes and creating useful new building land for people dispossessed by the fire. Once the grain ships from Egypt and the Black Sea, which fed the capital, had unloaded their cargo onto Rome's quays, they filled their empty holds with charred rubble before returning downstream. Dead bodies were removed without charge.

This was an impressive and well-designed prospectus. To dangle money in front of inflexible freeholders was probably the only way to persuade them to accept different and, doubtless for some, smaller parcels of land and to implement the new building regulations. When the work was finished (the sources do not reveal how long it took, but certainly several years), even those who mourned the old Rome had to admit that she was now more beautiful. More usefully, regulation worked; fires still broke out, but they were less frequent and less catastrophic than before.

Practical measures were not sufficient. The gods were angry and had to be appeased. The Senate consulted the Sibylline Books, as was its custom in times of crisis: These were a collection of prophecies in Greek that had originally been bought by Tarquin the Proud, a king of Rome long ago. They were destroyed by fire in the first century B.C., and a board of three replaced them with a group of similar oracular sayings gathered from around the Mediterranean. In response to the Great Fire, the authorities consulted the books for guidance and offered supplicatory prayers to Vulcan, divine blacksmith and god of fire; Ceres, goddess of the harvest; and her daughter, Proserpina, queen of the underworld. Married women conducted propitiatory ceremonies for Juno, on the Capitol hill and then on the nearest coast. From there they drew some water and sprinkled it on the temple and statue of the goddess. They also held ritual feasts and all-night festivals.

One of a series of monumental altars in honor of Vulcan has survived. It was erected by a later emperor, Domitian, who reigned from 81 to 96. An inscription explains that it was dedicated "in consequence of a vow that was undertaken but which had been neglected for a long time and not fulfilled, for the purpose of warding off fires when the city burned for nine days."

In other words, once the flames had subsided, Nero sacrificed a customary red cow and red pig to propitiate the god, but he failed to follow this up, as he had promised, with memorial altars. One of the emperor's official roles was as *pontifex maximus,* or high priest. This *pontifex* evidently had as little interest in the state religion as did (reputedly) his skeptical wife.

The city was still smoldering when people began to ask who was responsible for the fire. So great a tragedy could not have been an accident; someone had to be to blame.

It was whispered in the street that the emperor had donned his singer's costume and given a rendition of his epic poem *The Sack of Troy*. Some said he sang it on his private stage, others from the top of a tower in a park called the Gardens of Maecenas on the Esquiline hill, which was part of the imperial estate. He was quoted as delighting "in the beauty of the flames."

There were reports of criminal activity, according to Tacitus:

> And nobody dared fight the fire: there were repeated threats from numerous people opposing efforts to extinguish it, and others openly hurled in firebrands and yelled that they "had their instructions." This was to give them more freedom to loot, or else they were in fact under orders.

It was deeply suspicious that the fire had reignited near a property belonging to Tigellinus, the Praetorian commander. Opinion hardened against the princeps. Dio evokes the changing mood:

> There was nothing to be seen except the light of many fires across the city, as in an army camp, and nothing to be heard except con-

fused shouts. "This or that is on fire." "Where?" "How did it happen?" "Who kindled it?"

The last question had an easy answer. Nero was the guilty man, both ordinary citizens and critics in the Senate confidently asserted. He had set his heart on realizing a long-meditated plan to put an end to the city of Rome and the Roman empire. He liked to say that Priam, king of Troy, had been extraordinarily lucky to have seen his throne and his realm destroyed at one and the same time. Once, when someone in general conversation quoted from *Bellerophon*, a play by the Greek tragedian Euripides, "When I am dead, let the world be consumed by fire," he responded, "No, the first part of the line should read: 'While I live.'"

In Seneca's drama *Octavia*, the emperor's doppelgänger admits his real-life counterpart's culpability.

Then, let this city's roofs
Sink in the fires that I shall send upon her!
Let burning ruin, squalor, poverty,
Starvation and bereavement fall upon
Her sinful people's heads.

The fire gave Nero the opportunity to live up to these nihilistic words. It was said that he secretly sent out men who pretended to be either drunk or up to some other kind of mischief. They were under orders to set fire to buildings here and there about the city. These were the villains who had been seen at their dastardly work in the streets. Dio again:

> Many houses were destroyed for want of anyone to help save them, and many others were set on fire by the very men who came to lend assistance; for the soldiers, including the night watch, having an eye to plunder, instead of putting out fires, kindled new ones.

That the princeps was the arsonist was widely credited, although fear prevented him from being openly named. An oracular utterance, allegedly from the Sibylline Books, was on everyone's lips: "Last of the sons of Aeneas, a mother-murderer shall rule." Aeneas was the legendary Trojan prince whose genetic line led through the centuries to Julius Caesar and the Julio-Claudian emperors.

There is a final, damning piece of circumstantial evidence against the princeps. Two years after the fire, a Praetorian tribune called Subrius Flavus was on trial for conspiracy. Nero presided in his capacity as a judge. Subrius defended himself as well as he could, but when pressed, admitted his guilt. Tacitus gives his actual words:

> Interrogated by Nero on the reasons that brought him to forget his military oath, Subrius declared: "Because I hated you! None of your soldiers was more loyal to you while you deserved our affection. I began to hate you when you became the murderer of your mother and wife, and a charioteer, actor and arsonist."

The sting in the tail will have hurt. The tribune was executed.

What are we to make of these accounts? Dio and Suetonius are unremittingly hostile. They are certain that Nero burned Rome down either because he wanted to build himself a new palace or out of sheer spite.

The main evidence against the princeps are the reports of men setting fire to buildings and claiming that they were acting under orders. We have already noted the testimony of Tacitus and Dio. According to Suetonius, Nero

> set fire to the city so brazenly that several former consuls did not venture to lay hands on his servants although they caught them on their estates with tow and blazing torches. Some granaries solidly built of stone occupied space he had his eye on [for a new palace]. He used siege-engines to demolish the walls and then set the interiors ablaze.

An impartial judge will have noticed that basic facts are not in contention; it is the interpretations that differ. The demolition of buildings is not disputed, but the rationale for doing so is. There is in fact a clear path through the wood. Tacitus, by far the most authoritative of our literary sources, provides a convincing account of the fire's genesis in a shop at the Circus Maximus. It is wholly implausible that the emperor would have hired people to start the fire without any attempt at secrecy. In fact, as the historian points out, the supposed arsonists were men, *vigiles* one presumes and perhaps Praetorians, doing their best to create firebreaks, an unwelcome but necessary policy.

Other sinister accusations have equally innocent explanations. It is possible, even probable, that individual criminals seized their moment to loot or to act on private grievances. That said, most fires that, as reported, simultaneously broke out in different parts of the city will have been the consequence of embers blowing about in the hot wind rather than the machinations of an evil tyrant.

As for the well-known allegation that Nero fiddled while Rome burned, he may very well have done so, although Tacitus has it only as a rumor. (In any event he would have played a cithara rather than the not yet invented violin.) But he will have been too busy dealing with the aftermath of the catastrophe to give a major concert immediately. However, once life had returned to something approaching normal it would have been in character for him to perform an appropriate extract from his Trojan epic, which was considered his masterpiece (at least by him). This was not in the best of taste, but it became a full-scale public relations fiasco, remembered to this day, only when it was set alongside his supposed overall culpability.

At first sight, Subrius's accusations are damning. They are verbatim and date from only two years after the fire. They are that rare thing in classical studies, contemporary testimony. Unfortunately, they are not to be trusted, being the desperate insults of a man at the end of his tether. His reference to arson was designed to embarrass and hurt. He was not necessarily telling the truth, but retelling the common talk of the Forum.

Tacitus's inclination is to condemn the emperor at every turn. However, he ignored Subrius's assertion that Nero was an arsonist and did not adduce it elsewhere in his writings as evidence. One senses that he would have liked it to be true, but knew that it was not. He comments favorably on Nero's reconstruction program: "These measures were welcomed for their practicality, and they also enhanced the aesthetics of the new city."

In sum, the overall tenor of Tacitus's account, from the conflagration's tentative beginnings to Rome's rebuilding, points unequivocally to an accident rather than a conspiracy. And, in the manner of Claudius and Agrippina when faced with a similar emergency, Nero behaved exactly as was expected of a responsible princeps.

—

Why was the rumor about the emperor believed in the first place? The best answer is that people had lost their homes, their possessions, and in some cases their friends and relatives. They were angry and hit out at Nero, because as princeps he was in charge.

And he did make a bad mistake. Since the days of the republic, the state had distributed an allotment of free grain, called the *annona,* to Rome's poorer citizens, many of whom were underemployed or jobless. In the first century there were about two hundred thousand beneficiaries. The *annona* was a drain on the treasury, and, presumably panic-stricken at the cost of reconstruction, Nero began charging for the grain handouts. Anything more likely to enrage his support base is hard to imagine, and the reform must have been quickly abandoned, for we hear no more of it. Also, the price of commercial grain in the shops was held low. At about this time a coin was struck celebrating the *annona.*

The upper classes were hostile to Nero, but it is difficult to assess the reaction of the hard-pressed ordinary citizen by whom he was well liked. A best guess is that Nero's popularity dipped, but so far as we can tell it recovered soon enough.

—

Although the princeps was obviously aware of his own innocence, he feared that the public believed the rumors. The most efficacious way of dealing with this problem was to "contrive culprits" onto whose heads he could divert the blame.

He chose the Christians. The Romans knew little about them except that they caused trouble. They were seen as a sect within Judaism, rather than what it was in the process of becoming, a new religion whose founder had died thirty years or so before. Their attempts to win adherents infuriated their fellow Jews and led to civil unrest and riots. The Roman authorities resented being dragged into quarrels over arcane theological disputes. This was more than a minor irritation, for there were Jewish communities throughout the empire.

Both parties had form. Clashes between communities of anti-Semitic Greek speakers and of Jews in the cities of the eastern Mediterranean had long been a challenge to the Pax Romana. Now internal disputes involving traditional Jews and Christians were attracting attention. According to Suetonius, "since the Jews constantly made disturbances at the instigation of Chrestus [probably in error for Christus], Claudius expelled them from Rome." Dio disagrees, stating the emperor merely banned Jews, doubtless including Christians, from holding meetings. One way or another they were all of them a nuisance.

In 51 or 52 some Jews took the apostle Paul, Christianity's leading propagandist, to court in southern Greece. The presiding judge (and provincial governor) happened to be Seneca's elder brother, Gallio. He lost his temper and dismissed the case, saying: "Since this is an argument about words and names and your own law, you yourselves must settle it. I will not be the judge of such things."

Public opinion was hostile and ill-informed. Tacitus was typical:

> They were people hated for their shameful offenses whose founder, Christus, had been executed during the rule of Tiberius by the procurator Pontius Pilatus. The pernicious superstition had been temporarily suppressed, but it was starting to break out again, not just in Judaea, the starting point of that curse, but in Rome, as well, where all that is abominable and shameful in the world flows together and gains popularity.

Christians were supposed to hold cannibalistic rites, presumably a misunderstanding of the Eucharist, according to which (in some interpretations) bread and wine are transformed into Christ's body and blood before being consumed. They were also alleged to be sexually promiscuous. Jews loathed them for claiming to have produced the Messiah, or Savior, and to have built a false faith on ancient truths. A tireless traveling missionary, Paul was always being run out of town by angry locals. While visiting Jerusalem sometime around 57, he was seized by an angry mob that accused him of defiling the Temple by bringing gentiles into it. The Roman authorities took him into custody and decided to interrogate him by flogging. To extricate himself from an increasingly dangerous situation, he exercised his right as a Roman citizen to appeal to the emperor (*appellare Caesarem*), which averted the flogging. He was sent to Rome, where he lived under house arrest on remand.

A Christian community lived in Rome, perhaps across the Tiber in what is now the Trastevere. We do not know how large it was, but it was newly established and cannot have been numerous. Never one to let sleeping dogs lie, Paul immediately got in touch with Jews in the city, to whom he spoke of Jesus Christ's life, death, and resurrection. As usual, he sharply divided opinion.

According to Christian tradition, the apostle was condemned and decapitated at some point after the Great Fire and before 68. We are told that his severed head bounced three times before coming to rest, and that springs miraculously welled up where it touched the ground.

There was some sympathetic interest in Judaism and Christianity among the Roman elite. Stoics saw parallels with their philosophy. In particular its monotheism and its concern with the virtuous life were of stronger appeal than the examples of the dissolute gods and malicious goddesses of the state religion. Seneca, for one, thought in terms that a Christian would understand. He observed in a letter to a friend:

> God is near you, he is with you, he is within you. This is what I mean, Lucilius: a holy spirit indwells within us, one who marks our good and bad deeds, and is our guardian. As we treat this spirit, so are we treated by it. Indeed, no man can be good without the help of God.

The empress Poppaea showed some interest in Jewish affairs, according to the contemporary Jewish historian Josephus. Nero found in favor of the priestly hierarchy at the Temple in Jerusalem when adjudicating a dispute concerning Roman official tactlessness. Apparently he made this decision in order to gratify his wife, who, opines Josephus somewhat surprisingly, was "a religious woman."

———

Tacitus tells a strange and terrible story. By a grim coincidence, once the princeps had decided to invent a case against Christians, some members of the faith confessed to setting fires and were arrested. Their disclosures led to many more arrests. The motive for their crimes was obscure and, in Tacitus's less than convincing judgment, reflected more "their hatred of humankind than that they were genuine arsonists."

Their lives were ended cruelly, even by Roman standards. Some were covered with the hides of wild animals and torn to pieces by dogs. Others were fastened to wooden crosses, coated in tar, and set alight. The emperor made his gardens a public venue for these illuminations. He mingled with the crowds, costumed as a charioteer, and stood in his chariot.

So ghastly were the torments, Tacitus writes, that

> guilty though these people were and deserving [of] exemplary punishment, pity for them began to well up because it was felt that they were being exterminated not for the public good but to gratify one man's sadism.

The difficulty with this account is that the events described cannot have taken place.

The text contains contradictions: for example, it implies that Christians were at one and the same time innocent scapegoats and deep-dyed criminals. Some of those arrested volunteered confessions, but to what? There is no evidence that being a Christian was illegal at this time, so presumably they admitted to arson. They believed that the end of the world was nigh, but it stretches credulity that they burned Rome down in order to hasten the apocalypse. Modern practice suggests that confessions could have been beaten out of them, but the ancient texts do not even hint at this.

A more general objection is that the awfulness of the punishment does not accord well with Nero's known dislike of violent public entertainments.

On a technical point, Tacitus calls Pontius Pilate *procurator*—a schoolboy error when the correct title was Prefect (or *praefectus*). This is the kind of detail over which he habitually took great care.

Most seriously of all, he is the only classical historian to have referred to the executions, nor does any Christian author, before the fifth century. The Christian community in Rome would have remembered such a fearful experience and passed it down to subsequent generations, but no one did so.

A complete silence prevails.

Church fathers, such as Bishop Eusebius (author of the *Chronicon,* a world history, and the *Ecclesiastical History,* a history of the Church), condemn Nero for launching the first significant persecution of the new religion, but none of them mentions the terrible martyrdoms in the emperor's private park. It is conceivable that pagan authors decided to omit all reference to them or that their reports have been lost. However, this does not meet the point that Christian apologists were eager for news of pagan atrocities and would have publicized them if they had heard of them from their own sources.

The unavoidable conclusion is that nobody, apart from Tacitus, knew anything at all about the matter. Where, then, did he get *his* information from? The answer has to be from elderly Romans or Christians who witnessed what happened and informed Tacitus, writing half a century later, either directly or through intermediaries and descendants. If such informants told Tacitus, they would certainly have told others, and we would expect to find more than one description in ancient texts of the agony in the gardens.

The simplest explanation of a mystery is, as usual, the best. In this case, we are obliged to conclude that some person or persons unknown, perhaps a copyist, concocted the whole story around the end of the fourth century. Imitating the historian's writing style, he inserted it into a text of the *Annals*. The date is secured because a Christian author called Sulpicius Severus who flourished in the early fifth century is the first to have restated Tacitus's narrative. The forger's aim, one supposes, will have been to add weight to the data-thin Christian caricature of Nero as author of the cruelest of persecutions, as an inhuman monster, as a first sketch of the Antichrist.

The plan worked better than could have been expected. Nero was smeared for a crime he never committed, and the Roman Catholic Church still mourns the nonexistent martyrs of the Great Fire.

The fates were kind when they arranged that the artistic and exuberant Nero and the dynasty's disciplined and dutiful founder, Augustus, never met. Three emperors separated them. Had their paths crossed, they would have found they had little in common. However, they did share one grand passion: They were untiring builders.

Several ambitious projects got under way soon after Nero's accession. His great wooden amphitheater was completed within a single year, 57. Work started on a grand temple of the deified emperor Claudius. The baths and gymnasium complex in the Campus Martius opened its doors before 64, and a large market on the Caelian hill was dedicated in 59. The princeps also completed a harbor development at Ostia, which Claudius had begun, and a racetrack, the Circus Vaticanus, which Caligula had laid out.

At one point Nero considered extending the walls of Rome to the port of Ostia about fifteen miles away, perhaps creating a corridor similar to the Long Walls running from Athens to Piraeus. A canal was to be driven from the sea to the capital, thus increasing the shipping tonnage that could sail straight to its wharves rather than unloading at Ostia, which suffered from buildups of mud brought down by the river. The city's population seems to have been rising, and more housing was required, hence the infilling of marshland near the port with rubble from the Great Fire.

Despite the malevolent chatter, Nero's latest and most astonishing scheme was unplanned; however, it was enabled by the catastrophe. He was the biggest loser rather than its instigator. A grand new palace, the Domus Transitoria (House of Passage), was destroyed, and with it his fine collection of works of art. This was not a single structure but a ribbon of linked buildings and parks that ran down from the Palatine hill across a valley and up to the Gardens of Maecenas, on the Esquiline.

The princeps was fascinated by the art of architecture. At this time many innovations were introduced thanks to the increased use of concrete, which allowed the construction of vaults and domes. After the fire he decided to rebuild the Domus Transitoria and hired some well-known architects and engineers of the day, Severus and Celer, to design a palace for him. Their Latin names suggest that they were not Greek, as might have been expected of that race of town planners, but originated from the Latin-speaking or western half of the empire.

Tacitus thought them frivolous wastrels, but he says enough to indicate their talent: "They possessed the ingenuity and audacity to attempt to create by artifice what nature had denied—and to amuse themselves at the emperor's expense." It is a description that has been unjustly leveled at architects throughout the ages.

The plan that emerged was far more than a restoration project. Timber beams and posts gave way to concrete and a sophisticated use of vaulting. The basic trajectory of the Domus Transitoria was to be retained, as was its combination of parkland and buildings, what the poet Martial called *rus in urbe,* or "countryside in the city." However, neighboring freeholds were bought up to create additional space for them to realize the architects'—and the emperor's—vision. The whole complex covered an estimated 125 to 200 acres.

The outcome was so magnificent that it was universally known as the Golden House, or Domus Aurea. Only a little of it has survived, partly because it appears to have been unfinished and partly because it was built over by later emperors. What follows brings together ancient representations and the findings of modern archaeologists. It evokes the Golden House as it was intended to be; some years, we do not know how many, will have had to pass before it could be completed.

The Forum Romanum was more than a mere marketplace; it was Rome's sacred, judicial, political, and commercial space. From here the visitor to the Golden House made his way up the newly colonnaded Via Sacra (Holy Way) to the official entrance. A lofty vestibule, or *atrium,* was large enough to accommodate a colossal bronze statue, 116 feet high, of Nero (probably) as the sun god. It was taller than the Colossus of Rhodes, reputedly by ten feet. Beyond the vestibule a triple-pillared covered arcade ran for a whole mile.

The next extravagant surprise was an ornamental man-made lake (where the Colosseum was later to rise from the ground). It was so extensive that it was "like a sea." On the far side of the water, buildings made to resemble cities (presumably from different parts of the empire) could be seen, and a diverse landscape opened up. According to Suetonius, there were "tracts of country, varied by tilled fields, vineyards, pastures and woods, with great numbers of wild and domestic animals."

The vestibule nudged against the Palatine hill, which had suffered from the fire. Nero renovated the existing Domus Tiberiana, or House of Tiberius, on the eastern part of the hill overlooking the Forum and built a new palace at its western end. The two structures are best understood as a single complex. It may be here that the princeps spent most of his time and that the imperial civil service, with its Greek-speaking freedmen, lived and worked.

South of the lake, the long-promised and unfinished temple of Claudius was canceled and replaced by an elaborate fountain house watered by an aqueduct, the Aqua Claudia. To the west, some baths offered a choice between running sea water and sulfurous spring water.

Nearby, on the slope of the Oppian hill, an outsize two-story villa or pavilion was built with an overall frontage some four hundred feet long. The focal point of the whole development, it consisted of two wings attached to a great eight-sided hall in the center. It was topped by Rome's first example of a dome (albeit octagonal rather than circular). There were many concrete halls and, at the last count, one hundred forty-two rooms. Nero had a reputation for wastefulness, but here, surprisingly, there are some signs of economy; pillars and stone blocks were salvaged from the ruined city and reused. However, no expense was spared in the interior decoration.

Romans of this period were fascinated by ingenious mechanical devices. In Petronius's comic novel *The Satyricon,* the inexperienced Encolpius is a guest at Trimalchio's absurdly elaborate dinner party. He is astounded by one such gimmick:

> All at once the coffered ceiling began to rumble and the whole dining room began to shake. I jumped up in panic, expecting that some acrobat was about to come swinging down through the roof. . . . All at once the panels opened and an enormous circular hoop descended, with gold crowns and little alabaster jars of face cream hanging from it. We were told that these were all presents for us guests that we could take home. I stuffed my pockets with them.

Suetonius reports that the Golden House deployed similar architectural trickery. He writes:

> Every part of the house was overlaid with gold and adorned with gems and mother-of-pearl. There were dining-rooms with fretted ceilings of ivory, whose panels could turn and shower down flowers and were fitted with pipes for sprinkling the guests with perfumes.

The literary sources tell us that the ceiling of the Golden House's main dining room was circular and constantly revolved like the heavens. The motive power was provided by slaves. The whereabouts of this early planetarium are unknown. The octagon is one of the candidates, but it was more probably located in the Neronian palace on the Palatine hill. Its superstructure did not survive the following reign, but a cellar has been found with two concentric walls encircling a wide, hollowed-out pillar with a circular staircase inside it. This looks very much as if it was the foundation for a rotating mechanism of some kind.

What exactly was the Golden House for? If only its remaining stones could speak. However, its general purpose and function must have been obvious on arrival at the vast vestibule. This was not a despot's luxury palace, hidden behind walls and closed doors and accessible only to favorites and guards. Nero did not commission Severus and Celer to create a secluded retreat. The grand entrance must have been designed for partying crowds, as was (surely) the monumental fountain. The complex may also have been used for political ceremonies and the entertainment of distinguished foreign visitors and delegations. The impression the estate gives as a whole is of a contemporary theme park.

Except for the palaces on the Palatine, it seems unlikely that there were apartments or suites where a princeps might live; at least none has been found. A Roman's bedroom was often dark, windowless, and large enough only for a bed. Such rooms have yet to be unearthed, except for a residential area in the eastern wing. Likewise, archaeologists have not identified latrines or evidence of cooking facilities. (For large-scale events, equipment such as braziers and urinal jars would presumably have been brought in for the occasion.) A long line of rooms in the pavilion with exits onto open ground was most likely used as shops.

Martial called the Golden House that "arrogant park which stole the dwellings of the poor." With typical hyperbole, he wrote that "one single house was starting to occupy a whole city." This was an upper-class view, nose wrinkled against the vulgarity of the place. But even a critic such as Martial had to admit that the tyrant built well: "What is worse than Nero, what is better than Nero's baths?"

By contrast, Nero was no snob, and as we have seen, he enjoyed mingling with people of every social class. The Golden House could have been, and probably was, designed for public banquets à la Tigellinus and the kind of erotic evening concerts that Nero enjoyed in company with his young hooligans. As at the Campus Martius, its open spaces in the daytime may also have accommodated family picnics and athletic sports.

The Golden House was the origin of the inaccurate rumors of a plot to destroy the city so that a selfish despot could rebuild it as a private enclave. However, in the event, it was designed as a gift to the citizens of Rome. It reflected Nero's policy of deploying culture and entertainment to secure approval for his rule. Ordinary Romans were invited to enjoy a taste of imperial luxury. They were grateful rather than envious.

Nero famously said of the Golden House: "At last I can begin to be housed like a human being." He was referring not only to the splendors of his new home on the Palatine, but also to the pavilion and the park where he could pursue his populist politics and mingle with the crowds. He had created a stage on which the emperor of the known world could play his part as lead actor. He liked to pretend to be who he actually was. This was a new sort of principate, whose core priority was to please.

To summarize, the Golden House was a People's palace. As it rose, phoenixlike, from the ashes of the Great Fire, it allowed the princeps to face down the allegations of arson. We hear no more of them nor of complaints about shortages of food or shelter.

His reign was beginning to be a success.

12

ALL THE CONSPIRATORS

ONE NIGHT in the year 65, Caesellius Bassus dreamed a dream that was to change his life.

He was a mentally unstable *eques* of Punic stock who lived in Carthage, where he owned a farm. He put his faith in what had been revealed to him and set sail for Rome where he bribed his way into the emperor's presence. He announced great news: Prompted by his dream, he had found an immensely deep cavern underneath his land. It contained a vast quantity of gold, not minted into coins but in the form of unwrought and ancient bullion. Heavy ingots were strewn on the floor, and in another part of the cave the metal was piled in columns.

The treasure had lain there for centuries, hidden by Dido, the legendary founder and queen of Carthage, a merchant city on the coast of North Africa that matured over the centuries into a powerful maritime empire. She was a princess of the Phoenician city-state of Tyre. Handsome, clever, and rich, she escaped after the murder of her husband to try her fortunes elsewhere, bringing with her a sizable proportion of Tyre's population—not to mention her golden hoard. She chose the site of Carthage, and building had begun when, according to Vergil's *Aeneid,* Prince Aeneas, together with his exiles from the sack of Troy, arrived.

He fell in love with the queen, but immediately dropped her when instructed by Jupiter to fulfill his destiny and help found Rome. Before sailing away, the hero lamely excused himself by telling her:

"Italiam non sponte sequor" (I am not going to Italy of my own free will!). Angry and brokenhearted, Dido built a funeral pyre on which she immolated herself. (The story, however, was a later invention designed to explain the bitter relations between Rome and Carthage, which culminated in long wars and eventually the latter's destruction in 146 B.C.)

The impressionable Bassus claimed that Dido had concealed her gold while her city was under construction, on the grounds either that her young nation might be corrupted by too much wealth or that covetous natives might be tempted into war.

The princeps was convinced that Bassus was telling the truth, and he took no steps to check neither the man's credibility nor the facts of his revelation. Triremes were dispatched to Carthage to fetch the loot. Excitement rose in the court and the city. Nero began spending his windfall before he had received it.

The promise of fabulous wealth became the prime topic taken up by orators looking for material with which to eulogize the emperor. Tacitus amuses himself at their expense:

> "Earth is teeming with a new kind of fertility," they said, "and the gods are sending wealth we did not ask for." And there were other flatteries delivered with consummate eloquence to dupe a credulous emperor.

It was all a bubble. Bassus had been so confident that only now did he actually dig up his fields and the surrounding land. He was helped by soldiers and a crowd of locals in a delusory gold rush. Nothing was found, neither cave nor bullion. Bassus at last recognized his error, and took his own life.

The tale of the dream that did not come true illustrates the financial difficulties in which Nero found himself. The empire was very expensive to run and there was seldom any annual surplus. Matters deteriorated throughout the reign.

Financial values in the ancient world cannot be directly compared with those of today, because social and economic expectations then and now differ so greatly. Historians such as Tacitus showed little interest in money except when they wanted to highlight imperial extravagance.

The best that can be done is to take into account a basket of costs and prices in the basic Roman currency, the sesterce (or the denarius, worth 4 sesterces). So, for example, a private soldier in the legions earned 900 sesterces a year (if we ignore bonuses and deductions), a loaf of bread cost a reasonably priced half sesterce, and a donkey 500 sesterces. It is estimated that 115 sesterces would cover minimum subsistence for a year.

At the other end of the scale, a great fortune was measured in hundreds of thousands of sesterces—Pallas and Seneca were reputed to be worth 300 million sesterces each. An average Senator such as Pliny the Younger at the end of the first century might have disposed of 200,000.

The empire's gross domestic product (GDP) is estimated at between 9 and 20.9 billion sesterces, and the state's income from all sources may have amounted to 0.8 billion sesterces.

This was a large but inflexible budget, without a reserve. Transporting heavy specie to and from the capital was impractical and risky. Ships sank and bandits marauded. So tax revenue tended to be raised and spent in its province. Officials were often corrupt. Tax increases were deeply unpopular, and emperors did their best to avoid them.

At least 40 percent of the state's income went to the army, with its twenty-five legions and matching auxiliary formations. They added up to an estimated quarter of a million men. This was the least necessary to defend a frontier which ran from the North Sea to the river Euphrates. In addition, the Praetorians, the Urban Cohorts, the *vigiles,* and a fleet employing some forty thousand sailors had to be paid their wages.

Wars were a further expense and the unwarlike Nero faced three during his reign—the revolt of Boudica in Britannia, campaigning in the Black Sea, and the seemingly endless struggle with the Parthian empire over Armenia.

Military action was not the only drain on Nero's resources. Special payments were made to the Praetorians to buy their loyalty on his accession and to calm them after Agrippina's murder.

One of the qualities the public demanded of their ruler was open-handedness, liberality. He was expected to step in with assistance after natural disasters, and to provide entertainments for Rome's tricky and exacting inhabitants. He had to steer a course between the Scylla of extravagance and the Charybdis of avarice.

All these largely unavoidable costs made the maintenance of financial control extremely challenging.

How could Nero manage to balance the books?

Nero's upper-class critics gave him a reputation for overspending on a luxurious lifestyle, grandiose architecture, and populist cultural programs. This was largely undeserved. In fact, he took an interest in financial management, even though he was no expert and depended on well-judged senatorial advice and expertise as well as the input of his freedmen.

In 58 an incident occurred that throws light on Nero's seriousness. Following persistent public complaints he considered announcing the abolition of indirect taxes, such as harbor and customs duties. These were collected by commercial companies of businessmen who bid for the tax-raising contracts. They were rapacious, oppressive, and hard to regulate. Nero was well-meaning but inexperienced. Abolition would mean free trade and be very popular, for it would stimulate the imperial economy. But wiser heads advised a rethink. Before any beneficial effects could be felt, a large hole in the government's annual budget would have to be filled. Nero pulled back and replaced his plan with a set of practical but unambitious policies largely designed to encourage transparency and deter criminality. We may guess that the farmers soon found a way to circumvent the new measures.

Like his predecessors and his successors on the throne, Nero was obliged to plug projected deficits by fund-raising. The princeps regularly dipped into his vast personal wealth, the privy purse, or *fiscus,* to assist the state exchequer, or *aerarium*. He expected relatives and wealthy individuals to leave him a generous legacy when they died. Plotters against the regime usually had their estates confiscated in whole or in part. The property of convicted criminals throughout the empire could also be expropriated by state authorities. These were the *bona damnatorum,* the goods of the condemned.

As we have seen, coins were a powerful propaganda tool for sending messages from Nero to his subjects. In the wake of the Great Fire, he conducted a reform of the coinage, partly to redesign its imagery and partly to make the mint profitable by moderate reductions in the content of silver and gold specie. There seems to have been little adverse reaction.

Modern scholarship, working on a plausible analysis of major categories of expenditure and cost trends, suggests that extraordinary payments throughout the reign nearly equaled the regular budget in most years. The lion's share of 58 percent went toward military campaigns in Britain and the Middle East as against 20 percent spent on construction and the same again spent on life at court (gifts, salaries, and pensions).

As a rule, Nero did manage to cover his costs (thanks in part, we surmise, to the foundations laid by Agrippina and Pallas during their time in power). But after the Great Fire, strains began to show, and the wealthy found themselves under continual pressure to help the emperor out. The Golden House was a slap in their faces. The atmosphere in the Senate grew ever more irritable.

This was the backdrop against which the most serious challenge to Nero's rule played itself out.

In the early sixties, various dissidents complained about the princeps. From muttering they graduated to conspiring.

Small groups formed and gradually came to be aware of one another's existence. All kinds of malcontents joined a growing movement—Senators, businessmen (namely, *equites*), soldiers, and, surprisingly for a male-dominated society, a few women. An emperor felt secure only if he could command the loyalty of the Praetorians, so it was ominous that two of the key plotters were guardsmen—a military tribune, Subrius Flavus (whom we have already met), and a centurion. Perhaps Agrippina's death had unsettled them more than had appeared at the time.

Motives were mixed. Some were Stoics and idealists; as already discussed, their model was Julius Caesar's enemy, Cato, who refused under any circumstances to accept one-man rule. The usual toxic personal resentments of court life played a part. So maybe did expensive plans to rebuild the burnt city and to spend a fortune on the Golden House. But if there was one common theme, it can be traced to the emperor's extraordinarily successful debut at Naples. He had proved to himself that he could make a go of it as a professional artist and entertainer. So far the princeps had been a dilettante, a hobbyist, but now he had gone too far. His customary appearance was a visual summation of everything the aristocracy loathed. He always had his hair set in curls and often held audience in a silk dressing gown, worn effeminately without a belt. He completed the ensemble by wearing a scarf around his neck.

More seriously, Nero used the arts and sport as a means of communicating directly with ordinary Romans, with the masses. His legitimacy would no longer depend on the constitutional settlement which Augustus had agreed with the Senate, but on the direct approval of the People. To be bypassed in this way was an existential threat for the ruling class. It could not be permitted.

No one was advocating a return to the confusions of the republic, and there was an urgent need to locate a figurehead who would lead the conspiracy and was qualified to succeed Nero as emperor.

A name emerged which attracted widespread support—that of Gaius Calpurnius Piso, the model of a conventional aristocrat in all respects bar one—his wife, "a low born woman whose only asset was her physical beauty." He came from one of Rome's most distinguished families (a forebear was the Calpurnia who was Julius Caesar's last wife). Well connected among the nobility, he was also popular with the plebs. Tall and good-looking, he was an excellent public speaker and usually acted for the defense in court. He preferred the "mild warfare" of the law to a military career. Generous to his friends and affable to strangers, he had the common touch. He opened his doors to men of talent from disadvantaged backgrounds.

Piso had wide tastes, held in moderation and in private. He performed tragedies, wrote poetry, and composed for the cithara. He enjoyed playing ball and exercised his brain by playing a strategy board game called Little Bandits (*latrunculi*). He was a watered-down version of Nero.

Unfortunately, an attractive and kindly exterior masked weakness and self-indulgence. Tacitus had little time for Piso, who

> was far from possessing depth of character or moderation in his pleasures; he immersed himself in frivolity, luxury, and, sometimes, dissipation. And this had the blessing of most people who, surrounded by such sweet vices, do not want to see austerity or great strictness in the supreme power.

Piso was on the friendliest of terms with the princeps, whom he often entertained at his beautiful seaside villa at Baiae. Nevertheless, he accepted the invitation to join the conspiracy, although he seems to have adopted a somewhat detached attitude toward it. Some plotters noticed this and talked of dumping Piso once Nero was dead. They would kill him too and offer the throne to Seneca. It is uncertain whether the old Stoic knew what was under way and approved. Was he even an active participant? Dio believes he was, whereas Tacitus claims to be unsure, although his narrative points toward involvement.

One thing we do know is that Seneca was experienced in the shady art of political intrigue. A conspirator, an *eques* called Antonius Natalis, whom he happened to know, recommended that he meet with Piso. He replied that such an encounter would be to neither man's advantage, adding: "My own survival depends on Piso's safety." This cryptic remark implied that he knew more than he was revealing.

The emperor's longed-for creative renaissance was breaking down. Some of the conspirators were or had been members of Nero's artistic circle. The most famous of these was Seneca's nephew, the fashionable poet Lucan, who had been dropped by a jealous princeps and was hungry for revenge. Nero's intimate, the freedman Senecio, who had facilitated his affair with the lovely and loving Acte, had also given up on him for reasons unknown, although he pretended to be as close as ever.

The key activists appear not to have worried greatly about confidentiality and recruited whomever among their friends and acquaintances they judged likely to be sympathetic. Among them were two disreputable Senators, Flavius Scaevinus and Afranius Quintianus, who busied themselves beyond their abilities. If we believe Tacitus, Scaevinus's brain "was ruined by dissipation and he led a languid, sleepy life . . . The other was a notorious effeminate who had been insulted by Nero in a scurrilous poem and wanted to get his own back."

All these men, caught between hope and fear, spoke darkly among themselves and hesitated. The number of those in the know grew. Subrius brought along some more Praetorian officers. For a long time it was hoped that the Guards Prefect, Faenius Rufus, could be won over to the cause, but the fruit was too high to reach. He had no particular quarrel with Nero. However, the continual sniping by his fellow Prefect, Tigellinus, about his old friendship with Agrippina became intolerable. When at last he let it be known late in 64 that he endorsed the plot, there was relief all around, for Faenius was a leading man in the government and a great catch.

Then a woman called Epicharis put in a surprise appearance. Her name was Greek, and she was probably a freedwoman. She had ferreted out details of the conspiracy and was eager to join it. Her source of information is unknown but can be guessed. She was the lover of Lucius Annaeus Mela, Seneca's younger brother and Lucan's father. All roads led to the Senecas. She must have been briefed by one of them or deduced his secret from something said or done. It is possible that Seneca himself was worried by the inactivity of the conspirators and felt that Epicharis would get the project back on track.

FIRST EMPEROR

Augustus brought Rome's civil wars to an end and founded the Julio-Claudian dynasty. He was much admired by Nero, his great-grandson, especially for his cultural policies. VATICAN MUSEUMS, ROME.

THE FACES OF NERO

The young Nero, when he was being educated by the philosopher Seneca and trained to be emperor by his mother, Agrippina. Römisch-Germanisches Museum, Cologne.

Agrippina crowns her son Nero with a laurel wreath, as if to claim sole credit for making him emperor. Indeed, she meant to rule through him. Relief from the Sebasteion, Aphrodisias Museum, Turkey.

Nero made the most of the opportunities that being emperor gave him. But it seems he would rather have been a professional musician based in Alexandria, the ancient world's culture capital. Here he wears his hair long at the back in the fashionable Greek manner, as if he were a *cithara,* or lyre, player. CAPITOLINE MUSEUMS, ROME.

Nero seen through the eyes of an ordinary soldier, who left this sketch of the emperor in the basement of the imperial palace on Rome's Palatine hill. Although rough, it is a convincing likeness. GRAFFITO COPY, FROM P. CASTREN AND H. LILIUS, *GRAFFITI DEL PALATINO II, DOMUS TIBERIANA* (HELSINKI, 1970), 121, NO. 3.

Nero's disciplinarian mother, Agrippina, who plotted his route to the throne. This bust from around the year 50 captures the empress's intelligence and charm but hints at her underlying ruthlessness. GETTY VILLA COLLECTION.

Seneca, philosopher and statesman, who could never reconcile his great wealth with his moral principles. As Nero's chief political adviser, along with the Praetorian Prefect Burrus, he encouraged his inexperienced master to practice the art of good government but lived long enough to see him set aside his good intentions. MUSEO NEUES, BERLIN.

Poppaea Sabina, a noted Roman beauty, was eager for power. She became Nero's greatest love, but she died young when, in a fit of anger, the emperor kicked her in the belly during a pregnancy. He never forgave himself. Palazzo Massimo alle Terme, Rome.

The dining room of the Villa Poppaea at Oplontis, a holiday resort near Misenum on the Bay of Naples. It may have been here in 59 that Nero masterminded his mother's murder. In 79 the villa was buried—and preserved—by the eruption of Vesuvius.

A modern evocation of the flames engulfing the temple of Claudius at Camulodunum, today's Colchester. Boudica, queen of the Iceni tribe, led a rebel army that destroyed the magnificent edifice and slaughtered the town's defenders.

A personified Britannia falls to the Roman invader. In 61 Boudica fights back, but like the hapless female warrior in the marble relief, she too is defeated and destroyed. Aphrodisias Museum, Turkey.

The frieze on the Arch of Titus in Rome shows victorious legionaries looting the menorah from the Temple in Jerusalem. In 67, a revolt broke out in Judaea, and Vespasian, a competent general, was sent by Nero to suppress it. After a fierce struggle, the Romans were victorious. Resistance was over by 73, by which time Vespasian had succeeded Nero on the throne.

FIRE AND RENEWAL

Nothing is left today of ancient Rome's major racecourse, the Circus Maximus. Where it once stood, all that remains is a stretch of grassy scrub. But in its heyday it was a vast structure with stands, shrines, and shops and seated 150,000 spectators. Hereabouts in 64, the Great Fire of Rome broke out, probably in a fast food outlet or a small manufacturing business. Much of the city was burned down. The disaster was an accident, but the emperor got the blame. In the background of this photograph are the Palatine hill and the imperial palace.

Little is left of Nero's spectacular Golden House (Domus Aurea) in Rome, built over the ruins of the Great Fire. Here a large octagonal space, roofed with a concrete dome, survives. It was probably used as a banqueting hall.

Epicharis loathed Nero, although we do not know why, and was pushy and determined. She saw no reason for delay. Happening to be in Campania, she decided to subvert the loyalty of senior officers at the naval base of Misenum. She looked up the captain of a war trireme whom she knew. He was Vulsius Proculus, who had played a part in the murder of Agrippina. Our sources do not say, but he may have commanded, or at least sailed in, the doomed vessel that was meant to carry the empress mother to a watery grave.

Proculus had expected promotion for his assistance, or some other generous reward, and been disappointed. He complained bitterly to Epicharis about a thankless emperor. He told her: "I will settle the account, should the opportunity arise."

She was encouraged by what she had heard. Proculus might be persuaded to bring in other officers of the fleet. She mused that they could be extremely useful, since Nero delighted in going out on sea trips off Puteoli and Misenum that would offer plenty of opportunities to attack him.

Taking her courage in both hands, Epicharis went further and listed all the emperor's crimes. Nothing was left, she said, of the Senate's and the People's rights. A way had been found, however, to punish him for the ruin of his country. Proculus had only to stiffen his will and bring over the best men to the cause. This time he would be well rewarded.

Proculus considered his position. He came to the conclusion that despite his sense of grievance he would be wiser to maintain his present loyalty than to entrust his fate to the conspirators. He reported his conversation to Nero, and Epicharis was arrested. Nero in person confronted her with the informer and interrogated her under torture to discover what she might know of the plot. She endured the pain without revealing anything. She had been careful to name no names, so it was her word against that of Proculus. Her denials were convincing and, in the absence of witnesses, she easily refuted him.

Although she was judged to be innocent, Nero had a suspicion that there was more to her story than met the eye. He kept her in custody.

The arrest of Epicharis galvanized the plotters, terrified that she might betray them.

Everyone could see that the time for conversation was over and that a plan of action had to be agreed and implemented. For a time Subrius had set his heart on attacking Nero covertly during the Great Fire, when he was scurrying around the palace at night without guards. Alternatively, he could strike the tyrant down while he was singing onstage. Such an exploit would fire the imagination of all lovers of liberty. But what were the chances of his escaping with his life? The likely answer gave the tribune pause for thought.

A safer choice of location was, of all things, Piso's villa. Nero appreciated its charm and often dropped by for a bath or for dinner. From time to time he liked to dispense with his guards and escape from the "tedious magnificence of his position."

Piso objected. In Tacitus's words, his excuse was

> the hostile reaction they would face if the sanctity of the table, and the gods of hospitality, were stained with the blood of an emperor, however despicable. Better for them to do the deed in the capital—in that detestable palace built with the plundered wealth of Roman citizens, or else in some public place.

That was what Piso said. Secretly he was afraid that his absence from the city would create a power vacuum which somebody else would exploit by claiming the throne for himself. He was especially worried about Lucius Silanus, son of the "golden sheep." He was the last living direct male descendant of Augustus and like Nero his great-great-grandson. Piso also feared one of the Consuls for 64, the energetic Marcus Julius Vestinus Atticus. He might well present himself as a champion of senatorial liberty or, at least, act as kingmaker. All in all, it was best to stay in Rome, Piso thought.

In mid-April 65, as every year, crowds gathered after nightfall at the Circus Maximus to witness a bizarre and cruel ritual. Torches were tied to the tails of foxes and set alight, and the terrified animals were released onto the racecourse. The object of the exercise is uncertain. According to the poet Publius Ovidius Naso (Ovid to us), long ago a farm boy caught a fox stealing chickens and tried to burn it alive. It ran off in flames and set fire to the fields. The explanation is fanciful, and presumably the custom was somehow connected with the arrival of spring and the growth of crops. It was a high point of the Cerealia, a week-long festival in honor of the grain goddess, Ceres.

The final day was given over to *ludi,* or games. This was when and where the conspirators decided to carry out their great exploit. The princeps hardly ever left home, spending most of his time in the seclusion of his palace and gardens. However, he would be unable to resist a program of events that included a horse race and theatrical shows. His inattention to his personal security would make him easy to reach.

A detailed action plan was prepared at last. A Consul designate, Plautius Lateranus, was to make the first move. His main claim to attention was his affair with Claudius's scandalous wife Messalina, for which he narrowly escaped a death sentence. He had nothing personal against Nero and joined the conspiracy for a serious and disinterested reason—regret for the republic.

Lateranus would approach Nero and apparently beg for financial assistance. He would prostrate himself in front of the emperor, grab him around the legs, bring him down, and hold him to the ground. According to Tacitus, he was well equipped for this task, being "determined, enormous, and muscular."

Flavius Scaevinus would be the first to stab Nero. He had removed an ancient dagger on display in a temple for the purpose. He wore it all the time, as an instrument sanctified for a daring enterprise. Other plotters were expected to join in the subsequent mêlée as well as they could or dared.

Meanwhile Piso would be waiting eagerly for news in the temple of Ceres on the Aventine hill, which overlooked the Circus Maximus. Once it was confirmed that Nero was dead, Faenius Rufus would arrive and take Piso to the Praetorian camp, where he would be introduced as the new emperor. This would be a crucial encounter, for the approval of the Guards was of greater practical importance than that of an unarmed Senate. Unless they were brought on board, Piso's reign would not outlast the day, nor (most probably) would he.

To sweeten the pill, the two men would be accompanied by Antonia, Claudius's daughter, whom we have already encountered. She was the widow of Faustus Sulla, one of Nero's victims (see page 168). The new princeps intended to marry her and so link himself to the imperial family. Tacitus doubts the story, for Piso adored his lower-class wife. History teaches us, though, that ambition can trump the heart. From Antonia's point of view, involvement in such a risky project would bring few obvious advantages—unless she were to seek revenge for her husband's murder, which she almost certainly witnessed. Her presence in front of the soldiers would connect Piso to the glorious memory of Germanicus, and more likely than not she accepted the invitation to join him.

While Nero was careless about his safety, the conspirators were just as careless about secrecy. It is extraordinary that such a large and diverse group was able to remain undetected for so long. On the eve of the attempt their luck ran out.

For much of that day Scaevinus was moody and stressed. In case of failure, he decided to put all his affairs in order. He had a long conversation with a fellow conspirator, Antonius Natalis, after which he returned home and sealed his will. He drew his holy dagger from its scabbard and complained how blunt it was. He instructed a freedman in his household, a certain Milichus, to sharpen it on a whetstone "till the edge glittered." At this point he lay down to a more elaborate dinner than usual and gave his favorite slaves their freedom and in certain cases sums of money. He made desultory remarks with affected cheerfulness. Finally, he ordered bandages for wounds and tourniquets to staunch the flow of blood.

Milichus reviewed these curious events with concern. What could they portend? It was obvious that his employer was preparing the ground for a dangerous crisis during which blood might be shed, including his own. Scaevinus had no serious enemies, had not explained himself, and whatever he had in mind was keeping secret. Melodramatic though it must have seemed to the freedman, there was only one plausible interpretation which solved the mystery. Scaevinus intended to assassinate the emperor.

What should Milichus do? His first loyalty was owed to the man who had enfranchised him, given him work, and trusted him. He discussed the matter with his wife. She pointed out that he was not the only person to witness Scaevinus's odd behavior. Others in the household will have come to the same conclusion he had and would report what they had seen and heard to the authorities. "So one man's silence will change nothing," she said, "and the rewards will go to the informer who spoke first."

Her husband was persuaded and early the following morning the couple slipped away to the Horti Serviliani (the Servilian Gardens). This imperial property was a house in a park with a fine art collection, probably located in the southwest quarter of the city. Nero was spending time there, presumably to avoid the dust and noise of the building work under way on the Palatine as part of the Golden House development.

Milichus was turned away at the door, but when he insisted that he had grave and terrible news to tell, the doorkeepers escorted him to the emperor's secretary, the *libertus a libellis,* Epaphroditus. At the time he was the most powerful of the Greek freedmen who ran the administration—not so much for his handling of correspondence and petitions, but because he controlled physical access to the princeps, deciding who could see him and who not. (He also had the bizarre distinction of owning the greatest philosopher of the age, Epictetus, who happened to have been born a slave.)

Epaphroditus listened to the informant's story and decided it was important enough to warn Nero immediately. Once in the emperor's presence, Milichus reported everything he knew or guessed. He stressed the urgency of the case and the determination of the conspirators. As his pièce de resistance he produced the sharpened dagger and recommended that his patron be arrested at once.

Scaevinus was picked up by soldiers and taken to the Servilian Gardens for questioning. He assumed a mask of affronted innocence.

The dagger was a family heirloom, he said, and had been kept in his bedroom. His freedman had stolen it. He often reviewed his will and there was nothing out of the ordinary that he did so yesterday. He habitually enfranchised slaves and gave them money. He was particularly generous on this occasion because he had money troubles and needed to cut back on his household outgoings. As for his dinner he always ate well.

It was a self-assured performance, and when he concluded his defense by attacking Milichus as an unspeakable rascal, the freedman's case collapsed.

Or it would have if his wife had not reminded him of the suspiciously long and secret conversation his patron had had with Natalis. When he mentioned this to the emperor, Natalis was summoned. He and Scaevinus were placed in separate rooms and asked what they had discussed at their meeting. When their answers failed to tally, suspicion neared certainty, and they were put in chains. They were threatened with torture and shown the instruments. They broke down.

Natalis was the first to talk, and he did so with a will. He knew more details about the plot than Scaevinus did. He named Piso and reported his meeting with Seneca, but without implicating him. Tacitus believes that he may have mentioned the retired statesman only because he was out of favor at court and he wanted to please Nero. Once Scaevinus knew that Natalis was talking, he followed suit and named the rest of the conspirators, including Lucan, who, when questioned, implicated his mother, and Senecio, his best friend.

The cowardice of the men threw into bold relief the courage of a woman. Nero recalled that Epicharis was still in custody and had her brought before him and Tigellinus for further examination.

Believing that a woman's constitution could not endure pain, they subjected her to renewed torture. But neither flogging nor branding weakened her denials. Her irritated tormentors piled on the pressure so as not to be bested by a woman, but to no effect. On the following day she was brought back, but this time in a covered sedan chair or litter, for her limbs had been dislocated and she could no longer walk. On the way, she stripped off her breast band (a basic type of brassiere) and made a noose of it, which she put around her neck and fastened to the chair's canopy. She then pushed down with all her weight and throttled what little life was left in her. The guardsman accompanying the litter did not notice what had happened until the carriers set it down and he looked inside.

New names were brought forward and the city entered a military lockdown. The regime was determined to stamp out any sign of insurrection at home and to keep the wider empire, especially potentially rebellious frontier legions, in the dark. Tacitus evokes a climate of fear:

> Nero grew more and more frightened, despite having redoubled the guards surrounding his person. He virtually put the city under arrest, manning the walls with military units and the sea and river under close surveillance. There were also Praetorian foot soldiers and cavalrymen—interspersed with Germans, trusted by the emperor because they were foreigners. They were tearing about the forums and private houses, and even through the countryside and nearby towns. And so never-ending columns of manacled prisoners were being dragged to the gates of the Servilian Gardens and left there waiting.

Nero and Tigellinus presided over the interrogations. Guilt was assumed on the slightest scrap of evidence. Cheerfulness toward a known plotter, a chance conversation, a casual encounter, attendance at a dinner party or at a show in their company—these were enough to compromise, to convict, and to condemn. Suetonius reports that some men lost their lives on frivolous pretexts:

> one man was brought to trial and put to death for living near the Forum, and letting out some shops or for receiving a few friends in them; and another [C. Cassius Longinus, a famous jurist] because he possessed an image of the Cassius who assassinated Julius Caesar.

The coup was not over.

It could in fact still succeed. A number of conspirators had not yet been identified and arrested, some with direct access to the princeps. Nobody had fingered Faenius Rufus, the Praetorian Prefect, who joined the interrogation team and sought to prove his bona fides by asking prisoners the toughest of questions. At one point, Subrius Flavus, also still free, was standing beside the Prefect. He asked by a discreet gesture whether he should draw his sword and finish Nero off there and then. Faenius shook his head, and the moment of opportunity passed.

Along with a number of others, he tried to maintain his dual role as plotter and inquisitor. He was exposed when he pressed Scaevinus too hard during his interrogation. The latter observed with a sneer that nobody knew more about what had been planned than Faenius himself. Faenius was thunderstruck. His stammering reply betrayed his terror. Nero ordered a burly private who was standing nearby to seize and bind him. Faenius never recovered his nerve. He faced execution without resolve and even entered lamentations in his will.

In the meantime, while Milichus's revelations were fresh and the administration still reeling from them, there were those who advised Piso to make a decisive move while he still could. He should mount the rostra in the Forum and announce Nero's overthrow. Once his intentions were known, the impact on the public would be immense. His fellow conspirators should seize the hour and rally civilian opinion. Alternatively, and more wisely, Piso should go at once to the Praetorian camp with Faenius by his side and try to win over the Guards. This was risky, but if he succeeded, Nero would fall.

There was no salvation in inactivity. In Tacitus's words, Piso was warned that

> men would come to shackle him, and ultimately put him to a degrading death. How much more creditable to die for the good of one's country and calling for help for its liberty! Better that the soldiers abandon him and the plebs too—provided that he himself,

if his life must be prematurely taken, make his death a credit to his ancestors, and to his descendants.

Piso preferred to throw in his hand. He went out into the street, walked about for a while, and then returned to his house. Steeling himself against imminent death, he waited for the soldiers to arrive. When they did, they turned out to be raw recruits or men new to the service. Nero was unsure that experienced Praetorians would obey his orders.

Piso was permitted suicide. He cut the arteries in his arms. As with other casualties of the regime, he left behind a will that flattered the emperor in the hope of averting the confiscation of his estate. He wanted his wife to live on after him in appropriate style.

The plot failed because it was halfhearted and amateurish. For some it seems to have been a game without real commitment and (apparently) without real consequences. Too many people were involved to ensure secrecy and timely decision making. There appears to have been no consultation with the frontier generals, with whose legions power ultimately lay. Leading personalities were reluctant to launch the attempt on Nero's life. Above all, while many loathed the regime, there was no groundswell of opposition among either Senators or the citizenry at large, most of whom remained loyal during the crisis. Had Nero been killed, Piso and his friends would very probably have faced serious resistance and even civil war.

Did these men suspect that they had not made a convincing case against the princeps? Perhaps they did not altogether believe in it themselves. The emperor had handled the Great Fire competently, the Boudica rebellion had been quickly suppressed, and affairs in Armenia were proceeding well enough. All was quiet along the European marches. In what way would Piso represent an improvement on Nero? As a cynic put it, they would simply be exchanging a singer for an actor.

We know of forty conspirators, real or alleged, most of whom were punished after interrogation or summary trial. They were well-known public men, and to live through that time, waiting to learn their fate, was a painful experience. The ancient sources describe Nero's reaction as an indiscriminate "reign of terror," and certainly mistakes were made. However, he and his advisers took some care when determining penalties. These should be exemplary but seen to be reasonable. They wanted to avoid further disturbance of the status quo.

Death was restricted to the guiltiest. Up to twelve conspirators appear to have been executed and eight took their own lives (not counting a Praetorian who was acquitted, but killed himself all the same). Proculus and Natalis were pardoned for informing.

The Senate was treated with a degree of sensitivity: an estimated twelve members were merely sent into exile, plus Scaevinus's widow, as against seven executions or suicides. The uncertain loyalty of the Praetorians called for cautious handling too: Five Praetorians were put to death, including Faenius Rufus, and four were acquitted (among them the suicide reported above) or demoted. The guardsmen did not disgrace themselves when facing execution, although the same could not be said of their Prefect.

Two brave deaths deserve to be remembered. The tribune Subrius Flavus, an originator of the whole failed enterprise, was an old-fashioned soldier who was a stickler for duty and competence.

A fellow tribune was detailed to conduct the execution. He ordered a grave to be dug in a field nearby. Flavus had a look and said it was too shallow and narrow. "More bad discipline," he remarked to the soldiers in attendance. When the executioner told him to hold his neck out firmly, Flavus replied: "I only hope you strike as firmly." In fact, the tribune was shaking violently and only cut off the head after two blows. He recovered his nerve after Flavus was dead and boasted to the emperor of his brutality.

The Consul designate, Lateranus, was taken away with such speed that he was not allowed to kiss his children goodbye or have a minute or two to choose his method of death. He was rushed to a location reserved for the punishment of slaves and butchered at the hands of a Praetorian tribune who had himself been involved in the plot. Lateranus maintained a resolute silence, and did not give away his executioner. He stretched out his neck, but received a feeble blow. He pulled back for a moment and then stretched out his neck again, before making his quietus.

The impact on Nero of the conspiracy was almost life-threatening. He was deeply affected by the large number and diversity of those who wished him dead. He believed that he was genuinely loved and was dismayed that close friends such as Senecio had betrayed him. Tormented by his crimes, he had depended on people he trusted for acceptance. Once again, the timidity that underlay Nero's brashness darkened into fear and fear into rage.

He was especially unforgiving to those who were or had been members of his inner circle. One of the Consuls for 65 was Julius Vestinus Atticus. He had once been an intimate companion of his and they were now on bad terms: according to Tacitus,

> Nero's loathing of Vestinus had arisen from an intimate friendship. In the course of this Vestinus came to know well, and to despise, the emperor's cowardice, while Nero came to fear his friend's outspokenness. He had many times been the butt of his biting witticisms, which, when they have drawn largely on the truth, leave behind a bitter recollection.

A further offense was his marriage to an aristocratic beauty, Statilia Messalina, who had caught the imperial eye.

The emperor had confidently expected Vestinus's name to appear on the list of traitors. Surprisingly, nobody mentioned him. This was because he had not been invited to join the plot. Old feuds and a general feeling that he was headstrong and indiscreet had excluded him. Nevertheless, although he could not be brought to trial for lack of evidence, the princeps was determined to destroy the Consul by foul means if not by fair. He sent out a Praetorian cohort "to forestall the Consul's designs, capture what might be called his military headquarters and overpower his corps of youthful followers."

Vestinus maintained a house with a view of the Forum and a retinue of handsome slaves all of approximately the same age, of whom the authorities were evidently nervous. On this day he had finished his consular duties and was hosting a dinner party when soldiers entered and said that their commander was looking for him. Vestinus realized at once what their mission was and saw that resistance would be futile. He rose from his dining couch and made some necessary arrangements. He shut himself in his bedroom and called for his doctor who happened to be at hand. His arteries were sliced.

Before the effects were felt, Vestinus was carried to a steam bath and immersed in hot water. He did not allow himself a word of self-pity before expiring. Tacitus writes that the emperor amused himself with a cruel practical joke:

> Those who had been reclining at table with [Vestinus] were surrounded by guards and were not allowed to leave. The diners expected death to follow food. In his mind's eye Nero laughed at their dismay, but eventually he let them go, quipping: "They have paid a steep enough bill for their meal at the Consul's."

Lucan fared no better. Nero next ordered his death. As his blood ran, Lucan felt his feet and hands grow cold and his life gradually slip from his extremities. His chest was still warm, though, and his mental powers intact. At that moment he remembered some lines from his epic, *Pharsalia,* in which he described a wounded soldier experiencing a similar death:

> *From no-one who is dying, has life*
> *Rushed down so wide a path. The lowest part of his torso*
> *Handed over to death limbs empty of vitals;*
> *But where the swelling lung lies, where the organs are warm,*
> *The Fates stuck for a long time and, after a long struggle*
> *With this portion of the man, took all his parts with difficulty.*

Apparently, these were his last words. He was twenty-five years old.

Lucan's mother whom he had betrayed was left to go free, as much as to say that nothing worth believing could come from his lips.

——

The most famous of Nero's victims, and one of the earliest, was Seneca. The old man had been keeping himself occupied with his plays, essays, and correspondence. While he was careful not to comment on contemporary politics, he used tragedies on Greek mythological themes as safe spaces in which to speak his mind.

His *Thyestes* concerns two brothers at odds; one of them serves up the other's children in a stew for their father to eat. The play includes a damning definition of kingship that uncannily evokes Nero's weaknesses as a ruler:

It is not worldly wealth that makes a king
. . . nor the proud gaudiness
of golden halls or Tyrian purple dress.
A king is he who has no ill to fear,
Whose hand is innocent, whose conscience clear;
Who scorns licentious greed, who has not bowed
To the false favor of the fickle crowd.

It does not take much imagination to discern in these lines covert allusions to the Golden House and to Nero's lack of courage, his feelings of shame, and his populist policies.

Apart from Seneca's ambiguous exchange about a possible meeting with Piso, there was no evidence implicating him. It was odd that in the run-up to the planned assassination attempt, he had moved to a country house of his only a few miles from Rome. Perhaps he had wanted to be on call, but conjecture was nowhere near proof. He remained where he was while the conspiracy foundered.

He understood the risks he ran by associating himself, however cautiously, with the conspiracy. He once wrote to a friend: "The present letter is written to you with this in mind, as if death were about to call me away in the very act of writing. I am ready to depart, and I shall enjoy life just because I am not overanxious as to the future date of my departure."

Dusk was coming on when a Praetorian tribune and some troops surrounded the villa and delivered a message from the princeps to Seneca, who was dining with his wife, Pompeia Paulina, and a couple of friends. He wanted to know whether Seneca could confirm Natalis's account of their conversation about Piso. Seneca did so, and the tribune reported back. Nero, who was with Poppaea and Tigellinus, asked him whether Seneca looked as if he was about to kill himself. He replied that he detected no signs of alarm, nor any distress in his language or expression. He was therefore instructed to return and deliver the death sentence.

Unbeknownst to the authorities, the tribune was himself a conspirator. He did not return the same way he had come but made a detour to see Faenius (who had not yet been unmasked). He asked him whether to obey the order. Faenius told him that he should. Tacitus cannot resist observing: "Thus fate had made cowards of them all."

Back at the villa, the tribune felt he would not be able to control his emotions and sent in one of his centurions to tell Seneca he must die. The old man did not repine and calmly asked for his will. The centurion refused to allow this, and Seneca apologized to his guests for being prevented from showing his gratitude for their services.

For a Stoic, death is to be accepted willingly, even welcomed. This was the message Seneca preached throughout a long life:

> Before I became old I tried to live well; now that I am old, I shall try to die well; but dying well means dying gladly. See to it that you never do anything unwillingly. That which is bound to be a necessity if you resist it, is not a necessity if you wish it.

Now that his last moments were upon him, he needed to prove the sincerity with which he implemented these high principles. He was well aware that his contemporaries detected in his lifestyle a gap between the theory and practice of virtue. In a letter to a friend he imagined his critics asking, as they habitually did, "Why, then, do you talk so much more bravely than you live?" He recognized that the only answer he could give was "I am not a wise man. . . . Do not require me to be on a level with the best of humanity, but merely to be better than the worst."

Seneca's private dining room had become a public stage. What was said and done there would be discussed throughout the known world. His reputation with posterity depended to a large extent on how well he acted the part Nero had given him.

He rallied his weeping guests, saying: "I leave you my one remaining possession—the pattern of my life. Where has your philosophy gone, where your rational attitude to approaching evils, which you had studied over all these years? Who is unaware of Nero's cruelty? Or that having killed his mother and his brother, his inevitable next step was to murder his guardian and teacher?"

These and similar observations were clearly for general consumption. Seneca then kissed Pompeia Paulina and begged her after his death to console herself with memories of their loving marriage. She made it clear that she intended to accompany him to the shades and he accepted the decision. They each made an incision in their arm with a single stroke.

Seneca's aged body was emaciated from his spare diet, and his wounds bled only slowly, so he also severed the arteries in the legs and behind the knees. Worn out by racking pain, he was worried that his suffering might break his wife's spirit and that her misery might weaken his own resolve, so he asked her to withdraw to another bedroom. His mind still sharp, he called two of his secretaries and dictated revisions to a book he had been writing.

Nero kept in touch with the latest developments at Seneca's villa. He had no quarrel with Paulina and sent orders that she should be saved. Her wounds were bandaged and the bleeding checked. She survived for a number of years, loyal to her husband's memory. She never fully recovered. Her blanched complexion was a permanent reminder of that terrible April evening.

As for Seneca, death still came agonizingly slowly. He asked a certain Statius Annaeus, a physician and probably a family freedman, to give him some hemlock. This was the poison used in ancient Athens as a means of capital punishment. Its most famous victim was the philosopher Socrates, and it seems that Seneca wanted to associate himself with that celebrated miscarriage of justice. In any event, some hemlock juice was brought and Seneca drank it, but without effect. As a last resort he was placed in a bath of warm water. He sprinkled some of it on the slaves who had helped him, saying that it was a libation to Jupiter the Liberator.

Once again we have the dying man aligning himself with Socrates, whose famous last words were to have reminded his friends that he had vowed a cockerel to the god of healing, Asclepios, in thanks for being cured of the disease of life. For his part, Seneca was making much the same point when he thanked the king of the gods for freeing him from existence.

He was then transferred to a steam bath, where he suffocated. He was immediately cremated without any ceremony.

Seneca lived up to his wish to suffer an exemplary death. He was brave and endured pain and delay without complaint. However, one cannot resist the impression of an event that was staged. The comparison with Socrates was not to his advantage. According to the accounts of Plato and Xenophon, the final hours of the Greek philosopher were unforced and truly moving, whereas, if we follow Tacitus, Seneca offered a performance that elicited applause rather than sorrow.

It was time to rejoice. Nero had come within twenty-four hours of a violent death. By the merest chance a plot to kill him had been revealed and most if not all of the would-be assassins had been identified and punished. The gods had been kind to him.

Too many Praetorians for comfort had been among the guilty men, and the princeps steadied the Guard's support for him by meeting them on parade and announcing a bonus of 2,000 sesterces a man as well as free grain. He also gave it a new Prefect, one Nymphidius Sabinus, the son of an imperial freedwoman and, some claimed, of a gladiator. He himself put it about that his father was Caligula. Did he perhaps have his eye on the purple? At any rate, he was not in Tigellinus's pocket. Much of his career had been with the Praetorian Guard, and his promotion may have been a signal to his comrades that the emperor was on their side.

Nero explained what had taken place to the Senate. Members were sycophantic, especially those who had lost relatives and friends, and scrambled to save their own lives. Among all the congratulations Seneca's brother Gallio was denounced as a public enemy and "parricide of his country." In a rare instance of defiance, the charge was unanimously rejected and the prosecutor withdrew it. Later, after his brother Mela's suicide on a false charge, it seems that he too killed himself under orders. This marked the end of the Annaeus clan.

Ordinary citizens doubted that there really had been a major conspiracy and blamed the princeps for destroying many innocent lives from personal motives of jealousy or fear. In response, he published a rebuttal together with statements by informers and confessions. Just as it came to be believed that he was no arsonist, so anyone who looked into the matter eventually accepted his version of events.

There were widespread celebrations and festivals of thanksgiving to the gods. So, for instance, Egyptians living in Italy "vowed to make sacrifice for the preservation of Caesar. One hundred ox-felling axes stained the willing necks of the bulls with blood on the altars of heavenly Zeus." Offerings were especially voted to the sun god. He had an ancient shrine at the Circus Maximus, where the assassination was to have taken place. As the colossus commissioned for the Golden House showed, Nero identified himself with the sun, the ultimate victorious charioteer who drove his *quadriga* through the sky from sunrise to sunset and had miraculously brought to light the conspiracy.

The games of Ceres were to be extended with additional horse races and the month of April was to be renamed Neroneus after the emperor (he liked self-promotion of this kind and even thought about renaming Rome Neropolis). A Temple of Safety was promised and a memorial placed in the temple from which Scaevinus had taken the dagger. Nero himself carried the weapon up to the Capitol, where he dedicated it to Jupiter the Avenger. It was recommended that a temple should be constructed as soon as possible to the Divine Nero. This was too much even for him, and he vetoed the proposal. By convention, emperors were deified by the Senate only after their death, and he felt it would have been an unlucky omen for godhead to be conferred while he was still alive.

The general mood lightened.

The Senate faced a conundrum. Nero intended to appear in his first fully professional public performance in Rome on strictly equal terms with rival poets and musicians. At the same time, he expected to win every competition he entered. It was decided that he be awarded in advance the first prize in song and also a crown for eloquence.

This attempt to square a circle failed. Nero insisted that there was no call for favoritism, nor would it be right to hide behind the authority of the Senate. He would compete fairly and squarely. He would earn his distinction and rely on the conscientiousness of the judges.

The princeps was attacked by last-minute nerves, and although there was a general demand for him, he left the theater. The courtier Vitellius was presiding at the festival and called him back. The people were insistent, he said, and he came as their ambassador. A flattered Nero gave way to their entreaties.

He stood on the stage and began by reciting from his poem about the fall of Troy (the one he was supposed to have delivered among the flames that had engulfed his capital the previous year). None of that composition has survived, but an unknown versifier refers to the reading. His sycophantic argument was that because of the imperishable poetry it inspired in the emperor, Troy's destruction was justified:

Rejoice, you ruins; sing praises, you funeral pyres: 'tis your little child,
your descendant, that brings you back to life! . . .
Look! Homer too came, whose full beard and white hair
shone in undimmed honor. So when he filled Nero's ears
with accents divine, he undid the golden circlet from his noble brow,
and veiled the emperor's head with its deserved attire.

The crowd clamored for more. Tacitus claims to repeat their exact words: "Show us all you have got!" The princeps then came down into the orchestra, the circular space in front of the seating, dressed in the flowing robe of a citharode, or lyre singer, and resumed his performance. He strictly observed all the rules of competition: He did not sit down when tired; to wipe sweat from his face, he used only the costume he was wearing; and he concealed any discharge of saliva from his mouth and nose. Finally, on bended knee he nervously awaited the verdict of the judges.

It sounds as if the emperor's claque, the Augustiani, were present and in loud form. Praetorians were stationed along the benches. Some *equites* were crushed to death as they tried to leave through the theater's narrow exits. A down-to-earth general, Vespasian, had the misfortune to nod off during the show and was reprimanded by an imperial freedman. He avoided serious trouble only when his friends spoke up for him.

Tacitus has not a good word to say about the spectators' reaction:

> The city rabble . . . thundered approval in measured cadences and organized applause. You might have supposed they were enjoying themselves, and so perhaps they were—without giving a thought for the national dishonor.

The overtone of patrician disdain is intended to discredit what was quite clearly a hit show. The atmosphere seems to have resembled that of a modern rock concert. Tacitus tries to deny Nero's competence as a musician and performance poet who appealed to a mass audience, but he is too honest a historian to get away with it.

The first half of the year 65 had been catastrophic, but once the Pisonian crisis had played itself out, the political situation calmed down and Nero looked to the future with a degree of optimism.

The regime had settled into an informal triumvirate consisting of Nero; his wife Poppaea, with whom he was still deeply in love and who was pregnant again; and his close adviser, Tigellinus.

However, the fates were not done with him.

One day Nero came home late from the races. Poppaea was feeling out of sorts and complained. He lost his temper and jumped on her, feet first. The blow to her stomach killed her and her unborn child. It was uncertain whether he meant it to be fatal, and there was gossip about poison. Was he a generally abusive husband, or was this a disastrous aberration? The sources do not say. In fact, they claim that the princeps adored his wife—and certainly he was in pressing need of a male heir. Whatever the truth of their relationship, Poppaea's killer was agonized by guilt as well as by grief.

Poppaea was not greatly missed, although as a mark of respect the Senate voted her divine honors. Intelligent and loyal, she might have made a greater impact on her times if she had not left the stage early. She was heartily disliked by the political elite and criticized for her vanity and extravagance. Dio claims that the empress

> took the greatest pains to maintain the beauty and brilliancy of her person, and this is why, when she noticed in a mirror one day that she was looking unattractive, she prayed that she might die before she passed her prime.

Her wish was evidently granted.

The tittle-tattle about her bathing in asses' milk was the kind of resentful allegation that stood in for a woman's political ability, and it should not be taken too seriously. We have already seen how a male-dominated society did all it could to suppress female agency.

The same charge of profligacy was directed at the princeps. According to Suetonius, Nero

> never wore the same costume twice. He played at dice for four hundred thousand sesterces a point. He fished with a golden net drawn by cords woven with purple and scarlet threads. It is said that he never made a journey with less than a thousand carriages, his mules were shod with silver and their drivers clad in highly prized wool of Canusium. He was escorted by horses from Mauretania and outriders with bracelets and trappings.

These stories probably had some truth in them, but we should remember that splendor was expected of emperors and their spouses. A simple lifestyle merely attracted accusations of parsimony or avarice.

Nero's devastation at Poppaea's death took a curious turn. He learned of a woman who bore a remarkable resemblance to his dead wife. He sent for her and had her live with him at court.

The autumn saw a disaster of a different kind. Rome was struck by a plague. Like all ancient cities, its inhabitants lived in unsanitary conditions and in this case among the ruins of the Great Fire. The principle of antisepsis being unknown, they were prone to mass infections at not infrequent intervals. The symptoms of this epidemic have not been recorded, but contemporaries estimated thirty thousand deaths. Nero contracted a swollen larynx at this time, although whether this was caused by the epidemic or by straining his voice is unclear. He soon recovered.

As in a Greek tragedy, the events of 65 precipitated in Nero a *peripeteia*—namely, a drastic reversal or turning point in a protagonist's circumstances, after which the action moves steadily to its foregone conclusion. His sanguine mindset completely changed; if people wanted him to be a tyrant, he would become one. The time for Senecan clemency was over. A new phase in the drama of his life was opening.

He launched a second wave of executions, suicides, and banishments toward the end of the year, which continued into 66. The judicious moderation and confidence of the summer gave way to savagery. In total, out of twenty-seven named deaths, thirteen were Senators, six Senators' wives, and four *equites*. To these we can add an astrologer, whose fate is unknown, and a young Senator who was excluded from public office and handed over to his father's care. There appears to have been no overall rationale for the purge, except for a generalized fear that treason lurked around every corner. Political moderates were struck down who had nothing to do with the Pisonian conspiracy, yet for one reason or another were an affront to the emperor.

As well as acknowledgment of his power, or imperium, Nero demanded respect for his *auctoritas*—a word whose meaning combined moral authority and charisma. He expected Senators to support his policies and play an active part in the business of empire. For their part they grudgingly accepted the legitimacy of the imperial system, but insisted that their rights and privileges as aristocrats be maintained.

Increasingly they found fault with the administration and criticized Nero in public. In the early years of the reign a degree of license had been permitted. A few put on a show of dumb insolence and withdrew from politics into private life. They were members of the Stoic Opposition, whom we have met before. This loose grouping of austere, committed Stoics, members of noble families often linked through marriage, was an especial irritant to the regime.

The most celebrated of them was Thrasea Paetus. His mother-in-law was the famous Arria who had committed suicide alongside her husband on the orders of Claudius (see page 42). Thrasea had long been a thorn in Nero's side. He made his dissatisfaction with the regime very clear. However, he took care not to overstep the narrow line between acceptable and unacceptable activity, nor did he engage in serious criminality. He did not join the Pisonian conspiracy and at one point his relationship with the emperor even warmed into something like friendship. He may have regarded himself as a constructive critic. From about 63 he withdrew from political life, a step which Nero regarded as a hostile act.

In 66 he decided that Thrasea should be tried in the Senate on potentially capital charges. The prosecutor was a personal enemy of his and Tigellinus's son-in-law.

The case against Thrasea turned out to be a catalog of minor offenses, but taken together they added up to culpable absenteeism. As already mentioned, he had left the Senate debate on Agrippina and declined to appear onstage at the Juvenalia. According to Tacitus, it was alleged that

> at the New Year Thrasea evaded the regular oath [to uphold the acts of past and present *principes*]. Though a member of the Board of Fifteen for Religious Ceremonies he did not take part in its formal prayer meetings. He had never offered sacrifice for the emperor's safety or for his divine voice. He had not entered the Senate

in three years, though at one time he had attended diligently and tirelessly, taking sides on the most trivial proposals.

The charge sheet was sent to Nero for his endorsement, and Thrasea wrote him a note asking exactly what he had in mind. He would welcome the opportunity to rebut any allegations. The princeps read the note eagerly, hoping that Thrasea had been panicked into a humiliating comedown. The probability is that at this stage he did not intend to have him put to death.

However, once he knew that the Stoic intended to defend himself, Nero himself panicked and called an emergency meeting of the Senate, at which this obdurate opponent would be put on trial. By moving fast and firmly, the princeps may have hoped that Thrasea would maintain his boycott of the Senate, for a conviction would be easier to obtain if this experienced orator stayed away from the proceedings.

Thrasea asked his friends what they thought he should do next. Some argued that he should attend the Senate and speak in his defense with all the persuasive force at his command. If he captured the mood of the meeting, Nero might well change his mind and give way. If he insisted on the ultimate penalty, at least Thrasea would die an honorable death.

Others advised him to stay at home and avoid the unpleasantness of a trial. A strong rebuttal of the charges would not save him and could have grave repercussions for his family.

The young and enthusiastic Quintus Junius Arulenus Rusticus, a friend and follower of Thrasea, intervened. He said that he was a Tribune of the People for the present year and had the authority ex officio to veto any Senate resolution. He was willing to veto Thrasea's conviction. Thrasea refused the offer, saying that it would be a futile gesture, and would pointlessly destroy the Tribune's promising career.

"My own time is over," he said, "and I must not abandon my longstanding way of life." Later, he decided not to attend his trial.

The temple of Venus Genetrix (the goddess was hailed as mother and ancestor of the Julian clan) stood on a raised podium at one end of the colonnaded forum of Julius Caesar. It was here that on the following morning the Senate met to determine Thrasea's fate. Security was tight, indeed almost menacingly so. Troops were scattered around the city center and the temple itself was guarded by two fully armed Praetorian cohorts. The approach was crowded with men in togas who were ostensibly civilians but openly wore swords. They glared at the Senators as they arrived for their session.

Like the other principal in the case, the princeps judged it best not to attend and sent in his place a Quaestor to read out his speech. This named no names, but criticized Senators for absenteeism from their meetings. It was obvious that Thrasea was the target, and his accusers seized the weapon that had been given them. A barrage of personal attacks on him ensued.

The outcome was predictable. Thrasea was allowed a choice of how to die. So were a former Consul and his daughter, who had also been accused. In addition, a philosopher, and Thrasea's son-in-law Helvidius Priscus, who was an ardent republican, were banished from Italy. As already noted, a young nobleman was returned to the care of his father, who was a close friend of Nero.

Nero gave the prosecutors generous rewards—two of them received 5 million sesterces each and a third 1.2 million sesterces together with an honorary Quaestorship.

Dusk was drawing in when one of the emperor's Quaestors arrived to inform Thrasea of the Senate's sentence. He found the Stoic holding a party in his garden with a large number of distinguished men and women. The guest of honor was a celebrated thinker, a Greek from Corinth called Demetrius. Much admired by Seneca, he despised worldly goods. Caligula once tried to tempt him by offering him 200,000 sesterces. "He would have done better," said Demetrius, happy to entertain the thought of a despot without a job, "if he had offered me his entire empire."

Thrasea was deep in discussion with Demetrius about the nature of the soul and the relationship between it and the body. A guest interrupted and gave him the Quaestor's message. The news quickly spread among the company and Thrasea told them to leave at once;

otherwise they would be tainted by their association with a condemned man. His wife wanted to follow the example of her mother and namesake and die with her husband. He counseled her to stay alive and look after their young daughter. He then walked to a colonnade, where the Quaestor found him. He appeared to be in a cheerful mood because Helvidius had only been sent into exile. He took Demetrius and the Quaestor into his bedroom, where he had the arteries in his arms severed.

When the blood began to flow he called the Quaestor over. Sprinkling his blood on the ground, he said: "We are making a libation to Jupiter the Liberator. Look, young man. I pray the gods to avert the omen, but you have been born into a time when it is expedient to toughen the mind with examples of firmness."

Like Seneca, Thrasea staged his death to evoke that of Socrates and made his "libation" to the same deity. Taking care not to vilify Nero, he used suicide to assert his moral superiority—and to have the last word. He was a serious, thoughtful, and well-intentioned man, but his virtues were overshadowed by self-righteousness.

Another distinguished departure was unconnected with political or philosophical principle. Petronius, author of the low-life masterpiece *The Satyricon,* had the misfortune to anger Tigellinus. Both men were "experts in the science of pleasure" and were members of Nero's small circle of intimates. As Praetorian Prefect, Tigellinus was in a strong position to eliminate his talented rival. At a time when Nero was out of the way in Campania he indicted the author of *The Satyricon* for friendship with the traitor Scaevinus and bribed one of his slaves to incriminate his master. Tacitus tells the story:

> Petronius had gone as far as Cumae [presumably on his way to Nero], where he was arrested. He did not allow fear or hope to further delay him. However, he did not rush to end his life. Having cut his veins, he bandaged them and opened them again on a whim, in the meantime chatting with his friends, but not on serious matters or topics that would win him a reputation for forti-

tude. He listened to their words—not about the immortality of the soul or the doctrines of philosophers, but light songs and frivolous verses. He gave presents to some of his slaves, others received a whipping.

He took his place at dinner and drowsed a little so that his death, though compulsory, might look natural.

Petronius declined to produce a last will and testament that flattered Nero or Tigellinus, as many of his fellow victims had done in order to protect their loved ones. The Arbiter of Elegance left behind a cruelly elegant *envoi* to the author of his troubles. He wrote down a list of all the emperor's sexual encounters, naming each partner, male as well as female, and giving a precise description of the orgiastic novelties in which they had engaged. Petronius sealed the document and sent it to Nero. He then broke his signet ring to prevent its misuse. He also smashed his fluorspar wine dipper which had cost him 300,000 sesterces, so that the emperor's table would not inherit it.

The list was, as intended, a hilarious embarrassment and was soon, presumably, the talk of the town. Nero wondered where Petronius had obtained his information. An inquiry was set up, and the talebearer turned out to be a Senator's wife called Silia, member of an ancient and noble plebeian family. Tacitus tells us that she had been requisitioned by the princeps for sexual purposes; a close friend of Petronius, she told him all she had seen, enjoyed, or endured. Silia was sent into exile for her pains.

The regime had shown signs of nervousness when dealing with Thrasea Paetus. The intimidatory military presence and the emperor's uncertainty in the run-up to the trial suggests that the Senator was understood to be a real threat. It is hard to see why.

The Stoic Opposition was a cast of mind rather than a program of action. These gloomy nobles were incapacitated by a basic contradiction in their position. They hankered after the republic but accepted the bitter truth that a pugnacious collective of aristocratic families was incapable of running an empire. They had nothing better to propose than the system as it was—namely, the military autocracy Augustus had established. Piso came from the same stable as Nero, and had his coup d'état succeeded, few would have noticed any difference in their government. Stoicism, with its insistence on welcoming, or at least enduring, whatever an impersonal and universal force of nature might bring, was not a creed for revolutionaries. For Stoics, execution or suicide was a fate to be embraced. Tacitus, our chief literary source for the period, admits to being depressed by

> the sad continuum of deaths, honorable though they may well be, of our citizens. The servile acceptance of death, and the spilling of so much wasted blood, fatigue the mind and paralyze it with despondency. The only favor I ask of the reader is to allow me not to hate those who died so tamely. The angry gods were responsible.

The effect of Nero's two purges was not only to depopulate the Senate, but to cow its survivors. They had no answer to the bloodbath apart from insincere flattery. Nevertheless, the princeps found himself in a difficult position. Outside the palace and the barracks he had few friends ready to back him in the event of a crisis. The spirit of cooperation between emperor and political class that his mother had fostered in Claudius's time evaporated. Obedience became sullen.

If anyone were to have shared this analysis with Nero himself, he would probably have replied that openness and tolerance of opposition had been tried and had failed. It was better to acknowledge the autocracy as it was than to hide it.

A truer response to this new approach to governance may have been more psychological than political. The overreaction to the threat Thrasea Paetus posed suggests that Nero had not recovered from the shock of the recent conspiracy. He suspected everyone now, even his nearest and dearest friends, even somebody as delightful, affectionate, and above all uncompetitive as Petronius.

The emperor had had enough of ungrateful Rome and now revived his dream of visiting Greece, where artists were not assassinated but revered, and where he would be judged at his true worth.

13

THE ARMENIAN QUESTION

CORBULO HAD BEEN in charge of Roman armed forces in the east since 54, at the outset of Nero's reign. He was a fine figure of a man—tall, strong, and an excellent public speaker. A traditionalist member of the senatorial aristocracy, he believed in respect for one's elders, scorn for moral laxity, and honesty in the public service. He held a high opinion of himself, but not without reason.

Perhaps in his mid- to late fifties, he was the half brother of Milonia Caesonia, Caligula's fourth wife, murdered after her husband's assassination, and served as Consul during that emperor's short and violent reign. He was a capable commander, and his long career had been marked by an unbroken line of successes. He did not appreciate competition from his fellow commanders, and his relations with social equals were poor. By contrast, he got along well with his men, never asking them to do anything he would not undertake himself.

Corbulo's style of leadership was to insist on strict discipline. He kept his army under canvas through the harsh winters of the Anatolian plateau to acclimatize them to the snows of Armenia, a kingdom long the victim of a tug-of-war between Rome and the Parthian empire (see pages 13–14). Lightly dressed and bareheaded, he moved informally among his men and kept up their morale. For deserters, though, he had no mercy, and he put them to death without appeal.

Politically astute, the general understood the laws of survival. When he was campaigning on the German or the eastern frontiers, he made sure to stay within the objectives set by the emperor and his *consilium* of advisers. When circumstances changed, he always sent to Rome for new instructions before taking action.

It was a dangerous game, for the more battles Corbulo won, the more a Claudius or a Nero would worry that he might aspire to the purple and march his legions on the capital. One too many victories could lead to a letter inviting him to open his veins.

To guarantee his life, he built a reputation for unfailing loyalty.

Corbulo was awarded overriding authority in the east (*imperium maius,* literally "greater power"). As we have seen, he was tasked by the elderly Claudius with settling Armenia, where in 52, after a period of unrest, the newly crowned Parthian king Vologeses I had installed his younger brother Tiridates as monarch. This broke the terms of the entente between Rome and Parthia that Augustus had negotiated as long ago as 20 B.C. Since that time, Roman emperors had appointed pro-Roman kings of Armenia. They had no desire to annex or govern the unruly realm, regarding it merely as a useful buffer between the Roman and Parthian empires. They expected the Parthians to take the same view. On one point everyone agreed—all-out war between the two empires, as distinct from war between proxies, was out of the question.

With Claudius's death a couple of years later, the crisis was bequeathed to Nero, who had no military experience and had no wish to obtain any. It was seen as a test of the young man's competence. He instructed Corbulo to expel Tiridates from Armenia. Once he had accomplished his mission, he was to withdraw his legions. This was an intelligent plan, for it promised to restore the agreement between the two powers with the minimum use of force.

Corbulo and the Roman governor of the wealthy province of Syria tried negotiation before sending in the army. To begin with, the tactic worked. To show his good faith, Vologeses agreed to provide hostages as a prelude to negotiations. Then the Parthians unexpectedly evacuated Armenia for the second time—on this occasion because a son of Vologeses had raised the standard of revolt. This was a victory won without effort, but a victory nonetheless.

There was junketing in Rome. Nero was accorded an ovation (a minor triumph that took the form of a ceremonial entry into the capital). A national thanksgiving was declared, during which the princeps wore the robes of a triumphing general. This outrageously flamboyant outfit included the *corona triumphalis* (a coronet in the shape of a laurel wreath with gold ribbons); an ivory baton; the *tunica palmata* (a tunic embroidered with palm leaves); and the *toga picta,* or "painted toga." A statue of Nero was to be erected in the temple of Mars Ultor, the Avenger. He would now be justified in boasting his military credentials.

For a couple of years nothing much happened. It was obvious that a permanent settlement had not been reached, and Corbulo filled the time by training his army. He showed his mettle as a commander; Tacitus reports that

> his main difficulty was to counteract the lethargy of his men than thwart the enemy's treachery. Demoralized by long years of peace they showed a pronounced reluctance to put up with service conditions. It was a well-known fact that his army included veterans who had never been on a picket or a watch, and for whom ramparts and ditches were eccentric novelties. Owning neither helmets nor breastplates, they were polished and prosperous "civilian" warriors.

The sick and the elderly were discharged and a legion along with auxiliary infantry and cavalry was summoned from Germany as reinforcement. Gradually Corbulo transformed his troops into an effective fighting force.

That said, he believed that the dispute with Parthia would only be solved permanently by diplomatic rather than military means. He advocated a compromise: a Parthian prince—doubtless Tiridates—would be nominated by King Vologeses for the Armenian throne and would travel to Rome to be crowned by Nero. Both monarchs would be able to report a success to their domestic constituencies, and it was likely that a king appointed in this way would pursue nonaggressive and fair-handed policies.

Neither side liked the plan, but Corbulo kept it on the table. Vologeses was detained by yet another rebellion, and the Roman general advised Tiridates to petition Nero for the kingdom he would otherwise lose. "You might win a secure throne," he told him, "if you pursue an aspiration which is within your grasp." The two men met for discussions, but nothing came of them.

So war it had to be. In the spring of 58, Corbulo's legions, supported by pro-Roman client kings in the region, entered Armenia and captured its two main cities, Artaxata and Tigranocerta. Following an age-old tradition after a major victory, the legionaries spontaneously acclaimed Nero as Imperator (the nearest English equivalent is field marshal). More junketings. The Senate voted thanksgivings, statues, and triumphal arches. The dates of the victory and its announcement were to rank as public holidays. A witty Senator advised his colleagues that if they went on like this there would be no working days left in the calendar.

Having driven out Tiridates, Corbulo installed Nero's nominee for the Armenian throne, Tigranes VI, a great-grandson of Herod the Great and not a Parthian. He had been raised in Rome and had become acclimatized to Roman ways. The princeps may have followed the advice of newcomers to imperial politics, Poppaea and Tigellinus, when in 58 he crowned Tigranes in Rome. To help him establish himself in a kingdom he scarcely knew and where he was scarcely known, Nero allotted him a guard of one thousand legionaries, three auxiliary cohorts, and two companies of horse.

Corbulo waited in vanquished Armenia for the arrival from Italy of the new ruler. He did not much approve of Tigranes's promotion and looked for a means of distancing himself from him. Luckily, there was one to hand. He had long been worried that the Parthians could descend on the Roman province of Syria while the legions were preoccupied with Armenia. Some time previously, he had advised Nero that it would be difficult for one general to manage two theaters of war and suggested that he be appointed governor of Syria where he could develop the province's defenses against a possible Parthian attack across the river Euphrates. (The previous officeholder had died, opportunely but of natural causes.) Meanwhile another general should be charged with responsibility for Armenia. For the moment Rome took no action on this proposal.

King Tigranes turned out to be inexperienced and aggressive, an unlucky combination. He launched an attack on a neighboring vassal state of the Parthians. The last thing the Parthians wanted was an energetic and expansionist Armenia and so in 61 Vologeses reinvaded the turbulent kingdom. However, a strong response from the Romans prompted him to change his mind. He agreed to evacuate Armenia for the second time and sent a delegation to Rome to discuss the Parthian claim to Armenia and the conclusion of a stable peace. Corbulo took the opportunity to remove his legions from the province. We may not be wrong if we guess at a private understanding between the Roman and the Parthian.

At last Nero decided to implement the proposal to divide the command and dispatched Corbulo to Syria, where he was soon building forts along the Euphrates. The emperor was determined to keep his Romanized prince in place and sent an enthusiastic successor general to ensure stability in Armenia. He was Lucius Caesennius Paetus, Consul in 61. At the end of his term of office he made his way east to take up his new commission.

Great commanders understood the prime importance of securing a reliable food supply for their armies. Not so Paetus, and his men were weakened by hunger. He mendaciously announced victory, when in fact he had suffered a humiliating defeat. Vologeses's forces surrounded two legions at a place called Rhandea. Paetus appealed to Corbulo for help, but the wily general was in no hurry and took his time responding. Paetus asked to meet the Parthian king for a parley, who insultingly sent only his cavalry commander. In an attempt to please the enemy, the Romans built a bridge over the Euphrates for them. Vologeses dictated terms. The legions would be allowed to leave unharmed and Rome would abandon its claim over Armenia.

Roman children were brought up to remember the battle of the Caudine Forks, a military debacle long ago when Rome was battling for mastery of Italy. One of its armies had been "sent under the yoke," a public shaming when the soldiers of a defeated force passed under a yoke formed from spears.

Tacitus reports a rumor that this indignity was forced on Paetus's troops. Even if this was not the case, the actuality was almost as bad. Not only did the Parthians enter the camp

> before the Roman column had left. They lined the roads, identifying and dragging off slaves or transport animals that had been captured long before. Clothing was seized, weapons confiscated. Our terrified troops dared not resist in case they set off new hostilities.

Vologeses enjoyed a victory ride on an elephant. He piled up the weapons and corpses of the enemy fallen, but avoided watching the Romans march away, not wishing to be seen to gloat and so inflame an already tense situation. He sent a new delegation to Rome to negotiate a peace.

Corbulo had at last left his province to relieve Paetus, but arrived too late to save him. The two commanders and their armies met a few days after the capitulation. Tacitus has them discuss briefly their next move.

Corbulo complained: "My labor has been lost. My campaign could have ended with a Parthian rout."

Paetus replied: "We are still in a strong position. We have only to turn our legions round, join forces and invade Armenia together."

"I have no orders to that effect from the emperor," came the reply. "I only left my province because of the danger you were in. The Parthians are very unpredictable and I must get back to Syria."

Once he had regained his province, Corbulo and a Parthian representative held a prolonged meeting on Paetus's bridge, after first destroying its middle section. Both sides agreed to quit Armenia for good. The accord was carried out provisionally, until Nero could review the proposed settlement and talk directly with the Parthian delegation.

Paetus withdrew his hapless legions to the Roman province of Cappadocia, where they convalesced after their ordeal. He was not entirely candid about the failure of his campaign. It was not until the arrival in Rome of the Parthian envoys that the true extent of the disaster became clear.

Nero and (we presume) a selected group of advisers, his *consilium,* realized that both their client king and their general had shown themselves to be incompetent. Tigranes was dumped and Paetus recalled (to everyone's surprise, Nero forgave him). The princeps was forced to abandon his plan to establish a pro-Roman and non-Parthian ruler for Armenia.

There was now only one plan left—Corbulo's.

Nero gave it his assent, and from then onward the whole affair was handled with considerable skill.

For public consumption, the *consilium* voted unanimously to resume hostilities; privately, though, the Parthian delegates were given handsome presents when they left and hints were dropped that if Tiridates were to present himself in person to the emperor he might receive a much more positive response.

Once again Corbulo was awarded *imperium maius* over the eastern provinces where he proceeded to make ready a substantial army. In the last resort the Parthians were militarily weaker than the Romans and they realized that the game was up. Envoys from Vologeses and Tiridates visited the general in his camp. They were greeted warmly and sent back with some centurions bearing conciliatory messages from the Roman general. We can speculate that confidential discussions took place during which the script for what was to happen next was approved.

Not long afterward, Tiridates called for a public conference at which peace would be debated. An early date was agreed, and the Parthians suggested that the encounter take place on the site of Paetus's debacle. Corbulo made no objection to the implicit slur. Indeed, he went a step further: He ordered the defeated general's son, who was a military tribune, to take a detachment and bury the decaying remains of the blockade.

Corbulo's son-in-law, Annius Vinicianus, acting commander of a legion that had served under Paetus, visited the camp of Tiridates, partly as a compliment and partly to dispel any fear of treachery. He was accompanied by a well-regarded political fixer called Tiberius Julius Alexander, a wealthy, nonreligious Jew who mingled in the highest circles and may have been commissioned by Nero as a back passage to keep him posted on developments. Then the two principals, each accompanied by twenty mounted men, rode toward each other. As the Roman approached, the king jumped off his horse. Corbulo quickly followed suit, and the two men shook hands.

Speeches ensued. Corbulo congratulated Tiridates for rejecting adventurism in favor of a safe and well-intentioned policy. The king responded with a lengthy account of his noble ancestry. Eventually, he came to the point. Tacitus reports him as saying: "I will go to Rome, and bring the emperor an unfamiliar distinction—a Parthian prince voluntarily doing him homage without any military pressure." It was then arranged that Tiridates would lay down his royal diadem at the feet of a statue of Nero. He would travel to Rome and be given it back by the emperor in person. The conference concluded with a kiss.

A few days later the formal ceremony of abdication took place. Tacitus evokes its splendor:

> Both armies mounted a dazzling display. On the Parthian side, cavalry was ranged in squadron after squadron with their national emblems; on the other, stood the columns of our legions in a glitter of eagles and standards. Statues of the gods gave the scene something of the appearance of a temple. In the center, a Roman chair of state stood on a dais, and the chair bore an effigy of Nero.

Tiridates walked forward and after the usual animal sacrifices lifted the diadem from his head and laid it at the foot of the statue. For the time being he ceased being the king of Armenia. That concluded the business of the day, and the general offered Tiridates "courtesy and a banquet."

Like an enthusiastic tourist, Tiridates continually asked the reason for anything he noticed that was new to him—for example, the announcement by a centurion to mark the beginning of every watch, the sound of a trumpet that marked the end of a meal, and the firing of sacrifices on the altar outside the headquarters tent. Corbulo, by exaggerating every point in his answers, filled him with admiration for Rome's ancient traditions.

The next day, Tiridates asked for time to say goodbye to his brothers and his mother before starting on such a long journey, which was agreed. He handed over his daughter as a hostage, together with a formal petition to Nero for the gift of his kingdom. Vologeses was worried for his brother and sent special couriers to Corbulo asking him to make sure that Tiridates was treated with all due respect. When he met governors of the Roman provinces he would be passing through, it should be on equal terms. He should not be prevented from giving them formal embraces nor be kept waiting outside their doors.

In the autumn of 65, Tiridates set out on his trek. He did not go alone. He was accompanied by not only his own sons but also those of his siblings. The expedition was a unique opportunity for the royal boys to gain firsthand experience of their powerful, wealthy, and dangerous neighbor.

He was escorted by the promising legate Vinicianus, who was under orders from Corbulo to look after the prince and smooth over any difficulties. But there was something else the old general had in mind. He wished to signal to Nero that he knew he had been too successful and wanted to reinforce his loyalty by placing a close relative in the emperor's hands. Vinicianus was to be a guarantor of best behavior.

The Parthian's entourage included a large number of servants and, to use Dio's phrase, "all his regal paraphernalia." He was guarded by three thousand Parthian horsemen, more for the splendor of their appearance than from any real fears for his security. In addition, numerous Romans followed in his train—tour guides, doubtless, along with cooks, provisioners, and customer service officials to handle relations with the people through whose territory the Parthians would be passing.

The sudden appearance in a territory of armed men in large numbers, hungry and thirsty, was disruptive and usually unpopular among local inhabitants. When supplies were needed they were often seized rather than bought. However, Nero volunteered to pay all Tiridates's expenses at the astoundingly generous daily rate of 800,000 sesterces. So the Parthians had plenty of cash with which to make their purchases. The journey lasted nine months and must have strained the imperial cash flow.

In fact, Tiridates received a warm reception. His progress had something of the noisy optimism of a triumphal procession. He was in his prime and, writes Dio, "cut a fine figure by reason of his youth, beauty, family, and intelligence."

Tiridates's route from Syria took him to the Bosporus. It then ran across Thrace, through Illyria, on the eastern shores of the Adriatic, to Picenum, in northeastern Italy. He covered the whole distance to the Italian frontier on horseback, with his wife riding beside him. In place of a veil she wore a golden helmet, presumably with cheek guards so as not to defy her cultural traditions by letting her face be seen. Probably arriving in Italy in April 66, for the last part of his journey he traveled in a two-horse carriage provided by Nero.

The emperor and the prince met not in the capital, as might have been expected, but at Neapolis, in part because it was one of Nero's favorite places. More substantively, it gave the two men a chance to get to know each other and settle any difficulties before the public ceremonies that lay ahead.

Tiridates refused an order to put away his sword, but he had it nailed into its scabbard so it could not be drawn. When meeting the emperor, he knelt on the ground, called the emperor master, and, with arms crossed, did obeisance—all to Nero's delight.

Puteoli (today's Pozzuoli) was a busy commercial port near Neapolis where the Alexandrian grain ships unloaded their cargo, without which Rome's population would go short. Here, in the prince's honor, Nero presented a festival of entertainments, including a gladiatorial display—according to Dio, "a most brilliant and costly affair." Like many of his fellow countrymen, Tiridates was a skillful archer, and from his seat high up in the auditorium he shot and killed two bulls with a single arrow—a feat, one suspects, more honored in the telling than the event.

Black people were known in the ancient world, but only in enough numbers for them to be regarded as exotic. On one of the festival days, Dio thinks it worth recording that the theater was filled with Ethiopians of all sexes and ages (the term usually signifies any dark-skinned person). The intention must have been to demonstrate that Rome's power reached deep into Africa.

Once the festival was over, Nero took the prince up to Rome. The city was *en fête*. It had been transformed. Everywhere there were lights and garlands. Great crowds were out in the streets, the Forum being especially full. Dio writes:

> Civilians occupied the city center, gathered according to rank. They were clothed in white and carried laurel branches. Everywhere else there were soldiers, arrayed in shining armor, their weapons and standards flashing like lightning. The roof-tiles of all the buildings in the vicinity were completely hidden from view by the spectators who had climbed to the roofs.

The final arrangements were made overnight, and everyone was in their places at sunrise when Nero, accompanied by the Senate and wearing his triumphal robes, entered the Forum. The emperor ascended the steps to the rostra with its marble balustrade and facings and seated himself in a chair of state, made from ivory and resembling a campstool with curved legs and arms.

Then Tiridates and his suite entered the Forum between lines of Roman soldiers and stood next to the speaker's platform. The prince prostrated himself before Nero. This act of subservience was unfamiliar to most of those present, and a deafening roar went up that so alarmed the prince that he was speechless for some moments.

There was a call for silence, and, according to Dio, Tiridates recited a carefully prepared speech:

> Master, I am the descendant of Arsaces, brother of the kings Vologeses and Pacorus, and your slave. And I have come to you, my god, to worship you as I do Mithras. You will spin my destiny; for you are my Fortune and my Fate.

Nero replied in equally studied terms:

> You have done well to come here in person. By meeting me face to face you will be able to enjoy our favor, for what neither your fa-

> ther bequeathed you nor your brothers gave and kept for you, I grant you. I now pronounce you king of Armenia, so that both you and they understand that I have the power to take away kingdoms and bestow them.

There was another great roar and Nero gave the king a seat on his right. He closed the doors of the temple of Janus to signify that the Roman world was now at peace. The formalities were over.

It is telling, if puzzling, that the Parthian prince mentioned Mithras. Originally a Zoroastrian divinity, whose worship centered on Persia, he was expropriated by the Romans who cast him as the presiding spirit of a mystery cult. Open only to initiates, Mithraism was hugely popular in the western half of the empire especially among soldiers. Meetings were held in underground temples (many of them have been identified by modern archaeologists, including some hundreds in the city of Rome). No literary texts have survived, and the doctrines of the cult are uncertain. Statues and bas-reliefs have been found in the temples that show scenes from the god's life, in particular one of Mithras fighting and killing a bull.

By mentioning Mithras the prince may have wanted to suggest the connections between Roman and Parthian spirituality (in point of fact the relationship between Rome's Mithras and Parthia's Mithra is shadowy). Mithras was a god of light, and the reference to him was also perhaps a tactful acknowledgment of Nero's identification of himself with the unconquered sun, *sol invictus*.

According to Pliny the Elder, Tiridates was a Magus—that is, a member of a princely Persian caste or clan of priests. In Roman eyes he was a keeper of esoteric knowledge, an astrologer, and a practitioner of magic (the word derives from Magus). Pliny observes of Tiridates,

> he refused to travel by sea, for the Magi consider it sinful to spit into the seas or defile its nature by any other human function. He brought his fellow Magi with him and initiated Nero into their

> magic banquets. Yet although Tiridates had given Nero a kingdom he was unable to teach him the art of magic.

It was probably now that the princeps lost faith in the dark art (see magic page 76).

One way or another it hardly mattered. The show had to go on—and what a show. Rome's largest and grandest theater, and the first to be constructed from stone, had been dedicated by Pompey the Great about a century before. Doubling as a temple of Venus and containing a large formal garden, it was paid for from the loot Pompey brought back from his campaigns in the eastern provinces. A meeting hall at the end of the garden was notorious for being the room where Julius Caesar was assassinated. A display of statuary illustrated key moments in Roman history. In an external arcade a set of figures represented the fourteen nations Pompey had subdued, which included Armenia.

So this was not the most tactfully chosen venue for the next event in the day's schedule, a variety show at which Tiridates was the guest of honor. He made no complaint, though, and his attention will have been seized by the spectacle before him: the entire open-air stage and auditorium had been specially gilded for the occasion, as had the props used by the performers. Awnings to protect the spectators from the sun were dyed purple, the imperial color, and an image of the emperor as the sun god driving a chariot across the sky was embroidered on one of them.

The program has not survived, but it concluded with an expensive banquet. Afterward Nero sang in public to the cithara. He also drove a chariot, wearing the costume of the Green faction and a charioteer's helmet.

Tiridates was disgusted. That a powerful ruler should behave like a variety artiste was beyond comprehension. Kings didn't do things like that. He had spent months on his best behavior, but Nero infuriated him and every now and again the mask slipped. The Parthian greatly admired Corbulo, for his dignity, honesty, and reasonableness. He once blurted out to Nero: "Master, you have a good slave in Corbulo." What he must have meant between the lines was that he was surprised by Corbulo's continued loyalty. Apparently, the emperor failed to detect the subtext and took the remark at face value.

The Parthian shamelessly flattered him and wheedled his way into his confidence. The result was that he was showered with expensive gifts, reputedly worth 200 million sesterces. Tiridates also won permission to rebuild his capital, Artaxata, which had been razed by Corbulo, and when he set off for Armenia, he took with him craftsmen and city planners, some under orders from Nero and others independents lured by the promise of high wages.

We may assume that any resistance the king felt to traveling over water was dispelled by a desire to get back home as quickly as possible after so long an absence. He rode south along the Appian Way via the town of Beneventum to the south Italian port of Brundisium, where he took ship for Dyrrachium, a port on the western coast of Greece. From there he sped along the paved highway of the Via Egnatia, Rome's main link to the eastern Mediterranean.

Although the king had little time for the emperor, he was impressed by the empire. The Hellenistic cities of Asia Minor made a powerful impression on him. They were what he wanted his new Artaxata to look like. Once safely in Armenia, Tiridates made good use of his borrowed experts and began to reconstruct his capital. With astute gratitude, he renamed it Neronia. Archaeologists have identified the remains of their labors. There were aqueducts, drainage channels, and bathhouses on the acropolis. We also know that there was a theater, the first in Armenia.

Corbulo came to an unhappy end.

Details are missing thanks to the loss of Tacitus's chapters about the last years of Nero's reign, but, according to Suetonius, a conspiracy about this time to assassinate the emperor was both conceived and detected at Beneventum.

We know little about it, but the man behind the plot was Annius Vinicianus, who (as we have seen) was married to one of Corbulo's two daughters and had been sent to Rome as an informal hostage.

Nero had appointed Vincianus, a young and talented officer, to the command of a legion. He must have thought very highly of him, for his relatives were less than satisfactory. He came from a family of rebels and political assassins. His father had taken part in the killing of Caligula and later in an insurrection against Claudius. His brother had joined the Pisonian conspiracy and been punished with exile.

It may be that Corbulo's reputation for total loyalty to the Julio-Claudians threw an invisibility cloak over Vinicianus. The general remained in Syria and there is no reason to suppose that he knew anything about the legate's intentions, which may have been rapidly formulated in Beneventum to be carried out elsewhere, most probably thirty miles away in Neapolis. The fact that the second phase of post-Piso suicides, including that of his sister-in-law Servilia, and executions coincided with Tiridates's journey to Italy may have upset Vinicianus. By terminating Nero he could reasonably hope to halt the bloodshed in Rome.

It was not to be. A priestly society in Rome, the Arval Brethren, inscribed minutes of their meetings on stone tablets, many of which have survived. In mid-May 66 they celebrated the detection of a criminal plan, and again in mid-June, presumably referencing the exposure and presumed execution of Vinicianus.

The affair was yet another crushing blow to the princeps, at a time when he wanted nothing to distract from or diminish his Armenian achievement. For the second time he made arrangements for a state visit to Greece (the Roman province of Achaea) where he could practice his art uninterrupted and refresh his spirits.

So far as he was concerned, the days of partnership with the Senate were over. According to Suetonius, Nero

> boasted that no princeps had ever known how much power he really had, and he often threw out unmistakable hints that he would not spare even those Senators who were still alive. One day he would wipe out the whole Senatorial order and hand over the administration of the provinces and command of the armies to the *equites* and his freedmen.

Until now the emperor had chosen his generals and provincial governors on merit and seemed to be immune to fears of insurrection. His predecessors had tended to prefer loyal incompetence to ambitious brilliance. However, Nero cheerfully appointed two brothers, Publius Sulpicius Scribonius Proculus and Publius Sulpicius Scribonius Rufus to the strategically crucial provinces of Upper and Lower Germania. They had never done anything separately and were both capable and trusted in spite of the fact that they could easily amalgamate their legions and threaten the regime. As for Corbulo, we have seen the leeway Nero had allowed him as regards Armenia. The fact that his father-in-law had been exiled for involvement in the Pisonian conspiracy was tactfully set aside.

Nero's mood had darkened. In 67, during his tour of Greece (see the next chapter), he sent friendly messages to the Scribonii and Corbulo. He would very much like to see them and, it must be supposed, seek their advice on some undisclosed topic. Serious unrest had broken out in Judaea, and perhaps the emperor sought their opinion on how to handle the matter.

The brothers' expertise was not required after all. Dio is clear:

> Complaints of the kind in which that period abounded were lodged against them, but they could neither obtain a hearing nor get within sight of Nero. And as a result everybody treated them as being of no importance. They began to long for death and so met their end by opening their veins.

As for Corbulo, he received a deferential summons from the emperor in which he was called "father" and "benefactor." He obediently took ship from the east and disembarked at Cenchreae, one of the two ports of the inland city-state of Corinth, where Nero happened to be at the time. He was unarmed and it seems he did not believe he was in any danger. He could not have been more wrong. Tacitus remarks that in a private interview with the princeps, one of Corbulo's officers had maligned his character. The general was probably condemned to death in absentia at a secret trial. Nero ordered that the sentence be carried out on his finest commander before he even entered his presence.

Seeing, or sensing, what was afoot, Corbulo grabbed a sword from one of the greeting party and cried *"Axios!"*—Greek for "My due!" His meaning is ambiguous: perhaps that by working for such a ruler he deserved all he got. Alternatively, he might have been stating that like a victorious Olympic athlete, he deserved applause for his performance. If the latter, he was making much the same point as Augustus on his deathbed, when he quoted a well-known theatrical formula:

If I have pleased you, kindly signify
Appreciation with a warm goodbye.

Corbulo then dealt himself a mortal blow.

What are we to make of this unexpected denouement to a distinguished career? Our information is limited and the answer must be provisional.

First of all, Nero's general in the east made a fatal miscalculation. He believed that if he was innocent of plots, delivered victory on the battlefield, and consulted the emperor at every step during a campaign, he would be safe. He was the greatest general of his day and may have thought that he was too valuable for his services to be dispensed with.

Unfortunately his twelve years in the eastern provinces had delivered too much glory, too much preeminence, in a subject. He knew that he deserved the main credit for the Armenian settlement and did his best to push as much of it as he could onto Nero's shoulders. Hence, we speculate, the splendors of the coronation of Tiridates.

However, there were those with access to the princeps who took a negative view of the settlement. When all was said and done, they whispered, Nero's role had been merely symbolic. Corbulo had lost Armenia and a Parthian prince ruled there now instead of a Roman quisling.

His long absence from Rome meant that he was out of touch with the emperor's darkening personality and the deadly atmosphere at court. Death struck him out of left field.

It seems that Nero was running short of money. Tiridates's visit had been very costly, and Rome still had to be rebuilt. His planned expedition to Greece, which entailed transporting the entire imperial court away from Rome and Italy, would be another extraordinary item of expenditure. Suetonius writes that the princeps was "obliged to postpone and defer even the pay of the soldiers and the benefits due to the veterans." Here lay danger. Nothing was more liable to shake the throne than out-of-pocket and discontented legionaries.

Fund-raising became the order of the day. We are told that the princeps never appointed anyone to an office without adding: "You know what my needs are," and "Let us see to it that no one is left with anything." Unscrupulous methods were used to bleed the rich. They were bullied into increasing their legacies to the emperor. Imperial gifts were recalled and temples stripped of their treasures.

Nothing like today's international banking system existed in ancient Rome, but moneylenders were able to raise funds and provide letters of credit for wealthy travelers. Although little evidence survives, Nero would have been able to borrow large sums from them, and probably did. Suetonius draws our attention to a "monkey-faced" moneylender called Paneros (presumably a Greek, whose name translates as Love All). Nero lavished country estates on him and, when he died, buried him with almost regal splendor. We can safely assume that Paneros helped out the treasury in times of need.

One thing is clear. Nero had no intention of ceasing his spending.

It had been a very curious crisis. The two rival great powers headed efficient military machines. They were expected to fight each other. However, they gave every appearance of doing their best to avoid hostilities. Corbulo was trusted, even well liked by his opponents.

Vologeses could field fine fighters, and the Parthian cavalry was an outstanding resource on the battlefield. However, the king was domestically weak, and plots by close relatives and insurrections were constant distractions. If the Romans were to launch a serious invasion, the regime might well collapse.

For Nero and Corbulo, the Armenian question was one of saving face rather than resolving an issue of substance. Neither of them wanted to see Armenia transformed into a Roman—or for that matter a Parthian—province. Direct rule by Rome would be costly and troublesome; it would bring them uncomfortably close to the intermittently bellicose Parthians. Armenia was an invaluable no-man's-land. However, the two men did disagree on the emphasis of policy. By forcing a foreign monarch on Armenia, Nero hoped to enhance Rome's influence, whereas Corbulo believed that a lasting solution could only be found with the wholehearted consent of the parties.

It was to Nero's credit that once the inadequacy of Tigranes, compounded by that of Paetus, had been exposed for all to see, he was willing to change his mind and back Corbulo's plan, which had probably been cooked up with Vologeses and commanded broad approval. He added his own personal spin by transforming the coronation of Tiridates into a ludicrously expensive but memorable extravaganza.

The settlement of Armenia was a triumph of statecraft and the finest achievement of the reign. Its longevity refuted its critics, for it remained in place until the emperor Trajan in the following century unwisely annexed the kingdom. It remained a bone of contention between the two empires, with pro-Roman and pro-Parthian monarchs alternating angrily until the Sasanians in the third century conquered a Parthia fatally weakened by palace rebellions and, above all, by futile wars with Rome.

14

"I DREAM'D THAT GREECE MIGHT STILL BE FREE"

OLYMPIA WAS a quiet backwater in southern Greece. Lying between a broad but shallow river and a lofty wooded hill, named Kronos after the father of Zeus, king of the gods, it was not so much a human settlement as a congregation of temples, statues, and altars. Plane trees and olive trees, white poplars, vines, and flowering shrubs gave summer shade. Few people lived there and few visited.

Then, once every four years, this became the venue for the Olympic games, and it became briefly the center or capital of the Hellenic world. Its small, quarrelsome city-states were still fiercely independent-minded, albeit now incorporated into the Roman empire. For a month beforehand, armed hostilities among them were banned. Spectators and athletes who qualified as Greek were guaranteed unhindered passage to this remote spot. They came by the tens of thousands.

The games were held in honor of Zeus, whose large open-air walled sanctuary, called the Altis, enclosed temples in his and his wife, Hera's, honor. Greek and Roman temples were not used for worship but were primarily shelters for the cult statue of a god. Zeus was represented by one of the seven wonders of the ancient world—a colossal gold and ivory effigy of the seated god, some forty feet high. So much ivory had been needed that some wit claimed it to be the reason nature created elephants. Another cynic remarked that Zeus would not be able to stand up without banging his head on the ceiling. This extraordinary work of art was the masterpiece of the great Athenian sculptor Phidias, and it must have been as much of a draw as the games themselves.

A keen-eyed observer in Nero's day described the crush:

> Some unpleasant and difficult things do happen in life. At the Olympic games for one. Don't you swelter in the heat? Aren't you crammed in and jam-packed? Isn't it awkward getting a wash? Aren't you drenched whenever it rains? Don't the noise, the din and all the other irritations get to you? But I imagine that you can put up with all this by setting it off against the gripping spectacle you are about to witness.

The festival featured chariot and horse racing; wrestling, boxing, and a brutal amalgam of wrestling and boxing without rules called the *pancration;* the *stadion,* or long-distance footrace, and various other footraces; and the pentathlon (consisting of wrestling, the *stadion,* the long jump, javelin throwing, and discus throwing). Victors received only a crown made from the leaves of a sacred olive tree, but won great prestige and were laden with gifts and honors by their authorities at home. To accommodate the program of events, a gymnasium, a *palaestra* (a colonnaded courtyard for wrestling and boxing), a stadium, and a racecourse were laid out around the Altis.

Olympia had remained largely unchanged for centuries. Then in 66, on a corner of the Altis and near the start gates for the racecourse, a brand-new building neared completion. The interloper was a Roman villa. Elaborately but hurriedly built, it had an internal courtyard, many rooms, gardens, and a luxurious bathhouse. It was commissioned by Nero, who had decided to attend the games and needed somewhere of appropriate grandeur to stay, even if only for a few weeks.

The games organizers could not guess the surprises that lay in wait for them.

Nero was happy to see the back of the Parthians. He could now set off on his first foreign expedition. He had given thought to a shadowy proposal to invade Ethiopia, by which was probably meant unspecified lands beyond the southern frontier of Egypt. An alternative was to campaign in the lower Danube and the Black Sea region, a plan that Alexander the Great had had in mind and left unachieved at his death, and a region where a Roman general had recently scored some victories. Both projects would add much-needed military luster to an excessively civilian emperor. But they appear not to have appealed to him.

Instead, he intended to revive his expedition to Greece followed by a visit to Alexandria, canceled in 64. He had a highly original scheme in mind: He would campaign as an artist rather than as a warrior.

As well as those at Olympia, three other Pan-Hellenic games were held at various points during the four-year cycle of an Olympiad—in Corinth, in Delphi, and in Nemea, near Argos. They too featured athletic events, to which they added instrumental and singing competitions.

For some time these cities, which regularly promoted musical contests, had been sending all the relevant prizes to Nero, who accepted them with delight. He gave early audience to the envoys who delivered them. He invited them to eat with him at his private table. Very wisely, they begged the emperor to sing after dinner and greeted his performance with extravagant applause. He purred: "The Greeks are the only people who have an ear for music and they alone are worthy of my efforts."

The envoys returned home to report the unexpected fruit of their labor. Nero had let them know that he intended to spend the next twelve months or so in Greece, starting in the autumn of 66, and required them to rearrange their calendars so that during his stay he could compete in each Pan-Hellenic festival. Olympia was to add music making and singing to its program.

In August 66 the princeps and a large and colorful cavalcade left Rome along the Appian Way and proceeded south to Brundisium, where they took ship to Cassiope, a port on the island of Corcyra (Corfu). Not many miles south on the mainland lay Nicopolis, "City of Victory," founded by Augustus in the previous century, which overlooked the waters on which the sea battle of Actium was fought. Here Nero attended the Actian games before moving on. He may have called briefly at Corinth and then taken part in the Pythian games in Delphi, perched on the precipitous slopes of Mount Parnassus. This was the home of Apollo's oracle; in its long-ago heyday it was consulted by generals and politicians across the Mediterranean world, but it was now impoverished and underused.

A visit by the emperor of Rome was hugely welcome, for it promised a revival in the oracle's fortunes. However, there were stories that the encounter was not a great success. They tell of Nero's fury that a poor man's inquiry was dealt with before his own. The priestess, or Pythia, who tended the shrine and mediated the god's responses to ordinary mortals, is reported to have said, "I don't talk to mother-killers."

Apparently, Nero took drastic action to render the oracle inoperable. He threw some people down into the fissure that reputedly lay beneath the temple of Apollo and emitted a gas that sent the Pythia into a trance. In ordinary times she spoke in tongues, which temple priests translated into neat, ambiguous hexameters. On this occasion the séance must have been aborted.

But these are improbable anecdotes, and the emperor is more reliably said to have made a payment of 400,000 sesterces to the prophetess in return for favorable prognostications. He deposited metal copies of olive and oak-leaf crowns in Apollo's shrine, which, according to late sources, he may have helped restore.

What he did do, which seriously dented the goodwill he inspired, was to steal about five hundred statues from Delphi to adorn his Golden House, now rising from the ground. This was a crime, indeed, but not one unique to Nero. Rome's cultural inferiority complex vis-à-vis Hellenic art and literature began on its first contact with the Greeks at the end of the third century B.C. Invading generals and provincial governors turned themselves into connoisseurs and stripped bare of their aesthetic holdings great cities such as Syracuse in Sicily, Corinth, and even violet-crowned Athens. Nero was a latecomer, but he "collected" on an even more massive scale than his predecessors.

He chose only the very best. Among the artistic treasures he removed was a statue of Eros, or Cupid, god of romantic love. It was carved from marble by the world-famous Athenian sculptor Praxiteles. The god was worshipped by the citizens of the small town of Thespiae in Boeotia and the masterpiece was one of their dearest possessions. It was stolen by Caligula but respectfully returned by Claudius. Nero had no such qualms. He seized the statue and sent it back a second time to Rome (where some years before the end of the second century it was destroyed by fire). Gods easily take offense.

Bad news arrived from abroad. The Jews of Judaea were in open revolt. Rumblings of disaffection reached Rome in the spring of 66, shortly before Nero left for Greece. The local Roman authorities handled the situation incompetently and matters got out of hand. The new governor of Syria, Cestius Gallus, who succeeded Corbulo, marched a substantial army against Jerusalem in the vain hope of restoring order. The Roman troops were ambushed and a reported five thousand massacred.

Judaea was a small and, on the face of it, unimportant province. Appearances can deceive. Over time a Jewish diaspora had led to the emergence of noisy and dynamic communities throughout the Mediterranean and especially in large cities such as Alexandria and Rome. As already noted, frequent disputes between Jews and Greek speakers led to serious riots.

Jews themselves were divided. Some were happy to cooperate with the Romans and to participate in the Hellenic culture of the eastern half of the empire, with its polytheistic mythology. Others were fierce believers in their single god, Jehovah, and refused to have anything to do with the imperial cult that identified emperors as divinely sanctioned while alive and deified them after death. To avoid needless trouble, the Roman authorities tolerated the refusal of Jews to make sacrifices to the cult.

But Gallus's humiliation forced their hand. Even if it meant poking a hornets' nest, he would have to be avenged. The Judaean Jews made preparations to resist a punitive invasion.

Who was to lead it? This was a political as well as a military decision. Nero, now universally suspicious, did not want to appoint another Corbulo, who could become a threat to his employer. He needed a competent but obscure general. Vespasian came to mind. He was born into an undistinguished equestrian family and had made his name as a legionary commander during Claudius's conquest of Britannia, when he subjugated Vectis (the Isle of Wight). For this he was awarded a Consulship. He fell afoul of Agrippina and lived in retirement for twelve years. At one point he ran into financial difficulties. He mortgaged his estate and went into the mule trade, for which he won the nickname of Mulio (mule driver).

Vespasian's unfortunate lapse during one of Nero's recitals drove him into the political wilderness again, until his surprise appointment in February 67 to the Judaean command. He was provided with three legions, cavalry, and a large force of local auxiliaries and told to stamp out the revolt.

Nero went everywhere, relentlessly grabbing first prizes. He performed not only at the big four's international celebrations, but also at smaller, local fairs, in fact anywhere that would have him. He ended up with more than eighteen hundred wreaths and garlands. Oddly, he avoided Greece's two best-known cities—Sparta because its militaristic constitution was uncongenial and isolationist, and Athens, home of the unforgiving Furies.

His behavior as a contestant embodied honest contradictions. He knew that as emperor he could make happen whatever he wished. At the same time he suffered dreadfully from stage fright and, as if he were on a par with his rival performers, did all he could to throw them off their stride. Nero spoke politely to them while slandering them behind their backs. A late source claims he was so enraged when a talented competitor refused to give way that he had him killed. If true, it was as if he was regressing to the immaturity of his teen years.

According to Suetonius,

> before beginning he would address the judges in the most deferential terms, saying he had done all he could and the outcome was now in the lap of the gods. They however were men of sense and experience who would know how to exclude accidents from their deliberations. When they told him not to worry he calmed down a little. But he was still anxious, mistaking polite silence for sullenness and ill-will. He said: "I still have my suspicions of you."

What was to be done if Nero made an error that obviously merited disqualification? When he was performing a tragedy, he would speak or chant all the roles, as the rules required, while an accompanist played a flute and made mimed gestures as in a dumbshow. One day, when playing the role of a king, he accidentally dropped his scepter. He picked it up quickly but was terrified that he would be penalized. The accompanist swore that the spectators had not noticed the slip, so engrossed had they been by the emperor's performance.

By now Nero regarded himself as a completely professional and full-time artist. Did his audiences agree? Aristocrats with conservative tastes believed that the princeps's singing was unbelievably bad. A second-century dialogue titled *Nero*, about his time in Greece, takes a more balanced view, and one of its speakers argues that

> his voice deserves neither admiration nor yet ridicule, for nature has made him tolerably and moderately tuneful. His voice is naturally hollow and low, as his throat is deep set, and his singing has a sort of buzzing sound because his throat is thus constituted. However, the pitch of his voice makes him seem less rough when he puts his trust not in his natural powers but in gentle modifications, attractive melody and adroit *cithara*-playing, in choosing the right time to walk, stop and move, and in swaying his head in time to the

> music. The only disgraceful feature is that a king should seem to strive for perfection in these accomplishments.

However, those in his entourage who had to sit through all or most of his shows did have grounds for complaint. While he was singing, no one was allowed to leave the theater, even for the most urgent reasons. Unkind rumor had it, according to Suetonius, that some women in the audience gave birth during the performances. Many, worn out with listening and applauding, slipped over the back wall of the theater, or pretended to drop dead and were carried out as if for burial.

As well as music and the arts, the emperor enthusiastically watched athletic contests. He always had to be the center of attention and was upset when anyone else caught the public eye. He even won the right to be a festival herald, who made all the public announcements. Suetonius again:

> It was generally believed that after his victories as an artist he intended to compete as an athlete at the next Olympic games. He practiced wrestling constantly and wherever he was in Greece he always supervised the athletic events as if he were one of the judges. He used to sit on the ground beside the running tracks in the stadium and, if any of the pairs of contestants moved too far from their allotted positions, pushed them back with his own hands.

There was one sport that the emperor practiced wherever and whenever possible during his stay in Greece—chariot racing. It very nearly cost him his life. While in Olympia, he drove a chariot with a ten-horse team around the racecourse, in spite of the fact that in one of his poems he had criticized an oriental client king for doing the same imprudent and profligate thing. It seems he was in a race and was thrown from the driver's platform and almost crushed to death, probably at the racecourse's turning point. He was helped back in but was too shaken to continue.

Needless to say, he was awarded a victor's crown all the same. He rewarded the judges with the inordinately generous sum of a million sesterces.

Wherever the emperor went, so too did the court and the government. While abroad, Nero had to conduct or at least authorize business, whether routine or urgent. Most leading freedmen traveled with him, including the *a libellis* and *ab epistulis* secretaries. Together with senatorial and equestrian advisers, or *comites,* they were on call to administer the empire.

Members of the political elite were also expected to join the expedition; they were distrusted, and it was better to have them under the authorities' eye than let them get up to mischief in the deserted capital. When he received members of the Senate, the emperor teased them by wearing a short, flowered tunic and around his neck a gauzy scarf. Like a professional citharode, he had grown shoulder-length hair.

The Praetorians were present in force, and so, doubtless, were the princeps's personal German bodyguard. His cheerleaders, the noisy Augustiani, were on hand to guarantee enthusiastic audiences. A number of distinguished musicians, including Terpnus, one of his most influential tutors, were brought along to compete with the emperor—and to make sure to lose.

Nero's intimates and most trusted advisers made sure to stay close to him. Chief among them was Tigellinus, of whom Dio observes: "I consider him a mere appendage to Nero, because he was constantly with him." His new wife, Statilia Messalina, previously one of his lovers, whom he married shortly before leaving for Greece, accompanied him. She was witty and attractive, but perhaps not in her first youth. We know little more about her, except that she was no Poppaea.

There was one sudden departure from Nero's inner circle. The actor and pantomime artist Paris, once a bosom friend, was put to death, apparently, because of his "incapacity" to teach the emperor dancing. More probably, if there is any truth to the report, he foolishly allowed himself to outshine his patron.

For the time being Rome was no longer the center of events, but it still needed good governance. Helius, an experienced freedman, was left behind to rule the metropolis in his absence.

Nero had not gotten over Poppaea's death and was still infatuated with her. When he was onstage he made sure that she remained with him, writes Dio:

> The masks that he wore [according to the conventions of classical drama] were sometimes made to resemble the characters he was portraying and sometimes carried his own features; but the masks for women's roles were made to look like Poppaea, in order that, though dead, she might still take part in the show.

He found the most bizarre of remedies to dull his pain and guilt. One day at court he noticed a boy whom he judged to be the spitting image of Poppaea. He was probably a *puer delicatus,* or "dainty slave-boy," a juvenile court jester in many wealthy households and often sexually exploited. He may have been as young as twelve and not older than in his late teens.

He was called Sporus. This was probably a lewd nickname, for *sporus* is the Greek for seed or semen. To prevent the boy from entering puberty, Nero had him castrated, and from then on he treated him as a reincarnation of Poppaea, calling him by the late empress's personal name, Sabina. Despite already being "married" to the freedman Pythagoras, Suetonius writes that the emperor

> went through a wedding ceremony with him—dowry, bridal veil and all—took him to his house with a great crowd in attendance, and treated him as a wife . . . He dressed Sporus in *haute couture* clothes fit for an empress. While in Greece he took him in his own litter to the assizes [over which, as emperor, he presided] and marketplaces. Later at Rome they went to the Sigillaria [a high-class shopping street], where they kissed amorously now and then as they wandered about.

Tigellinus gave the bride away, according to convention. Celebrations throughout Greece were held in honor of the marriage, and the usual good wishes were uttered, even to the extent of praying that legitimate children might be born to the happy couple. Sporus was now addressed as Lady or Empress. A near contemporary reports that he wore his hair parted, young women attended him whenever he went for a walk, he wore women's clothes, and he was "forced to do everything else a woman does in the same way." What Statilia Messalina, Nero's female wife, thought of all this is not recorded, but she could not compete with a love from beyond the grave.

Dio comments sardonically: "After that Nero had two bedfellows at once, Pythagoras to play the role of husband, and Sporus that of wife."

The contradictory aspects of Nero's sexuality now appear to have melded—the serial monogamy of a faithful adult and the misogynistic promiscuity of a brawling adolescent.

The treatment of Sporus was cruel, agonizing, and demeaning. So far as we can tell, nobody thought to ask him how he felt, and it is too late now even to sketch his personality. Could he have avoided the humiliation of his fate? Almost certainly a slave, he will have thought twice before trying to escape. The odds on a juvenile runaway vanishing for good and starting a new life, hidden from the authorities, were poor.

The impression given by the sources is that Sporus was of a forgiving nature and entered into the spirit of the arrangement. He enjoyed a luxurious quality of life and was content to play the part of an imperial consort. A noblewoman called Calvia Crispinilla was entrusted with his care and was appointed his mistress of the wardrobe. She possessed a substantial fortune and invested in the lucrative wine trade. Tacitus claims that "she tutored Nero in vice," although it is debatable that he needed instruction.

Nero had a bright idea. What if he had a canal cut through the Isthmus of Corinth? This was a strip of land more than three and a half miles across its narrowest extent.

Centuries previously, a ruler of nearby Corinth had built a limestone pathway, called the Diolkos, along which unloaded cargo or ships themselves could be hauled from one sea to the other. This was still in operation and was an alternative to the dangerous trip around the reef-strewn and windy coastline of the Peloponnese. However, it was time-consuming, potentially damaging to vessels and merchandise, and expensively labor-intensive. Most maritime traffic probably preferred the risk of shipwreck.

It is likely that the emperor launched the canal project in the spring of 67. He emerged from his tent singing a hymn in honor of the divinities of the sea. A trumpet sounded, and he was the first to break the ground with a mattock to clapping and cheers. A detachment of the Praetorian Guard was present and started digging. Their labor was ceremonial, for the real effort was to be undertaken by slaves and convicts (including, it is said, the celebrated Roman thinker Musonius Rufus, implicated on trumped-up charges in the Pisonian conspiracy). The ground was rocky and the going hard. Vespasian was making gratifyingly rapid progress in Galilee, which he depopulated; as a promise of future victory, he sent six thousand sturdy Jewish prisoners of war, who were put to work on the canal.

Once the ceremonies were over, Nero left, carrying a basket of earth on his back. After a couple of months, though, he announced that he had changed his mind. He explained that he had been informed (wrongly, of course) that the sea levels on either side of the Isthmus were different and that the island of Aegina would be flooded if the canal was built.

It is an unlikely tale, and the real reason for cancellation may have been cost or difficulty. Whatever the fact of the matter, the project was terminated after only half a mile had been dug.

In 196 B.C., in the heyday of the Roman republic, a victorious Proconsul made an astonishing announcement to a great assembly of Greeks at Corinth.

For a long time they had been ruled by the kingdom of Macedon, which lay north of Greece, but now that kingdom had been conclusively defeated by Rome. The Greeks waited to learn what the future held for them. Would they remain under Macedonian control or become a Roman province? Might they even be granted independence?

The youthful Proconsul, one Titus Quinctius Flamininus, was a passionate admirer of Greek culture. He declared to the assembly that from now on the Greeks would be free from outside control.

> At first the proclamation was by no means generally or distinctly heard, but there was a confused and tumultuous movement in the stadium of people who wondered what had been said, and asked one another questions about it, and called out to have the proclamation made again. When silence had been restored, and the herald [repeated his announcement], a shout of joy arose, so incredibly loud that it reached the sea. . . . Ravens which happened to be flying overhead fell down into the stadium.

The promised independence lasted little more than fifty years before Rome annexed Greece again. Nevertheless, this had been a remarkable moment, and Nero, with his feeling for theatrical effect, decided to restage it. He ordered a gathering of all the Greeks at Corinth on November 28, 67. An inscription has been found that records Nero's address verbatim. He probably wrote it himself. If so, these are the only words that we know to be his—competently put together, if a little tactless:

> For you, men of Greece, it is an unexpected gift which, even though nothing from my generous nature is unhoped-for, I grant to you, as great a gift as you would be unable to request. All Greeks inhabiting Achaia and what is now known as the Peloponnesus, receive freedom with no taxation! . . . Would that Greece were still at its peak. . . . It is not out of pity for you but out of goodwill that I bestow this benefaction. . . . Other leaders have liberated cities, [only Nero] a province.

Even Greeks who disapproved of Nero and were infuriated by his art thefts and the hijacking of their sacred games endorsed the liberation of their homeland. (It is an unusual great power that voluntarily turns its back on tax revenues.) The geographer Pausanias commented: "When I consider this action of Nero, I think that Plato was telling the purest truth when he said that the greatest and most daring crimes are not the product of ordinary men, but of a noble spirit corrupted by a perverted education."

Although little is discussed in the sources, the aborted canal and Greek freedom were examples of imperial thoughtfulness. The eastern half of the Roman empire was economically less developed than the western. Simplifying and speeding up sea communications would boost international trade in the region.

In Roman eyes, contemporary Greeks were slippery wheeler-dealers who did not deserve their roll call of great ancestors. Imperial officials spread bad blood by lording it over their subjects. Changing the constitutional status of the land that had seen the birth of Hellenic civilization would enhance its political and cultural reputation, just as the abolition of central taxation would stimulate economic activity.

Back in Rome, Helius faced opposition. Shockingly for Roman eyes, true-blooded citizens were having to obey a Greek freedman. Apparently, he spent much of his time extorting money from the rich by means of obligatory legacies to the emperor.

In the summer of 67, Helius sent the first of a succession of anxious letters to Nero, who was then competing in the Olympic games. He reported that affairs of the city required his presence and begged the emperor to cut short his trip. Nero was not interested in going home and wrote back: "However much it may be your advice and your wish that I return speedily, you ought rather to advise me and to hope that I may return worthy of Nero." In other words, he would leave Greece only when he had acquired enough prizes.

Eventually Helius grew so alarmed that in November 67 he decided to brave the dangerous winter seas, sail to Greece, and brief the emperor in person. He revealed a new conspiracy against the regime that required Nero's immediate intervention.

A difficulty presents itself. We hear no more of this plot and wonder whether it ever existed. After the deaths of the Scribonius brothers, the German legions had new commanders and the frontiers were quiet. But something must have prompted Helius's emergency journey. In all probability the freedman found himself out of his depth. Time and again the upper classes may have behaved with stubborn insolence and declined to work with him, thus provoking him to a severe response. This irritable ball game continued until eventually Rome began slipping out of control. Nero's presence was needed to restore order.

The princeps was alarmed by Helius's urgency and agreed to bring his Greek adventure to an end, although this would mean abandoning his longed-for stopover in Alexandria. It looks as if he brought forward to November the Isthmian games at Corinth and his final coup de théâtre, the liberation edict. Then he and his multitudinous retinue set sail for Italy across inclement seas.

Despite this enforced change to his plans, the princeps was in an excellent mood. He was proud of all the prizes he had won and ordered a massive celebration for the people of Rome. He continued practicing wrestling intensively, and most people expected him to take up athletics seriously. According to Suetonius,

> He was hailed as Apollo's equal in music and the Sun's in driving a chariot; he now planned to match the exploits of Hercules as well. They say that a lion had been specially trained for him to kill naked in the amphitheater, with a club or by the clasp of his arms.

Whatever Helius might have thought, all was well.

15

DOWNFALL

NERO RETURNED to Rome as if he were a victorious general fresh from battle, but with one crucial difference: His conquests were not of foreign enemies but of his rivals at the Greek games.

First, he entered Naples, that much-loved city. A section of its walls had been demolished, the Greek custom when a wreathed winner at the games came back home. This was repeated at two more towns, and finally he staged a grand march around the capital. Men carrying his multitudinous crowns led the way, followed by the princeps in the chariot Augustus had used when celebrating his many military successes. He wore the purple and gold tunic of the Triumphator. He was crowned with wild olive from Olympia and held in his hand a laurel branch from Delphi. Then came his cheerleaders, the Augustiani, shouting that they were the emperor's escort. All along the route animal victims were sacrificed to the gods. Every so often the streets were sprinkled with perfume. Songbirds, as compliments to Nero's voice, ribbons, and confectionary were showered on him.

The procession wound its way into the Circus Maximus (an entrance arch had been dismantled to make more room) and through the Forum. It then climbed the Palatine hill, where it came to a halt at the temple of Apollo (not, as a regular military triumph did, at the temple of Jupiter on the Capitol). The mood on the streets was exuberant. Romans knew that Nero could throw a party and they seized the opportunity to have a good time. Dio reports that the city

> was decked out with garlands. Lights blazed and burnt incense reeked. The entire population, the Senators most of all, kept shouting in chorus: "Hail, Olympian victor! Hail, Delphic victor! Augustus! Augustus! Hail to Nero, our Hercules! Hail to Nero, our Apollo! The only victor on the Grand Tour [that is, a winner at all four Greek games], the only one from the beginning of time! Augustus! Augustus! Divine Voice! Happy are those who hear you!"

After the celebrations, Nero withdrew to the palace, where he laid out his wreaths on the beds in his sleeping quarters. He set up statues of himself as a cithara player and had a coin struck with the same design.

Nero felt he had reached the pinnacle of artistic practice and was unwilling to sacrifice his creative achievements—and indeed his creative future—on the altar of political duty. The story of his life from the moment in his teens when he had recognized his vocation as musician and poet had been a process of incremental gains. Gradually he had pushed outward the boundaries of acceptable aspiration as princeps. Winning the support of the man in the Roman street, he was able to face down carpers in the Senate. Greece allowed Nero to express his passion fully in the open. In his eyes he had won a famous victory after a lifetime of patient effort. He had transformed the principate from a military and political system into a cultural institution. (Or apparently so, for events impended that were to remind him of the traditional realities of power.)

No longer would Nero make concessions to his opponents. If Suetonius is right, it never occurred to him to stop singing now, or even to sing a little less. He saved his voice by addressing the Praetorians only by letter. He would not attend any entertainment or deal with official business unless he had a voice trainer on hand to warn him to spare his vocal cords and hold a handkerchief to his mouth. He would judge somebody to be a friend or enemy according to the warmth, or lack of it, of his applause.

Delighted but exhausted by his labors, Nero withdrew to Naples. Uninterested in the chores of government, he paid scant attention to external events. After thirteen years as princeps, at last he was master of Rome, fully and on his own terms.

In March 68 trouble broke out in Gaul and cast a shadow over Nero's hopes.

Gaius Julius Vindex was an example of the Roman state at its most moral. He was a Gallic nobleman from Aquitania (today's Aquitaine), a forebear of whom had been given Roman citizenship, probably in the days of Julius Caesar. His father was appointed to the Senate by the emperor Claudius. The enfranchisement of leading provincials and their recruitment into the Roman political elite was one reason why the empire won the cooperation of its inhabitants, or at least of those wealthy men who were in charge of local government.

Vindex was thirty-one and, according to Dio, "physically strong and intellectually astute. He was an experienced soldier and full of daring for any great enterprise. He had a passionate love of freedom and was hugely ambitious." Gaul was divided into provinces and Vindex was the governor of one of them, Gallia Lugdunensis (Lugdunum, now Lyon, was its capital).

He saw himself as a Roman of the old school and loathed everything Nero stood for. Dio catches his disgust in a speech he composed for him:

> I have seen [the princeps as a theatrical performer] in chains, hustled about as a criminal, heavy with child, yes, even in the pains of childbirth. . . . Will anyone call such a person Caesar and emperor and Augustus? Never! Let no one abuse these deeply respected titles.

Early in the year he decided to rebel. It says something of his quixotic nature that at the time he had neither an army to command nor a successor to Nero to propose.

We do not know what drove him to such a desperate enterprise, some enraging straw, perhaps, that broke the camel's back. It is claimed that a continuous flow of emergency taxes infuriated the Gauls, but this does not seem sufficient to have provoked Vindex to revolt. More likely, it was his idealism that moved him to take up arms. He struck coins with boldly republican slogans. These included SPQR [SENATE AND PEOPLE OF ROME] FOR CITIZENS RESCUED FROM DEATH; THE MILITARY STANDARDS OF THE ROMAN PEOPLE; and THE SALVATION OF THE HUMAN RACE.

He understood very well that Rome would not tolerate an emperor from Gaul. Ever since a Gallic tribe briefly captured and, as noted, set fire to the city around 390 B.C., barbarian hordes from the north were the stuff of nightmare. So Vindex had to locate an acceptable candidate. To ferret one out, he wrote to provincial governors and proposed an insurrection. Most of them did not reply and simply forwarded the letters to Nero.

Vindex had very few troops (just a cohort to guard the Lyon mint). If he could not win to his cause the powerful armies on the German frontier, one or other of them would soon temporarily leave its post to hunt down and destroy him. It looked as if he was facing a predictable doom.

On this occasion, however, fortune favored the headstrong. Vindex found both the soldiers and the replacement for Nero that he needed. He called on Gallic tribes to send him their militias and soon commanded something approaching an army, although its quality was untested.

The candidate for the throne who emerged uncertainly into the light was Servius Sulpicius Galba. He was rich, old, and stingy (his enemies said senile). He boasted a long noble lineage. As a boy he had actually met Augustus, who once pinched his cheek, saying: "You too, child, will taste something of this power of mine." He was adopted by the empress Livia, to whom he was distantly related: She left him 50 million sesterces in her will, her single largest bequest.

Sixty-nine years old, Galba was of average height, very bald, with blue eyes and a hooked nose. His hands and feet were so distorted by gout that he could not bear to wear a shoe for long, unroll a book, or even hold one for reading. He suffered from a large hernia that protruded from his right side to such an extent that it could hardly be held in place by a bandage. He had a copious appetite, eating up other people's leftovers.

Galba lived simply, and his only eccentricity was a taste for sex with mature men. He was a competent general, albeit something of a martinet, and had spent the last seven years as governor of Hispania Tarraconensis (that is, the northern half of Spain), where he commanded a garrison legion together with two squadrons of cavalry and three infantry cohorts. When he received Vindex's letter, he ignored it and took no action either way.

This must have been negligence on his part, for he was not yet ready to show his hand and will have known that silence would be interpreted by the authorities in Rome as treason. And so it fell out. The fate of the Scribonius brothers and Corbulo showed that sudden death was Nero's preferred method of managing his provincial generals. He sent a secret order for Galba's execution to his official agents in Spain (finance officers, or *procuratores,* for the most part). The governor's hand was forced when the communication was intercepted and forwarded to him. Motivated by fear rather than ambition, he replied positively to another letter from Vindex that called on him to "make himself the liberator and leader of mankind."

Nero was not especially worried by the letters from Vindex that had been forwarded to him. It was clear that the generals' loyalty was mostly undisturbed. Galba was the exception and, the princeps was sure, he would soon be dead.

Vindex rose in arms in mid-March. He may have chosen the fifteenth of the month, known as the Ides, an auspicious date, for it was the anniversary of Julius Caesar's assassination in 44 B.C. Nero was enjoying himself in Naples when the news arrived on March 23, this date an inauspicious one, for it was the anniversary of his mother's death. He did not even bother to send a letter to the Senate about it or make any public announcement. In fact, he was so calm and uninterested that people around him thought that for some inscrutable reason he was pleased. Going straight to the gymnasium, he watched some athletic contests with close attention. When he was interrupted at dinnertime by an even gloomier dispatch, he had nothing to say beyond threatening to punish the rebels.

Nero remained in Naples, but a series of insulting edicts issued by Vindex provoked him to set a price of 10 million sesterces on his head. He urged the Senate to avenge him. He was particularly upset by being called a hopeless player of the cithara. He observed: "The taunt is especially unfair when one thinks of all the time and energy I have put into training myself in the art." He apologized for not being with them in person, but explained that he was suffering from a sore throat.

Vindex also addressed him by his birth name, Ahenobarbus, implying that Nero had not the slightest right to the imperial throne. Oddly enough, according to Suetonius, the princeps had no objection to being named after his father and giving up his adoptive and imperial appellations. Tired of the endless problems of government, was he toying with the idea of retiring into private life and setting himself up as a jobbing musician? We do not have enough information to say, but it may have been so.

It would not have been the first time such a thought had entered his head. We have already heard of his youthful pipe dream of living as a musician in Alexandria. A visit to the city was to have been a highpoint after his year of music making in Greece, Apparently, when Nero's astrologers warned him that he would lose his throne one day, he famously replied, "A simple craft will keep a man from want." In other words, he believed he could live off his earnings as a performance artist.

In early April, Galba was to preside over the assizes at Nova Carthago (New Carthage, today's Cartagena) when he received news that the revolt in Gaul had started. He had been expecting it and was ready. He mounted the judge's dais, on the pretense of conducting routine ceremonies for enfranchising slaves. In fact, Galba had something more important in mind, as he made clear by setting up in front of him as many statues of Nero's victims as he could find. After a speech in which he deplored the state of the times, those present hailed him as princeps.

He replied with caution, merely proclaiming that he was their governor and thereby represented the Senate and People of Rome. The statement was crafted with care, but it was enough to attract Nero's full attention when it was reported to him.

The fact that Galba did not mention him by name made his meaning clearer than if he had: The incumbent emperor was not even worth considering. He implied that the succession was for Senators to decide, but this was no more than politeness. Those who remembered Claudius's accession recognized that the transfer of power would lie in other hands.

Like Vindex, Galba did not command enough soldiers to challenge the substantial forces under Nero's control, so he raised a new legion from local recruits and added it to his small army. This strengthened his military position, but not decisively so. He seems to have been unsure of the loyalty of his troops, for he replaced his bodyguard of regulars with young *equites* who stood watch at night over his sleep. He also appointed a *consilium* of experienced men who would offer him advice as necessary. He was joined by Otho, Nero's onetime nocturnal playmate and for the last eight or nine years governor of Lusitania. His adherence was helpful if not conclusive.

Galba was taking an enormous gamble on which his personal survival was at stake. Favorable portents were reported, but his chances were not improved by the poor state of his health.

For his part, Vindex must have hoped to win the support of the Rhine legions, or at least their tacit goodwill. It was a sign of his poor judgment that this did not materialize. He was greatly relieved when Galba declared his claim to the purple, and gave him his enthusiastic endorsement.

Nero was no general and could not be relied on to plan military action himself or to lead his troops in the field. However, it is abundantly clear that his staff and advisers knew exactly what needed to be done, not only to destroy Vindex but to dissuade any provincial governor from joining him.

They immediately began the time-consuming and complicated process of assembling a large army in northern Italy, where there was extensive flat land in the Po River basin suitable for a major battle. It consisted of two new legions, XIV Gemina and, originally designed for the putative Black Sea expedition, I Italica. To these were added detachments from Britannia, the two Rhine frontier armies, and the Danube. Units were summoned from as far away as Egypt. Another legion was being raised from the marines in the Misenum fleet. The task of this force was to protect the capital and seat of government and, when the time came, to march against Vindex in central Gaul. On the assumption that by now the only candidate for the throne, Galba, was dead, this defense force would face more of a police action than a military campaign.

Nero alternated between airy optimism and black depression. As usual, his timidity sparked rage. According to Suetonius,

> At the very beginning of the revolt it is believed that he formed many appalling plans, not at all out of character, to depose and assassinate all army commanders and the provincial governors, because they were all united in a conspiracy against him; to massacre all exiles everywhere and all men of Gallic birth in Rome . . . to turn over the Gallic provinces to his armies to ravage; to poison the entire senate at banquets; to set fire to the city.

These threats were the fantasies of a mind under intolerable pressure and did not represent a rational plan of action.

Harassed by dispatch after dispatch, Nero returned to Rome in a panicky frame of mind. He did not personally address either the Senate or an assembly of the People, doubtless not wishing to contribute to a sense of crisis. Instead, he summoned some leading politicians to the palace who were members of his *consilium* and briefly discussed the situation with them. He devoted the rest of the day to demonstrating a new type of water organ and lecturing on the theory and complexity of different models. He promised to exhibit them in

Pompey's Theater, adding, as a joke, "by kind permission of Vindex."

About April 7, Nero had just taken his bath and was at breakfast when he was told that, after all, Galba had foiled the plan to kill him and the Spanish provinces had risen in revolt. He was so upset that he pushed his table over and fell down in a deep faint. He soon regained consciousness and composure, and later took to staging grand banquets whenever good news was reported and composing satirical verses set to sexy music that mocked enemy personalities.

Nero took two sensible practical measures: He appointed himself sole Consul and arranged for the Senate to declare Galba a public enemy. These were welcome signs that he was taking personal charge of the crisis and would lead his forces in person.

His once close woman friend Calvia Crispinilla had been Sporus's duenna, but she now took ship for the province of Africa, where she persuaded the governor, Lucius Clodius Macer, to join the revolt and cut off the grain supply to the capital. This was a clever move, for shortages were likely to spark discontent and even riots. To further irritate public opinion, a ship from Egypt was reported to have docked carrying sand for the court wrestlers.

In general, though, the auguries were good. The army that was gathering in the Po valley would be a powerful deterrent to treason. Vindex and Galba were not strong enough to pose an existential threat. The frontier legions along the Rhine were loyal, or so it appeared, and showed no sign of a falling away from the princeps. Surely they would prefer a descendant of Augustus to a sick and superannuated Galba. The evidence suggested that the empire was holding steady.

Lucius Verginius Rufus was governor of Upper Germany and commanded three legions as well as a similar number of auxiliaries—in sum, more than thirty thousand men. He supported Nero.

His soldiers agreed and disapproved of Vindex. He and his ragtag force were the image of the Gallic horror that had haunted Romans for centuries. They supposed him to be leading an anticolonialist insurrection and regarded him as a male Boudica. In this they were completely mistaken. Vindex wanted to get rid of Nero and nothing more.

Presumably on instructions from Rome, Rufus led his troops into Gaul to hunt down Vindex and terminate both him and the revolt. They found the gates of Vesontio (today's Besançon) closed to them. The inhabitants may have wished to avoid the massive inconvenience of a military occupation and hoped that they were unimportant enough for the Romans to leave them alone.

After all, 120 miles south lay the far more tempting target of Lugdunum, a sizable city loyal to Nero, which Vindex and his irregulars were blockading. In fact, Rufus decided to capture Vesontio and laid siege to it. Vindex left Lyon and came to the town's aid. He encamped not far away from Rufus.

It is hard to understand the two commanders' motives for their puzzling behavior. Vesontio was a place of no great strategic interest and was hardly worth the trouble they were taking. An explanation may lie in their next step: Once they were close enough to each other, they met for confidential discussions with no one else present. The two commanders sheltered behind a cover story concerning the struggle for Vesontio, for it was essential that suspicions of betrayal not be prematurely aroused among the soldiers of either party.

So what did they actually talk about? Dio says that they came to a secret deal against Nero, but adds "as is conjectured." There must have been a compact of some sort, for after their encounter, Rufus gave permission for Vindex to enter Vesontio unopposed.

All this is speculation and we will never know the truth, for destiny intervened. When the Gauls began to move through the Roman lines, as agreed during the discussions, Rufus's legionaries interpreted this as an attack on them and, without their officers' permission, charged. Plutarch writes that the armies "compelled their leaders, like charioteers who had lost control of the reins, into the crash of a great battle."

Rufus withdrew, speechless and despairing, to his tent while his forces won a complete victory. Vindex, dismayed by this accidental rout, killed himself, and Rufus mourned his death. He lived a long life, and when discussing his intentions later, he adjusted his account to the prevailing political winds.

To offer a guess at the truth, he sympathized with Nero but above all else wished to avoid the misery of a civil war. At Vesontio he may have tried to arrive at some kind of peaceful settlement. Whether that would have favored Nero or Galba is unclear. Rufus's legions called on him to accept the purple himself. He firmly refused and persuaded his men to renew their allegiance to the princeps. When Galba wrote to him proposing an alliance, he did not trouble to reply.

Vesontio was a feather in Nero's cap and a disheartened Galba withdrew to Clunia, a remote town in the highlands of Tarraconensis nearly three hundred miles from the provincial capital of Tarragona. Here, with bitter regret for what he had done, he awaited the arrival of an emissary from Rome requiring his suicide.

Events now took a dizzying turn and slipped into reverse. The person responsible was the princeps himself. The new sole Consul was greatly relieved by the death of Vindex, but was dismayed when he heard of the offer of the throne which the legions of Upper Germany had made to Rufus.

A mistaken idea lodged itself in his head that he had lost both the German armies, whereas in fact they preferred him to Galba. Then he heard a rumor that the commander of the army in northern Italy, Publius Petronius Turpilianus, an elderly loyalist who had picked up the pieces as governor of Britannia after the Boudican debacle, had changed sides. This too was incorrect, although Petronius may have tried to position himself in such a way that he could survive the unlikely event of his defeat.

The emperor knew that his chances would be greatly improved if he took the field himself, but he failed to act decisively and appropriately on his fears. Suetonius recounts that

> as he was leaving the dining room after a banquet, leaning on the shoulders of his comrades, he declared that immediately on setting

foot in the province he would go before the soldiers unarmed and weep and weep. In this way he would lead the rebels to change their purpose. Next day he would rejoice among his rejoicing subjects and sing paeans of victory, which he ought at that very moment to be composing.

Nero may have intended to join his army, but we are told that when making his preparations he mainly worried about how many wagons he would need to carry all his stage equipment. He arranged that female staff members who were to accompany him on campaign were given male haircuts (presumably to conceal their gender and so protect them from sexual assault).

Short of ready cash, he announced an emergency income tax and tried unsuccessfully to raise fresh troops from Rome's citizenry. Grain prices rose, probably due to supply difficulties from Africa, but the princeps got the blame.

None of this helped his cause. What he ought to have done was to convey a sense of energy instead of irresolution and frivolity. He seemed paralyzed by his timidity. A flaw of his principate had always been its military inexperience. It was too late to do much about this now, but his friends at least expected him to lead, if only as a figurehead, the powerful forces assembled to save his throne. He never did so.

On the home front it was essential to keep on the side of the Praetorians, waiting on events in their barracks. He should have learned this from his mother, daughter of the charismatic Germanicus, and his adoptive father, Claudius, both of whom recognized the Guards' role as a bulwark of the imperial regime. So far as we know, Nero made no move to meet them, lift their morale, and confirm them as guardians of the Julio-Claudian family.

Instead, he placed his trust in the two slippery Praetorian Prefects, Tigellinus, ill and thinking about a shift to Galba, and the ultra-ambitious Nymphidius Sabinus, who was already considering a bid for the throne.

Dispatches were delivered to the palace at dinnertime on June 8, reporting fake news of army defections. The princeps tore them to pieces and for a second time knocked over his table in a rage. Two favorite crystal drinking cups, which he called Homeric because they were engraved with scenes from the epic poet's work, fell to the floor and were smashed.

Nero was slowly coming to a decision to abdicate. Courage was not his strong suit. He wanted to run away from Rome and all it stood for. This was a terrible error of judgment. To vacate one's chair and leave the room changes everything, for it cancels oaths and obligations. Trusted aides were losing confidence in his ability to hold on to power. When he ordered his most reliable freedmen to Ostia, where they were to get a fleet ready, he was shocked that some of them refused and the others prevaricated. One of them even quoted a line from Vergil: "Is it so dreadful a thing to die?"

He obtained some poison from Locusta, who was still at work solving the problems of the mighty with her prescriptions, and placed it in a gold box, just in case he were to need it. Then he walked across the Servilian Gardens and tried to persuade the Praetorian tribunes and centurions on guard there to join him as he made his escape from the city. They declined the invitation.

Where was he to go? Nero turned over in his mind his dwindling options. The accord over Armenia must have stored much goodwill for him at the Parthian court; perhaps they would grant him asylum. It would take an age to negotiate, though. Would Galba treat him kindly if he prostrated himself before him?

Alternatively, he could walk down to the Forum and address the People from the rostra. He would beg forgiveness for his past shortcomings. If they refused to pardon him, they would surely at least allow him the Prefecture of Egypt. He began to draft the speech but left it unfinished on his writing desk. He dared not deliver it for fear of being torn to pieces by the mob. Mentally fragile, was he still being pursued by the Furies and his vengeful mother?

Nero was wrong about the public mood; there is little evidence that his long-standing popularity among the masses was taking more than transitory hits. The grain supply crisis, we may assume, was soon resolved, for we hear no more of it. The plebs knew that if they discarded this princeps they were unlikely to find another one who shared their appetites and interests.

Putting off his deliberations to the following day, he went to bed, but awoke at midnight. He found that his bodyguard had left. He leaped up and called for his servants and friends. No reply came back from anyone, so he went to their bedrooms, accompanied by the few followers who were left. The doors were locked and nobody answered when he called and knocked. He went back to his room. It had been stripped bare in his absence, and the caretakers had absconded with his bed linens and the gold poison box.

Nero abandoned hope and summoned his favorite gladiator, Spiculus, who was an officer of the German bodyguards and ought to have been on duty, or any other efficient executioner who could deliver a painless death. Again, no one appeared, and he said: "Don't I have either friend or foe?" He dashed out of the palace intending to throw himself into the Tiber, then changed his mind.

A handful of loyalists appeared and Nero asked if anyone knew of some secluded spot away from the city where he could hide and collect his thoughts. They discussed Nero's best course of action. He repeated his wild schemes to massacre the Senate or burn down the already burned-down city. He returned to his idea of sailing to Alexandria and making a living as a musician. "Even if we are forced out as emperor, this little talent of mine will support us."

He accepted the offer by a senior freedman, Phaon, his finance minister (*a rationibus*), of a suburban villa four miles out of town. There he could lie low for a while. From then onward, only four supporters stayed with Nero during his night flight from Rome. They included Phaon, Epaphroditus, the minister for petitions (*a libellis*), and a freedman about whom nothing is known apart from his name, Neophytus.

The fourth member of the group was, of all people, Sporus, the pseudo-Poppaea. That he remained true to a cruel and selfish master suggests a remarkably tolerant and empathetic nature. That indeed seems to be the case if we can judge from a new year's present he gave Nero: a ring on which was carved the rape of Persephone, daughter of the harvest goddess, Ceres, who was kidnapped by the king of the underworld and became his queen. The legend echoed Sporus's acceptance of his role as empress.

Nero left his residence (probably the Servilian Gardens) as he was, barefoot and wearing a tunic. He put on a faded cloak and mounted a horse. To avoid being identified he covered his head and held a handkerchief to his face. He was startled by a thunderclap and a flash of lightning full in his face. He and his companions passed the Praetorian barracks and heard soldiers shouting "Death to Nero!" and cheering the name of Galba.

They encountered some travelers on the road and heard one of them say, "These people are after Nero," and another asked them, "Any news in town about Nero?" Then his horse took fright at the smell of a dead body that had been thrown out onto the road; the cloak fell back from his face, and a retired guardsman recognized him and saluted.

When the riders came to a bypath leading to the villa, they turned their horses loose. Nero pushed his way along a track among bushes and brambles. He struggled through a stretch of marshy reeds and reached the back wall of the house only when someone threw down a garment for him to walk on.

Phaon evidently suspected that their hideout had been discovered and wanted them to enter the building unobserved. He urged Nero to lie down out of sight for a while in a nearby sandpit while a secret tunnel was dug, but he answered: "I refuse to go underground while I am still alive." He scooped up with his hand some water from a puddle and drank it. Referring to his own concoction of distilled water cooled in snow, he remarked: "So this is now Nero's favorite drink!" While he waited, he spent time removing thorns that had torn his cloak. Everyone who went past on the road he suspected had come for him.

When a narrow passage had been excavated Nero crawled through on all fours into the villa. The first room he entered was a cramped space probably used by slaves. He lay down on a couch with a shoddy mattress on it, covered by an old cloak. Although he was hungry and thirsty, he refused some coarse bread and only sipped a little lukewarm water.

He was struck by the irony that he was now living out for real the kind of part he had played in the theater. He could not get out of his head a line about Oedipus: "My father and mother order me to a lamentable death."

The mood of the group had changed. There was no longer a question of escape to Egypt or indeed to anywhere. Everyone begged Nero to avoid the degrading fate that awaited him when he was found. Eventually he asked them to dig a grave for him of the right size. They were then to collect any pieces of old marble they could find with which to decorate it, and to bring water to wash his corpse, and wood to cremate it.

While this was being done, he wept continuously, repeating all the time: "God, what an artist is dying with me!"

While he hesitated, a courier arrived with a letter for Phaon. Nero snatched it from his hand and read that the Senate, meeting in emergency session, had declared him a public enemy. They were looking for him so that he could be punished in the ancient fashion. He asked what that was. He was told that he would be stripped naked, fastened by the neck in a V-shaped wooden fork, and beaten to death with rods.

Terrified out of his mind, Nero produced two daggers he had brought with him, tested their tips, then put them away again, saying that the fateful hour had not yet come. He begged Sporus to begin the ceremony of mourning by keening for him. Then he asked one of the freedmen to set him an example by killing himself first. Nobody volunteered.

He kept whining about his cowardice: "How ugly and vulgar my life has become," and, in Greek, "This is no credit to Nero, no credit at all. Come on, pull yourself together."

The sound of horses' hooves could be heard. A troop of cavalry was galloping up the road with orders to capture Nero alive. Time had expired. He quoted a line from *The Iliad:* "Listen to the sound! It is the trampling of swift-footed horses."

With the help of Epaphroditus, he pushed a dagger into his throat. He was half dead when a centurion rushed in. Taking in the scene, he pretended that he had come to help Nero, not arrest him, and tried to stanch the wound with his cloak. Nero gasped: "Too late!" and "What loyalty!" He died, his eyes glazed and bulging from their sockets.

It is tempting to be touched by the fidelity of Nero's companions, but all may not have been as it seemed. Another sinister possibility presents itself. The contemporary orator and philosopher Dio Chrysostom refers to a mysterious betrayal. In his essay *On Beauty,* he writes that Sporus

> in anger disclosed the emperor's designs to his retinue; and so they revolted from him and compelled him to make away with himself as best he could. Indeed the truth about this has not come out even yet; for so far as the rest of his subjects were concerned, there was nothing to prevent his continuing to be emperor.

The meaning is unclear, but Sporus may have revealed to the Senators or to the Praetorians Nero's plan to hide in Phaon's villa while arranging to escape from Rome to Alexandria. If that is what happened, the *puer delicatus* broke faith. According to one of Dio's epitomators, Nero was furious and wanted to kill Sporus, who then fled the scene.

Of course, the word "retinue" may refer only to members of the emperor's personal staff. In that case, Sporus would have been acting helpfully if he had alerted them to Nero's whereabouts.

Dio Chrysostom realizes that he may have gotten his facts wrong and is repeating inaccurate gossip. However, his report does explain the speed with which the emperor was tracked down and is perhaps reinforced by the fact that, soon after Nero's death, Sporus was picked up and employed by Nymphidius Sabinus, Nero's treacherous Praetorian Prefect.

This account is not without interest, but is unconvincing. If he was minded to inform against Nero, Sporus must have done so while the emperor was still in Rome. So why did he not run away then rather than accompany Nero on his frightening journey through the night?

The fact that a letter was delivered to Phaon from one of his contacts in the city suggests that the imperial whereabouts were not a total secret. But Dio does not implicate Sporus in wrongdoing and claims that after making urgent inquiries, the Praetorians discovered Nero's location for themselves and dispatched a posse.

Should Nero have been betrayed, it is odd that nobody spoke or wrote about it—except for Dio Chrysostom's puzzled (and puzzling) comment.

In the last analysis the hypothesis of treachery is superfluous. The story as we have it of Nero's last hours stands up on its own terms without requiring the intervention of a scheming eunuch. On balance, it is safest to believe that Sporus was true.

The first important visitor at the death scene was a freedman called Icelus, who was Galba's representative in Rome. When his master announced his revolt, he was imprisoned, and was immediately released on the news of Nero's suicide. He wanted to check that he really was dead. While at Phaon's villa, he agreed that the corpse should not be mutilated, a possibility that had worried Nero, and authorized a decent funeral.

This turned out to be quite a deluxe affair, costing 200,000 sesterces, fitter for an emperor than an enemy of the people. The dead princeps was laid out in a white robe with gold embroidery and cremated in the presence of members of his household, including Sporus. His ashes were not lodged in the Mausoleum of Augustus, the resting place of the Julio-Claudians, as might have been expected, but in the tomb of the Domitii, his genetic family. They were deposited by his old nurses, Egloge and Alexandria. The ceremony was attended by Nero's first and perhaps deepest love, the freedwoman Acte.

His sarcophagus was of porphyry, with an altar of marble from Luna (today's Carrara) standing above it, and was enclosed by a balustrade of white marble from the island of Thasos.

16

LOOSE ENDS

The freedman Icelus brought to Galba, who was en route from his Spanish province to Rome, the good news of Nero's death. He was so delighted that he showered the freedman with kisses and told him to get ready to have sex with him immediately.

In the interval before Galba's arrival in Rome, the Praetorian Prefect, Nymphidius Sabinus, was the leading man in the state. On Galba's behalf, he persuaded his guardsmen to abandon Nero in return for a handsome bonus. He assumed the sole credit for Nero's downfall and made a bid for the purple himself.

Once in the capital, though, Galba took charge. Alarmed by the poor state of the public finances, he declined to pay the Praetorians their promised bonus. He told them: "It is my custom to levy troops, not buy them."

The Praetorians believed they had been misled and were angry with both men. They murdered Nymphidius when he had the temerity to visit their barracks. They looked around for a replacement to Galba and found Otho, Nero's old drinking buddy. He too went to meet them, with a better result. The Praetorians listened to him, liked him, and hailed him as princeps. He reinstated the bribe and made sure the bill was quickly settled.

Otho sent a cavalry detachment to kill Galba and his newly nominated heir, an innocuous young nobleman, in the Forum. Galba's reign had lasted only a few months. In Tacitus's lethal assessment, he was "perfect for the job of emperor, if only he hadn't become emperor" (*capax imperii nisi imperasset*).

Otho's imperium was insecure. He presented himself as Nero's natural successor and was popular in Rome. The first grant he made was one of 50 million sesterces for finishing the Domus Aurea. However, the legions on the German frontier, which had supported Nero against Vindex, now opted for one of their own generals. In place of Galba, they nominated the commander of Lower Germany as emperor. This was the affable Aulus Vitellius, whose father, Lucius, had been the friend, and indispensable bootlicker, of emperors. He was a gourmand for whom food was as tasty as power. On his first day as emperor, he promoted Asiaticus, his sex slave, to the rank of *eques*.

Vitellius defeated Otho in a great battle in northern Italy. For once, someone in this long story acted honorably. Reinforcements were on their way, but Otho decided that it would be wrong to prolong the civil war, and after three months in office he killed himself in the national interest.

In Judaea, Vespasian turned out to be in safe hands. Ably assisted by his son Titus, he was winning the Jewish war. His legions proclaimed him emperor. The army of the Danube concurred and marched on the capital. It fell after a bloodbath during which many thousands lost their lives. Vitellius was dragged from a hiding place and tormented half naked before being put to death. He was heard to say: "And yet I was your emperor once." So he had been, for nine months.

At last the civil wars were over during which four emperors briefly ruled, Vespasian being the winner. He sailed to Rome from Egypt where he had been awaiting the call. He was competent and durable, and not a drop of noble blood ran in his veins. For once Rome had a princeps with straightforward sexual tastes. His wife bore him two sons and a daughter, and after her death he lived with the love of his life, a middle-aged freedwoman.

As in a tragedy by Seneca, few of the dramatis personae were left standing by the last act. Readers may care to learn the fates of two players in Nero's story.

One of the first decisions of Nymphidius Sabinus during his brief period in power was to take Sporus into his household "while Nero's body was still burning on its pyre." He maintained the boy's female identity and, according to Plutarch, treated him as his consort, as Nero had done, and called him Poppaea.

Sporus seems to have been a popular boy or girl. After the death of Nymphidius, he passed into the hands of Otho, who gave shelter to many in Nero's household. According to Dio, their relationship was "intimate." On Otho's suicide, Sporus was taken in by Vitellius. Here the plot takes a darker turn. The new emperor enjoyed a luxurious lifestyle, and one of his pleasures was to organize gladiatorial combats. As a dramatic interlude,

> it was proposed that Sporus should be brought onto the stage in the role of a virgin being raped, but he would not endure the shame and made away with himself beforehand.

The chosen theme was a bitter humiliation, for it echoed Sporus's own experience, and it was also the subject of the ring he gave Nero. We know no more of what was planned, but it may have been one of those entertainments in which the abuse on display was real rather than simulated.

Even by the standards of the day, Sporus lived a bizarre and tragic life. If he was indeed a *puer delicatus,* as is plausible, he may have been only a boy when he died.

Tigellinus was ill with tuberculosis during the crucial days of Nero's downfall, and Nymphidius Sabinus relieved his fellow Prefect of his duties. Galba was under pressure to execute him, but he bought his life with lavish gifts to an influential member of the new regime. What was the point, Galba mused, of executing a man about to die anyway from a fatal disease (as Caligula had done with regard to Seneca)? According to Plutarch, Tigellinus spent his last days having sex with prostitutes, "clutching after them as his life painfully ebbed away."

Otho was unforgiving. He sent a messenger to fetch him from Sinuessa Spa where he was taking the waters; it was near the coast and there was a risk that he would escape by ship. Tigellinus tried to bribe the messenger with a large sum of money to let him go free. Even when that failed, he still gave him presents.

He begged the man to wait till he had shaved. Then he picked up his razor and cut his own throat, demonstrating that if nothing else he had a sharp sense of humor.

For a long time after his death, people used to lay spring and summer flowers on Nero's tomb. They had statues made of him wearing his distinctive fringed toga and set them up on the Speakers' Platform. They even circulated his edicts as if he were still alive and would soon return to confound his enemies.

While the ruling elite, the Senators and the Stoics, were delighted by Nero's demise, the people at large were dismayed. On Otho's accession, enthusiastic crowds called him Nero, and he was happy to have his name associated with the dead emperor. According to Suetonius,

> he even made use of that surname in his state correspondence and his first letters to some of the provincial governors. It is certain that he allowed Nero's busts and statues to be reinstated, and reappointed his procurators and freedmen to their former posts.

Vitellius also recognized the political advantage of adopting the Neronian model of government. He made funerary offerings to Nero in the middle of the Campus Martius, attended by a large crowd of official priests. At the usual banquet, a flute player was warmly received, and the emperor

> openly called for him to perform something from the Maestro. When he began to play Nero's songs Vitellius was the first to jump to his feet and applaud.

Word got about that Nero was not dead after all. One contemporary observer remarked: "There was nothing to prevent his continuing to be Emperor for all time, seeing that even now everybody wishes he were still alive. And the great majority do believe that he still is." It was widely thought that he had fled to Parthia, where he intended to recruit a large army and come back to Rome to destroy it.

In late 68 or early 69, a personable slave from Pontus who could play the cithara claimed that he was the emperor. Tacitus writes that "the great name of Nero attracted many who pined for revolution and hated the existing state of affairs." The provincial authorities in the east were thrown into a panic, but they need not have upset themselves. The pretender was more interested in piracy than politics. He was soon captured and put to death.

In the reign of Vespasian's eldest son, Titus, a second pretender appeared. He was an Asiatic called Terentius Maximus. He looked and sounded like Nero, and he too sang to the accompaniment of a cithara. He claimed to have escaped from the Praetorians who had arrested him and to have lived in hiding for many years. He attracted some followers in Asia Minor, and the farther east he traveled, the more popular he became.

The Parthians missed Nero and were tempted to believe the bona fides of Terentius when he took refuge among them. He joked, in character, that they owed him a reward for handing over Armenia to them. The Parthian king, Artabanus, was on poor terms with Titus and set about promoting his cause in Rome. However, Terentius's true identity became known, and since a false claimant had no value for the king, he was put to death.

Twenty years after Nero's suicide, during the reign of Vespasian's younger son, Domitian, a third pretender emerged, as Suetonius recalls:

> When I was a young man, a person of uncertain rank appeared, who gave out that he was Nero, and the name was still in such favor with the Parthians that they backed him vigorously and only handed him over with great reluctance.

Nero was not remembered kindly by Jews and Christians. The former had watched him send an army to suppress the revolt in Judaea with frightening violence, and the latter believed he had put to death the founding fathers of their church, Peter and Paul. He became a favorite hate figure in the imagery of eschatological literature and was enrolled as the second Beast in the book of Revelation. At the end of the world, Belial the Antichrist will manifest himself as the incarnation of the dead Nero.

In the fifth century, one of the greatest church fathers, Augustine of Hippo, wrote of Nero:

> Some suppose that he shall rise again and be the Antichrist. Others, again, suppose that he is not even dead, but that he was hidden that he might be supposed to have been killed, and that he now lives in concealment in the vigor of that same age which he had reached when he was believed to have perished, and will live until he is revealed in his own time and restored to his kingdom.

So Nero, a reluctant ruler, ended up as the once and future emperor, a Mediterranean King Arthur. He finds himself where he would most wish to be: embedded in the collective imagination.

In one of his essays, Plutarch, who was a teenager when Nero died and may have heard him sing, imagines his fate in the afterlife. Demons pierced him with red-hot nails as a punishment for his crimes. But once justice had been served, underworld technicians used to prepare dead souls for rebirth. Nero was to be reincarnated as a viper, a creature that was believed to enter the world by gnawing through its mother's womb—a suitable fate for a matricide.

Then a great light suddenly shone and a voice came out of it, saying that Nero had been punished enough and deserved some reward from the gods for freeing Greece. So the technicians devised something milder: They transformed Nero into a creature that frequents lakes and marshes, and croaks. He became a frog and now sings his songs to his heart's content, in the same husky tones he is said to have commanded in his previous life.

A happy ending of a sort.

Nero's life was one long act of resistance, to his mother and to the Roman political class.

Was he a great poet and music maker? His tragedy is that he was not. He seems to have had a real but middling talent. One has the impression that he himself did not know whether he was any good. We do not know either, but what is certain is the seriousness and application he devoted to his creative work.

The new Flavian dynasty (so named after Vespasian's family name Flavius) justified itself by blackening Nero's reputation. And indeed the dead emperor did commit many crimes. The mud stuck, for even today Nero is a byword for decadence and despotism.

However, although he gave little time to running the empire, he was a more effective ruler than he has been given credit for. His first advisers, Seneca and Burrus, carried much of the burden in the early years of his reign and he learned from them how to supervise government rather than to govern. The handling of the Boudica rebellion was, after a shaky start, competent and the Armenian settlement was an example of far-sighted statecraft. The rebuilding of Rome after the fire was intelligently planned. Nero dealt decisively with the Jewish revolt, although it was not finally suppressed until the arrival of the Flavians. Much of the credit for these achievements must go to his team of efficient Greek freedmen, but he appointed and presided.

In his teens the emperor was allowed, perhaps encouraged, to misbehave. He delighted in ordinary pleasures and came to see that his "pop star" image allowed him to engage directly with ordinary citizens. Personal taste matured into his strategy of spectacle. This was a real success. His approval level seems to have been consistently high throughout the reign. Later emperors took the point and did their best to follow suit. It was Vespasian, his immediate successor, who built the most celebrated venue for spectacle in history, the Colosseum.

Perhaps Nero's most serious mistake was not to plan for his successor. He sensed a potential threat from other members of the imperial family and one by one he eliminated them, even if they were unambitious and avoided conspiracies. By the end of the reign execution and suicide had wiped out the dynasty of Augustus. This exercise in realpolitik could be explained as essential to the safety of the state, but in the light of Nero's failure to produce an heir it left him as vulnerable as ever.

Another weakness was Nero's lack of military experience and his reluctance to acquire any. The Roman empire was a disguised monarchy held in place by the legions. Rulers such as Augustus, Tiberius, and even the disabled Claudius led armies and won wars. Generalship was a skill expected in a princeps, and Nero might have saved his skin had he possessed it.

Nero's interest in the Greek-speaking half of the empire was before its time. Half a century later, Hadrian, perhaps the greatest of the emperors, adopted a similar concern with considerable success. In the long run it was the eastern provinces that outlasted the west and survived as the Byzantine empire until the fifteenth century.

What was Nero like as a person? This is hard to say, for the literary sources are insufficient and heavily biased against him. From what we can tell, he combined fearfulness and obstinacy camouflaged by swagger. Once he had committed a crime, he was racked with guilt. Remarkably, he went on to share his anguish with his public, who never lost its affection for him.

Nero's most admirable quality was the purity of his commitment to art. Unfortunately, performances vanish as soon as they conclude, and none of his poetry has survived in written form.

So we know next to nothing about what he most cared for.

ACKNOWLEDGMENTS

We are greatly indebted to Molly Turpin, our editor, and Nancy Delia, who was in charge of production, at Penguin Random House, New York, and to my agents, Christopher Sinclair-Stevenson and Jeff Gerecke, for their wise guidance and unfailing enthusiasm. As in the past, Professor Robert Cape of Austin College, Texas, has very kindly read a draft and offered useful comments and suggestions. We are grateful to David Grocott for his expert advice, to Andrew Shrubb for his wisdom, and to Jamie Sawyer for his hard work.

TIMELINE

The timeline is selective and reflects themes in the book. It is comprehensive for Nero's reign.

B.C.		
63	*September 23*	Birth of Octavius (later Octavian, later still Augustus)
49		Julius Caesar launches civil war
46	*April*	Suicide of Cato
45	*March*	Julius Caesar wins civil war
44	*March 15*	Julius Caesar assassinated
43		Octavian Consul. Triumvirate formed (Octavian, Mark Antony, and Lepidus)
42	*October*	Battles of Philippi; defeat of Julius Caesar's assassins
41		Antony in Asia, meets Cleopatra
40	*Summer*	Octavian marries Scribonia
		Antony marries Octavia, Octavian's sister
		Herod granted throne of Judaea
38		Octavian divorces Scribonia, marries Livia
36		Antony invades Parthia
34		Donations of Alexandria
34–27		Augustus in Gaul and Spain
33		Triumvirate lapses
31		Antony divorces Octavia
	September 2	Battle of Actium
30		Suicides of Antony and Cleopatra
29		Doors of temple of Janus are closed
28		Mausoleum of Augustus started
27		Octavian announces his settlement, is titled Augustus
25		Marriage of Julia, Augustus's daughter, to Marcellus, his nephew
		Closing of the doors of the temple of Janus

23		Illness of Augustus; he receives *imperium maius proconsulare* and *tribunicia potestas* for life
		Death of Marcellus
21		Marriage of Agrippa, friend and deputy of Augustus, and Julia
20		Tiberius crowns Tigranes king of Armenia
20–19		Agrippa in Gaul and complete pacification of Spain
16–13		Augustus in Gaul, Agrippa in the East
12–9		Tiberius campaigns in the Balkans, Drusus in Germany
9		Accidental death of Drusus, Tiberius's brother
7		Tiberius recalled
6		Tiberius withdraws to Rhodes
5		Gaius Caesar, son of Julia and Agrippa, Consul
4		Death of Herod, his kingdom divided among his sons Philip, Herod Antipas, and Archelaus
		Lucius Caesar, son of Julia and Agrippa, *princeps iuventutis*
1		Gaius Caesar in the East
A.D.		
2		Agreement between Gaius Caesar and Phraates, king of Parthia; Ariobarzanes installed as king of Armenia
		Lucius Caesar dies at Massilia
		Tiberius returns from Rhodes
4		Gaius Caesar dies of wound
		Augustus adopts Agrippa Postumus and Tiberius, who himself adopts Germanicus, son of Drusus
9		Three legions lost in German ambush
12		Germanicus takes command in Gaul and Germany
14	*August 19*	Death of Augustus
		Accession of Tiberius
		Murder of Postumus
	Autumn	Germanicus and Drusus put down mutinies
15	*November 6*	Agrippina, daughter of Germanicus, born
16		Germanicus recalled
17		Germanicus sent to the East to install new king of Armenia
19	*October 10*	Death of Germanicus, allegedly by poison
		Birth of Tiberius Gemellus
20		Trial and suicide of Calpurnius Piso, "murderer" of Germanicus
23		Death of Drusus, Tiberius's son
26		Quarrel between Agrippina the Elder and Tiberius

		Tiberius leaves Rome and settles in Capri
		(?) Pontius Pilate, *praefectus* of Judaea
28		Death of Julia, Augustus's daughter
		Marriage of Agrippina the Younger, Germanicus's daughter, to Gnaeus Domitius Ahenobarbus
29		Death of Livia
		Exile of Agrippina, Germanicus's wife, and her son, Nero Julius Caesar
30		Suicide of Nero Julius Caesar
31	*October 18*	Dismissal and death of Sejanus, favorite of Tiberius
		Caligula joins Tiberius on Capri
32		Consulship of Gnaeus Domitius Ahenobarbus
33	*October 18*	Death of Agrippina, Germanicus's wife
		Death of Agrippina's son, Drusus
35		Tiberius names Caligula and Gemellus heirs to his estate
36		Pontius Pilate removed from his post
37	*March 16*	Death of Tiberius
		Accession of Caligula; his three sisters, including Agrippina, honored
		Claudius, brother of Germanicus, Consul with his nephew Caligula
		Gemellus put to death (or forced to kill himself)
	Autumn	Caligula seriously ill
	December 15	Nero born (Lucius Domitius Ahenobarbus)
38		Death of Caligula's sister, Drusilla
		Caligula marries Lollia Paulina
		Trouble between the Greek and Jewish communities of Alexandria
39		Caligula divorces Lollia Paulina, marries Milonia Caesonia
		Caligula in the Rhineland
		Conspiracy discovered
		Caligula's surviving sisters, including Agrippina, implicated and exiled
		Birth of Octavia, daughter of Claudius
39–41		Nero cared for by his aunt, Domitia Lepida
		Claudius marries Messalina
40		Death of Nero's father, Gnaeus Domitius Ahenobarbus
		Preparations for invasion of Britannia
		Caligula orders a statue of himself to be displayed in the temple at Jerusalem
		Caligula back in Rome
41	*January 24*	Assassination of Caligula

Year	Date	Event
		Accession of Claudius
		Recall of Agrippina and Livilla
		Birth of Britannicus, son of Claudius and Messalina
43		Invasion of Britannia
46		Exile of Seneca
47		Corbulo in the Rhineland
		The Troy Game incident
48		"Marriage" and execution of Messalina
49	*January 1*	Marriage of Claudius and Agrippina
		Seneca appointed Nero's tutor
50	*February 25*	Claudius adopts Nero
		Agrippina declared Augusta
51		Burrus Praetorian Prefect
		Nero recognized as adult, assumes the *toga virilis*
		Nero *princeps iuventutis*
		Caratacus, British leader, defeated and brought to Rome
		Vologeses king of Parthia
51–53		Nero presents petitions to the Senate by various cities
		Gala opening of the Fucine lake tunnel
53		Nero Praefectus Urbis (City Prefect)
		Nero marries Octavia, daughter of Claudius
		Parthians annex Armenia, Tiridates king
54	*October 13*	Death of Claudius, probably poisoned
		Accession of Nero
54–66		War in the East
54 or early 55		Corbulo appointed to Eastern command against Parthia and Armenia
55		Agrippina and Nero quarrel over Acte
		Britannicus murdered
		Dismissal of freedman Pallas
		Agrippina leaves the palace
		Agrippina charged with conspiracy
		Agrippina's influence revives
		Seneca's *On Clemency*
56		Nero *pater patriae*
		Treasury transferred from Quaestors to Praetors
56/7		Agrippina honored on Alexandrian coins
57		Proposal that Nero be Consul Perpetuus rejected
		Corbulo attacks Tiridates and captures Artaxata, capital of Armenia
58		Nero's relationship with Poppaea Sabina starts (?)

Year	Date	Event
		Otho governor of Lusitania (or 59)
59		Nero arranges assassination of his mother, Agrippina
		Corbulo captures Tigranocerta
		First Iuvenalia festival; Nero shaves his first beard
60		Armenia subjugated; Tigranes, great-grandson of Herod, appointed king
		Corbulo governor of Syria
		First Neronia festival
		Faustus Sulla and Rubellius Plautus exiled
60–61		Revolt of Boudica
61		Tigranes invades Adiabene in Assyria; Vologeses threatens Syria
62		Death of Burrus, replaced as Praetorian Prefect by Ofonius Tigellinus and Faenius Rufus
		Allegations against Seneca
		Seneca retires
		Murders of Faustus Sulla and Rubellius Plautus
		Nero divorces Octavia and marries Poppaea Sabina
	June	Execution of Octavia
		Caesennius Paetus, commanding general, sent to Cappadocia, surrenders to Vologeses at Rhandeia
63		Birth and death of Claudia Augusta, daughter of Nero and Poppaea
64		Nero performs in public at Naples
	July 18–23	Great Fire of Rome
		Alleged persecution of Christians
		Financial crisis, currency reform
64–68		Reconstruction of Rome
		Construction of Domus Aurea (Golden House)
65	*April*	Conspiracy of Piso
		Suicide of Seneca
		Neronia festival, again
		Death of Poppaea Sabina
		Grain fleet wrecked in storm
		Work starts on canal from Lake Avernus to Ostia
66		Conspiracy of Vinicianus
		Suicide of Thrasea Paetus
		Suicide of Petronius
		Nero marries Statilia Messalina
		Tiridates crowned king of Armenia in Rome; settlement of the Parthian question
66–68		Nero tours Greece

		Nero proclaims freedom of Greece
		Nero takes part in the Greek games, wins many prizes
		Work starts on canal across Isthmus of Corinth
66		Suicides of Corbulo, Scribonius Proculus, and Scribonius Rufus
67		Revolt in Judaea; Vespasian appointed to put it down
68		Nero returns to Rome
		Revolt of Vindex
	April 2 or 3	Galba acclaimed emperor by troops in Spain
		Battle of Vesontio, suicide of Vindex.
		Vespasian reduces Samaria and Idumaea, prepares siege of Jerusalem
		Revolt of Clodius Macer in Africa
	June 9 or 11	Suicide of Nero
		Galba proclaimed princeps
		First Nero impostor
	Autumn	Galba arrives in Rome
69	*January 15*	Otho proclaimed princeps
		German legions rise against Galba, proclaim Vitellius princeps
		Murder of Galba
	April 14	Otho defeated at Bedriacum by Vitellius's troops
		Suicide of Otho
		Revolt of Civilis and the Batavians
	July 1	Vespasian proclaimed princeps in Alexandria, then by the army in Syria and Judaea
70	*January*	Vespasian confirmed as princeps by the Senate in Rome
79/81		Second Nero impostor
81/96		Third Nero impostor

GLOSSARY

Africa Roman province in northern Africa comprising Tunisia and parts of Algeria and Libya.

Augusta Revered One (female). Name/title bestowed on senior imperial women.

Augustiani Cheerleaders for Nero at his music/drama performances.

Augustus Revered One. A name awarded to Octavian. Over time it became a title.

auxiliaries Military units recruited from men in the provinces who were not Roman citizens. They served alongside the legions.

centurion Officer in a legion, in command of a century, a unit of about eighty men.

circus A racecourse for chariot racing.

cithara Lyre, musical ancestor of the guitar.

colonia An urban settlement of veterans. They were a military reserve and encouraged Romanization in the local native population.

comites Companions. These were men who, as members of an ad hoc committee, or *consilium,* or as individuals, gave advice to the princeps on upcoming decisions.

Consul One of two annual chief executive officers of the Roman republic. They were elected by the People. Under the early emperors they lost most of their powers. They were elected by the Senate, usually on the emperor's nomination. The Consul Ordinarius started the official year, which was named after him and his colleague; in his place one or more Suffect Consuls were appointed as required. Consuls went on to serve as provincial governors and generals.

cursus honorum The sequence of public offices in the republic and the early principate. They were usually held at or after minimum ages:

Viginivirate	18
Military tribune	21–22
Quaestor	25
Tribunes of the People	(often omitted)
Aedile	(often omitted)
Praetor	30–35
Propraetor / second-rank governor	30
Consul	37
Proconsul/governor	38

Elysian fields A place in the underworld reserved for the righteous and those favored by the gods.

eques, plural ***equites***. Literally a horseman or knight. Member of Rome's second social class after Senators. Usually wealthy businessmen or men who qualified for the senatorial class but chose not to enter politics.

Gaul A region comprising France, Luxembourg, Belgium, most of Switzerland, and parts of Northern Italy, the Netherlands, and Germany, particularly the west bank of the Rhine.

imperium Executive military power conferred on senior government officials.

legatus Senior military officer, commander of a legion. Governor of an imperial province, deputizing for the emperor.

maiestas "Diminishment of the majesty of the state," or treason. Informers (*delatores*) initiated prosecutions.

military tribune Staff officer of a legion, junior to a *legatus* and senior to a centurion, often recruited from young men of equestrian rank.

pantomime Dramatic entertainment in which a solo performer mimed a mythical story, supported by a choir and a small instrumental ensemble.

Praetor An annually elected executive officer, junior to a Consul. Praetors exercised important legal powers and presided over courts.

Proconsul A former Consul acting on behalf of a Consul. Governor of a senatorial province.

procurator Either governor of a small province or treasury official.

Propraetor Governor of senatorial province.

quadriga A chariot with four horses driven abreast.

Stoicism A philosophical school that attracted many supporters among the Roman aristocracy. Held that divine reason controls the universe and the wise man accepts whatever happens.

Suffect Consul A Consul appointed to replace one who has vacated his office.

triumph A military procession into Rome to celebrate a general's victory in battle.

A NOTE ON SOURCES

Nero's life and times are described by three main literary sources: *The Annals* by Publius (or Gaius—the evidence is contradictory) Cornelius Tacitus; *Lives of the Caesars* by Gaius Suetonius Tranquillus; and *Roman History* by Lucius Cassius Dio.

Possibly a native of Narbonese Gaul, **Tacitus** was born in 56 or 57 and so was in his early teens when Nero died. He began a successful senatorial career under Vespasian. In 77 he married the daughter of Gnaeus Julius Agricola, a distinguished general and governor of the province of Britannia. He was Praetor in 88 and a Suffect Consul in 97. His writings include *Agricola,* a tribute to his father-in-law and his achievements in Britannia; *Germania,* an ethnographic study of German tribes; and *Dialogue on Oratory,* which discusses the decline of public speaking and the principles of rhetoric. His experience of life as a senior official under the despotic emperor Domitian marked him and contributed to his bleak view of the imperial system. He died sometime after 117.

The two masterpieces on which his high reputation as a historian chiefly depends are *The Histories* and *The Annals*. Between them they covered the era from the death of Augustus in 14 to Domitian's assassination in 97. Unfortunately, large portions of both books are lost. After the fall of the Roman empire in the fifth century there was no demand for the works of non-Christian authors, copies were not made, and much of Latin literature vanished.

Most of *The Annals* has come down to us, but two years of Tiberius's reign, all of Caligula's short reign, half of Claudius's, and Nero's last two years are missing. Only one-third of *The Histories* survives, which deals with the Year of the Four Emperors. These are grievous losses, not altogether compensated elsewhere.

Tacitus writes a highly condensed Latin, packed with aphorisms. He is a rich pleasure to read, but his style and prejudices can cloud rather than clarify the event he is describing. Like other ancient Roman authors, he does not touch on economic or social topics and restricts himself to high politics and military tactics. He regarded history as a subset of rhetoric; plain facts were written up to convey emotion and color, to draw moral lessons, and to grasp the attention of the reader (or listener, for books were often recited). The historian should ensure, he observed, that "virtues are not left unrecorded and that evil words and deeds are made subject to the fears inspired by posterity's denunciation."

He claims to write "without anger or partisanship." This is not strictly true. As a member of the senatorial elite, he looked back fondly on the republic and was disinclined to give the emperors the benefit of any doubt. He accepted, bitterly, that the imperial system was here to stay, but he was pessimistic about its ability to produce a good ruler.

Tacitus draws much of his information from earlier authors (mostly lost), but he also consulted the senatorial archives and spoke to eyewitnesses who were still alive. He does not usually identify his sources as modern historians do.

A cutting skepticism pervades his history writings, which today's readers need to discount when evaluating his work. If they do this, they will find that Tacitus is a reliable narrator who interprets facts according to his opinions but does not invent them.

By contrast with Tacitus, **Suetonius** does not moralize; rather, he assembles information that interests him and usually avoids making judgments.

He was born in about 70 to an equestrian family in Hippo Regius, a small town in the province of Africa (today's Annaba in Algeria). His father served as a military tribune and was present when the emperor Otho decided to kill himself. While studying in Rome to be an orator he became a close friend of a Senator, Gaius Plinius Caecilius Secundus, known as Pliny the Younger (nephew of the encyclopedist Pliny the Elder), who admired him for his sense of honor and his integrity and encouraged his writing career. He accompanied his patron when he was appointed governor of Bithynia and Pontus.

Suetonius rose to the highest positions in the imperial bureaucracy, serving under the emperors Trajan and Hadrian as secretary *a studiis,* probably responsible for writing speeches, and *ab epistulis,* in charge of the emperor's correspondence. He published a series of brief biographies of all kinds of famous people from prostitutes to Roman kings, poets to orators, historians to philosophers. He also wrote lighthearted essays on such topics as Roman games and Roman dress.

He was dismissed by Hadrian for some unknown but minor offense regarding the empress Sabina. He appears to have regained favor before he died, but nothing more is known about the rest of his life and death.

Suetonius's most substantial and popular work is *Lives of the Caesars,* a collection of biographies of Julius Caesar and the eleven subsequent emperors. Although it is an entertaining and instructive book, it creates certain difficulties for the reader. First, the author is a biographer; he is interested only in personality. He is especially attracted to salacious, damning personal details about his subjects. He offers no historical analysis—nor even much in the way of description. In his *Life of Nero,* for example, he omits almost all mention of important events in Britannia and Parthia/Armenia. He was a stickler for accuracy but was uncritical in his choice of sources. For all his weaknesses, Suetonius is an important source, because he had access to the imperial archives and materials that others would not have seen. Second, when structuring his biographies, Suetonius largely abandons chronological order. They follow a broadly similar pattern. They open with his subject's family background, youth, and education, and describe his early career. He then abandons narrative in favor of treatment by topics, such as military successes, legislation, character, private life, behavior as a citizen, and physical characteristics. He treats each topic as if it were a basket into which he drops relevant data or anecdotes, drawn from the entire life, that have caught his eye. These compilations are unmoored from context and date. It is often unclear when events took place and what their significance was.

Suetonius concludes by describing the omens and portents of the emperor's death, the number of years of his reign, and his funeral.

Lucius Cassius **Dio** (about 164 to about 235) was a Greek from Nicaea in Bithynia on the Black Sea. He was the grandson of Dio Chrysostom and belonged to a wealthy family. He enjoyed a long and highly successful political career. He became a Senator during the reign of the unsatisfactory Commodus and served as Consul under Septimius Severus and, after living through the eccentricities of the boy emperor Elagabalus, for a second time under Severus Alexander. At various times, he was governor of the provinces of Asia, Africa, and Pannonia Superior.

Dio's magnum opus was his *Roman History*. It tells the story of Rome in eighty books, from the legendary landing of the Trojan hero Aeneas on the shores of Italy to the then present day in A.D. 229. Written in Greek, it contains little analysis apart from a tendency to moralize. It is as good or bad as its sources.

Only about a third of the original text has survived. The rest exists only in fragments or abridgments. Nero's reign is covered chronologically in books 61 to 63 and can be accessed only in Epitomes, or précis, produced by two Byzantine monks, Xiphilinus in the eleventh century and Zonaras in the twelfth. They do not offer summaries but quote or rewrite sections that attract their attention. Neither is very assiduous.

A number of other valuable sources fill gaps in the record. **Seneca** (c. 4 B.C. to 65) and **Petronius** (c. 27–66) belonged to Nero's court. The former was his tutor and was not only a statesman but also a prolific letter writer, essayist, and author of tragedies in the Greek manner. He penned the satirical *Apocolocyntosis*. He opens a window into the mind of a leading statesman and Stoic.

Octavia is Seneca's only play on a contemporary theme: Set in Nero's court, it dramatizes the fall of his first wife. The weight of scholarly opinion holds that it was written by an anonymous hand soon after the emperor's death because that death is described in the play. However, it is done in very general terms when the actual details will have been well known and available to a postmortem author. So the tragedy is best seen as a prediction rather than a report. Seneca appears very much as he regarded himself. For an alternative view, see Rolando Ferri, ed., *Octavia: A Play Attributed to Seneca* (Cambridge Classical Texts and Commentaries No. 41, Cambridge University Press, 2003).

Petronius's proto-novel *The Satyricon* is the only Latin text that describes the low life of the time and what today we would call youth culture. Both his and Seneca's writings are discussed at various points in the body of this book.

Pliny the Elder (23/4–79) was extraordinarily productive, writing books on cavalry tactics, oratory, grammar, and history. None of them has survived except for his most remarkable work, *Natural History,* a vast encyclopedia itemizing all that was thought to be known. It is full of errors and bizarre "facts," but it also contains much useful and entertaining information about first-century Rome. A number of references are made to Nero, all of them critical. Pliny died in the eruption of Vesuvius, which buried the town of Pompeii.

The Life of Apollonius of Tyana by **Philostratus** (c. 170 to 247/250) was written in the early third century and purports to be a biography of the celebrated philosopher and miracle worker, who lived through Nero's reign. It contains historical material mixed with what appears to be fiction; it is difficult to tell which is which.

Plutarch, the Greek philosopher, biographer, and essayist (about 46 to after 119), wrote lives of Galba and Otho. In contrast to Suetonius, he preferred a strictly chronological approach in which he mingled a series of anecdotes with some brief digressions.

Nero encouraged the poets of his day, although they did not always respond with appropriate gratitude. The most prominent was Seneca's nephew **Lucan** (39–65), whose epic *Pharsalia* described the civil war won by Julius Caesar. Calpurnius **Siculus**, whose dates are unknown, wrote bucolic verse in the manner of Vergil's eclogues.

Persius (34–62) was a Stoic and satirist. These writers comment, usually flatteringly but on occasion unfavorably, on Nero.

BIBLIOGRAPHY

Most of the ancient texts cited below are available in translation, in particular by the Loeb Classical Library and, for leading authors, Penguin Classics.

Acts of the Apostles Acts
Augustine, *City of God* Aug City
Augustus, *Res Gestae* Res Gest
Aurelius Victor, *Liber de Caesaribus* Vic
Caesar, Julius, *Civil War* Caes Civ
Caesar, Julius, *Gallic War* Caes Gall
Cassius Dio, Lucius, *History of Rome* Dio
Cicero, *Letters to Atticus* Cic Att
Cicero, *On the Agrarian Law* Cic Agr
Cicero, *On the Nature of the Gods* Cic De Nat Deor
Cicero, *Pro Sestio* Cic Sest
Clement, *First Epistle to the Corinthians* Clem
Dio Chrysostom, *To the Rhodians* Chrys
Diodorus Siculus, *Library of History* Diod
Diogenes Laertius, *Lives of Eminent Philosophers* Diog
Einsiedeln Eclogues
Epictetus, *Discourses* Epi
Euripides Eur
Fronto, *Preamble to History* Fronto PH
Gaius, *Institutes* Gaius
Greek Anthology Anth
Homer, *Odyssey* Hom Od
Horace, *Odes* Hor Odes
Inscriptiones Latinae Selectae (ed. Dessau) ILS

Josephus, *Antiquities of the Jews* Jos Ant
Josephus, *Jewish War* Jos Jew
Josephus, *Life of Flavius Josephus* Jos Vita
Justin, *Epitome of the Philippic History of Pompeius Trogus* Just
Juvenal, *Satires* Juv
Laus Pisonis Laus
Livy, *Books from the Foundation of the City* Livy
Lucan, *On the Civil War,* or *Pharsalia* Lucan
[Lucian], *Nero* [Luc] Nero
Macrobius, *Saturnalia* Macr
Martial, *Epigrams* Mart
Martial, *Liber Spectaculorum* Mart Spec
Ovid, *Fasti* Ovid Fasti
Parthenius, *Erotica Pathemata* Parth
Paul, *Letter to the Galatians* Gal
Pausanias, *Description of Greece* Paus
Persius, *Satires* Pers
Petronius, *Satyricon* Petr
Philo, *Against Flaccus* Philo Flacc
Philo, *Embassy to Gaius* Philo Gaius
Philostratus, *Life of Apollonius of Tyana* Phil
Plato, *Republic* Plat Rep
Pliny, *Epistles* Pliny Ep
Pliny, *Natural History* Pliny NH
Plutarch, *Concerning Those Whom the Gods Are Slow to Punish* Plut De Sera
Plutarch, *Life of Cato the Younger* Plut Cato
Plutarch, *Life of Flamininus* Plut Flam
Plutarch, *Life of Galba* Plut Galba
Plutarch, *Life of Julius Caesar* Plut Caes
Plutarch, *Life of Otho* Plut Otho
Polyaenus, *Stratagems* Poly Strat
Polybius, *The Histories* Polyb
Quintilian, *Education of an Orator* Quint
Seneca, *Consolation to Helvia* Sen Helvia
Seneca, *Epistles* Sen Ep

Seneca, *Natural Questions* Sen QN
Seneca, *Octavia* Sen Oct
Seneca, *On Anger* Sen Ang
Seneca, *On Benefits* Sen Ben
Seneca, *On Clemency* Sen Clem
Seneca, *On Peace of Mind* Sen Peace
Seneca, *On the Happy Life* Sen Hap
Seneca, *On the Shortness of Life* Sen Short
Seneca, *Thyestes* Sen Thy
Seneca the Elder, *Controversiae* and *Suasoriae* Sen Eld Con *or* Sua
Strabo, *Geography* Strabo
Suetonius, *Life of Augustus* Suet Aug
Suetonius, *Life of Claudius* Suet Clau
Suetonius, *Life of Gaius* Suet Gaius
Suetonius, *Life of Galba* Suet Galb
Suetonius, *Life of Julius Caesar* Suet Caes
Suetonius, *Life of Lucan* Suet Lucan
Suetonius, *Life of Nero* Suet Nero
Suetonius, *Life of Otho* Suet Otho
Suetonius, *Life of Passienus Crispus* Suet Pass
Suetonius, *Life of Persius* Suet Pers
Suetonius, *Life of Tiberius* Suet Tib
Suetonius, *Life of Titus* Suet Tit
Suetonius, *Life of Vespasian* Suet Vesp
Suetonius, *Life of Vitellius* Suet Vit
Tacitus, *Annals* Tac Ann
Tacitus, *Histories* Tac Hist
Tacitus, *On Orators* Tac Orat
Terence, *Andria* Ter Andria
Varro, *Re rustica* Var
Vegetius, *On Military Matters* Veg
Vergil, *Aeneid* Verg Aen
Vergil, *Eclogues* Verg Ecl

MODERN COMMENTATORS—A SELECTION

Balsdon, J.P.V.D. *Life and Leisure in Ancient Rome*. London: Bodley Head, 1969.

———. *Roman Women, Their History and Habits*. London: History Book Club, 1966.

Barrett, Anthony A. *Agrippina: Sex, Power and Politics in the Early Empire*. London: Routledge, 1996.

———. *Livia, First Lady of Imperial Rome*. New Haven and London: Yale University Press, 2002.

———. *Rome Is Burning: Nero and the Fire That Ended a Dynasty*. Princeton, N.J.: Princeton University Press, 2020.

Bartsch, Shadi, et al., eds. *The Age of Nero*. Cambridge: Cambridge University Press, 2003.

Bastomsky, S. J. "The Emperor Nero in Talmudic Legend." *Jewish Quarterly Review,* vol. 59, no. 4 (April 1969), pp. 321–25, University of Pennsylvania Press.

Bedoyere, Guy de la. *Roman Britain, A New History*. London: Thames and Hudson, 2013.

Bowman, Alan K., Edward Champlin, and Andrew Lintott, eds. *The Augustan Empire, 29 B.C.–A.D. 69*. Cambridge Ancient History. Cambridge: Cambridge University Press, 1996.

Bradley, K. R. "The Chronology of Nero's Visit to Greece A.D. 66/67." *Latomus* 37 (January–March 1978), pp. 61–72. Brussels: Société d'Études Latines de Bruxelles, 1978.

———. "Nero's Retinue in Greece, A.D. 66/67." *Illinois Classical Studies,* vol. 4, pp. 152–57. Champaign and Urbana: University of Illinois Press, 1979.

Brunt, P. A., and J. M. Moore. *Res Gestae Divi Augusti*. Oxford: University of Oxford Press, 1967.

Buckley, E., and M. T. Dinter, eds. *A Companion to the Neronian Age*. Wiley-Blackwell, 2013.

Canter, H. V. "Conflagrations in Ancient Rome." *Classical Journal,* vol. 27, no. 4 (January 1932), pp. 270–88. Classical Association of the Middle West and South.

Champlin, Edward. *Nero*. Cambridge, Mass., and London: Harvard University Press, 2003.

Courtney, Edward. *A Companion to Petronius*. Oxford: Oxford University Press, 2001.

Craver, Scott E. "Urban Real Estate in Late Republican Rome." *Memoirs of the American Academy in Rome,* vol. 55, pp. 135–58, University of Michigan Press for the American Academy in Rome, 2010.

Drinkwater, John F. *Nero: Emperor and Court*. Cambridge: Cambridge University Press, 2019.

Frier, Bruce W. "Roman Same-Sex Weddings from the Legal Perspective." *Classical Studies Newsletter,* vol. 10, winter 2004, University of Michigan. academia.edu/profile/Bruce Frier.

Griffin, Miriam T. *Seneca: A Philosopher in Politics*. London: Oxford University Press, 1976.

———. *Nero: The End of a Dynasty*. London: B. T. Batsford Ltd., 1984.

Hersch, Karen K. *The Roman Wedding: Ritual and Meaning in Antiquity*. Cambridge: Cambridge University Press, 2010.

Hornblower, Simon, and Antony Spawforth, eds. *Oxford Classical Dictionary*. Revised 3rd edition. Oxford: Oxford University Press, 2003.

Jackson, Steven. "Apollonius and the Emperors." *Hermathena* 137, pp. 25–32. Trinity College Dublin, 1984.

Kennell, N. M., "Nerwn Periodonikhs," *American Journal of Philology,* vol. 109, no. 2 (Summer, 1988), pp. 239–51. Baltimore: Johns Hopkins University Press.

Levick, Barbara. *Claudius*. London: B. T. Batsford, 1990.

Mattingly, Harold. *An Imperial Possession: Britain in the Roman Empire, 54 B.C.–A.D. 409*. London: Penguin Books, 2006.

Newbold, R. F. "Some Social and Economic Consequences of the A.D. 64 Fire at Rome." *Latomus* 33, pp. 858–69. Société d'Études Latines de Bruxelles, 1974.

Olson, Kelly. *Masculinity and Dress in Roman Antiquity*. London and New York: Routledge, 2017.

Oost, Stewart Irvin. "The Career of M. Antonius Pallas." *American Journal of Philology,* vol. 79, no. 2 (1958), pp. 113–39. Baltimore: Johns Hopkins University Press.

Pease, Arthur Stanley. "Is the 'Octavia' a Play of Seneca?" *Classical Journal,* vol. 15, no. 7 (April 1920), pp. 388–403. Monmouth, Ill.: The Classical Association of the Middle West and South.

Perrottet, Tony. *The Naked Olympics*. New York: Random House, 2004.

Richardson, L., Jr. *A New Topographical Dictionary of Ancient Rome*. Baltimore and London: Johns Hopkins University Press, 1992.

Sansone, David. "Nero's Final Hours." *Illinois Classical Studies,* vol. 18, pp. 179–89. Champaign and Urbana: University of Illinois Press.

Sherk, Robert K. *The Roman Empire: From Augustus to Hadrian*. Cambridge: Cambridge University Press, 1988.

Smallwood, E. Mary. *The Jews Under Roman Rule from Pompey to Diocletian*. Leiden: E. J. Brill, 1976.

———. "The Alleged Jewish Tendencies of Poppaea Sabina." *Journal of Theological Studies,* New Series, vol. 10, no. 2 (October 1959), pp. 329–35. Oxford: Oxford University Press.

Swaddling, Judith. *The Ancient Olympic Games*. London: British Museum, 1980.

Syme, Ronald. "Domitius Corbulo." *Journal of Roman Studies,* vol. 60 (1970), pp. 27–39. London: Society for the Promotion of Roman Studies.

———. *The Augustan Aristocracy*. Oxford: Oxford University Press, 1986.

Tomlin, Roger. *A Five-Acre Wood in Roman Kent*. In J. Bird, M.W.C. Hassall, and H. Sheldon, eds. *Interpreting Roman London: Papers in Memory of Hugh Chapman*. Oxford: Oxford University Press, 1996, p. 209 et seq.

Toner, Jerry. *Popular Culture in Ancient Rome*. Cambridge, UK, and Malden, Mass.: Polity Press, 2009.

van der Horst, P. W. *Chaeremon: Egyptian Priest and Stoic Philosopher.* Leiden: E. J. Brill, 1984.

van Hooff, Anton J. L. *From Autothanasia to Suicide: Self-Killing in Classical Antiquity*. London and New York: Routledge, 2011.

Wright, Thomas. *Paul: A Biography*. San Francisco: HarperOne, 2018.

On the Boudican Rebellion

Aldhouse-Green, Miranda. *Boudica Britannia: Rebel, War-leader and Queen*. London and New York: Routledge, 2014.

Bauman, Richard A. *Crime and Punishment in Ancient Rome*. Abingdon, UK, and New York: Routledge, 1996.

Bédoyère, Guy de la. *Roman Britain: A New History*. Thames and Hudson, 2006, revised 2013.

Champion, T. C. "Britain in the European Iron Age," *Archaeologia Atlantica*, vol. 1, no. 2 (1975).

Crummy, Philip. *City of Victory: The Story of Colchester—Britain's First Roman Town*. Colchester Archaeological Trust, 1997.

Cunliffe, Barry. *Iron Age Communities in Britain*. 4th ed. London and New York: Routledge, 2005.

Davies, John. *The Land of Boudica: Prehistoric and Roman Norfolk*. Oxford: Oxbow Books, n.d.

Dunnett, Rosalind. *The Trinovantes*. London: Duckworth, 1975.

Ellis, Peter Beresford. *The Druids*. London: Constable & Co., 1994.

Evans, David. "Agamemnon and the Indo-European Threefold Death Pattern." *History of Religions,* vol. 19, no. 2 (November 1979).

Fields, Nic. *Boudica's Rebellion A.D. 60–61*. Oxford: Osprey Publishing, 2011.

Frere, Sheppard. *Britannia*, vol. 7, *History of the Provinces of the Roman Empire*. London: Routledge and Kegan Paul, 1967.

Hingley, Richard, and Christina Unwin. *Boudica: Iron Age Warrior Queen*. London and New York: Hambledon Continuum, 2006.

Hodgson, Tom, and Philip Wise. *Colchester Castle: 2000 Years of History*. Peterborough: Jarrold Publishing, 2015.

Hutton, Ronald. *Blood and Mistletoe: The History of the Druids in Britain*. New Haven and London: Yale University Press, 2009.

Joy, Jody. *Lindow Man*. London: British Museum Press, 2009.

Mattingly, David. *An Imperial Possession: Britain in the Roman Empire, 54 B.C.–A.D. 409*. London: Penguin Books, 2007.

Oppenheimer, Stephen. *The Origins of the British*. New ed. London: Robinson Publishing, 2007.

Parrott-Sheffer, Chelsey, research ed. "Briton." In *Encyclopaedia Britannica* 2010, revised entry, Britannica.com, retrieved August 2021.

Phillips, Andrew. *Colchester: A History*. Stroud: Phillimore, 2017.

Piggott, Stuart. *The Druids*. London: Thames and Hudson, 1975.

Rackham, Oliver. *Trees and Woodlands in the British Landscape: The Complete History of Britain's Trees, Woods and Hedgerows*. London: Phoenix Press, 1976, revised 2002.

Rigley, Valery, and Simon James. *Britain and the Celtic Iron Age*. London: British Museum Press, 1996.

Webster, Graham. *Boudica: The British Revolt Against Rome A.D. 60*. London and New York: Routledge, 1993.

Welch, Col. George Patrick. *Britannia: The Roman Conquest and Occupation of Britain*. Middletown, Conn.: Wesleyan University Press, 1963.

Wheeler, R. "Belgic Cities of Britain." *Antiquity* 7(25), (1933). doi:10:1017/S0003598X00007602.

NOTES

PREFACE

xix **Napoleon Bonaparte** Comment to Henri Gatien Bertrand, quoted in Georges Roux, *Néron,* Paris 1962.

xix **When Nero perished** *Don Juan* Canto 3 119.

xx ***Rex quondam*** Sir Thomas Malory, *Le Morte d'Arthur* 21 7.

xxi **She deserves her own book** As a matter of fact she has gotten it, by Anthony A. Barrett (see bibliography). She wrote her own life story, sadly lost.

xxi **"left in the decent obscurity"** Edward Gibbon, *Memoirs of My Life* (1796), ch. 8.

1. THE NEW ORDER

3 **The youth was seventeen** Suet Nero 51.

3 **This was Nero** Nero is the family name of a subgroup of the Claudii, a patrician clan whose lineage stretches back to Rome's beginnings.

3 **The ceremony unfolded** The description of the Campus Martius and Claudius's funeral is a reconstruction indebted to Polyb 6 53–55, Suet Aug 100 2–4, and Strabo 5 3 8 (236); also to Richardson (entries Mausoleum Augusti and Ustrinum Augusti). Tac Ann 12 60 makes it clear that Claudius's last rites followed the pattern set by those of Augustus.

4 **"present to the eye the appearance"** Strabo 5 3 8 (216).

5 **"all together and as if alive and breathing?"** Polyb 6 53 10.

6 **called *Res Gestae*** The document was rediscovered in modern times.

6 **"At the age of nineteen"** Res Gest 1 2 3 25.

8 **"After I had extinguished"** Ibid. 34 1–3. "Influence" is the best translation in English for the original word, *auctoritas*. It signifies moral authority, prestige, reputation, and charisma—in a fashionable contemporary phrase, soft power.

10 **"I gave three gladiatorial games"** Ibid. 22 1 and 3.

10 **"I produced a naval battle"** Ibid. 23 1.

11 **found Rome a city of brick** Suet Aug 28 3. Res Gest 19, 20, and 21 give a complete list of Augustus's construction projects.
11 **"the personalities and principles"** Livy Pref 9.
12 **"riven by civil faction"** Hor Odes 3 6 13.
12 **"The age has proved fertile"** Ibid. 3 6 17.
12 **"perfects the arts"** Ibid. 3 6 22.
12 **"Careless of whom"** Ibid. 3 6 24–26.
12 **a tiny building** See Richardson for more on the shrine of Janus (entry Ianus Geminus).
13 **"It was the will of our ancestors"** Res Gest 13.
13 ***"Tu regere imperio populos"*** Verg Aen 6 851.
13 **"I extended the territory"** Res Gest 26.
14 **"I compelled the Parthians"** Ibid. 29 2.

2. A FAMILY AT WAR

15 **infant mortality** Toner, *Popular Culture,* p. 67.
15 **"It is in the due order of nature"** Pliny 7 8 46.
15 **Caligula, or Little Boots** Properly he should be called Gaius, but today he is far better known as Caligula, so that is the name I use in this book.
15 **imperial villa at Antium** See Barrett, *Agrippina,* p. 56. Some ruins survive, no thanks to the encroaching sea and Allied artillery in the Second World War.
16 **"He can kill me"** Tac Ann 14 9.
19 **"If you are not empress, my girl"** Suet Tib 53 1.
21 **He often consulted her** Suet Aug 84 2.
21 **"remember that she was a woman"** Suet Tib 50 3.
21 **"Ulysses in a frock"** Suet Gaius 23 2.
23 **they stroked the man's beard** Suet Nero 1 1.
23 **"Should his bronze beard really surprise"** Ibid. 2 2.
24 **he once attempted to kill himself** Ibid. 2 3.
24 **a more attractive personality** He is the Enobarbus of Shakespeare's *Antony and Cleopatra*.
24 **"haughty, extravagant, and cruel"** Suet Nero 4.
24 **"detestable in every aspect of life"** Ibid. 5 1.
24 **a bath annex** Sen Contr 9 4 18.
24 **passionate chariot driver** Ibid. 4 1.
26 **"*You* will kill him"** Tac Ann 6 46.
27 **"And I will not value my life"** Suet Gaius 15 3.
27 **"Good fortune and happiness"** Ibid.
28 **"it was his habit to commit incest"** Ibid. 24 1.

28 **As a culminating humiliation** Dio 59 22 8.

29 **"I have swords as well as islands"** Suet Gaius 29 1.

30 **young man called Gaius Ofonius Tigellinus** These entertaining, plausible, but not necessarily reliable details come from the Scholia on Juvenal Satires 1 155.

30 **"I made for a coign of vantage"** Hom Od 10 148–49.

31 **a modern Circe** I am grateful to Barrett, *Agrippina,* p. 69, for this insight.

32 **The flamingo struggled** For the flamingo, see Jos Ant 19 87 and Suet Gaius 57 4. For my reconstruction of Caligula's assassination, see Suet Gaius 57–59, Dio 59 29, and Jos Ant 19 1–113.

32 **"Jupiter," he replied** Suet Gaius 58 2–3.

32 **"I am still alive"** Ibid.

33 **Some spat on the man** Dio 59 30 1a.

33 **"I wish I had"** Ibid. 30 2, Jos Ant 19 159.

3. THE IMPROBABLE EMPEROR

34 **Claudius had left the show early** For Claudius's accession, see Suet Clau 10–11, Jos Ant 19 1–273, Jos Jew 204–14, and Dio 60 1–2 1.

35 **His childhood was marred** On Claudius's appearance and disabilities, and his family's reaction to them, see Suet Clau 2–5 30.

35 **"a monster whom Nature had not finished"** Suet Clau 3 2.

36 **"The poor fellow is unlucky"** Ibid. 4 5.

36 **"more for want of taste"** Ibid. 41 3.

37 **"Any child born to me and my wife"** Suet Nero 6 2.

37 **Agrippina had not been allowed** For the chief account, brief and unsatisfactory, see Suet Nero 6.

37 **handed over to his aunt Domitia** It is uncertain whether it was she or her younger sister, Domitia Lepida, who took the baby Nero in. It is more likely the former, for Lepida was generous and tried to spoil him some years later. Suet Nero 63.

37 **"There is nothing either of you needs"** Quint 6 1 50.

38 **"grim and threatening"** Tac Ann 12 64.

39 **"I prefer the broad daylight"** Quint 1 2 9, 29.

40 **One of the curiosities** This section on Roman suicide is indebted to van Hooff, *From Autothanasia to Suicide.*

40 **Cato attended a last supper** For Cato's death, see Plut Cato 67–70.

41 **a spectacular example** Caes Gall 5 37.

42 **"It doesn't hurt"** Pliny Ep 3 16. Thrasea Paetus was the Paetuses' son-in-law.

42 ***"Victrix causa diis placuit"*** Lucan 1 128.

42 **"shameless"** According to Suet Galba 5 1.
42 **Caligula . . . asked him in confidence** Suet Pass.
43 **"There never was a better slave"** Tac Ann 6 20.
43 **"We leave the door"** Sen QN 4 pr 6
43 **she poisoned him** So reports the unreliable Juvenal Scholium. See Juv 4 81, and Syme, *Augustan Aristocracy,* "Domitius Corbulo," p. 160. The timing was convenient for the lady, and the charge is plausible.
43 **Asconius Labeo as a guardian** Tac Ann 13 10.
44 **"a speaking tool"** Var 1 17 1.
44 **"Though the laws allow a slave to be ill-treated"** Sen Clem 1 18 2.
44 **"I am glad to learn"** Sen Ep 47 1–8.
44 **"get away from his boyhood"** Sen Ep 47 7.
45 **A terrible case occurred in 61** Tac Ann 14 42–45.
46 **"slave and yet son"** ILS 7479.
46 **Freedmen were very unpopular** Tac Ann 13 26–27.
47 **"I have seen standing in a queue"** Sen Ep 47 9–10.
47 **thirty large onyx columns** Pliny NH 36 60.
47 **"Experience had taught him"** Tac Ann 11 29.
48 **"when one day Claudius"** Suet Clau 28.
48 **"in virtual control of the state"** Tac Ann 13 14.
48 **"content with the honor"** Ibid. 12 53.
48 **"The Senate's decree was engraved"** Ibid.
49 **an indelible portrait** See Juv 6 117–35 for the satirist's demolition of Messalina's character.
50 **"reeking of ancient blankets"** Juv 6 121.
50 **"with her clitoris inflamed and stiff"** Ibid. 129.
50 **Belle de Jour** Catherine Deneuve starred as a bored housewife who resorts to prostitution in Luis Buñuel's 1967 film.
51 **"understood the scandal and the peril"** Tac Ann 11 12.
51 **divorce her husband** Ibid. 11 30.
52 **"A terrible storm over Ostia"** Ibid.
52 **"Am I still emperor?"** Ibid. 11 31.
53 **"Your life is over"** Ibid. 11 37.
53 **"I have added no touch of the marvellous"** Ibid. 11 27.
53 **what Claudius believed** Suet Clau 36.
53 **"We don't have to wait"** Tac Ann 11 26.
54 **adopting Silius as his son** The device was also used by Hadrian, with great success. He adopted Antoninus Pius, who in turn and at the same time adopted Marcus Aurelius.

4. YOUNG HOPEFUL GENTLEMAN

55 **"The execution of Messalina"** Tac Ann 12 1.

56 **"at a perfectly ordinary dinner party"** and **"obtained from loot gained in the provinces"** Pliny NH 9 117.

58 **"I am a citizen among citizens"** Tac Ann 12 5.

58 **"In his exceptionally arduous duties"** and **"Her exceptionally illustrious birth"** and **"I admit that marriage with a brother's child"** Vitellius's speech as cited here is Tacitus's version—Tac Ann 12 5–7.

59 **"From this moment, the state was transformed"** Tac Ann 12 7.

60 **In the first half of the reign** Ibid. 12 7. See following paragraphs for an account of Agrippina's relations with the Senate.

60 **"She realized her policies"** Dio 61 32 2.

61 **"[The princeps] must consult the national interest"** Tac Ann 12 25.

62 **"of the highest character as a soldier"** Ibid. 12 42.

62 **Titus, son of an up-and-coming general** Later, both became emperors.

62 **Britannicus was a changeling** Suet Nero 7 1.

62 **in "a kind of imprisonment"** Dio 61 32 6.

63 **"If I wanted to hear a clown's jokes"** Sen Ep 50 2–3.

63 **"The story sounds incredible"** Ibid.

63 **"You can see clearly"** Ibid.

64 **"You talk one way," you say, "and live another"** Sen Hap 18 1.

65 **a cameo appearance in the Acts of the Apostles** Acts 18:12–17.

65 **"In each of them [there is] cause for delight"** Sen Helvia 18 2.

65 **"a perverse ambition"** Tac Ann 16 17.

66 **One of his dramas, *Octavia*** See Note on Sources, page 371.

66 **mere "school textbook orator"** and **"sand without lime"** Suet Cal 53.

67 **may have been tuberculosis** Dio 59 19.

67 **"a sort of continuous last gasp"** Sen Ep 54 3.

67 **"Only the thought"** Ibid. 78 2.

68 **"took delight in adolescent boys"** and **"they were the wrong sort of lips"** Dio 61 10 4. The anecdote is obscure.

68 **"By freedom a boy's spirit grows"** Sen Ang 2 21 3.

69 **"Law: A son who strikes his father"** Sen Eld Con 9 4 1. I have paraphrased the Latin.

69 **"for making complete fools"** Petr 1.

70 **"I shall state the best paradigm"** Sen Clem 1 7.

70 **"You did what the situation at the time demanded"** Tac Ann 14 55.

70 **"In case those looking after him"** Dio 61 4 4.

70 **On March 17, 51** My reconstruction of Nero's coming-of-age ceremony assumes that he took part in the Liberalia procession on March 17. It is likely

that he did so, but another date could have been chosen for the ritual at home, any record of which is lost.

71 **an earthquake rumbled** Dio 61 33 2c.

73 **One of the Mouseion's senior officials** See van der Horst, *Chaeremon*.

73 **"You won't be so keen"** Mart 11 56 (I paraphrase the poetry).

73 **he had a passion for horses** Suet Nero 22 1.

74 **a criminal under sentence of death** From later in the century, but typical of the age. Mart Spec 9 7.

75 **In the event of serious injuries** Pliny NH 28 238.

75 **One day he was bemoaning the fate** Suet Nero 22.

76 **"practiced with water . . . fraudulent"** Pliny NH 30 14–15.

76 **"lively mind"** Tac Ann 13 3.

76 **"the rudiments of culture"** Ibid.

77 **"gave speeches and wrote poems"** Suet Titus 3.

77 **"Notebooks and papers"** Suet Nero 52.

78 **Nero was not allowed** I draw this conclusion from accounts of his engaging in these activities after his accession as being novel—see Suet Nero 10–12.

5. A DISH OF MUSHROOMS

80 **thirty thousand laborers** Suet Clau 20 2. Where would they all go? A tunnel in process of construction is a limited space. Perhaps the number refers to the sum of all the workers employed season by season over the eleven years. The Fucine lake was not completely emptied until 1878. It is now rich farming land.

80 **"The shores, the hills, the mountain-tops"** Tac Ann 12 56.

81 **"Hail Caesar! We salute you"** Suet Clau 21 6.

81 **"Despite being criminals the men fought"** Tac Ann 12 56.

82 **"her feminine imperiousness"** Ibid. 57.

82 **the case of Ilium (or Troy . . .)** Tac Ann 12 58.

83 **a temporary Prefect, or *praefectus urbi*** The City Prefect was temporary during the Roman republic. Augustus made the post permanent, but it appears that in Claudius's day the republican arrangement was revived.

84 **"Just being the princeps's wife"** Suet Nero 35 1.

84 **nobody was talking about Britannicus** Dio 61 33 9–10.

85 **in physical development** Ibid. 61 1 1.

85 **advised him to grow up quickly** Suet Claud 43.

85 **"The hand that wounded you"** Ibid.

85 **"Whoever comes to the throne"** Tac Ann 12 65.

86 **"I myself seem fated"** and **"It is my destiny"** Suet Clau 43, and Tac Ann

12 64. These could be different versions of the same event or repetitions of the same opinion on different occasions. I choose the second option. Old men forget.

86 **"Nothing seemed to satisfy her"** Dio 61 33 12.

87 **"womanly quarrel"** Tac Ann 12 64.

87 **"She could give her son an empire"** Ibid.

88 **"an artist in her field"** Tac Ann 12 66.

88 **"chosen a poison"** Ibid. 4 8.

88 **"much loved by his master"** Ibid. 4 10.

88 **A famous witch** Hor Sat 2 1 56.

89 **"would happily see their husbands die"** Juv 6 654.

89 **"What recommended itself"** Tac Ann 12 66.

90 **The next day, dinner was served at the palace** Ibid. 12 67, Suet Clau 44, and Dio 61 34. All the ancient sources say that Claudius was murdered. They vary in detail but agree on the basic story. Some modern scholars reject this proposition in favor of a natural death. They may be right. Claudius could well have expired from a heart attack or a stroke. We know he suffered from poor health. Also, it is argued that it would have been irrational for him to have altered his hard-won succession plan. But politicians do not always act rationally and often make mistakes. Agrippina must have been an overbearing and unconstitutional partner. If Claudius survived another few years, Britannicus would be an adult—and a player. It was increasingly obvious that the boys did not get along and that there would be a clash with the emperor's ferocious wife. The succession plan was looking increasingly fragile. It is tempting to tidy up history, but evidence is more helpful than speculation. The mushroom trick rings true (even if the second doses do not). Agrippina had to act. Murder is the most plausible verdict.

90 **Writers alive at the time** Tac Ann 12 67.

90 **Halotus who sprinkled the poison** Suet Clau 44 2.

90 **a performance by some comic actors** Sen Apoc 4.

90 **an envenomed feather** A similar tale is told of Alexander the Great in the "fake news" account of his alleged murder.

91 **"Apparently heartbroken"** Tac Ann 12 68.

92 **His mother was tactfully absent** An inference from silence. If she had been there, we would certainly have been told. The sources do not mention her.

92 **The speech, again ghostwritten by Seneca** The deification of Claudius may have been agreed at a later Senate meeting, but Tacitus includes it in the address on the day of his accession. Tac Ann 12 69.

93 **"the best of mothers"** Suet Nero 9.

93 **"The good spirit of the world"** Sherk 61.

93 **"mockeries of sorrow"** and **"I have advice"** Tac Ann 13 4.

6. BEST OF MOTHERS

95 **"You are afraid of death"** Sen Ep 77 18.
95 ***"For the lower-income guests"*** Juv 5 146–48.
95 **"Accept no dish at dinner"** Ibid. 6 629–31.
95 **"It's true"** and **"play the fool"** Suet Nero 33 1.
96 **"His last words heard on earth"** Sen Apoc 4.
97 **"Friends everywhere!"** Ibid. 13.
99 **bad-tempered and lethargic** Tac Ann 13 1.
99 **"the golden sheep"** Ibid.
100 ***"The shades of night"*** Sen Apoc 4.
100 **"Oh if only I had never learned"** Suet Nero 10 2, Sen Clem 2 1 2.
100 **"Wait until I have deserved them!"** Ibid. 10 2.
100 **"makes princes safer"** Sen Clem 1 11 4.
100 **"dyed the sea with Roman blood"** Ibid. 1 11 1.
100 **the story of a young Roman aristocrat** The bones of the story, Sen Clem 1 9 1–12, may be historical, but we are not obliged to credit the nocturnal conversation. Its purpose is to assert the value of mercy. Dio Cassius 55 14–22 1 gives a similar account, but at greater length.
102 **An aged, penniless, and licentious poet** For the anecdote that follows, see Petr 85–87.
103 **"He spent his days sleeping"** Tac Ann 16 18. It is supposed that the courtier in Tacitus's pages and the author of *The Satyricon* are one and the same person. We do not know at what point in Nero's reign he became friends with the princeps. Petronius's forename may have been Titus.
104 **an absurdly opulent banquet . . . Trimalchio** Trimalchio is a Falstaffian vulgarian. While he is not a parody of Nero, certain aspects of the banquet echo aspects of the emperor's lifestyle, as doubtless it did those of other rich Romans. Petronius's skit was intended to amuse, not to annoy.
104 **"We had no torch"** Petr 79.
105 **Nero, still in his teens, used to dress up** For Nero's night wanderings, see Suet Nero 26–29, Dio 61 8–9, and Tac Ann 13 25.
105 **"So he *knew* that he was hitting Nero"** Tac Ann 13 25, and Dio 61 9 4.
105 **raffish company of theatricals** Ibid.
106 **"corrupted by luxury"** Plut Galba 19 2.
106 **Another court habitué** For the Vitellius paragraph, see Suet Vit 3 2, 4, 5.
106 **"to their mutual pleasure"** For the career of Asiaticus, see Ibid. 12.
110 **"For a long time Nero excluded"** Suet Nero 15 2.
110 **"He acquired some knowledge of music"** Ibid. 20 1.
111 **"I didn't realize"** Dio 61 5 4.
111 **"partners of his dissipation"** Tac Ann 13 12.

112 **"as women do"** Ibid. 13 13.

112 **"my rival the ex-slave"** and **"my daughter-in-law the housemaid"** Ibid.

112 **frequent threats to abdicate** Suet Nero 34 1. The threats are undated, but they must have been made in the early months of the reign.

113 **"This change from excessive severity"** Tac Ann 13 13.

114 **"exercised virtual control over the monarchy"** Ibid. 13 14.

114 **For Agrippina to have the cup dashed** Ibid. Modern academic opinion sees Tacitus as overconcerned to create a dramatic composition. However, the empress's behavior, foolish as it was, is psychologically true.

114 **"whole dark history"** Ibid.

115 **"Heaven and myself are to be thanked"** Ibid.

115 **"a Greek concubine's son"** Ibid. 12 44.

116 **"where gossip thrives"** Ibid. 13 6.

116 **"a sign," observes a surprised Tacitus** Ibid. 13 8.

116 **"when its members were pleading"** Ibid. 13 5.

117 **It was late afternoon** The main meal of the Roman day usually took place in the late afternoon or at sundown. For the death of Britannicus, see Tac Ann 13 15–17.

117 **"This is nothing out of the ordinary"** Ibid. 13 16.

119 **"So you think I am afraid"** Suet Nero 33 2.

119 **"tried it on a young goat"** Ibid. 33 3.

120 **corpse's skin darkened** Dio 61 7 4.

120 **those who died prematurely** Servius *Aeneid* 11 143 and Seneca Short 20 5.

120 **"autocracy knows no partnership"** Tac Ann 13 17.

121 **"conscience-struck by his crime"** Ibid. 18.

122 **"Veneration of power"** Ibid. 19.

122 **"a woman of no morals and uncertain age"** Ibid. 13 19.

123 **"But everyone must be given"** Ibid. 13 20.

123 **"I defy anyone to accuse me"** Ibid. 13 21.

124 **Her birthday was officially celebrated** As recorded in inscriptions of the activities of the Arval Brethren.

7. "MY FOOLISH LOVE"

126 **"The whole gulf is quilted"** Strabo 5 4 8.

126 **small town of Oplontis** Pompeii, Herculaneum, and Oplontis were overwhelmed by the eruption of Vesuvius in A.D. 79. Much of Poppaea's villa has been excavated.

127 **"She paraded respectability"** Tac Ann 13 45.

127 **Poppaea tended her complexion** Juv 6 461–63, and Dio 62 28 1.

127 **Nero probably fell for Poppaea** See Tac Ann 13 46 for Tacitus's version of Nero's falling in love with Poppaea, and for the alternative, Suet Otho 3 1–2, and Dio 61 11 2.

128 **"I am devoted to Otho"** Tac Ann 13 46.

128 **"enjoyed her together"** Dio 61 11 2.

128 **the princeps drenched himself** Plut Galba 19 3.

128 **"as truly as you may expect to see me"** Dio 61 11 2.

129 **"We have every reason to believe"** Suet Otho 3 2.

129 **Nero decided to kill his mother** For the death of Agrippina I make use of Tacitus, Dio, and Suetonius, as well as the source closest in time to the murder, Seneca's tragedy *Octavia*. Their stories differ in various particulars but follow the same broad course. My version is an amalgam of the most plausible events.

130 **"nagged and mocked him"** Tac Ann 14 1.

130 **"Cluvius states that Agrippina's passion"** Cluvius Rufus's work is lost, but he is cited on a few occasions by Tacitus, as here: Tac Ann 14 2. He was a contemporary and eyewitness, so his testimony is of value. Like many people at the time, he credited (mistakenly, I believe) the incest rumor.

131 **Nero was having an affair** Dio 61 11 4.

131 **"Nero postponed no further"** Tac Ann 14 1.

132 ***hinc illae lacrimae*** Ter Andria l 126.

132 **Another unexpected expiry at dinner** Suetonius (Nero 34 2) claims three attempts to poison Agrippina and one to arrange the ceiling panels in her bedroom to fall on her. See also Tac Ann 14 3. The reports do not convince, for had these incidents happened, Agrippina would surely have taken countermeasures about which we would have heard. Also, could ceiling panels, even robust ones, have been depended on to kill her?

133 **attended a theatrical show** Dio 61 12 2.

133 **trireme's timbers to be loosened** Dio 61 13 3–4, Tacitus 14 3, and Suetonius Nero 34 2 imagine a bolder design in which the ship breaks asunder or ceiling panels fall on her. According to Dio, the ship was a replica of the theatrical one. It is all too complicated. The simplest explanation is the most plausible.

133 **vacationing in the gulf of Naples** This section deals with the murder of Agrippina. The three chief sources give a lot of fascinating color, but they frequently disagree on points of detail. For instance, Dio writes that the empress mother came for several days, whereas the others limit her planned visit to one day. Either is possible, but Dio's version seems more likely. None of the sources has a clear idea of the topography of the area; I reconstruct the movements of the parties where the sources are unclear or contradictory. Tacitus can be too brief (thus Agrippina waking up a household is inferred from the mere statement that she was carried home in a litter). But I trust him more than the others.

133 **"One has to put up with it"** Tac Ann 14 4.
134 **Otho, Nero's partner** Suet Otho 3 1.
134 **Nero conversed freely** Tac Ann 14 4.
134 **"I really must get back"** Suet Nero 34 2.
134 **"saw her on her way"** Tac Ann 14 4.
134 **"the last sight of his doomed mother"** Tac Ann 14 4.
134 **"All best wishes, mother"** Dio 61 13 2.
135 **"the waves soon resounded"** Sen Oct 313–18.
135 **"Help, help! I am Agrippina"** Tac Ann 14 5.
135 **was carried home** Agrippina may have owned another villa somewhere near the Lucrine lake. Alternatively, she could have returned to the villa at Bauli where she was quartered. If Bauli was located between Misenum and Baiae (which it probably was), this would have been quite a long journey and would have entailed passing Nero's villa. We do not know enough to solve the puzzle.
135 **She thought hard about the events** Agrippina's reflections are drawn from Tac Ann 14 6.
136 **"She may arm her slaves"** Ibid. 14 7.
136 **unaware of the plot** Dio 61 12 1 implausibly has it that Seneca knew and approved of the plot because it would lead to Nero's downfall.
136 **"Anicetus," Burrus concluded** Tac Ann 14 7.
136 **"This is the first day of my reign"** Ibid. 14 7.
137 **"If you have come to visit the sick"** and **"Strike here!"** Ibid. 14 8.
137 ***"You would have died"*** Sen Oct 636ff.
139 **"Sometimes dumb and motionless"** Tac Ann 14 10.
139 **"reliable authorities"** Suet Nero 34 4.
139 **"I had no idea"** Dio 61 14 3.
140 **"I won't bring you up"** Dio 61 16 2.
140 ***"Alcmaeon, Orestes, and Nero"*** Suet Nero 39 2. The translation is by the poet Robert Graves in *Suetonius, The Twelve Caesars* (London: Penguin Classics, 1957.
140 **"Goodbye father, goodbye mother"** and **"The underworld awaits!"** Ibid. 39 3.
141 **"He often admitted that he was hounded"** Ibid. 34 4.
141 **Canace, who slept with her brother** Ibid. 31 3.
142 **"The fact that I am still alive"** Quint 8 5 18.
142 **"She had hoped to be joint ruler"** Tac Ann 14 11.
144 **"Nero may kill me"** Dio 61 15 4.
144 **"flushed with pride"** Tac Ann 14 13.
145 **"When you shave"** Suet Nero 34 5.

8. FREE AT LAST!

146 **"like a driving wind"** Homer Il 20 492f.

146 **"The axle-tree under his chariot"** Ibid. 20 498ff.

147 **"The dust that rose from underneath"** Ibid. 365ff.

147 **"Charioteering was an accomplishment"** Tac Ann 14 14.

147 **between the Janiculum and Vatican hills** Saint Peter's Basilica stands above part of the circus today.

148 **On the right bank of the Tiber** This section deals with the Juvenalia. The sources—Suet Nero 11, 12, Tac Ann 14 15 and 15 33, and Dio 62 19–20—sometimes confuse the festival for Agrippina, the Juvenalia, with the Neronia. I attempt a fair allocation of attractions.

148 **a wooden amphitheater** We understand that this rapidly built edifice was the chief venue for the Juvenalia. But this was a theater festival for which an amphitheater (usually used for gladiatorial shows, animal hunts, and the like) was unsuitable. Perhaps another theater was built but not mentioned.

149 **a favorite gladiator called Spiculus** Suet Nero 30 2.

149 **with the aid of an emerald** Drinkwater, *Nero,* pp. 304–305, and Pliny NH 37 64. Exactly how the device worked remains a mystery. It seems not to have been used as a lens (as in the film *Quo Vadis*). By "emerald," Romans might mean fluorspar, green vitrified lava (or green Icelandic agate, as it is called), green jasper, or green glass.

149 **"good character"** and **"It was murder"** Sen Epist 7 2 4, and 5.

150 **"Some of them played the flute"** Dio 61 17 3.

150 **"There were many volunteers"** Tac Ann 14 15.

151 **"a man of loose morality"** Tac Hist 3 62.

151 **Thrasea Paetus, that most conservative** Tac Ann 16 21.

151 **"with his sigh and his word of praise"** Ibid. 14 15.

151 **"Honorable members, be so good"** Dio 61 20 1.

152 **the Augustiani** Suet Nero 20 3 and Tac Ann 14 15.

152 **"weak and husky voice"** Dio 61 20 2.

153 **some of them were reprised in public** Suet Vit 11 2.

153 **Among the trees and bushes** The atmosphere, magical and licentious, must have resembled that of the famous Vauxhall Gardens in London during the eighteenth century.

153 **"Nero affected a zeal for poetry"** Tac Ann 14 16.

154 **listening to "their disputatiousness"** Ibid.

155 **astoundingly prolific, insufferable twenty-year-old . . . Lucan** Only fragments survive, but apart from the *Pharsalia,* we know, among others, of *Journey to the Underworld, Story of Troy, Orpheus, Address to Polla* (his wife), ten books of *Woods, Saturnalia,* speeches for and against the murderer in a *crime passionnel,* and so forth.

156 **"No one ever befriends"** Lucan 8 535.
156 **"Lucan is fiery and passionate"** Quint 10 1 90.
156 **some scurrilous verses** Tac Ann 15 49 and Suet Dom 1 1. The two victims were Afranius Quintianus and Claudius Pollio.
156 **throw living men to crocodiles** Suet Nero 37 2–3.
156 **"In a ruler," he advised** Sen Clem 1 7 4.
156 **"cannot feel any sympathy"** Sen Contr 2 4 13.
156 **a nobleman read out** Tac Ann 14 48. He was Antistius Sosianus.
157 **"had grossly abused the emperor"** Ibid. 14 49.
157 **the princeps had planned to commute** Ibid. 14 48.
157 **promising young poet, Aules Persius Flaccus** Suet Pers. Aules was the Etruscan for Aulus.
157 **a poetry recitation as a sex show** Pers 1 13–23.
157 **"Who has not an ass's ears?"** Pers.
158 **He asked his circle how many "books"** Dio 62 29 2–4.
158 ***"You, when your duty is fulfilled"*** Lucan 1 40ff., translated by Susan H. Braund.
159 **"piqued because Nero"** Suet Nero Luc.
159 **"The citizens of Rome are kept in line"** Fronto PH 17. He was Marcus Cornelius Fronto, a cynical but truthful politician. Emperor Antoninus Pius appointed him as tutor to his adopted sons, the future emperors Marcus Aurelius and Lucius Verus.
160 **he focused on Paris** Servius ap Verg Aen 5 370.

9. THE TURNING POINT

161 **like a tranquil pool** Fronto PH 1 7.
162 **the Aqua Marcia was distributing** Frontinus, *De aquaeductu urbis Romae,* edited by R. H. Rodgers (Cambridge: Cambridge University Press, 2004), p. 67.
162 **Nero paid a high price** Tac Ann 14 22.
162 **"No matter how many people you kill"** Dio 61 18 3.
162 **"Memmius Regulus" came the ironic response** Tac Ann 14 47.
163 **"whether from destiny"** Ibid. 13 12.
163 **"When I have spoken about something"** Dio 62 13 1–2.
163 **"All right then, but give back her dowry"** Ibid.
163 **when Burrus died** See Tac Ann 14 51 for an account of Burrus's passing.
164 **"the grandeur of his mansions"** Tac Ann 14 52.
164 **"He allowed no one to be called a good orator"** Tac Ann 14 52.
165 **"It is nearly fourteen years, Sir"** Ibid. 14 53.
165 ***"Let others scale"*** Sen Thy 391ff., translated by E. F. Watling, Penguin Classics.

165 **"You are enjoying a vigorous old age"** Tac Ann 14 56.
166 **suborned one of his old tutor's freedmen** Tac Ann 15 45.
166 **an autocrat who worked within the law** This was not so fanciful an aim as it appears at first sight. Later in the first and second centuries, Vespasian, Nerva, Trajan, Hadrian, Antoninus Pius, and Marcus Aurelius were civilized rulers and governed (by and large) moderately and well.
167 **"consider the importance of calm"** Tac Ann 14 22.
168 **whose inveterate stupidity** Ibid. 13 47. I follow Tacitus's character assassination of Sulla.
168 **prolific sex after dark** I am told that the Ponte Milvio attracts young lovers to this day.
169 **"Sulla doesn't have any money"** Tac Ann 14 57.
170 **"Escape a passive end"** Ibid. 14 58.
171 **His widow clasped his spouting neck** Tac Ann 16 10.
171 **"I had no idea he had such a big nose!"** Dio 62 14 1.
171 **"turbulent spirits"** Tac Ann 14 59.
171 **he could at last safely discard his wife** For Octavia's last days, see Tac Ann 14 60–64.
172 **"My mistress's cunt is cleaner"** Dio 62 13 4.
173 **Nero had a nightmare** Suet Nero 46 1.
174 **cruel necessity** A phrase supposedly spoken by Oliver Cromwell as he stood beside the body of Charles I after his execution in January 1649, as quoted in Samuel Harden Church, *Oliver Cromwell: A History* (New York: G. P. Putnam's Sons, 1894), p. 321.
175 **A growing self-confidence** For the Naples gig, see Tac Ann 15 33–34 and Suet Nero 20 2.
175 **even when he took a short break** Suet Nero 20 2.
177 **The princeps ignored the rule** For Nero's collapse, see Suet Nero 19 1–2.
177 **He began to shake all over** Tac Ann 15 36.
177 **he had raped a Vestal** Suet Nero 28 1.
177 **"I have heard the whispered complaints"** Tac Ann 15 36.
178 **The emperor still balanced his vocation** Tigellinus's banquet is described in Dio 62 15 and Tac Ann 15 37.
178 **On one never-to-be-forgotten occasion** Dio 62 15 1.
178 **as if it were his own palace** Tac Ann 15 37.
179 **"Nero himself was defiled"** Ibid.
179 **"Nero moaned and groaned"** Suet Nero 29 1.
179 **"Bearded Callistratus married rugged Afer"** Mart 12 42.
180 **"Don't believe his looks"** Ibid. 1 24.
180 ***"Marriage documents were signed"*** Juv 2 119–20.
181 **"in the usual manner"** Mart 12 42.

182 **"He so prostituted his own chastity"** Suet Nero 29. Pythagoras is a correction for another freedman, Doryphoros, who died in 62. Suetonius nodded.

10. THE QUEEN IS DEAD

185 **Cicero (along with others)** Cic De Nat Deor 2 88 15, Pliny NH 4 119, Caes Gall 5 13, and Tac Agr 10 2.

186 **spread widely across the Continent** R. Williams and C. Le Carlier de Veslud, "Boom and Bust in Bronze Age Britain," *Antiquity* 93 (371), 1178–96.

186 **"They prepare the tin"** Diod Sic 5 22 1–2.

186 **"It bears grain, cattle, gold, silver, and iron"** Strabo 4 5 2.

187 **The seas** Tac Agr 10 6.

190 **"This battle being ended"** Caes Gall 2 28.

196 **Caesar was almost respectful** Caes Gall 6 13–19.

197 **The Druids—for that is the name** Pliny NH 16 95.

198 **They used to strike a human being** Strabo 4 4 5.

198 **Having devised a colossus of straw** Ibid.

198 **Today's jihadists** M. Aldhouse-Green, *Boudica Britannia,* 47

199 **There is also that custom** Strabo 4 4 5.

199 **There was a grove** Lucan 3 399–452.

201 **"in strong terms to do no harm"** Caes Gall 5 22.

202 ***". . . the Nile, who still conceals"*** Hor Odes 4 14 45ff.

203 **"No one had the least idea"** Suet Gaius 46.

205 **Cartimandua herself came to grief** Tac Hist 3 45.

206 **"If my high birth and my luck"** For the Caratacus story, see Tac Ann 12 36–38.

206 ***pius,* which was often applied to Aeneas** Vergil, author of the national epic *The Aeneid,* liked to call Aeneas *pius.*

206 **"And can you, then"** Dio 60 33 3c.

208 **"To some I will offer assistance"** Sen Hap 24.

210 **Legio XX Valeria Victrix** It is not clear where or when the honorific title Victrix (Victorious) was conferred on the legion, but it appears most likely that it was awarded after the Great Illyrian Revolt of A.D. 6–8 under the command of Marcus Valerius Messala Messalinus (A.D. 6–8).

212 **"The Britons themselves submit"** Tac Agr 13 1.

213 **"the very man who enslaved Britain"** Webster, *Boudica,* p. 89.

213 **suicide missions** Caes Gall 6 14.

214 **"Londinium, which did not have the distinction"** Tac Ann 14 33.

215 **"If," cried they, "we bend our necks"** Tac Agr 1–3.

215 **"Men chosen as priests"** Tac Ann 14 31.
217 **"a woman of royal race"** Tac Agr 16 1.
218 **parcels of land for auction immediately** Welch, Britannia, pp. 91–92.
218 **"the foremost Britons"** Ibid.
219 **Venta Icenorum** Antonine Itinerary, Tier 9.
220 **the most significant assaults** Tac Ann 14 31.
222 **"who, not yet broken by servitude"** Ibid.
222 **strange and disturbing omens** Tac Ann 14 32.
224 **"They [the city's population]"** Ibid.
225 **"Those who were taken captive"** Dio 62 7 1–2.
226 **through the roof** Crummy, *City of Victory,* pp. 25–26.
227 **"The victorious Britons"** Tac Ann 14 32.
227 **"Reassured by their general"** Tac Ann 14 30.
227 **"What they found appalled them"** Frere, *Britannia,* p. 88.
228 **"they considered it a duty"** Tac Ann 14 30.
229 **cut down his journey** Ibid.
229 **"The laments and tears"** Tac Ann 14 33.
230 **"He [Paulinus] chose a position"** Ibid. 14 34.
231 **hostile trouble in Winchester** This theory is extrapolated from Frere, *Britannia,* p. 90. Winchester was originally the headquarters of a Belgic tribe, with only a standard Roman fort. It is generally thought that the full Roman settlement was established after the revolt.
232 **"Recall this I say"** Dio 62 5–6.
233 **"Now is the time"** Ibid. 62 10 1–2.
234 **"The barbarians would assail"** Ibid. 62 12 3.
234 **"All this was going on"** Ibid. 62 12 5.
235 **rapacity of the procurator** Ibid. 62 2 1.
236 **any tribes that were vacillating** Tac Ann 14 38.
236 **but his real task** Ibid. 14 39.

11. FIRE! FIRE!

237 **The moon shone brightly** There was a full moon on the night of July 17, 64.
237 **"Turn your thoughts to this city"** Sen Clem 1 6 1.
237 **A small fire broke out** For the principal sources for the Great Fire, see Tac Ann 15 38–45, Suet Nero 16 31–38, and Dio 62 16–18 5.
239 **"Should a fire appear"** Sen Clem 1 25 5.
240 **The emperor and his wife, Agrippina** Dio 60 33 12.
240 **the loss of statues of the Muses** We know that the temple of Felicitas (Happiness) was burned down, and I assume that the sculptures that embellished it were destroyed, as they are not heard of again.

240 **"It outstripped all defensive measures"** Tac Ann 15 38.
241 **"at last, on the sixth day"** Tac Ann 15 40.
242 **at least ten to twelve thousand *insulae*** Newbold p. 858.
242 **man with partial civic rights** Gaius 1 33.
242 **fires still broke out** Drinkwater, *Nero,* p. 251.
244 **"in consequence of a vow"** Barrett, *Agrippina,* pp. 108ff.
244 **"in the beauty of the flames"** Suet Nero 38 2.
244 **"And nobody dared fight the fire"** Tac Ann 15 38.
244 **"There was nothing to be seen"** On Nero's guilt, see Dio 62 16–18.
245 **"When I am dead"** Suet Nero 38 1.
245 **"Then, let this city's roofs"** Sen Oct 832–33.
245 **"Many houses were destroyed"** Dio 62 17 1.
245 **"Last of the sons of Aeneas"** Ibid. 62 18 4.
246 **"Interrogated by Nero"** Tac Ann 15 67.
246 **"set fire to the city so brazenly"** Suet Nero 38 1.
247 **Tacitus has it only as a rumor** Tac Ann 15 39.
248 **"These measures were welcomed"** Ibid. 15 43.
248 **"contrive culprits"** Ibid. 15 44.
249 **"since the Jews constantly made disturbances"** Suet Clau 25 4.
249 **Dio disagrees** Dio 60 6 6–7.
249 **"Since this is an argument about words"** Acts 18:14–15.
249 **"They were people hated"** Tac Ann 15 44 2–3.
250 **"God is near you"** Sen Ep 41 1–2.
251 **"a religious woman"** Jos Ant 20 195.
251 **a strange and terrible story** See Tac Ann 15 44 for this grisly episode. The tar is presumed.
251 **"their hatred of humankind"** Ibid.
251 **"guilty though these people were"** Ibid.
251 **The difficulty with this account** For a full analysis, see Barrett, *Agrippina,* pp. 143–74.
253 **the Circus Vaticanus** Its site is now partly overbuilt by St. Peter's Basilica.
253 **extending the walls of Rome** Griffin, *Seneca,* p. 130f, and Suet Nero 16.
254 **"They possessed the ingenuity"** Tac Ann 15 42.
254 ***rus in urbe*** Mart 12 57.
254 **covered an estimated 125 to 200 acres** Drinkwater, *Nero,* p. 249.
255 **taller than the Colossus of Rhodes** Pliny NH 34 41–45.
255 **"like a sea"** Suet Nero 31 1.
255 **made to resemble cities** If so, the Golden House may have inspired the emperor Hadrian, whose "villa" at Tivoli was a similar mix of buildings and open ground, evoking different places in the empire (e.g., Canopus in Egypt).
255 **"tracts of country"** Ibid. 31 2.
255 **some baths** They were further developed by the emperor Titus.

256 **"All at once the coffered ceiling"** Petr 60.
256 **"Every part of the house"** Suet Nero 31 2.
257 **"arrogant park"** Mart Spect 2 8.
257 **"one single house"** Ibid. 2 4.
257 **"What is worse"** Mart 7 34.
257 **enjoyed mingling with people** Suet Nero 10 2.
258 **"At last I can begin to be housed"** Ibid. 31 2.

12. ALL THE CONSPIRATORS

259 **One night in the year 65** 16 1–3.
259 **Handsome, clever, and rich** I use Vergil's version of Dido's sad story.
260 ***"Italiam non sponte sequor"*** Verg Aen 4 361.
260 **"Earth is teeming"** Tac Ann 16 2.
260 **took his own life** According to another account, Bassus was briefly imprisoned and all his property confiscated. Tac Ann 16 3.
260 **The empire was very expensive to run** This section on the imperial finances leans heavily on Drinkwater, *Nero,* pp. 326–68.
262 **between the Scylla** Scylla and Charybdis were mythical monsters on opposite sides of the Strait of Messina.
263 **Modern scholarship** For example, Drinkwater, *Nero,* pp. 326–68.
264 **His customary appearance** Suet Nero 51.
264 **"a low born woman"** Tac Ann 15 59.
265 **"mild warfare"** Laus 28.
265 **"was far from possessing depth of character"** Tac Ann 15 48.
265 **"My own survival depends"** Ibid. 15 60.
266 **two disreputable Senators** Ibid. 15 49.
266 **"was ruined by dissipation"** Ibid.
266 **a woman called Epicharis** Tac Ann 15 51, also Poly Strat 8 62.
267 **"I will settle the account"** Tac Ann 15 51.
268 **"tedious magnificence of his position"** Ibid. 15 53.
268 **"the hostile reaction they would face"** Ibid. 15 52.
269 **According to the poet Publius Ovidius Naso** Ovid Fasti 4 679–712.
269 **"determined, enormous, and muscular"** Tac Ann 15 53.
270 **On the eve of the attempt** I follow Tacitus for the betrayal of the Pisonian plot; Plutarch (*Moralia* 505 c and d) offers a completely different account and must be referring to a different incident. His version concerns a shackled prisoner who is cryptically warned in the street by a conspirator about the imminent attempt on Nero's life and reports the exchange to the emperor. It is possible that the incident took place after the discovery of the plot and before the death of Piso, when the assassination of Nero was still feasible.

270 **"till the edge glittered"** Tac Ann 15 54.
271 **"one man's silence"** Ibid.
272 **may have mentioned the retired statesman** Ibid. 15 56.
273 **"Nero grew more and more frightened"** Ibid. 15 57–58.
273 **"one man was brought to trial"** Suet Nero 37 1.
274 **"men would come to shackle him"** Tac Ann 15 59.
275 **exchanging a singer for an actor** Ibid. 15 65.
275 **We know of forty conspirators** For the fate of the conspirators, see Drinkwater, *Nero*, pp. 212–13.
276 **He stretched out his neck** Tac Ann 15 57.
277 **"Nero's loathing of Vestinus"** Ibid. 15 68.
277 **"to forestall the Consul's designs"** Ibid. 15 69.
278 **"Those who had been reclining at table"** Ibid.
278 **"From no-one who is dying"** Lucan Phar 3 641–46.
279 **"It is not worldly wealth"** Sen Thy 344–52.
279 **"The present letter is written to you"** Sen Ep 61 2.
280 **"Thus fate had made cowards of them all"** Tac Ann 15 61.
280 **"Before I became old I tried to live well"** Sen Ep 61 2.
280 **"Why, then, do you talk"** and **"I am not a wise man"** Sen Hap 17 1, 3.
281 **"I leave you my one remaining possession"** Tac Ann 15 62.
283 **"parricide of his country"** Ibid. 15 73.
283 **"vowed to make sacrifice"** Sherk 70 A.
283 **renaming Rome Neropolis** Suet Nero 55.
284 **"Rejoice, you ruins"** Einsiedeln Eclogues 1 40–47.
284 **"Show us all you have got!"** Tac Ann 16 4. Tacitus has Nero perform on the stage, or *scaena,* before proceeding to the *theatrum*. In my reconstruction, I assume an open-air Greek-style theater with a raised stage, a circular or semicircular orchestra space, and a semicircular auditorium. The emperor performs first on the *scaena* and then descends to the orchestra.
285 **A down-to-earth general, Vespasian** Ibid. 16 5. Later the emperor Vespasian. Another version of this anecdote can be found at Dio 66 11.
285 **"The city rabble . . . thundered approval"** Ibid. 16 4.
286 **"took the greatest pains"** Ibid. 62 28 1.
286 **"never wore the same costume twice"** Suet Nero 30 3.
288 **"at the New Year Thrasea evaded"** Tac Ann 6 22.
289 **"My own time is over"** Tac Ann 16 26.
290 **"He would have done better"** Sen Ben 7 11.
291 **"We are making a libation"** Tac Ann 16 35.
291 **"experts in the science of pleasure"** Ibid. 16 18.
291 **"Petronius had gone as far as Cumae"** Ibid. 16 19.
292 **smashed his fluorspar wine dipper** Pliny NH 37 20.
293 **"the sad continuum of deaths"** Tac Ann 16 16.

13. THE ARMENIAN QUESTION

296 **"his main difficulty was to counteract"** Tac Ann 13 35.

297 **"You might win a secure throne"** Ibid. 13 37.

297 **A witty Senator advised his colleagues** Ibid. 13 41.

299 **this indignity was forced on Paetus's troops** Ibid. 15 15. Suetonius reports this as fact (Suet Nero 39 1).

299 **"before the Roman column had left"** Ibid. 15 15.

299 **"My labor has been lost"** Ibid. 15 17.

299 **meeting on Paetus's bridge** Dio 62 22 2–3.

301 **"I will go to Rome"** Tac Ann 15 29.

301 **"Both armies mounted a dazzling display"** Ibid. 15 29.

301 **"courtesy and a banquet"** Ibid. 15 30.

302 **Tiridates set out on his trek** It is at this point that Tacitus's manuscript of *The Annals* breaks off and the historian has to make do with Dio's epitomes and Suetonius's chatter. Tiridates's coronation journey is described in Dio 63 1 7 and Suet Nero 13 and 30 2.

302 **"all his regal paraphernalia"** Dio 63 1 2.

303 **"cut a fine figure"** Ibid. 63 2 1.

303 **"a most brilliant and costly affair"** Ibid. 63 3 1.

304 **"civilians occupied the city center"** Ibid. 63 3 4.

304 **The prince prostrated himself** There were different levels of *proskinesis,* of which full prostration was the most extreme. It seems likely that this was what Tiridates was compelled to perform.

304 **"Master, I am the descendant"** and **"You have done well"** Dio 63 5 2–4.

305 **Open only to initiates** Mithraism had some of the characteristics of a secret society with religious overtones, such as today's Freemasons.

305 **"he refused to travel by sea"** Pliny NH 30 17.

306 **"Master, you have a good slave"** Dio 63 6 4.

307 **a conspiracy about this time** I assume that Vinicianus's plot was laid near the end of Tiridates's journey from the east. As the Parthian's escort, he would have been physically close to him and accordingly to Nero. In the general excitement, security may have relaxed. It is possible, of course, that the attempt was planned somewhat later, when Nero was en route for his visit to Greece and probably passed through Beneventum on the Via Appia. But on this journey he will have been surrounded by his entire court and much less accessible.

308 **"boasted that no princeps"** Suet Nero 37 3.

309 **"Complaints of the kind"** Dio 63 17 4.

309 **in a private interview with the princeps** Tac Hist 3 6.

310 ***"Axios!"*—Greek for "My due!"** Ibid. 63 17 6.

310 **"If I have pleased you"** Suet Aug 99 1.
311 **"obliged to postpone and defer"** Suet Nero 32 1.
311 **"You know what my needs are"** Ibid. 32 4.

14. "I DREAM'D THAT GREECE MIGHT STILL BE FREE"

313 **"I dream'd that Greece might still be free"** From *The Isles of Greece,* Lord Byron.
314 **A keen-eyed observer** The slave philosopher Epictetus. Epi 1 6 23–29.
314 **a brand-new building** The mosaics and the arched roofs of the bath are still well preserved. The building replaced the Sanctuary of Hestia as well as other buildings of the fifth and fourth centuries B.C.
315 **"The Greeks are the only people"** Suet Nero 22 3.
316 **"I don't talk to mother-killers"** Champlin, *Nero,* p. 133.
316 **400,000 sesterces** Dio 63 14 2.
317 **a statue of Eros** Pau 9 27 3.
318 **Vespasian came to mind** Suet Vesp 4.
318 **he avoided Greece's two best-known cities** Dio 63 14 3.
318 **he was so enraged when a talented competitor** [Luc] Nero 9.
319 **"before beginning he would address"** Suet Nero 23 3.
319 **"his voice deserves neither admiration"** [Luc] Nero 6.
320 **some women in the audience gave birth** Suet Nero 23 2.
320 **the right to be a festival herald** Ibid. 24 1. Dio disagrees, saying that Cluvius Rufus acted as herald.
320 **"It was generally believed"** Ibid. 53.
320 **While in Olympia, he drove a chariot** Ibid. 24 2.
320 **an oriental client king** Called Mithridates, but which of the many kinglets so named is uncertain.
321 **When he received members of the Senate** Dio 63 13 3.
321 **"I consider him a mere appendage to Nero"** Ibid. 63 12 3.
321 **not in her first youth** Syme, *Augustan Aristocracy,* p. 240.
321 **his "incapacity" to teach the emperor dancing** Dio 63 18 1.
322 **"The masks that he wore"** Dio 63 9 5.
322 **the late empress's personal name, Sabina** Poppaea, or, in the masculine form, Poppaeus, was a clan or family name.
322 **"went through a wedding ceremony"** Suet Nero 28 1–2.
323 **"forced to do everything else"** Dio Chrys 21 7. So writes Dio Chrysostom, orator, writer, philosopher, and historian.
323 **"After that Nero had two bedfellows"** Dio 63 13 1–2.
323 **The treatment of Sporus was cruel** Was Sporus a transexual *avant la lettre*?

We cannot tell, but if he was, Nero will possibly have been doing him a huge favor. Today he might be receiving treatment for gender identity development at the Tavistock Centre.

323 **"she tutored Nero in vice"** Tac Hist 1 73.

324 **celebrated Roman thinker Musonius Rufus** Phil 5 19.

324 **the project was terminated** It was not until 1893 that a canal across the isthmus was opened.

325 **"At first the proclamation"** Plut Flam 10 3–6.

325 **"For you, men of Greece, it is an unexpected gift"** Sherk 71 ILS 8794.

326 **"When I consider this action of Nero"** Pau 7 17 3.

326 **"However much it may be your advice"** Suet Nero 23 1.

327 **A difficulty presents itself** Drinkwater, *Nero,* p. 365.

327 **"He was hailed as Apollo's equal"** Suet Nero 53.

15. DOWNFALL

329 **"was decked out with garlands"** Dio 63 20 1–5.

329 **it never occurred to him to stop singing** Suet Nero 25 3.

330 **"physically strong and intellectually astute"** Dio 63 22 1 2.

330 **"I have seen [the princeps as a theatrical performer] in chains"** Ibid. 63 22 5.

331 **coins with boldly republican slogans** Drinkwater, *Nero,* p. 390.

331 **"You too, child, will taste"** Suet Galba 4 1.

331 **Sixty-nine years old, Galba was of average height** For this paragraph, see ibid. 21.

331 **unroll a book** In ancient Rome, books were handwritten on long papyrus rolls, quite inconvenient to read from.

332 **"make himself the liberator"** Suet Galba 9 2.

333 **"The taunt is especially unfair"** Suet Nero 41 1.

333 **the princeps had no objection to being named** Ibid.

333 **"A simple craft will keep a man from want"** Suet Nero 40 2.

335 **"At the very beginning of the revolt"** Ibid. 43 1.

336 **"by kind permission of Vindex"** Suet Nero 41 2.

336 **He was so upset that he pushed his table over** Plut Galba 5 3. Suetonius has Nero faint and tear his robe; see Suet Nero 42 1.

336 **His once close woman friend** Tac Hist 1 73.

336 **a ship from Egypt** Suet Nero 45 1.

337 **a male Boudica** I owe this striking image to Drinkwater, *Nero,* p. 402.

337 **"as is conjectured"** Dio 63 24 2.

337 **"compelled their leaders"** Plut Galba 6 3.

338 **"as he was leaving the dining room"** Ibid. 43 2.

340 **Dispatches were delivered to the palace** See ibid. 47–50 for Suetonius's blow-by-blow account of Nero's last hours. David Canzone argues, ingeniously but unconvincingly, that Suetonius's account is largely a moralizing fiction modeled on the story of Er in Plato's *Republic*. But the points of comparison are strained. For instance, in Suetonius, Nero's cloak is snagged by brambles, while Plato has the wicked bound, flayed, and impaled on thorns. Not quite the same things.

340 **"Is it so dreadful a thing to die?"** Verg Aen 12 646.

341 **"Don't I have either friend or foe?"** Suet Nero 47 3.

341 **"Even if we are forced out as emperor"** Dio 63 27 2.

342 **a thunderclap and a flash of lightning** Suet Nero 48 2. Suetonius reports an earthquake, but that is inconsistent with the flash of lightning.

342 **"I refuse to go underground"** Ibid. 49 2.

343 **He was struck** Dio 63 28 4.

343 **"God, what an artist is dying with me!"** Ibid. 49 1 and Dio 63 29 2.

343 **"How ugly and vulgar"** Ibid. 48 3.

344 **"Listen to the sound!"** Hom Il 10 535.

344 **"in anger disclosed the emperor's designs"** Dio Chrys 21 9–10.

344 **Nero was furious and wanted to kill Sporus** Loeb Dio vol. 8, p. 192; Joann. Antioch (fr. 92 M. v. 62–74n).

16. LOOSE ENDS

347 **he showered the freedman with kisses** Suet Galba 22.

347 **"It is my custom to levy troops"** Suet Galba 16 1.

348 **(*capax imperii nisi imperasset*)** Tac Hist 1 49.

348 **"And yet I was your emperor once"** Tac Hist 3 85.

349 **"while Nero's body was still burning"** Plut Galba 9 3.

349 **treated him as his consort** Ibid.

349 **their relationship was "intimate"** Dio 64 8 3.

349 **"it was proposed that Sporus"** Dio 65 10 1.

349 **"clutching after them"** Plut Otho 2 1–3.

350 **spring and summer flowers** See Suet Nero 57 1–2 for this section on reactions to Nero's death.

350 **"he even made use of that surname"** Suet Otho 7 1.

350 **"openly called for him to perform"** Suet Vit 11 2.

351 **"There was nothing to prevent"** Dio Chrys 21 10.

351 **"the great name of Nero"** Tac Hist 2 8.

351 **"When I was a young man"** Suet Nero 57 2.

352 **"Some suppose that he shall rise again"** Aug City 20 19 3.

352 **In one of his essays, Plutarch** Plut De Sera 32.

A NOTE ON SOURCES

368 **"virtues are not left unrecorded"** Tac Ann 3 65.

368 **"without anger or partisanship"** Ibid. 1 1.

PHOTOGRAPH CREDITS

Page 1

Till Niermann/WikimediaCommons
https://upload.wikimedia.org/wikipedia/commons/3/36/Augustus_of_Rome.jpg

Page 2

Top: MrArifnajafov/Wikimedia Commons
https://commons.wikimedia.org/wiki/Category:Bust_of_young_Nero_(R%C3%B6misch_Germanisches_Museum_K%C3%B6ln)#/media/File:Nero_Claudius_Caesar_Augustus_Germanicus.jpg
Bottom: Carole Raddato/Wikimedia Commons
https://upload.wikimedia.org/wikipedia/commons/d/d5/Relief_from_the_Sebasteion_depicting_Nero_and_Agrippina%2C_Aphrodisias_Museum%2C_Turkey_%2820481225182%29.jpg

Page 3

Top: Carole Raddato/ Wikimedia Commons
https://commons.wikimedia.org/wiki/File:Portrait_of_Nero_dating_from_AD_59-68,_later_reworked_as_Domitian_and_restored_in_the_modern_era_as_Nero,_Capitoline_Museums_(14381804955).jpg
Bottom: Wikimedia Commons
https://upload.wikimedia.org/wikipedia/commons/d/d6/Nero-graffito.jpg

Page 4

Top: Dave Hill and Margie Kleerup/Wikimedia Commons
https://upload.wikimedia.org/wikipedia/commons/b/b9/Head_of_Agrippina_the_Younger._Getty_Villa_Collection.jpg
Bottom: Calidius/Wikimedia Commons

https://upload.wikimedia.org/wikipedia/commons/4/44/Seneca-berlinantikensammlung-2_copy.jpg

Page 5

Top: TcfkaPanairjdde/Wikimedia Commons
https://upload.wikimedia.org/wikipedia/commons/7/73/Poppea_Sabina_-_MNR_Palazzo_Massimo.jpg
Bottom: AlMare/Wikimedia Commons
https://upload.wikimedia.org/wikipedia/commons/b/bd/Oplontis_Triclinium_Room_24.jpg

Page 6

Top: Colchester and Ipswich Museum Service: Colchester Collection
Bottom: Dosseman/Wikimedia Commons
https://upload.wikimedia.org/wikipedia/commons/3/39/Aphrodisias_Museum_Claudius_and_Britannica_4638.jpg

Page 7

Wikimedia Commons
https://commons.wikimedia.org/wiki/File:Detail_from_Arch_of_Titus.jpg

Page 8

Top: Jensens/ Wikimedia Commons
https://commons.wikimedia.org/wiki/File:Circus_Maximus_SE.jpg
Bottom: Andy Montgomery/Wikimedia Commons
https://upload.wikimedia.org/wikipedia/commons/2/27/Domus_Aurea%2C_Nero%27s_Golden_House_%2836453906275%29.jpg

INDEX

Names of very well-known people or places are cited by their popular Anglicized names—thus, Rome rather than Roma. Individuals are usually listed according to the Latin names by which they are generally known—for example, Corbulo, Gnaeus Domitius rather than (as is correct) leading with the family or clan name, Domitius Corbulo, Gnaeus.

Acte, Nero's first lover, 111–13, 126–28, 129, 130, 181, 266, 346, 360
Actium, battle of, 6, 7, 24, 100–101, 357
Aemilius Lepidus, Marcus, 28–30
Aeneas, Trojan hero, 82–3, 206, 246, 259–60, 370, 395, 397
Agricola, Gnaeus Julius, 367
Agrippa, Marcus Vipsanius, 16, 85, 178, 241, 358
Agrippa Postumus, 358
Agrippina, the Elder, 17–18, 19–20, 115, 358
Agrippina, the Younger, xxi, 15–16, 18, 20–21, 27–28, 38–39, 42–43, 49, 50, 54, 56, 57, 62–63, 67–69, 71, 72, 73, 75–76, 80, 82, 84, 85–86, 91–92, 93, 94, 96, 100, 109, 111, 112, 113–14, 116–17, 118–119, 120, 121, 122–24, 128, 129, 144, 145, 167, 173, 176, 206, 240, 248, 263, 264, 266, 267, 288, 318, 359, 360, 361, 383, 387, 389, 390, 391, 392, 397
  as empress, 97–99
  assassinated, 134–39, 140–43
  assessment of, 138–39
  early years, 21–22, 23, 25
  exiled by Caligula, 28–31
  gives birth to Nero, 36–37, 126
  her murder planned by Nero, 132–33
  holiday with Nero, 133–34
  marries Claudius, 58–60
  plans Claudius's murder, 87–90
  political position weakens, 114–15
  rumors of incest with Nero, 130–31
Augustus, 17, 24, 25, 31, 32, 36, 38, 40, 47, 50, 53, 54, 57, 72, 74, 85, 90, 97, 99, 100–01, 107, 108–09, 115, 118, 148, 153, 154, 159, 160, 173, 174, 200, 202, 203, 239, 241, 253, 264, 268, 293, 295, 310, 316, 328, 330, 331, 336, 345, 354, 357, 358, 363, 367
Alexander the Great, 72, 315, 387
Alexander, Tiberius Julius, 300
Alexandria, Egyptian city, 72, 73, 77, 176, 242, 315, 317, 327, 333, 341, 344, 357, 362

Alexandria, nurse of Nero, 346
Anicetus, tutor of Nero, admiral, 43, 132–36, 172–73, 391
Annaeus Mela, 65, 155
Annius Vinicianus, Corbulo's son in law, 300, 307–8
Antichrist, Nero as, 253
Antistius Sosianus, 393
Antium, seaside resort, 15, 126, 131, 133, 174, 237, 241, 382
Antonia Minor, 22, 28, 35–36, 49
Antonius, Marcus (Mark Antony), 7
Apollo, god of music, 140, 147, 152, 157, 316, 328, 329, 402
  Nero his equal as musician, 327
Apollonius of Tyana, 371
Aristotle, 184
Artabanus, king of Parthia, 351
Arulenus Rusticus, Quintus Junius, 289
Atrebates, British tribe, 190, 192, 201, 203
Augustine, bishop of Hippo, 352
Augustus,
  assassination of adoptive father, Julius Caesar, 6–7
  conservative social legislation, 11–12
  entente with Parthian empire, 13–14
  founds Julio-Claudian dynasty, 16–17
  mausoleum, 5
  negotiates with two Britannic rulers, 13
  policy of spectacle and architecture, 9–11
  "Res Gestae," 6–11
  wins civil wars, devises imperial system, 8–9

Baiae, seaside resort, 133, 134, 135, 137, 139, 141, 142, 265, 391
Beryllus, tutor of Nero, 43
Boudica, 217, 218, 261, 275, 337, 338, 353, 361, 403
  beaten and daughters raped, 220–21
  crowned queen of the Iceni, 219
  dies, 235
  gives pre-battle speech, 232–33
  heads rebellion, 226, 229, 230
Britannia, description, 183–89, 191–92
Britannicus, son of Claudius, 50, 52, 53, 54, 57, 72, 80, 84, 87, 91–92, 114, 121, 122, 132, 142, 173, 387
  angers Nero, 62
  birth, 360
  Claudius warms toward, 85, 89
  probably poisoned, 117–20, 125, 147, 360
Brutus, Marcus Junius, 42
Burrus, Sextus Afranius, 62, 91–92, 98, 111, 113, 115, 116, 118, 122–23, 124, 134, 136, 141, 147, 151, 152, 163–64, 166, 168, 171, 353, 360, 361, 391, 393

Caesar, Gaius, son of Julia and Agrippa, 358
Caesar, Lucius, son of Julia and Agrippa, 358
Caligula (or Gaius), emperor, 21, 22, 26–27, 31, 37, 42–43, 47, 56, 58, 66, 68, 97, 99, 106, 138, 148, 200, 203, 253, 282, 290, 308, 317, 349, 359, 382
  assassinated, 32–33, 34
  "Little Boots," 15
  his sisters' plot, 27–30
Calpurnius Siculus, pastoral poet, 372
Calvia Crispinilla, 323, 336
Campania, 142, 172, 267, 291
Camulodunon/Camulodunum (Colchester), capital of the

Trinovantes, later of Britannia, 201, 207, 212, 214, 215, 222, 223, 224, 225, 226, 234
Cantii, Kentish tribe, 192, 214
Capri (Capreae), 22, 25, 26, 43, 57, 359
Caratacus, British leader, 205–7, 360
Cartimandua, queen of the Brigantes, 205
Cassius Dio, Lucius, historian, 370
Cassius Longinus, Gaius, 273
Cassivellaunus, ruler of the Catuvellauni, 195, 201
Cato the Younger, Marcus Porcius, 40–41, 42, 68, 264, 357
Catus Decianus, corrupt procurator, 214, 215–16, 217, 215–20
flees Britannia, 225–26
Catuvellauni, British tribe, 192–93, 195, 201, 202–3, 207, 214, 223, 229
Celer, architect of the Golden House, 254, 257
Cerealis, Quintus Petillius, 226
Chaeremon of Alexandria, 73, 77
Cicero, Marcus Tullius, orator and statesman, 88, 185
Cinna Magnus, Gnaeus (or Lucius) Cornelius, conspirator, 100–102
civil wars, 49 to 31 B.C., 8, 24, 36, 40, 64, 101, 155, 202, 348
Civilis, Julius, 362
Classicianus, Gaius Julius Alpinus, procurator, plans clemency for vanquished Britons, 236
Claudia Antonia, daughter of Claudius, 57, 168, 270
Claudius, emperor, 38, 41, 48, 49, 50–54, 66, 67, 71–72, 73, 76, 77, 82–85, 86–87, 92, 93, 98, 99, 106, 108, 111, 112, 113, 114, 116, 117, 121, 129, 143, 162, 166, 168, 171, 181, 200, 208, 212, 213, 214, 215, 218, 223, 224, 240, 241, 248, 249, 269, 270, 288, 293, 295, 308, 317, 318, 330, 334, 339, 354, 359, 360, 367, 386
accession, 34–35
adopts Nero, 61–62
assessment, 90–91
building developments, 253, 255
character, 35–36
fall of his wife Messalina, 50–54
Fucine lake incident, 79–82
funeral, 4–5, 381
invades Britain, 203–5
looks for new wife, marries Agrippina, 55–61
pardons Caratacus, 205–7
poisoned, 87–90, 140, 387
satirized, 95–97
Claudius Nero, Tiberius, Livia's first husband, 16–17
Claudius Senecio, confidant, 111, 266, 272, 277
Cleopatra VII Philopator, Queen of Egypt, 74, 88, 357, 382
Clodius Macer, Lucius, 336, 362
Cluvius Rufus, Marcus, 130, 190, 401
Commius, British ruler, 193, 194, 201, 202
Corbulo, Gnaeus Domitius, general, 116, 169, 170, 294–95, 297–98, 306–7, 308, 311, 318, 332, 360, 361, 362
agrees Armenian settlement, 300–302
assessment, 310–12
imperium maius, 294, (second time) 300
relieves Paetus, 299–300
suicide, 309–10
trains army, 296
Corinth, Greek city, 290, 309, 315, 316, 317, 323, 324, 325, 327, 362
Cunobelin, British ruler, 202–3, 205

Delphi, Greek oracle, 315, 316, 328
Demetrius, philosopher, 290–91
Dido, legendary queen of Carthage, 259–60
Dio Chrysostom, 344–45
Dionysus, god of out-of-body experiences, 149, 152
Domitia, aunt of Nero, 37–38, 42, 144–45
Domitia Lepida, aunt of Nero, 25, 38, 49, 53, 86–87
Domitii Ahenobarbii, clan history, 22–25
Domitius Ahenobarbus, Gnaeus, Nero's father, 22, 25, 37, 38, 359
Doryphorus, imperial freedman, 111
Druids, 195–200, 209, 212–13, 221, 222, 227–28
Drusilla, sister of Caligula, 28, 359
Drusus Caesar, son of Germanicus, 359
Drusus Germanicus, Nero Claudius, father of Claudius, 358
Drusus Julius Caesar, son of Tiberius, 88, 358
Dumnonii, British tribe, 190

Egloge, Nero's nurse, 346
Epaphroditus, imperial freedman, 271, 341, 344
Epicharis, conspirator, 266–68, 272–73
Epictetus, philosopher and slave, 271
Eusebius, Christian apologist, 252

Faenius Rufus, Lucius, Praetorian Prefect, 164, 266, 269, 276, 361
  exposed as conspirator, 274
False Neros, 351–2
  Nero as Antichrist, 352
  Reportedly, still alive, 352
  Terentius Maximus, a false Nero, 351
fire of Rome, 237–42
  reconstruction, 242–44
Flamininus, Titus Quinctius, liberator of Greece, 325
Flavius Scaevinus, conspirator, 266, 269, 271–72, 283, 291
  betrays Faenius, 274
Fronto, Marcus Cornelius, 393

Gaul, 21, 108, 129, 169, 186, 189–90, 191, 192, 193, 194, 195, 200, 201, 202, 209, 213, 216, 217, 226, 236, 238, 330, 331, 333, 335, 357, 358, 364
Galba, Servius Sulpicius, 42, 335, 336, 338, 339, 340, 342, 345, 347–48, 349, 362, 371
  character, 331–32
  claims the purple, 333–34
Gallio Annaeanus, Lucius Junius, 65, 151, 249, 283
Gallus, Gaius Aulus Didius, governor of Britannia, 209
Gallus, Gaius Cestius, governor of Syria, 317
games, 73–76,
gay marriage, 179–82
Germanicus Julius Caesar, brother of Claudius, 17, 18–19, 22, 26, 28, 29, 34, 41, 50, 54, 56, 57, 61, 72, 88, 113, 120, 136, 139, 141, 270, 339, 358

Halotus, food taster, 90
Hector, prince of Troy, 75, 147
Helius, imperial freedman, 99, 322, 326–27
Helvidius Priscus, Stoic philosopher and politician, 290–91

Hercules, 141, 185, 327, 329
Herod Antipas, ruler of Galilee and Perea, 216
Homer, 21, 30, 39, 66, 75, 146, 284
Horace (Quintus Horatius Flaccus) poet, 11, 12, 39, 65, 202

Icelus, freedman of Galba, 345, 347
Iceni, East Anglian tribe, 201, 205, 208, 216, 217, 218–19, 220, 221–22, 223, 235

Janus, temple of, 12–13, 305, 357
Jewish revolt, 318, 324, 348, 353, 362
Jugurtha, king of Numidia, 207
Julia, Augustus's daughter, 16, 17
 marries Marcellus, 357
 marries Agrippa, 358
 death, 359
Julia Livilla, sister of Agrippina and Caligula, 28, 29, 30, 67, 360
Julius Caesar, Gaius, 8, 24, 40, 138, 155, 156, 185, 201, 202, 246, 290, 330, 357, 369, 372
 assassination, 7, 36, 273
 campaigns in Britannia, 190–91, 192–95
 on Druids, 195–200
 Gallic wars, 41, 189–91
Juno/Jupiter, rulers of the gods, 55, 71, 83, 100, 118, 148, 192, 259, 282, 283, 291, 328
Juvenalia, festival, 148–53
Juvenal, satirist, 49–50, 89, 95, 180, 383

Livia, wife of Augustus, 16, 20–21, 22, 35, 59, 86, 90–91, 331, 357, 359
Locusta, poisoner, 88–89, 90, 119–20
Londinium (London), 214, 219, 228, 229
Lucan (Annaeus Lucanus, Marcus), 42, 155–56, 157, 158–59, 266, 272
 author of *Pharsalia,* 155, 199
 death, 279
Lucullus, Gardens of, 52

Mandubracius, king of the Trinovantes, 201
Marius, Gaius, 210
Martial, satirist, (Marcus Valerius *Martialis*), 179–80, 181, 254, 257
Minerva, goddess of wisdom, 55
Mithras, 304–5
Mithridates, eastern king, 401
Musonius Rufus, Gaius, 324

Narcissus, imperial freedman, 48–49, 57, 79, 82, 85–86, 87, 89, 96–97, 204
 and Messalina, 51–54
Nero, emperor, *passim* as well as key citations below.
 accession, 92–93
 adoption by Claudius, 61–62
 Agrippina, relations with, 97–98, 111–13, 115–17, 120–24, 130–38, 145
 appearance, 3
 artistic practice, 77, 78
 assessment, 173–75, 329–30
 attempt on his life, 50–51
 attends Claudius's funeral, 1–5, 14
 betrothal/marriage to Octavia, 61, 84
 birth and infancy, 15–16, 37
 and Britannia, 209–10, 217, 223, 232–33, 236

Nero (*cont'd*):
building projects, 253–55
Golden House (Domus Aurea), 254–58, 348
cared for by aunts Domitia and Domitia Lepida, 37–38, 87
chariot racing, 74–76, 98–99, 146–48
clemency, and the first five years, 100–102, 206–7,
comes of age, 70–72
death of Britannicus, 117–20
death, 344
divorces/executes Octavia, 163, 171–73
education/guardianship, 39–40, 43, 68–70, 76–77
encouragement of literature and the arts, 153–60
fascinated by "magic," 76
finance and administration, 107–9, 260–63
coinage reform, 263
fire of Rome, 237–42
Nero wrongly blamed, 244–48
Christians wrongly blamed, 249–53
first professional premiere
in Naples, 175–76
in Rome 284–85
gladiatorial games, 148–49
Greece, tour of, 176–78, 313–27, 315–316
announces freedom of Greece, 324–26
at Delphi, 316–17
chariot accident, 320
competes, wins 1,800 first prizes, 318–21
Corinthian canal, project, 323–24
returns to Rome as *triumphator,* 326–29
hooliganism, 104–7
illnesses, 162
improves Aqua Marcia and Rome's aqueducts, 161–62
introduction to public life, 82–84
learns from Augustus's policies, 6–14
loyalty to childhood tutors and carers, 43, 132, 133
marries Poppaea Sabina, dies, 285–87
marries Statilia Messalina, 181, 277, 321, 361
Nymphidius Sabinus, Gaius, Praetorian Prefect, 282, 339, 345, 347, 349
personality, 125, 140–41
Pisonian conspiracy, 263–70, 361
aftermath, 282–83
impact on Nero, 276–78, 282–83
plot uncovered, 270–75
second wave of post-Piso punishments, 287–93
revolt of Vindex and Galba, 330–34
kills himself, 343–44
leaves Rome by night, 341–43
loses heart, 340–41
mistakenly believes reports of betrayal, 338–99
raises army, appoints himself sole consul, declares Galba an enemy of Rome, but fears the worst, 332–36
sex life, 179–82
Pythagoras "marries" Nero, 179, 181, 182, 322, 323, 395
Nero makes Sporus a pseudo-Poppaea, 322–23
Sporus remains loyal, 341–42, 344–45
spectacle, policy of, 147–53, 178–79
tutors, 38, 63, 72–73
work and leisure, 109–12

Nero Julius Caesar, brother of Claudius, 31
Neronia, festival, 154

Octavia, Senecan tragedy, 66, 133, 134–35, 137, 245, 371
Ollius, Titus, 126
Olympia/Olympic games, 154, 313–14
  also games at Corinth, Delphi, and Nemea, 315
Ordovices, kingdom in north Wales, 228
Ostorius Scapula, Publius, governor of Britannia, 205
Otho, emperor, 106, 111, 127, 134, 334, 347–48, 349–50, 361, 362, 368, 371
  quarrel with Nero over Poppaea, 127–29
  sent to govern Lusitania, 129
Oxyrhynchus, 93

Paetus, Aulus Caecina, 41–42
Paetus, Lucius Caesennius, 298–300, 312, 361
Pallas, Marcus Antonius, imperial freedman, 48–49, 51, 57, 61, 85–86, 98, 168, 263
  fall of, 114, 360
  wealth, 261
Paris, famous pantomime artist, 122–23, 124
  executed, 321
Paris, son of Priam, 55, 56, 160
Parthia, 115–16, 295, 296, 312, 351
Passienus Crispus, Gaius Sallustius, second husband of Agrippina, 43
Paul, the apostle, 65, 249–50, 352
Paulinus, Gaius Suetonius, governor of Britannia, 210, 211, 212, 213, 214, 219, 221, 223, 226
  attack on island of Mona, 227–28
  battle of Watling Street, 230–35
  cavalry dash to London, 229
  plans campaign, 230–31
  victorious, seeks revenge, 235–36
Peter, the apostle, 352
Petronius, Gaius, 156, 370
  author of the *Satyricon,* 102–4
  suicide, 291–92, 293, 361
Phaon, imperial freedman, 341–42, 343
Philostratus, sophist, 371
Piso, Gnaeus Calpurnius, "murderer" of Germanicus, 18, 41, 358
Piso, Lucius Calpurnius, 264–65
  heads conspiracy, 268, 269–70, 272, 274–75, 279, 280, 293, 308, 358
Plautus, Rubellius Gaius, 167–68, 170–71
Plautius Lateranus, conspirator, 269
Pliny the Elder (Gaius Plinius Secundus), encyclopedist, 47, 56, 75, 76, 197, 305, 369, 393
Pliny the Younger (Gaius Plinius Secundus), letter writer, 261
Plutarch, essayist and biographer, 106, 337, 349, 352–53, 371
Pompeius Magnus (Pompey the Great), Gnaeus, 155
Poppaea Sabina, wife of Nero, 126–30, 131, 133, 134, 163, 171, 172, 173, 174, 181, 251, 280, 285–87, 297, 321, 322, 341, 349, 360, 361
Poenius Postumus, deputy *legatus*, 231
Pontius Pilate, Prefect of Judaea, 31, 58, 216, 252, 359
Poppaeus Sabinus, Gaius, 126
Praetorian Guard, 9, 26, 32, 34, 35, 52, 61, 62, 81, 120, 121, 124, 136, 141, 142, 151, 163–64, 169, 269–70, 273, 274, 277, 279–80, 290, 324, 340, 342, 347

Prasutagus, king of the Iceni, 205, 217, 218
  death, 216
Pytheas, geographer and explorer, 185–86

Roman Republican constitution, 7–8
Roman soldiers in battle, 211
Rome, city of, 3–4, 10–11, 45, 64, 159, 161–62, 237, 240,
Rubria, Vestal virgin, 177

Saturnalia, festival of misrule, 204
The Satyricon, 69, 103–4, 156, 181, 256, 291, 371
Scribonia, second wife of Augustus, 357
Scribonius Proculus, Publius Sulpicius, 309, 327, 332, 362
Scribonius Rufus, Publius Sulpicius, 309, 327, 332, 362
Sejanus, Lucius Aelius, 30, 49, 56, 88, 126, 162, 359
Seneca, Lucius Annaeus, 44–45, 47, 63, 64, 66–68, 72, 75–76, 77, 82, 84, 92, 95, 98, 104, 110–11, 113–14, 115, 116–17, 118, 123, 129, 130, 141, 142–43, 151, 152, 154, 155, 157, 162, 171, 176, 237, 239, 249, 250, 283, 290, 291, 348, 349, 353, 360, 361, 370–71, 372, 387, 389, 390, 391
  adultery with Livilla, 67
  Apocolocyntosis Divi Claudii, 96–97, 99–100, 156
  death, 280–82
  financial investor, 208, 212, 215, 217, 261
  Octavia, 133, 134–35, 136, 137, 245, 369
  On Clemency, 100–102, 287,
  on gladiatorial shows, 149
  perhaps joined Piso's conspiracy, 265, 266, 272, 279–80
  retires from public life, 164–67
  tutor to Nero, 63, 68–70,
Severus, architect of the Golden House, 254, 257
Severus Alexander, emperor, 370
Silanus, Marcus Junius, 98–99
Silana, Junia, false plot,122–24
Silanus, Lucius Junius, 97, 268
Silanus, Marcus Junius, 98–99
Slavery and freedmen, 43–49
Sporus
  "marries" Nero, 322–23
  stays loyal to Nero, 341–42, 344–45
  suicide, 349
  taken in by Nymphidius Sabinus, then Otho, then Vitellius, 349
Stoicism, 40, 44, 65, 73, 144, 167, 169, 171, 173, 280, 288, 292–93
Subrius Flavus, Praetorian tribune, 246, 264, 274, 276–77
suicide, culture of, 40–42
Suetonius Tranquillus, Gaius, author, 367, 368–70
Sulla Felix, Faustus Cornelius, 168–70

Tacitus, Publius (?) Cornelius, historian, 367–68
Tasciovanus, father of Cunobelin, 202
Terentius Maximus, a false Nero, 351
Thrasea Paetus, Publius Clodius, 143, 144, 151, 157, 174, 288–89, 288–291, 292, 293, 361
Tiberius, emperor, 17, 18, 19, 20, 22, 25, 32, 43, 49, 54, 56, 57, 61, 88,

91, 106, 112, 122, 162, 202, 239, 241, 249, 255, 354, 358, 359, 367
  death, 25–27
Tigellinus, Gaius Ofonius, Praetorian Prefect, 30, 164, 169, 172, 174, 178–79, 244, 258, 266, 272, 273, 280, 282, 285, 288, 291, 292, 297, 321, 323, 339, 349–50, 361, 383
Tigranes VI, king of Armenia, 297, 298, 299–300, 312, 361
Tincommius, son of Commius, 13, 202
Tiridates, king of Armenia, 115, 295, 296, 297, 300–302, 310, 312, 361
  journey to Rome, 302–3
  receives crown from Nero, 304–7
Titus, emperor, 62, 77, 117, 348, 351
Togodumnus, British leader, 205
Torquatus, Decimus Junius Silanus, 176
Trinovantes, British kingdom, 192, 201, 202, 203, 207, 208, 212, 213–15, 216, 221, 222, 223, 224, 226, 230, 235
Troy/Ilium, 55, 75, 82, 146, 160, 244, 245, 259, 284
  Troy Game, 50, 360
Turpilianus, Publius Petronius, army general, 338

Velosenus, sea captain, 194
Venus, goddess of love, 55, 102, 289–90, 306
Vercingetorix, king of the Arverni, 201, 207
Verica, son of Commius, 203
Verginius Rufus, Lucius, governor of upper Germany, 336
  meets Vindex and wins unintentional battle, 337–38
  Veranius, Quintus, 209–10
Verulamium (St. Albans), 229–30, 234
Vespasian (Titus Flavius Vespasianus), 62, 117, 285, 351, 353
  appointed to quell Jewish revolt, 317–18, 324, 348
  becomes emperor, 348, 367
  builds Colosseum, 353
Vestinus Atticus, Marcus Julius, conspirator, 268, 277–78,
Vindex, Gaius Julius, governor of Gallia Lugdunensis, 330–31, 332–33, 334–35, 336–38, 348, 362
Vitellius, Aulus, emperor, 106, 107, 284, 348, 349, 350, 362
Vologeses I, king of Parthia, 115, 295, 296, 297, 298, 299, 300, 302, 304, 311, 312, 360

women in Roman society and politics, 17–18

ABOUT THE AUTHORS

ANTHONY EVERITT, a former visiting professor in the visual and performing arts at Nottingham Trent University, has written extensively on European and classical culture. He is the author of *Cicero, Augustus, Alexander the Great, Hadrian and the Triumph of Rome, The Rise of Rome,* and *The Rise of Athens*. He has served as secretary general of the Arts Council of Great Britain.

RODDY ASHWORTH is an award-winning investigative journalist. He is a former national news editor and visiting lecturer in media ethics at City University London.

The authors live near Colchester—formerly Camulodunum, the first Roman city in Britain.

ABOUT THE TYPE

This book was set in Bembo, a typeface based on an old-style Roman face that was used for Cardinal Pietro Bembo's tract *De Aetna* in 1495. Bembo was cut by Francesco Griffo (1450–1518) in the early sixteenth century for Italian Renaissance printer and publisher Aldus Manutius (1449–1515). The Lanston Monotype Company of Philadelphia brought the well-proportioned letterforms of Bembo to the United States in the 1930s.